# PRISONER 302

A FIJIAN PRIME MINISTER'S STORY OF HIS LIFE;
OF MILITARY REBELLION, NATIONAL
OPPRESSION, AND A HANDFUL OF MIRACLES

LAISENIA QARASE

# CONTENTS

ISBN 979-8-9861477-0-3
Cover Design: Alonso De La Fuente
Photo Credit: Getty Images, Ronald Kumar (Fiji Sun), The Fiji Times

*I dedicate Prisoner 302 to my wife, Leba, who inspired me to write this book and who stood by me throughout my ordeal, before the trial, during the trial and when I was incarcerated.*

# amazon Gift Receipt

## Send a Thank You Note

You can learn more about your gift or start a return here too.

Scan using the Amazon app or visit
**https://a.co/d/3DFOLNd**

**Prisoner 302**

Order ID: 112-1391049-8615447    Ordered on January 4, 2023

# A NOTE FROM THE QARASE FAMILY

Laisenia Qarase began this final draft of his memoir manuscript, aged 70, in 2012; he completed it aged 76 in 2018 after a struggle with health issues brought on, we believe, by harrowing events described in this book. He passed away in 2020. We, his surviving family and publishers, in turn, dedicate this publication to our great and beloved hero, its author, and to the legacy of goodness he gave to the people of Fiji.

# FIJI

Fiji, with its approximately 330 islands, is strategically located in a large area of the Southwest Pacific Ocean. It is an economic, commercial and transport hub for many small Pacific nations. The islands of Fiji lie 3,100km northeast of Sydney, 2,100km north of Auckland, 5,100km southwest of Honolulu, and 7,100km southeast of Tokyo.

Viti Levu, Fiji's biggest island, has an area of approximately 10,389 square kilometers. It's the home of the busy cosmopolitan capital city Suva, the seat of government and a centre for regional and international organisations.

Fiji's main industries include tourism, sugar growing and milling, fisheries, forestry, manufacturing, educational services, telecommunications, and other service sectors.

The second largest island, Vanua Levu, covering about 5,587 square kilometers, also hosts sugar farms, forestry and some tourism.

Fiji's population of approximately 880,000 comprises the majority native Fijians, descendants of immigrants from India and groupings of smaller ethnic communities.

After gaining independence from Britain in 1970, Fiji experienced 17 years of stable government under the leadership of Ratu Sir

Kamisese Mara, a paramount chief. Ratu Mara maintained a policy of multi-racialism. However, a military coup in 1987 reflected underlying ethnic tensions. Since that first military takeover, Fiji has gone through a series of coups and is still trying to find a model of governance capable of creating unity from a very diverse population.

# MAP OF FIJI

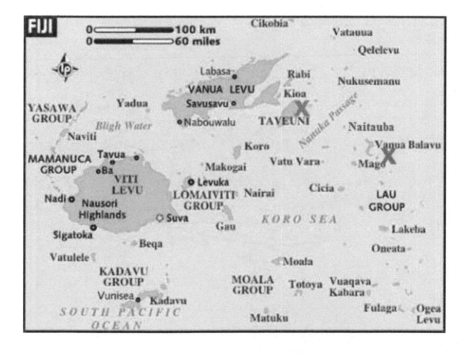

# PRONUNCIATION GUIDE

b/B – as in ti<u>mb</u>er

c/C – as in <u>th</u>at

d/D – as in san<u>d</u>

g/G – as in so<u>ng</u>

q/Q – as in fi<u>ng</u>er

# FOREWORD

*Prisoner* 302 is a powerful and inspirational book. It is the life story of one man and grows into a penetrating narrative of his nation. Laisenia Qarase, born in an outer island of Fiji, tells of growing up, schooling, moving into the center of the island nation's life, gaining a love for civic service with a desire to serve others. He is unexpectedly appointed prime minister at a time of great crisis when democracy had been reduced to ruins. For the next six years, he went through many ups and downs and great challenges as he took Fiji back to legal parliamentary rule and embarked on the difficult task of rebuilding a divided country.

What is most impressive is his description and assessment of his work with countless others to develop the art of governing, of working for the public good, of trying to bind many peoples with different languages, together in the common bond of a nation.

The same intelligence and feel for political reality shown in those constructive efforts comes to the fore in a powerful way when he writes about being ousted in a coup by military leader Frank Baini-marama and his side-kick Sayed- Khaiyum, who then take Fiji down into the darkness of their authoritarian dictatorship. Mr. Qarase endures imprisonment and other abuses. The entire country operates under ruthless and cruel military rule.

And then, the most touching part of the book comes with his story of being renewed in Christian belief in the fellowship of prisoners living out their faith in God's strength.

I was especially moved and inspired by this very Christian, public-servant story at this moment in American history when President Donald Trump in my country is violating so many norms and obligations of our constitutional state. Dictatorial tendencies are evident daily in his speech and actions. The United States may well be entering its worst political crisis since the Civil War. And those of us that are trying to foster wise citizenship and just governance are asking, 'What must we do?' One of the first things I will tell my friends and colleagues that what we need to do, is to read "Prisoner 302." It is a biography of truly Christian statesmanship for our time.

*James W. Skillen, BD (Bachelor of Divinity), PhD, DD*

*Political Scientist, retired founder-director, Centre for Public Justice Birmingham, Alabama*

# PREFACE

Since its first coup of 1987, and particularly since the promulgation of the 1997 Constitution, Fiji has been a tumultuous mix of democratic instability and military-imposed order. In this context, we need to hear from Laisenia Qarase, and this is his book you have in your hands.

As Fiji's twice-elected prime minister appointed to power in the ruins of George Speight's failed putsch of 2000 until he himself was toppled by a coup in 2006, Qarase knows the precarious character of political legitimacy, the difficulties of governing a post-colonial multi-cultural Pacific nation, and what it is to suffer for the sake of one's principles.

The former PM tells his story from humble beginnings on a remote Fiji island, to rising to the top in Fiji's civil service, managing a national development bank, to ascending to national leadership in a time of crisis.

With Christian conviction and a clear conscience, Qarase reminds us of his Soqosoqo Duavata ni Lewenivanua (SDL) government's vision to try and bring indigenous Fijians opportunities in commercial enterprises they lacked, and to introduce affirmative action policies on their behalf – all the while ensuring other ethnic communities were rewarded for their achievements. For this orientation, he worried entrenched economic interests and alienated political rivals who rallied behind the military to support his overthrow in December 2006. And their anti-SDL agenda did not stop there – the military government pursued Qarase and his party through the law and by oppression, eventually landing the former PM in jail in 2012 on charges relating to obscure events in 1992.

Qarase cinematically describes the case against him, his trial, sentencing, and imprisonment. Along the way, he offers insightful assessments of the government that displaced him. He is understandably critical of the post-2006 leadership and of the country's current policy direction. The impact that the post-SDL regime has had on Fiji's indigenous people are a major concern. In all of this, Qarase is measured and factually philosophical; on matters of personal hardship and family impact, his book is emotionally honest and surprisingly good-humored.

General readers and lovers of Fiji will find much in it to argue about; students of Fiji's political history will appreciate Qarase's depth and breadth of perspective.

And for those too young to appreciate what Fiji has been through on their behalf, this is a must read – it is a manual on how-not-to-do government at the end of a gun.

Qarase rediscovered his Christian core in prison, and despite the vindictive character of his persecution, his faith in democracy, justice, human rights, and equality for all in Fiji is unwavering. I am in awe of his integrity and courage. As someone who has known and admired him for 27 years, and who has had the privilege of working for the causes he espoused, I heartily commend this volume to the people of Fiji and to defenders of democracy the world over – there is much we can learn from Laisenia Qarase's story.

*Robert Wolfgramm, MA (Monash), PhD (La Trobe)*
  *Ringwood, Australia*

# FURTHER ACCLAIM FOR PRISONER 302

**When a son of Vanuabalavu** island In Lau, accounting and economics graduate and head of the Fiji Merchant Bank, Laisenia Qarase, accepted the initial role of interim prime minister during the serious troubles of 2000, with parliament taken over and the streets in uproar, his address to the nation declared that the citizens of Fiji belonged together, all had contributed to its development, and the challenge for everyone was to devise ways of reinforcing the foundations for living peacefully and harmoniously in their multiracial and multicultural society.

This was going to be an uphill task, pretty much as it had been since independence in 1970, as well as to some extent during colonial days too. And from this autobiography the reader will learn a great deal more about Fiji's world in general, Mr Qarase's challenges and difficulties of government following success in two general elections up until the end of 2006, and the later severe experience of confinement in Suva Gaol combined with a particularly close acquaintanceship with God of *Prisoner 302*.
In government and following a distinguished role in the life of Fiji,

Mr Qarase, the prisoner himself, paid a high price for venturing to promote indigenous rights, even though these are well accepted internationally since the desire to preserve identities and cultures is pretty well known across the world.

Autobiographies, histories, essays, poems have very fortunately been coming from the varied communities of Fiji for some time now, much to the benefit of people from elsewhere in the world who, like me, are fortunate to have family and friends in these Islands, and this new volume, *Prisoner 302*, with its evocations of childhood and then of recent experiences, is a particularly valuable addition to existing shelves of books.

*Deryck Scarr, BA, PhD, Emeritus Faculty Member, Australian National University*

---

**Laisenia Qarase's story** has to be told. *Prisoner 302* is a stimulating and challenging read. It is about a Fijian island village boy who became prime minister, and then suffered a most harrowing political persecution. Mr Qarase writes this account of his life and career from a very personal perspective, complete with political failures that are his responsibilities.It should be read by his village and island community, his political comrades and opponents, the wider population and in fact by everyone interested in Fiji.

Mr Qarase is not the corrupt person depicted by those who ousted him. Not at all. Here is a man who has weathered prolonged vilification while keeping true to the Christian values of his upbringing and they sustain him still. The campaign against him was driven by lust for power and the agenda of a dictatorship that has negatively shaped not only Fiji's politics, but more importantly its system of public governance, its civil society and electorate. It may take decades to overcome this.

Sayed-Khaiyum's student thesis played its part in what has happened to Fiji. The thesis is remarkable for flying in the face of reality. The attempt by Bainimarama and Sayed-Khaiyum to redefine who a Fijian is by State decree, presupposes the childish notion that a government, rather than respecting the ethnicity of its citizens, can somehow redefine reality by legislation.

In outlining the many serious problems confronting Fiji, Laisenia Qarase in this autobiography, steers clear of any notion of vengeance against those who seized his government by force. He is motivated by a desire for all the people of Fiji to come together through a process of dialogue and an adherence to the rule of law. These are the factors that will lead the nation to resolutely take the path of public justice for all.

*Dr Bruce Wearne BA (Monash 1972), MSocSc (Waikato NZ 1979), PhD (LaTrobe 1986) - Australian academic, researcher in sociological theory and writer and publisher of works on the religious and philosophical basis of that discipline. Seeks to contribute to the renewal of an authentic Christian way of life in the South West Pacific.*

---

***Prisoner 302* is about the life** of Laisenia Qarase from his birth and childhood in a traditional Fijian village; his education in Fiji and overseas; his rise as a senior civil servant and then into top banking positions. He was later influenced to move into politics and became prime minister in 2000 after a civilian uprising. He won power in two elections and led the country through a sustained period of economic growth.

But in 2006 Frank Bainimarama, Fiji's army leader, unhappy with the Fiji government, instigated a coup and took control. Under his military dictatorship, the legal system was hobbled, there was internal chaos, the media was censored, and many citizens feared for their lives and rights were abused. Fiji was internationally isolated. Following this coup Mr Qarase was convicted on dubious and seemingly trumped up charges and spent eight months in the antiquated Korovou prison in Suva. In 2018, although Mr. Qarase has still been denied his full political rights, he continues to play a role as a productive citizen of Fiji.

This thought-provoking book is a must read, not only for the people of Fiji seeking to understand the state of their nation and its future, but also for the wider international community. Credit to Laisenia Qarase for producing *Prisoner 302*.

*Dr Barry Ellem, BA Hons (Monash), MEd (Monash), PhD (Monash), CELTA (Cambridge) – Australian sociologist analyst.*

# ACKNOWLEDGMENTS

## BACKGROUND, ACKNOWLEDGEMENTS AND THANKS

I acknowledge and offer thanks to many people for inspiring me to produce *Prisoner 302*. My wife Leba is first on the list. She pushed me to put pen to paper. The first draft was limited to my time in Korovou gaol and drew on comprehensive notes I kept. It had the working title '243 Days in Prison'.

But with Leba's support I decided that the fuller story should be told. It is divided into three parts and takes in certain events and occurrences until near the end of 2017 when I finished the text.

The love of my wider family, especially grandchildren, was very important to me throughout my persecution.

I thank God for the privilege of leading the government of Fiji from 2000 to 2006. I thank my colleagues in the SDL party for their support and confidence in my leadership. I thank many thousands of supporters throughout Fiji and trust the governments I led contributed well to the development and welfare of the country and its people.

A summary of our main achievements makes up eleven appendices (starting on page 483). A timeline of relevant dates and events, maps, and a short glossary of Fijian terms, titles and abbreviations (for the non-Fijian reader) is at the back of the book. Endnotes elaborating on points raised in the body of the text are also placed there. A short list of my main source documents constitutes the final section.

I want to record my big "thank you" to those who made my life reasonably comfortable in prison. I appreciate the support of many citizens who followed my trial and extended their good wishes and prayers, particularly the large crowd that gathered around the High Court during sentencing. They gave me moral comfort when I needed it. I thank the prison officers and inmates at Korovou for their kindness and respect. I thank friends who visited me in prison, as well as those who wished to but were not allowed. I thank the pastors/ministers who offered prayers in Korovou for me and the other inmates. I thank the many individuals and prayer groups who were concerned for my welfare. All these people and what they did helped me enormously in dealing with an ordeal.

My special gratitude goes to James W. Skillen, for his foreword; and to Bruce Wearne, Barry Ellem and Deryck Scarr for their commendations. Dr Scarr contributed also to the project by reviewing texts, and making consequential recommendations and suggestions on the structure of the book. Robert Wolfgramm provided substantial assistance by preparing a preface, editing, arranging layouts, drafting appendices, a glossary and endnotes. Matt Wilson, whose services as a consultant and speechwriter I had used for many years, gave much editing support and many suggestions for improving style, presentation and quality. Jioji Kotobalavu, who was my permanent secretary and was recognized as one of Fiji's most distinguished and knowledgeable public servants, gave great help in reviewing the initial draft and offering comments. I thank Tanya Waqanika, Bachelor of Law, for taking the time to scrutinize the overall text from the legal perspective and for making recommendations.

I am indebted to Ranjani Riashni Chand for typing the original manuscript and to Davina Rounds Kaitu, who typed and formatted the edited text through numerous drafts to the final version and assisted with fact checking and liaison work.

*Laisenia Qarase, Suva 2018*

Note: I take full responsibility for the contents of *Prisoner 302*. I have checked them for accuracy. If any mistakes have crept in, they are my fault.

# PART I

## 1

# HOW HAD IT COME TO THIS?

This is not a scholarly work and is not meant to be a comprehensive, fully annotated historical record. It is a very personal narrative of my life, from my youth in a remote Fijian village on the shores of a lagoon, through overseas university education and a career in the public service, banking and commerce, to my fateful decision to enter politics. I became the fifth elected prime minister of Fiji, succeeded in two elections and enjoyed high approval ratings.

Then I was the target of a military coup and eventually served time in prison for trumped up charges of abuse of office that pre-dated my accession to power.

There is a concentration in these pages on the tumultuous developments that culminated in the coup, my forcible removal from office and eventual consignment to Korovou gaol in Suva, Fiji's capital, where I was a guest of the government for 243 days, from the 3$^{rd}$ August 2012 to the 3$^{rd}$ April 2013. I was the first prime minister of Fiji to end up in a prison cell after sentencing by a court. In this case it was a court presided over by a judge appointed by a military dictatorship. My official identity during my incarceration was Prisoner No. 302.

How had it come to this for someone who had always tried to conduct himself as a responsible citizen devoted to public service?

How had the legal holder of Fiji's highest political office become a common convict living with murderers, rapists, child molesters, thieves, violent robbers, and fraudsters? I shared a cell with someone serving a life sentence. There were other occupants of the cell too: bed bugs so fierce their bites left my blood on the sheets.

The story of the fall from power of Prisoner No. 302 and its aftermath is one of treachery, military insubordination, deception and lies, a manufactured national crisis, violence, injustice, threats and persecution and illegal use of force. A number of innocent people were killed.

My experience took a severe personal toll. The legal bills left me virtually broke. The prime minister's pension due to me was withheld until 16$^{th}$ December 2014. At the time of writing this, the government had still not given me all my legal entitlements provided under the *Prime Minister's Pension Act No. 16* of 1994. This was another phase of my punishment by those in power. There is something else which to my mind is further evidence of their vindictiveness. They included in their imposed 2013 constitution a provision that a person convicted of an offence and sentenced to imprisonment for 12 months or more cannot seek election to parliament during the eight years following release from prison. I have a suspicion that this was aimed specifically at me. Consequently, I was not able to contest the 2014 general election and will also be barred from the 2018 poll. I feel I have been sentenced twice and that my political rights have been violated. I compare the treatment meted out to me for alleged "abuse of office" which, God knows, I did not commit, and the non-accountability of the coup-makers. They continue to lead a dictatorship government protected by comprehensive immunity to cover their multiple crimes.

It was very obvious that I was hated with a passion by the military government and their hangers-on. Hate is a strong word, but I believe it accurately described the feelings towards me of some in the army leadership and their supporters. On more than one occasion I was threatened with arrest and death.

Apart from my tribulations, the entire country suffered from the excesses of a military dictatorship that imposed a reign of terror, intimidation, and abuse of rights, and clung to power for eight years. Apart from those who were killed, numerous citizens were subjected to torture, ill treatment, and humiliation.

The people were warned of the consequences of speaking out against the regime. The head of the Fiji Military Forces, Commodore Frank Bainimarama, made it very clear in his public pronouncements that he believed the military was "all powerful" and those opposing it would be placing themselves "in harm's way".

What did he mean by "all powerful"? More powerful than the people? Yes, in his mind. The power he spoke of was that of armed might and a willingness to use that against unarmed, defenseless civilians.

What did he mean precisely by "harm's way"? A light beating or a savage assault? The hot water treatment similar to that administered to the son of a former parliamentarian or other forms of barbaric torment such as sodomy with a stick?

Informers were everywhere; suspicion of large-scale corruption was rife and financial mismanagement widespread. The full account of where taxpayers' money went during the military reign has not yet been told; neither have those responsible for the crime of treason and for certain brutal murders and deaths been brought to justice.

The rule of law was compromised and so was the judiciary. Due process was often ignored. Our legally appointed chief justice was forced out of office by soldiers and proper procedures were not followed in the appointment of an acting chief justice. Later the entire bench of the court of appeal resigned.

Despite an assurance by Commodore Bainimarama that press freedom would be respected, there was a crackdown against the media. Censors decided what people would be allowed to read. The Australian publisher in Suva of a daily newspaper was abducted from his home at night and flown to Sydney the next morning. He was snatched without money, a change of clothing, or even a toothbrush. His abductors cut him off from contact with his family, who were left to wonder, in a state of quiet dread, about his fate. Later another publisher got his marching orders.

For the first time I describe here my escape from house arrest in Suva as the military clamped down on the capital following their take-over of government on 5$^{th}$ December 2006. Accompanied by my private secretary disguised as a policeman, my wife and I drove through several checkpoints manned by armed soldiers, before flying by chartered plane to my home island of Vanuabalavu. I thought at the time that we got through the military cordon because God was watching over us.

I was later sentenced to twelve months in prison in a high court case brought by the *Fiji Independent Commission Against Corruption* (FICAC) relating to my involvement in some share transactions in Fijian Holdings Limited (FHL), while I was a director of that company back in 1992. There is an account in these pages of the legal proceedings.

FICAC also initiated another case against me. *High Court Case No. HAC 26 of 2009* was about my involvement in a Native Land Trust Board (NLTB) decision taken in 2004. At that time, in addition to my responsibilities as prime minister, I was also minister for Fijian affairs. In this latter role I was chairman of NLTB. I was charged by FICAC for "abuse of office" in that I approved the investment of certain trust funds. FICAC considered this unlawful. After four years of court hearings from 2009, and after great financial and personal cost to me, the case was withdrawn in June 2013. That was a relief, but of course I had already been punished by the protracted and expensive court process. I believe that was intended. The case is described in some detail in this book.

In the FHL case (*High Court Case HAC. 27 of 2009*) there were six charges of abuse of office and three others based on the same facts. The charges arose from FICAC's allegations that I applied for, facilitated, and approved the allotment and issuance of FHL shares to three companies in which it was alleged I had interests. I was found guilty by the court on all the charges. Later I appealed but this was ultimately dismissed by the Fiji Court of Appeal.

When I was taken from the courthouse in Suva to the 130-year-old Korovou gaol and the gates slammed shut behind me, I found myself in a grimy, run-down, overcrowded institution, with rules for nearly every aspect of existence.

Living space was very limited. Mealtimes, leisure, visiting hours, work and lights-out in the evenings are all regulated. A prisoner has virtually no choice in these matters. It is a strange and challenging environment requiring quick adjustments on the part of new prisoners. I tried my best to adapt rapidly. I was fortunate to be treated with respect and kindness by fellow prisoners as well as by prison officers. Mostly they called me 'Mr Qarase' or 'prime minister'. It was evident many had voted for my political party!

In truth I did not find it excessively difficult to settle down in this authoritarian environment because it had some marginal similarities to my boarding school experience! Some personal issues were sorted out quickly and I established good relations with fellow inmates, particularly those living at Makosoi dormitory where I was accommodated.

Thanks to the law of unintended consequences, I can testify that I owe Korovou gaol a great debt of gratitude. I did not anticipate this when I had my first taste of being a criminal behind bars. As I came to terms with life inside, I found a haven and inspiration in my Christian faith. It became even more deeply embedded in my being. I gained greater knowledge and understanding of the Word of God due to many hours of spare time devoted to Bible reading. Sharing the Word with my cellmates was deeply rewarding. I discovered that most of the Korovou convict community - these lawbreakers who had put themselves outside society – followed their religious beliefs steadfastly. Some later became church ministers.

I was assigned routine work in the prison office. It helped greatly in passing the time. Apart from my prisoner colleagues in the office I came into contact with many other inmates. I learned much about the circumstances that brought them into prison.

I befriended a mouse I named Rupert and a rat I called King Kong because of his size. He became my unlikely early morning walking companion. I never liked rats but being brought into close contact with one as a prisoner helped me get over my rodent aversion. Rupert and King Kong both gave me peace and comfort. I was reminded that people and animals were created by God for different purposes. There was another difference between them and me. I was in prison; Rupert and King Kong were free.

The letters from my granddaughters and the visits from them, my wife, children, and other immediate family members, were precious and boosted my spirits. Visits by a few close friends and prayers

from individuals and prayer groups also contributed immensely to my psychological and spiritual wellbeing.

The experiences and events I have mentioned in this introductory chapter are described at greater length in the pages that follow. Source material encompasses documents and speeches, news reports and other data.

Some of it is available on-line. My descriptions of my time in prison draw on notes I kept. The first draft of the book was based on this. But Leba and I decided that the fuller story should be told. It is divided into three parts and takes in certain events and occurrences until late 2017 when I finished the text. I know it is a matter of public interest involving someone who reached the top political office in the land and enjoyed high approval ratings before becoming Prisoner No. 302. I hope the readers get a clearer perspective of what happened to me and why. It is important for history for the truth to be known, especially in light of all the lies told by the Bainimarama coup makers. Many of these falsehoods are related in these pages.

This book, therefore, aims to set the record straight and provide for the people of Fiji and abroad and to a wider audience an account of why my government of 2006 was subjected to a military takeover, why I was targeted for criminal prosecution, and why important freedoms have been taken away from me.

The heading for this chapter asks, "How had it come to this." That question is not just about me. It is about Fiji. We suffered an ordeal, came through and now we are in the grip of another type of tyranny. Why?

Maybe the reader will find an answer in these pages. I state once more that I remain unequivocally clear in my mind that I did not commit the offences that put me behind bars. I was sacrificed for revenge. Now, I look to the future with the love of Jesus Christ and the counsel of the Holy Spirit as my constant guide. For as that great Apostle Paul reminds us: "For what is life? ... It is Christ!" (Philippians 1:21)

# A LIFE-LONG LOVE AFFAIR

I am married to Leba Laveti of Dravuwalu village, Totoya, in Fiji's Lau group of islands. I wish to pay her a tribute right at the start of this story. We have been together since 1968. For all these years Leba has been my loving partner, a great helper, a faithful friend and companion and comforter. We look forward to celebrating our golden jubilee of marriage on 16th September 2018.

Leba was born at Dravuwalu Village, Totoya, Lau, on 4th December 1946. Her father, Eroni Taole was a native of Dravuwalu; her mother Seini Lewatani hailed from Vanuavatu village on Vanuavatu island. This is part of the district (*tikina*) of Totoya, Lau. Leba belongs to the *tokatoka* (sub-clan) kaiwa, *yavusa* (clan) Korowaiwai. She was the eldest of Eroni and Seini's three children. Her brother Jone Soko died in 2007. Tragically Seini died when she gave birth to Wati, Leba's sister. Wati, sadly, passed away before she reached her first birthday.

Leba's father Eroni enjoyed a long life. He died at Dravuwalu in 2005 aged 86. Leba and I could not be at his funeral. But thankfully Leba, with three of our children, was able to visit him just before he passed on.

When she was four, Leba and her younger brother Jone moved from Dravuwalu to Vanuavatu village. There they would be looked after and raised by their aunt Seruwaia and her husband Volau Taivei.

Leba remembers the emotion of saying farewell to her father. They would not see each other again for a number of years. From Vanuavatu the new family moved to Mago Island in northern Lau where her uncle Volau was a labourer on the Borron family's copra estate. After several years at Mago, the family moved to Suva. Here Eroni, Leba's father, was reunited with his children. There were then moves to Nadi and Waiyavi, in the city of Lautoka, where they made their permanent home.

Leba enrolled at the Lautoka Fijian Primary School in 1958. A certain Voreqe Bainimarama was a student at the school but as he was much younger, Leba did not socialise or study with him. It is a commentary on the often-strange course of human affairs that Leba has family relationships with Bainimarama, this man who was to cause her so much turmoil and emotional pain. Her sister's daughter married into the Bainimarama family. The husband of her sister is related to the family on his mother's side.

Leba moved on to Sila Central Secondary School at Nausori before her admission to the Fiji School of Nursing in Tamavua in 1963. She graduated from there in early 1968.

Our first meeting was in 1967 at a welcome home party in Suva for a cousin of mine serving at the time in the Special Air Services (SAS) of the British Army. It was, as they say, love at first sight. Our courtship was short and sweet.

In that year of '67 Leba was in her final phase of studies at the Fiji School of Nursing. In spite of the distraction of frequent dates with me Leba passed her final examinations. I remember during one of many visits to the Nursing School to see her I was chased by the school dog, Chop Suey. Later I learned that, on that same night, two other adventurous young men were driven off by Chop Suey. But there was no way this hound could permanently out-manoeuvre those of us who had regular evening appointments at the Nursing School.

Early in 1968 Leba was to be posted out of Suva's CWM Hospital, but before that happened, we decided she should leave nursing and move in with me. We were married soon after. Our behaviour – living together before marriage - was culturally and morally unacceptable and earned the disappointment of our parents. Our marriage ceremony was not very auspicious. It was conducted in the office of the Registrar of Marriages. Our witnesses were the late Spike Padarath, a good friend and his wife Lavinia, who rose to prominence in the Fiji Labour Party (FLP). She was elected to parliament on a FLP ticket and succeeded Jokapeci Koroi as party president after Mrs Koroi's death.

For our wedding 'breakfast' after taking our vows at the Registrars, we had a *roti* parcel each. That was it. Some months later relatives from both sides of our families conducted traditional wedding rituals with a proper celebratory feast.

Leba and I have raised a family of six, one girl and five boys. All are married with children of their own. We are blessed with 14 grandchildren and two great-grandchildren, a boy and a girl.

We experienced many difficulties particularly in the earlier part of our marriage. We quarrelled many times, often due to my wayward behaviour. There were periods of financial pressure. But fundamentally nothing threatened our union. We thank God for bestowing his grace and favour on us. I thank Him for Leba's love, support and understanding.

My trial and subsequent imprisonment were very stressful for the family. I know that Leba suffered greatly but she endured everything with admirable calmness and fortitude. During my time in prison Leba took over my role as head of the family. She looked after the house and our two granddaughters Senikau and Fane. Her regular visits to me in prison were always a bright ray of light in Korovou's daily routine.

# HISTORY, MYTH & LEGEND

I was born on 4<sup>th</sup> February 1941, at Mavana village, located by a lagoon at the island of Vanuabalavu, in the far-flung Lau Islands. Mavana was, and is, picture-book perfect, except when battered by cyclones, as it was when the terrible Cyclone Winston hit Fiji in February 2016 causing much damage.

The islands of Lau lie in the eastern section of Fiji. There are up to 50 of them ranging in size from 800mtrs to 32kms in length. Geologically they are composed of a mix of volcanic rocks and limestone.

Mavana is on Vanuabalavu, third largest island in the archipelago. It has a land area of some 53sq.kms with a maximum height of 283mtrs. There are some fairly steep cliffs; the soil is generally fertile and there are a few pine plantations. Vanuabalavu has an airstrip at Malaka and a wharf close to the main village of Lomaloma. Here there are some shops, government offices, a small hospital, secondary school and a Bible training school. A public road network links the island villages.

Mavana with an immediate population of some 200 is located on the coast in the mid northern section of Vanuabalavu. Avea Island lies about three kms offshore from our village.

Like many places in Fiji, the ancient history of Mavana is based on accounts passed down orally. There are sometimes contradictions and stories are disjointed. It is often impossible to separate myth and legend from fact. But this is what has come to us through the centuries. Also evident are the intricate relationships between communities and clans. These relationships extend far beyond Mavana. We have relatives all over Fiji. It's the same with other villages' populations.

The reader will notice in the narrative that follows how our forebears gave names to many places such as caves, hills, forest areas and anchorages.

These names have endured; they are still used today. The storytellers often focused on details such as food preparation, a small spring of fresh water, or the site of a fire.

In Mavana's case the village was probably established a considerable time after the Fiji Islands were first settled some 3,500 years ago. We cannot identify a precise date. The academic Robert Wolfgramm, son-in-law of Mesake Koroi who acts as my traditional spokesperson, says our ancestors came from Moala Island to the southwest; from Cakaudrove to the northwest; from Samoa to the far northeast and from the Kingdom of Tonga to the southeast. Dr Wolfgramm writes of the warrior Ravuravu and his role in our history. At the start of the 19th century, our settled existence began to change with the arrival of the Tongan warrior prince Ma'afu, European Christian missionaries, and traders. Ma'afu had subdued Vanuabalavu by 1865 and installed as the first 'Tui Lau' in 1869.

The information we have accumulated in the village about our ancient origins differs somewhat from the academic research and writings of Dr Wolfgramm. Our legends and stories tell us that the founders of Mavana started out on a journey by foot from the landmass of Viti Levu before embarking by canoe on the perilous voyage which brought them to the eastern islands of the group. The Viti

Levu track would have been very hazardous as they made their way through forests and over mountains.

They were on this odyssey at a time when Fiji was afflicted by bloody tribal warfare. So, I think they probably had to defend themselves from hostile chiefs and warriors as they pushed forward with their journey to an unknown destination. I do not know what drove them to seek a new home. Perhaps it was the insecurity caused by constant conflicts.

The oral accounts tell us that our ancestors were quite numerous which is why they were known as Yavusalevu (big tribal group), and other names such as Yavusatinitini, Yavusaudolu or Yavusamanumanu, indicating large numbers. Their leader was known by a number of titles including *Tui* Wai (King of the Seas), Tui (King) Sawa or Tui (King) Sawani. The ancestral god of the clan was Komainasavalevu who manifested himself as a dog. Their traditional symbols included the yaro tree, the secala (kingfisher) and the mulu fish.

On their great journey in Fiji, they appear to have started from Nakauvadra and moved through the villages of Burelevu and Tokaimalo in what is now Ra province. From there they went to Navuniyaro, Lutu, and Wainibuka in Waimaro in what became the Naitasiri province. Eventually they reached the coast. Here they paused and made temporary homes as they pondered on what they would do next. The sea was in front of them; it had new horizons. Moved by the enduring spirit of those who had earlier voyaged through the vastness of the Pacific to discover the islands of Fiji, the Yavusalevu decided they would make another journey over the waters. They were going into an empty space of uncharted ocean. But the hope of finding a secure place to settle was a powerful force. Employing their skills as boat builders, they used tools made of stone to hew planks, and sinnet cord from coconut palms to bind the structures. Big sails were woven from the voivoi plant. The ships they manufactured were examples of the double-hulled canoes recognized as amongst the finest sea-going craft of the ancient worlds. It is not known how many they built, but our legends tell us that one was called Rogovoka, named for one of the canoes that landed the first inhabitants of Fiji at Vuda in the west of Viti Levu. In more modern times that name continued to be used especially for government vessels. Another of the canoes built for the voyage was called Dakuiviti.

And so they set out, men, women and children, with their possessions and foodstuff, and maybe even a few animals. Fires on the deck, built on earth and sand platforms and ignited by the friction of dry sticks rubbed together were used for cooking. These were seafarers probably without parallel anywhere. They navigated by the stars and were driven by the wind, the tides and currents; birds and vegetation floating in the water indicated when land might be near. It is said that some of the Yavusalevu passengers disembarked in the Lomaiviti islands, particularly at Yadua village on the island of Gau.

The main group, however, continued until they reached Moala, a 62.5 sq km island in southwestern Lau. Here they toiled upwards through the trackless bush, carrying their belongings. When they reached the highest point of the island, at some 457.2m, this became the location for their new home.

It was called Delaimoala meaning it was at the top of the land-mass; it was presumably easy to defend in case of attack. The village they established there was called Korobasaga. They built a communal centre with the name Katubatini meaning ten doors, although legend has it that it actually represented the ten children of the chief Tui Wai and Vereacagi, one of his wives.

After a while Tui Wai's clan was joined by other groups including one led by a certain Kubunavanua, a prominent figure in early historical accounts of Fiji and Lau. There were relationship links between Tui Wai and Kubunavanua. These helped to create an environment of peace. Leadership was eventually granted to Rovarovanaivalu, one of Kubunavanua's kin, who was of the Tura-galevu clan and had the title of Tui Nasau.

The next milestone in the story is of Kubunavanua and his

followers leaving Moala – for reasons that are not clear – and relocating to nearby Totoya Island. One of those accompanying Kubunavanua was Ravovo, with the title of Turagalevu, who became leader of a Totoya village called Yaro. He was to become a major player in what followed.

The story is somewhat complex at this point; there is no straight historical narrative. It appears that Turagalevu and Takala his brother, escorted by warriors, voyaged through very rough weather, some 211kms, to Naselesele on Taveuni. This was the third largest island in Fiji, ruled by the Tui Cakau.

The wet, cold and weary voyagers struggled ashore and stored their possessions at a spot they named Raviravi. The Tui Cakau got word that they had come ashore and sent out an invitation for them to visit him. The account that has come to us through the ages says the visitors were so cold and drenched by rain that when they were approaching the Tui Cakau they had their arms wrapped across their chests as protection against the cold.

Tui Cakau invited Turagalevu's group to stay. In another twist to the tale, Turagalevu married Adi (Princess) Levu, daughter of Tui Cakau. She gave birth to twins, Ratu Saunamoli and Ratu Tavai (or Tavaiyaro). Turagalevu, a restless person, felt his new family and followers should move on from Taveuni and asked Tui Cakau for permission to leave. The Taveuni high chief spoke to his grandchildren, the twins, as follows: "My grandchildren you are leaving us, and if you decide later to visit us, I ask you to fold your arms when you come. This will tell me and my people who you are." This tradition continues today; when people of Mualevu (Mavana included), arrive at Somosomo in Taveuni, they fold their arms.

Turagalevu and his people reportedly built another canoe called Vesitagitagi or Druatabua, which was named after his twin sons. They started out from Taveuni and after a few days of sailing encountered bad weather and had to offload some of their belongings. They ended up in a narrow passage leading to the island of Vanuabalavu. They named the passage Qilaqila, and an inner lagoon

Cautininapoupou. This name signified that the canoe had to be navigated carefully because of the limited area of water in the lagoon. Eventually they made landfall at a small beach where they needed to carry out some repairs. They named this place Navau.

After sailing further along the coast, they spent the night in a cave under a shelter made of coconut fronds for warmth. They named the cave Buresasa. Turagalevu sent Takala and others to look for food and water.

When Takala and his group returned they found the area deserted and the canoe had gone. This was an inexplicable act of abandonment and Takala naturally was very angry. Takala and his followers began to walk along the coast and soon felt hungry and thirsty. A cave that provided a resting place was named Qaratutu and its location became Biaurogotoa because of the sound of waves against the rocks. As they walked further along the coast they paused at a spot they called Naituturaki. It was not long after this that they discovered a spring of fresh water where they quenched their thirst. It was named Todrou.

Proceeding further they saw the canoe in the distance but it seemed to be deserted. Turagalevu had anchored it at a small beach. A party from the canoe searched for food and water at a location they called Korowaiwai. Finally, they constructed a village, Delaikorolevu, on a hill but made sure to return regularly to the coast to check the condition of the canoe.

One day they saw Takala mending its sail. Turagalevu went to his sibling and his group and asked them to stay with them at Delaikorolevu. Heated words were exchanged between the two. Takala shouted: "You own the land, I own the sea." Turagalevu agreed that his brother owned the sea and the coast and that he should have the title Tui Wai (King of the Sea). The newly anointed Tui tried to make arrangements for his wife and family to move to the coast but could only manage to take with him his children. There is an account of Tui Wai making food in a lovo (earth oven) for his offspring. Then inexplicably his wife appeared, running towards them. They boarded their canoe and sailed away in a hurry without consuming the food. This is a puzzling episode, but it is what has come down to us from history.

With Tui Wai were people from the clans of the Matanivanua, Tui Rara, and Yaro in Totoya. This community accompanying Tui Wai became the Yavusa Valika. They travelled by canoe from place to place naming the areas they visited and eventually decided to stay at Avea Island, just off the coast of Vanuabalavu, not far from where Mavana was eventually established.

Later Turagalevu found out that the Vesitagitagi canoe was not at its usual mooring position. He took his people to a high peak; one of the reasons for doing this was to keep a watch for Vesitagitagi. By this time relations between the brothers were not good. One day Tui Wai, as he was looking out to sea from Avea, thought of his elder brother Turagalevu. His thoughts were of violence. He wanted to kill his brother. Then he lit a fire naming the spot for this as Koma (Komo). Turagalevu, also watchful, spotted the smoke. He interpreted the lighting of the fire as a challenge to fight and gave instructions for his people to start a blaze in return. Tui Wai's anger and his desire to use violence against his brother began to subside when he thought about their blood relationship.

It is recorded that Tui Wai, using Avea as his base, was a frequent traveler by canoe. One day the canoe Vesitagitagi was returning to Avea through heavy seas and wind and ran onto a reef, which became known as Cakaunidruatabua. The canoe was destroyed.

Takala's people tried to save the hull at a beach location which they named Vatukatavo. Walking along the coast they observed parts of the canoe scattered over an extensive area. A fragment of the hull was discovered at a site they called Vokavu. Suddenly someone saw a girl in the sea clinging to a piece of wood. She was rescued. This site is known as Poutu (or Potu). It was here that they stayed. This is where Mavana, my village home, was built.

This story tells of Takala lighting another fire. Turagalevu spotted the flames and smoke. Again, he wondered whether this was some form of challenge. He dispatched some men. It was at this point that Takala announced that he wanted to reconcile with his brother. But that was not all. Takala wanted Turagalevu to be installed as Tui Mavana at the very place where he lived. It was called Buliya.

Turagalevu agreed and would come to Mavana with his people for the installation ceremony. Takala would take on three traditional roles for this – kingmaker, *bete* (priest), and *matanivanua* (spokesperson). This was an extraordinary adaptation of culture. Normally the three roles would be handled by separate individuals. And so the preparations were made. The kin from the two groups assembled; Turagalevu and his tribe came from their hilltop village Delaiko-rolevu and joined with Takala's followers at the new village site of Mavana. In accordance with protocols, *bati* (warriors) stood guard.

The reunion of the brothers produced a mixture of emotions. There were tears and laughter. Takala announced: "We will install you here. This is my village Mavana and this is my land Valika." The leaders of the clans took up their positions. There was complete silence. Then to formally seal the installation Takala moved towards his brother and tied a strip of fine *masi* (mulberry bark cloth) on Turagalevu's right arm.

Then he pronounced: "Look at me my brother. I am tying the *masi* of my *vanua*. It is Tui Mavana's *masi*. The *yaqona* is also ready for you to drink today. You now have the titles of Sau Ni Vanua and Tui Mavana. Have compassion and love for the land. Love your people. So that your name will be blessed, and the land may prosper during your leadership."

Just after this a large feast was prepared and served by the people of Valika. There was unity. The land was named Yaro and Navuni-yaro or Waimaro. The different yavusas offered gifts to the Tui Mavana and pledged their total allegiance. The names Nautu and Qalitu originated from this time.

This history and these legends were very much in my mind when on 1ˢᵗ January 2009 I was elected traditional head of Yavusa Qalitu of Mavana with the title Tui Kobuca. I succeeded Josefa Cagi, a cousin, who died in 2008. The traditional structure of Mavana revolves around the Yavusa of Qalitu. The *mataqali* (sub clans) are Tota, Vatulami, Valika and Valevono. Tota is the chiefly sub clan. Vatulami provides the *bete* (priest) and *matanivanua* (spokespersons). This is the way it has been from the time of the ancients.

The procedure for electing the Tui Kobuca follows a set pattern which evolved from the past. A meeting of the *mataqali* Tota is held to decide which elder is the most suitable choice. After that a gathering of the villagers is informed about the selection. This involves the presentation of a *tabua* which was usually accepted by the villagers. They would reciprocate by presenting a *tabua* (a whalestooth, the most sacred of the objects in traditional ceremonies) to *mataqali* Tota, signifying approval. After that a *yaqona* ceremony would be accorded to the new chief.

In my case I wished to combine tradition with Christianity. Established custom was followed except there was no *yaqona* ceremony. Instead the late Reverend Josateki Koroi, a former president of the Methodist Church of Fiji, offered a simple prayer of thanksgiving. On the next Sunday, the Rev. Inia Vukialau, superintendent of the Mualevu Methodist Circuit, conducted an "installation" during the morning service at Mavana village church.

Rev. Vukialau had carefully prepared declarations including an undertaking in which I committed before God and the congregation to fully perform my duties and responsibilities as the new Tui Kobuca. I was happy with what transpired and felt confident I was the chosen one for the village at that time.

As chief of Yavusa Qalitu I am expected to lead on matters relating to the *vanua* (the chiefs, land and people), *lotu* (church), *matanitu* (governance), and the general welfare of members of the clan. The education I received, which I could not have attained without my parents, my work experience and my spiritual life, have helped me immensely to fulfill my chiefly role.

4

## CARING PARENTS

My parents Josataki Mate and Vika Fane were ordinary villagers, living a life bound by tradition, culture and the Methodist Church, largest Christian denomination in Fiji. They cared for me and my younger brother Satini Lakepa in a way that gave us security, a proper understanding of our culture and a grasp of the moral and Biblical values that would shape our lives.

Our father was a member of the *mataqali* (sub-clan) Tota, *yavusa* (clan) Qalitu, of Mavana. Mataqali Tota is the chiefly *mataqali* of the village. For a brief period, he acted as *turaga-ni-koro* (village headman) with responsibility for implementing development projects and nurturing the general welfare of the community. Apart from his stint in this supervisory role, he was a typical villager. He was quiet, humble, hardworking and unassuming and knew how to divide his time between caring for his family and contributing to communal work in the village.

I was to find out that this ordinary person was actually extraordinary. He uprooted himself from his settled existence in Mavana patterned on centuries of history and culture and took me on my first sea voyage to a new life and then built the foundation for it.

Our father-son relationship revolved around Vanuabalavu custom and the strict protocols of the time. There was no casual conversation and easy chit chat between us. We never had a "real" discussion even on important family issues. In view of what eventually happened it seems odd that my father did not even talk to me about my education.

Typically, he would simply give me an instruction. It might be something like helping with the yam planting or contributing to tidying up the village. I was expected to do what I was told. There was no room for sidestepping. Often what I said to my father would be in the form of requests – "is it ok if Satini and I go fishing tomorrow or play cricket?"

The requests would normally be granted. On many occasions our communication would be through a third party such as my mother. This was also a normal procedure in families.

I was thankful that my father lived to see me carve out a successful career in the civil service and as managing director of the Fiji Development Bank (FDB). He had the satisfaction of knowing that his judgment about my abilities and the sacrifices he made, with my mother, to give me a good education, had produced the kind of result he was looking for. But I doubt that his aspirations for me included election as the prime minister of Fiji.

The traditional role of men in our part of the country, Lau province, is to provide income, rootcrops, vegetables, and a decent family house. My father fulfilled his responsibilities well. Although only a few coconut trees were shared by the members of our clan (*mataqali*) my father was still able to generate income from copra to meet the costs of educating my brother and I and also daily groceries. On occasion there would be new clothes for the family. That was always a pleasant surprise.

He excelled at tending his plantation; we were never short of regular produce. In fact, I can remember that other villagers would sometimes help themselves from the fruit of his labour. Years later his farming experience was a great asset as we settled into a *bure* home at

Laqere near Suva, as explained elsewhere in these pages. Here he worked for daily wages for a Mr Pritam Singh who had extensive landholdings. My father managed to keep the family going with his meager income. He must have been a good worker because Mr Singh employed him until he was able to find a more permanent job with the Department of Forestry. Looking back, I used to wonder how a simple villager with very limited resources was able to provide for his family, including the education of my brother and I up to secondary school and beyond. It could only have come from a devoted commitment to his family, sheer hard work and perseverance. He was 74 when he died in 1986. He was also buried at Suva's main cemetery at Lovonilase.

My mother more than made up for the quietness of our father. She could converse for hours if she was in a talkative mood. In fact she was usually the dominant conversationalist and I always had the feeling she was in control of the home. She cared very much about our education at the Mavana school. She kept our uniforms clean and neat and our school books and other materials were always ready for us to take to class. In later years I marveled at the way my mother looked after us, given our poor finances. I had the sense that the little money we did have was devoted largely to education of Satini and myself, and to the Sunday church collections.

She lived to the ripe old age of 89. She had stayed with us in Suva, but spent the last few years at Mavana. She became wheelchair- bound and we engaged a couple to care for her. I remember that she was happy for me in 2000 when I was appointed prime minister, but I could detect some hidden anxiety and fear for what the future might hold for me. A few months before she died in 2003, I stopped by Mavana to spend time with her during one of my official prime ministerial visits to Lau. It was then that she told me she had experienced a premonition of adverse events that would eventually affect me. I reassured her that all would be well and that she should not worry. It was the last time I saw her alive.

Leba and I flew to Vanuabalavu the morning after she passed

away. Since there is no mortuary on the island, burials usually took place within 24 hours after death. Hundreds of relatives and people from the villages of Vanuabalavu came to Mavana for her funeral service at the village church. The burial took place two hours after our arrival and within 24 hours of her death. This was fitting because my mother was born a Jew.

# 5

## PARADISE

Shortly after I came into the world on 4<sup>th</sup> February 1941, a severe cyclone struck Lau. Josateki and Vika feared for my life. As the ferocity of the wind increased and the posts of our thatched house, close to the beach, started to tilt, they decided that their baby boy should be evacuated. I was placed into a Chinese-made wooden suitcase they owned and carried in this through the raging storm to a house where other villagers were sheltering. I was protected well by the sturdy case and arrived safely at the refuge.

Mavana's village green, adjacent to a white sandy beach, is surrounded by the homes of the villagers, the church and a school. Wooded hills rise behind the village. Satini and I were brought up in the traditionally built *bure* (house) which had only just survived the 1941 cyclone. Like the other homes it had an outside toilet and kitchen and no power or running water. We used firewood and kerosene for cooking and light. Water came from the village well.

Jone Rarawa, a cousin whose mother died when he was an infant, stayed with us. Life for us boys was very much circumscribed by the rules and expectations of the village community.

Village existence was different in virtually every way from an urban upbringing. Although we lacked town amenities and services, our environment was generally more relaxed. It was also exciting and challenging. God, Christianity, the church and Sunday school were central to everything in those formative years in Mavana. We were brought up to be humble and respectful towards family, neighbours, friends and elders. Honesty, hard work and perseverance were impor-tant and so was culture and tradition. These principles and ideals stayed with me throughout my adult life and formed the moral and ethical framework which guided me. They still do.

Fijian indigenous culture is very rich and varied. One aspect of it had gained a notoriety which sometimes embarrasses Fijians. We practised cannibalism. To my knowledge the last time it happened was in Seaqaqa, Macuata, between the years 1910 to 1915 after the

last tribal wars in the area. In Lau it appears not to have been widespread. There is an absence of recorded incidents. However, in Mavana there were many stories about the alleged former cannibal who lived in our midst. He was an elderly man who always seemed to be a bit eccentric, muttering to himself and gesturing. He was obvi-ously a victim of some form of dementia. We young boys used to whisper about his supposed past and tease him. He died around 1946-47. The village talk was that he must have been in his twenties by the end of the 19th century and if the rumours about him were correct he must have practised cannibalism about this time. But where these acts took place and if they did happen was never confirmed. We will never know whether he was Mavana's last cannibal.

Despite the need for conforming culturally and socially, village existence offered children the freedom to roam in the sunshine along the beaches and coastal tracks. We went fishing; took expeditions into the bush; climbed trees and swam in the creeks. In Lau kirikiti (crick-et), not rugby, was the big game. We played our own casual version using the middle part of a palm frond as a bat and a "vutu" – a kind of chestnut – as a ball. The cricket pitch was anywhere convenient: the beach, the village green or a clearing in the forest. It was all, in a real

sense, a paradise for boys. Looking back now I considered my
Mavana upbringing a privilege and a blessing.

We often walked about 5kms from Mavana to the Masomo lake,
covering about 10 acres. It has the appearance of the extinct peak of a
volcano. It is very deep at its centre; no one has ever measured the
actual depth. The water is muddy and brackish. The site belongs to
*mataqali* Valevono. There are traditional *bete* (priest) for the lake who
come from *mataqali* Vatulami. One particular fish, the *yawa*, thrives
here and is a great delicacy. Yawa can also be caught in the ocean but
their taste is quite different from the species in the lake. Special
fishing expeditions at the lake are called *ulidrano*. They are organized
every two years or so to ensure that the *yawa* stock is sustainable.
Masomo lake is surrounded by complex rituals which have survived
from the distant past.

The legend of Masomo goes something like this:
   One warm sunny day Volavanua, an elderly man from
*mataqali* Valevono, was resting at his plantation about three kilometers northwest of Mavana. He was tired and thirsty. Then he saw a
huge bird flying past carrying two women who appeared to have
containers made from leaves. Volavanua, for some reason, thought
they would have some water and he called out to them for a drink.
But they did not oblige. Volavanua became angry. He chopped about
half a meter from the stem of a tree and threw this at the bird. This
missile pierced the containers woven from leaves which contained
water, mud and fish. These all dropped to the ground and Masomo
Lake was formed. The giant bird continued on its way still carrying
the two women. Laucala Island near Taveuni was their final destination. When they arrived, they found that their containers had only
carried water and mud. At Laucala there is a lake similar to Masomo;
but it only had water and mud, and no fish. I know that legend is not
very precise but that is often the way it is with these ancient stories.

The Masomo fishing expeditions – commonly called fish drives -

are governed by long standing traditions and protocols. When it is decided to hold a fish drive, the village elders approach the priestly clan *mataqali* Vatulami and request permission. This is usually granted. Then all the *mataqali* begin their preparations. Young men are sent to cut "floats" about two meters in length from the trunk of the *makosoi* tree, which is known to be very buoyant. The women, meanwhile, prepare their attire for the fish drive – a skirt is made from the *Qai* leaves, from the same tree that Volavanua used to make his missile to throw at the giant bird and the two women as they flew overhead. The leaf skirts are worn by men and women and are the only item of clothing permitted during a fish drive, not even underwear is worn.

On the day before an expedition, the villagers travel to the lake and gather in *mataqali* groups. Each have their own shelter for the night. Before darkness comes, *mataqali* Valevono approaches *mataqali* Valika to form a bond of mutual support. A whole *yaqona* plant is used for this, then the *mataqali* Valevono and Valika combine and approach *mataqali* Tota. Later these *mataqali* approach *mataqali* Vatulami, which in turn presents another *yaqona* root to the village chief, giving him authority to decide on all aspects of the fish drive, and a *yaqona* session follows.

In the early hours of the next morning the person designated as the spokesperson for the fish drive signals the beginning of the event. Scores of men and women put on the Qai leaf skirts. Coconut oil has by then been applied generously over their bodies. The participants then enter the lake and swim around in groups using the *makosoi* floats. All these movements stir up the water and mud. If a large number of people are taking part in the fish drive, the *yawa* float to the surface and are easy to catch. If the catch is good this means that the traditional rituals were followed properly. If it is poor, this is because they were not conducted properly. These customs practised at Masomo lake have continued through the centuries.

When I took the title of Tui Kobuca, I decided that I would gradually try to end these ceremonies. For me they are left over from a pagan past; and are a kind of devil worship.

---

I attended classes at Mavana Village School from 1947 to 1952, taking lessons from class one to six. When I enrolled, the school consisted of one long thatched building to accommodate six classes. The floor consisted of mats of coconut leaves (*tabakau*). There were no desks or chairs. We simply sat on the floor. The school was near the shoreline, about 30 feet in front of my family house – no school bus needed! The roll was between 80 to 100 children, including some from other villages.

To assist in teaching arithmetic each student was required to have a bag of reeds cut into six-inch lengths. It was our rudimentary version of the Chinese abacus. The reeds were used for learning addition, subtraction and division. I found it easier to understand the subject using this teaching aid. No calculators in those days.

Classes were not separated by partitions. This meant there was usually a chorus of competing noises. One class would be counting aloud; another would be spelling; and yet another reciting short sentences in English.

For most of us school was enjoyable. Class work was complemented by sports such as soccer, athletics and our local brand of cricket. I developed some skills in high jumping and continued this through to secondary education at Queen Victoria School. But I was never a great sports type. I liked studying better.

A village council meeting decided to build a new school at the back of the village. We moved into the new premise in about 1949. It consisted of classrooms built from concrete blocks, timber and roofing iron. There were three teachers' quarters and a playground. The facilities were certainly better than the single thatched building of the old school.

I did reasonably well from class one to class six. In 1950 Master

Samuela Jale of Yale, Kadavu was appointed head teacher of Mavana school. He was a good teacher, leader and disciplinarian. His role in my life was important. Master Samuela saw some potential in me and was persuasive in encouraging my parents to send me for further education in Viti Levu. They were already thinking about this.

As with most of the other Mavana families, we were always short of money but never went hungry. Several times a week we would trek with our father about four kms along the coast to the family planta-tion on three acres of land allocated to us from our *mataqali* (clan). There we would either harvest or plant crops such as cassava, sweet potato (*kumala*), yam; banana and the nutritious green vegetable, *bele*. There was always weeding to do as well. My father did not actively teach us about farming. But we watched and learned from the way he tended the gardens. We would return home weighed down with produce and firewood for the outside kitchen. These working visits to the plantation instilled in me a sense of family responsibility and taught that hard effort was required to achieve something positive.

Sometimes we harvested mature coconuts for processing into copra. Each nut had to be chopped in half with an axe, for the white flesh to be extracted with a special knife. On a good day we could gather 50kgs or more for sale at the village store. This was essentially the only source of income for villagers. Each family had the right to harvest nuts from the *mataqali* land on a "first come first served" basis. The proceeds from copra were just sufficient for basic needs, including, of course, church contributions. My farming and harvesting skills were very useful at boarding school and later when I was exiled in Mavana during the military insurrection, I became Qarase the farmer, well-known for the quality of his yams.

# 6

# PRUSSIA TO MAVANA

Not many of my friends are aware that I have Jewish blood. My mother, Vika, was a member of *mataqali* (sub clan) Valika, *yavusa* (clan) Qalitu of Mavana. Vika's father was John Bowman, one of the few Jews in Fiji at the time and certainly the only one in the Lau Islands. I believe John Bowman (or Jone Pomani in the vernacular) was the only son of Isaac Bowman and a Scottish lady, Fane Osborne. Isaac Bowman and Joseph Osborne, father of Fane Osborne, came to Vanuabalavu in the 1860s as traders. My mother was named after Fane Osborne, who was her grandmother.

John Bowman married Asinate Ole from Yavusa Munia on Avea Island opposite Mavana village. They had five children Vika was the only girl. The children were accepted for registration in the Vola ni Kawa Bula (VKB) (Register of Indigenous Fijians) of Mavana, Avea and Malaka villages on Vanuabalavu.

The fuller story of how a Melanesian Fijian like me, from a remote island, came to have a Jewish maternal grandfather who lived near the beach at Mavana is worth relating.

The Bowman family genealogy I have researched goes back to

one Schmerrill Bowman, born in Prussia, Eastern Europe in the early 1800s. It is a big jump from Prussia to a group of small islands in the Pacific.

Schmerrill Bowman's only son Alexandar Schmerrill Bowman came into the world on 7th July 1847 in Schneidemuhl. Due to the changed map of Europe, Schneidemuhl is today in Poland and known as Pila.

Alexandar moved across the world to Australia where he passed away on 14th July 1909, in Sydney, NSW. But records show that in 1875 he was living at Lomaloma, Vanuabalavu, where he owned a trading store. The *Sydney Morning Herald*, on 10th August 1891, carried a report that his Lomaloma store was totally destroyed in a fire. Fortunately for Alexandar, copra he had in store had been shipped for milling the previous day.

He was known in Vanuabalavu by the very Jewish name 'Isaac'. He had married Sara Annette Solomon (a good Jewish surname) on 25th July 1877, in Levuka. Sara was the daughter of Philip Solomon and Catherine Cohen of New Zealand.

There is some confusion about John Bowman's parentage. According to one account John Bowman was the child of Alexandar and Sara. That may be so, but my ancestor – also known as John Bowman - was in fact the offspring of Isaac and Fane Osborne. Fane's father was either John, or Thomas Osborne, originally from Scotland, and also owned a Vanuabalavu trade store.

John Bowman had the middle name Ma'afu, derived from the Tongan warrior prince, Enele Ma'afu, who had become overlord in the area. In June 1903 John married Asinate Ole of Avea. Their daughter, Vika, was my mother. So migration from Prussia of Alexander Schmerrill Bowman created a lasting legacy, not only for me but for a wider network of descendants. By 2016 there was a large extended family of Fijian Bowmans tracing their origins to the marriage of John and Asinate.

I had a close relationship with my maternal grandfather and regularly visited his small, thatched *bure* at one end of the village. A stocky person of medium height, John was fluent in the Vanuabalavu dialect, and of course spoke English. His residency in this quiet Pacific backwater did not detract from his cultural observances as a member of the Jewish faith. I can remember he always wore his traditional Jewish Yamulke headgear.

Grandfather Bowman was a very good fisherman. He used one of two outrigger canoes in the village for his expeditions. There is a story that is now part of village lore about him becoming impatient one day when bad weather drove the fish away. He was determined to find the means of putting seafood on the menu. He is said to have gone out at low tide and collected pieces of coral and edible seaweed. The coral purportedly joined the seaweed in some kind of a soup that he boiled up and allegedly consumed. I have never heard of anyone else making "soup" from coral rock!

In 1954, during my Christmas school vacation, he invited me to go fishing. It was a memorable trip. We paddled out in one of the outriggers to a submerged reef about 500 metres from the village. Using small crabs for bait, my grandfather dropped his line over the side, while I watched. Within two hours he had hauled in a big catch of sabutu, a grade one reef fish. We returned triumphantly to the village; there were many happy families that evening.

# 7

# THE GREAT LIBERATOR

I have always believed that a good education is key to progress in life. When I became a politician, I referred to it as the great liberator and ensured it was the centerpiece of the policies I put to the people. Education made it possible for islanders like me to break away from the traditional lifestyle, and its related financial poverty and earn qualifications for a professional career. My political preoccupation with education undoubtedly came from my parents. Unknown to me at the time they had already decided their boys would go beyond Mavana. Their own educations were basic but that did not limit their vision and ambitions for my brother and me. When I understood the extent of their commitment and devotion, I resolved to study hard, succeed and get good jobs. I very much wanted to repay my father and mother for the sacrifices they had made for me. To a certain extent I was able to do this. One of my regrets is that I did not do enough for them before they passed away.

In 1952 I passed the intermediate schools entrance examination. By then Master Samuela, the headmaster, had really started pushing for me to go to the main island, Viti Levu, to advance my schooling. Of course, he knew my parents were poor and would find it extremely difficult to fund a boarding school education for their eldest son. They were caught between a hard rock and the deep blue sea. They wanted very much to send me, and Satini, to Viti Levu, but their lack of money stared them in the face. They must have spent hours talking about how it could be done. The same dilemma faced the other village families.

It was during this period that, according to family lore, my father had a dream as he took a nap at his plantation. He saw a big man standing beside him who said something like, "Take your eldest son for further education. He will occupy some important positions in the future." He hurried to the village and told my mother about his experience.

Finally, the momentous decision was reached. I was to go to Ratu Kadavulevu School in Lodoni, Tailevu on Viti Levu, for the start of the first school term in 1953. I did not know for certain where my father found the funds to do this, but I believe he was granted a loan from our village co-operative society. I think my mother's prized possession, a Singer sewing machine, was offered as security.

I was to say goodbye to Mavana, which till then had been the cradle of my existence. I would travel for the first time the 200 kilometres to the capital city Suva. Something told me that I would not be returning to Mavana to live. That was what normally happened when children sailed away to the main island for schooling.

I learned that my father would accompany me on the voyage and then establish a new home for the family in Viti Levu. This 42-year-old, virtually penniless, was born and bred in Mavana. Apart from a short period of service in the territorial forces based in Suva in World War II, the village was all he knew. It shaped and defined him. Now he was taking himself away from everything that was familiar for the unspoken love of a son. Supported strongly by my mother, he wanted me to have the education he never had. He knew this would open up opportunities that had been denied to him.

His mind must have been filled with doubts and fears as we prepared for the journey, but typically he did not share them. One morning early in January 1953 our family gathered the luggage together. My mother and Satini would stay behind for now while my father established some sort of living arrangement on Viti Levu.

Satini, who is two years younger than me, also went to RKS and then Queen Victoria School. He took a course in maritime studies, became a sea captain and served on a number of overseas ships. Later he worked for the Ports Authority of Fiji from where he retired.

# 8

## EMOTIONAL GOODBYE

We voyaged to Suva in January 1953 on the motor vessel "Tovata" owned by the big island trading company W. R. Carpenter Limited. It carried basic consumer goods to the islands and collected return cargoes of copra for Suva. Although the Tovata was the most modern inter-island ship of that time, it did not have passenger accommodation. Those who travelled in her had to find their own space on deck. Their meals came from home-cooked food they brought on board.

When the Tovata arrived at Mavana on that January morning, a crowd of villagers had gathered at the co-operative store to farewell those traveling to Suva. Four of us were bound for secondary school. My father was joined by other parents travelling with their offspring. A handful were going to the capital for a variety of purposes. As final farewells were said, many tears were shed. As I have mentioned, when a child left Mavana like this, they were unlikely to come back to their village to live. It was the end of one part of their young lives. And so it was with me. We were in effect internal migrants who were expected to find a job after schooling on Viti Levu and then establish a home and family in one of the urban centres. We would build our lives there while providing support for the villagers we had left behind.

I was emotional and sad about departing from Mavana. But the sadness mixed with excitement and anticipation at the prospect of seeing the great city of Suva for the first time and attending a secondary school in a totally different environment. My luggage comprised a bundle of mats for bedding at RKS; another mat and a pillow for the voyage and a suitcase for my clothing.

The family had two suitcases: the large wooden model made in China, which was used to protect me from a hurricane as a baby; and a smaller case made of some thin iron material. It was this one I took with me. I came to dislike it intensely. I thought it looked strange and was too big for an 11 year-old boy. When I got to RKS I discovered it was the only one of its kind at the school.

When I was travelling to and from RKS, I felt very self-conscious and awkward lugging it into the Suva bus stand and placing it into the bus luggage area. I was sure everyone was watching me and laughing. But I was stuck with the horrible thing because I had no money to buy a replacement. It was my dislike of it that spurred me to join the carpentry classes at RKS.

My aim was to make a case that was lighter and looked better. I gave it my best effort and, thank goodness, was able to put together a more presentable wooden case. Although wooden models were also rare at RKS, at least what I had made was an improvement on the metal version from Mavana. It was not until I entered Queen Victoria School in 1955 that I was able to buy a new case. My schoolboy obsession in this matter only developed after we left Mavana and Vanuabalavu.

We spent the first night of the Tovata voyage at Cicia island, about 50 miles southwest of Vanuabalavu. We stayed at the home of a relative at Tarukua village. The son of the household, Kini Bera, was also getting ready for the journey to RKS. We had a hot meal and then went aboard again just before daybreak. The ship left Cicia shortly afterwards and arrived in Suva the following morning. The life-changing voyage was uneventful. It was a boring and tiring two days. Sleeping on the deck in a confined space was far from comfortable.

For those of us who were traveling to Suva for the first time, the capital was a world which had existed only in our imaginations. The reality was awesome. We marveled at the large concrete buildings, the wharf, the big ships, the busy roads, the vehicles and the general hustle and bustle.

For me the village was now far, far away and I was glad to be in Suva. From the wharf my father and I travelled by bus to stay with a family from Mavana who had settled with relatives on a five-acre farm at Laqere, about eight miles from the city.

# 9

# LABOURING HARD IN OUR NEW LIFE

In our new life at Laqere my father was a labourer working for Pritam Singh who had some landholdings in the area. His wages were about $20 to $30 for a five-day week. The work, harvesting Mr Singh's crops and weeding, was casual depending on demand. The income was small, but it was just enough to keep us going. At one point my father was so short of money that he had to send off an urgent telegram to the chairman of the Mavana Co-operative. He sent it under his surname 'Mate'. The English translation was something like, "Mate problem, money zero". (Fijian: "*Mate leqa, lavo sega*".) Of course, there are few secrets in a tightly knit village, so before long Mate's telegram was a popular saying especially in grog drinking circles. Thankfully the co-operative approved a further loan.

After a while my mother and Satini joined us. Things looked up financially when father found a better job in a Forestry Department mahogany plantation beside the *bure* where we lived. This involved keeping the plantation undergrowth under control. We knew our situation was getting a bit better when fish in lolo was served occasionally for dinner, particularly on Sundays.

Our thatched *"bure"* was built by my father, with the help of some neighbours. It was typical of residential structures found in Fijian villages. Its floor area was about 20 feet by 16 feet and the roof was made of palm leaves stitched together. The posts and rafters were fashioned from trees from the area. The walls were of the same material used for the roof. About 30 meters from the house was a pit-latrine. A small spring was our source of water for cooking and bathing. The *bure* was comfortable and cool during sunny days. But during rainy periods it leaked badly. We used to plug the leaks with anything we could find, from pieces of cardboard to flattened out biscuit tins.

When my brother and I enrolled at Ratu Kadavulevu School and later Queen Victoria School, both boarding establishments, part of the burden on our parents was removed. But they still struggled to support our education and day in and day out had to bear the discomfort and inconvenience associated with the lack of amenities at the Nasinu *bure*.

Then, suddenly, came the news that I had been awarded a Sukanaivalu Scholarship based on my results in the intermediate school entrance exam in 1952. The awards, in memory of the Victoria Cross winner, Corporal Sefanaia Sukainavalu, were allotted to the top 10 indigenous students competing in the examination. The scholarship was a great relief to my parents.

# 10

## FEELING FINE AT RKS

I went to Ratu Kadavulevu School [RKS] in 1953 when I was 12 and studied there for two years. The school in Lodoni is a very well-known boarding institution. Founded as the Provincial School Eastern in 1924 by a high chief, Ratu Penaia Kadavulevu. The school was later renamed in his honour.

I remember clearly the day my father took me there. I was dreading going because I did not know what to expect. Some of my fears were eased when I met the duty teachers. They were friendly and helpful. I was taken to my dormitory and shown the wooden bed allocated to me. I had to make it comfortable with two mats, a pillow and mosquito net I had brought with me. My father watched approvingly as I made my RKS bed for the first time. I saw other parents and their sons going through the same routine. Then I briefly met students from different parts of Fiji, including some from Vanuabalavu. The anxieties I had felt when we left Suva that morning evaporated. RKS seemed quite a friendly place. When my father said goodbye, I felt fine.

The school roll then was probably about 300. Most of the school buildings were sturdily built of concrete blocks, timber and roofing iron. There were many huge mango trees in the compound. Outside the compound the terrain was covered with bush and more trees, except for flat land separating RKS from Lawaki Village. Here there were crops of cassava, *bele* and more vegetables. A dairy farm and piggery added to our diet.

Breakfast was normally porridge or bread and tea. Lunch and dinner were invariably tinned fish with cassava and *bele*. You had to be careful with the *bele* because it often had small worms in it, which were not washed out when it was cleaned. On Saturdays we broke up into small groups to hunt for wild yams, crabs, prawns from the nearby creeks and sometimes the occasional mongoose (*manipusi*), which were caught in traps. Typically, one end of an approx. eight ft. long tree branch was stuck firmly into the ground while the other end was bent over in a half circle. The bait, usually cooked cassava or bread, was prepared and the trap was made ready. When an unfortunate mongoose stepped on it to get to the bait, the trap was sprung. If it worked, the mongoose was left hanging from the end of the branch. All the stuff we collected on these Saturday expeditions ended up in a *lovo* (earth oven). They were a very welcome complement to a pretty boring weekly menu.

Hard physical work was always part of the daily routine. At school parades each morning, every student was expected to turn up with a coconut leaf basket and a cane knife. If you didn't have these, you were penalised by working extra hours in the afternoon or on a Saturday. We spent a lot of time cutting down mango trees, clearing the dense bush around the school, planting new cassava and *dalo* plantations and rows and rows of *bele*.

The principal, Mr M. J. Bay from New Zealand, and his assistant Master Rupeni from Somosomo, Taveuni, were disciplinarians of the old-fashioned kind. It was a question of "spare the rod and spoil the child". Those who got into trouble found themselves working in the gardens for an extra two to three hours on a Saturday. When a boy really stepped out of line, Mr Bay and Master Rupeni produced their canes made from reeds. Punishment was usually between six and 12 strokes. This really hurt, and you could feel the after effects of the sting for days. One very bad memory revolves around an incident prior to the Secondary School Entrance Examination in late 1954. The candidates were required to arrange the desks on the evening before the examination. Two of us were carrying a desk from point A to point B. Before we reached point B, my friend's sulu slipped. When he grabbed it to save himself from embarrassment, he lost his grip on the desk which fell to the floor and broke in two. We had to report to the principal's house where we received six strokes each. Needless to say, when I took my seat for the examination, I was more than a bit uncomfortable. To this day I still feel we were treated unjustly. We did not break any rule and the incident was an accident. However, despite my sore backside I passed the exam and in 1955 moved on to Queen Victoria School (QVS).

# 11

# QUEEN VICTORIA SCHOOL

Queen Victorial School named after a British queen of the colonial era was the elite educational institution for indigenous boys. It is beautifully located at Matavatucou on the Eastern coast of Viti Levu, about a two-hour drive from Suva. Qoma Island with its village is about 200 metres offshore. In the distance you can see the islands of Ovalau and Naigani. This scene reminded students like me from the outer islands of our home environments.

QVS was originally at Nanukuloa in Ra and was moved to Matavatucou in Tailevu in 1952. Initially the institution was perceived by many as being reserved for boys from chiefly families. The aim was to train these scions of the traditional nobility for leadership roles in the public service and the broader community. However, in reality, boys who did not come from the chiefly ranks were admitted. By 1955 when I started at QVS, students from ordinary families were very much in the majority. Admission was based on academic achievement. The principals were carefully selected from top schools in England. Many students who studied there went on to play leading roles in the public service, professions, commerce and politics.

When I arrived at the school, the amenities were far superior to those of RKS. Beds, for instance, had a comfortable spring mesh. We had lockers for keeping some of our personal possessions. You could say that the food was "five-star" quality in the context of those times. We often had a combination of cassava, *dalo*, beef, pork, vegetables and fresh fish. The school was more or less self sufficient in produce. It had a dairy farm and piggery, and its own extensive gardens. The work programme for students was much easier than RKS. We did about one hour in the morning before breakfast and were free after school in the afternoons and spent a lot of time on sports and study. Study periods in the evenings and weekends were ample. Attending church on Sundays was compulsory.

I had three external examinations ahead of me, the Fiji Junior, Senior Cambridge and the New Zealand University Entrance. I was determined to study hard and pass all of them. In 1956 I succeeded in the Fiji Junior, with a Grade A pass, the Senior Cambridge in 1957, and the New Zealand University Entrance in 1958. Unfortunately, my results fell short of the requirements for a scholarship for a university degree.

In 1959 I enrolled in the Upper Sixth in the then Suva Boys Grammar School. (My parents continued to live at Laqere). Five of us from QVS who had moved to the Boys Grammar School were accommodated at the Fiji Medical School just outside Suva. The sixth form at the Grammar School was the forerunner of the present form 7. Attaining a government scholarship was determined by your performance at this level. There were about 10 of us sixth formers including Lionel Yee, who became first local chief executive officer of the Fiji National Provident Fund; the late Savenaca Siwatibau, who went on to pursue a distinguished career in the civil service and academia and was first local governor of the Reserve Bank of Fiji; and Yogesh Patel, who became a great success in the medical profession in New Zealand.

# 12

# AUCKLAND UNIVERSITY AND A COMMERCE DEGREE

I n 1960 government scholarships were limited to two or three a year. I missed out initially and had to wait until 1963 when I was awarded a scholarship to study for a Bachelor of Commerce degree at Auckland University in New Zealand. In the meantime, I was employed as an executive cadet in the Fijian Administration under a scheme for training for future leadership positions in the civil service or private sector.

I went on study leave to Auckland from 1963 to 1966. Mavana school with its one thatched classroom seemed even more remote now. I lived in a rented flat in Auckland's Grafton Road, which was within walking distance of the university campus. Other students from Fiji shared the flat. They were the late Mosese Qionibaravi, who became finance minister in Ratu Sir Kamisese Mara's Alliance government; Savenaca Siwatibau, Jioji Kotobalavu who went on to become an eminent civil servant and diplomat and served as my permanent secretary when I was PM; and Ratu Jone Y. Kubuabola who served with distinction internationally as an economist, went on to lead the RBF, and was finance minister in my governments.

We did our own cooking and cleaning, but I doubt it was up to standard.

Auckland University was education at a completely new level. In a sense I was my own boss. I could attend lectures/classes or stay away. It was my choice. For my B.Com Degree I chose accounting as my major and economics as my second. The course also included commercial, company and trustee law.

I was determined to work hard. In the first year I passed all three subjects of my study course. But failure struck in the second year. I attributed this to the many distractions of university social life for a lad from the islands; distraction like drinking beer, and staying up late at student parties.

Come the third year, I was on top of my game again and in 1966, my fourth year, I completed the full B.Com. programme. The lesson was clear. University education is not necessarily all that difficult, as long as you put in the required effort and fully apply your mind.

At the time of my higher education I was venturing along a path not usually followed by indigenous Fijians. Their horizons often did not extend beyond the cultural confines of village life, with its communal activity, traditional farming and fishing. University was not much talked about. When the topic did come up, it seemed beyond reach, not to mention the perennial problem of lack of money.

The great statesmen, paramount chief and reformer, Ratu Sir Lala Sukuna led the way, earning a Bachelor of Laws degree from the UK. Ratu Sir Kamisese Mara, Fiji's first prime minister, elected head of government for 17 years and then president, was a graduate of Oxford University with a Master of Arts degree and earned a Diploma in Economics and Social Administration from the London School of Economics. There was a steady trickle after that. Many of those who earned degrees also went on to serve in important positions. I think of people like Rusiate Nayacakalou, Fiji's first Ph.D.; Sir Timoci Tuivaga, who became our first local chief justice; Josevata

Kamikamica, first Fiji general manager of the Native Land Trust Board; and Savenaca Siwatibau.

But compared to the academic achievements of other communities the Fijians were far behind. There were complex reasons for this to do with history, cultural attitudes, communal living and sharing and lack of finance. But the bottom line is that if you want to get on in any field of endeavor you have to strike out on your own, make sacrifices and work hard.

# 13

## CO-OPERATIVES AND BUTADROKA

I returned to Fiji with my new degree and began a public service career, which covered a period of 16 years to 1983. In 1967 I joined the Department of Co-operatives. In 1969 I went on a 12 months course on co-operative development from July of that year at the Co-operative College at Loughborough, in the United Kingdom. This was just outside Leicester city. Loughborough University was about 15mins drive from the Co-operative College. I took a course leading to a Diploma in Co-operative Development, which was part of the Loughborough University programme. To round off my academic credentials, I became an associate member of the Chartered Institute of Secretaries (ACIS) through a study programme of the Auckland Technical Institute. This was an excellent course for company secretaries and executives in the public and private sectors.

The Co-operative Department was the ideal place to begin my employment in the public service. My B.Com. Degree assisted me to progress fairly quickly. I travelled extensively throughout Fiji during those 10 years with the department. It was the heyday of the co- operative movement. There were hundreds of village consumer co- operative stores in every part of Fiji. Similarly, sugarcane areas had hundreds of "thrift and credit" co-ops. Other co-operative groups included agricultural marketing societies, land purchase and transport co-ops. The department's function was to advise on organization, procedures, business principles and development. We conducted meetings with co-op members; gave accounting services and conducted audits. I enjoyed the work. It gave me further insights into the everyday social and economic problems of rural people, which differed depending on location and terrain. I learned how rural economies operated, and the role in them of culture and group activity.

Initially I was given responsibility for the eastern division, which took in the provinces of Lau, Kadavu and Lomaiviti. Consumer cooperatives dominated. They bought store goods from Suva and sold copra – dried coconut flesh - to the Island Industries coconut oil mill in Suva. High prices for copra during the 1960s helped to create a thriving co-operative network in the eastern areas. Good dividends were a strong incentive for villagers to support the movement.

Soon I was appointed assistant registrar of co-operatives, then senior assistant registrar. By 1976 I was registrar, which meant I was head of the department.

Mr Sakiasi Butadroka was a great influence in my co-operatives career. He came into prominence as a fiery, outspoken political personality in the 1970s and 1980s, distinguished by his red bow tie. Mr. Butadroka was my boss in the department. As a junior officer I used to accompany him to many co-operative meetings, large and small. I found him to be intelligent and sharp. He was an eloquent and persuasive speaker in the Taukei language. He had a very clear vision, particularly on matters relating to the advancement of the indigenous Fijians. He was passionate about this and often provocative in his pronouncements. For instance, he wanted all land in Fiji including freehold to revert to Fijian ownership. His ambition was for national leadership to remain in Fijian hands at all times.

Once Mr Butadroka had made up his mind it was difficult to

persuade him to change. Finally, he moved into politics and was elected to parliament. He ended up being sacked from Ratu Sir Kamisese Mara's Alliance Party because his principles were not consistent with the multiracialism of that party. He went on to form his own party, which, at its peak, gained support from about a quarter of the indigenous electorate. It was enough to unseat the Alliance in the first election of 1977. But in the next election of that year, the Fijians returned to the Alliance fold and Mr Butadroka's star began to fade.

I have never publicly disclosed that he asked me to suggest a suitable name for his party. I gave him two or three options including Fijian Nationalist Party. That was the name he registered.

Later I felt uncomfortable about this. I was still a civil servant. And yet, I had provided the name for Mr. Butadroka's party, which was in direct opposition to Ratu Mara's Alliance. I had no idea whether the high chief knew this. But he never raised the issue with me.

I learned certain things from Butadroka. In particular I was impressed with the way he controlled and managed public meetings of the indigenous Fijians. His delivery was often aggressive and unsettling for non-Fijians. You could not, however, fault how he structured and propagated his message. His arguments were always aimed at persuading and convincing his Taukei audience, and they usually succeeded. For me Butadroka's speaking talents were a good lesson for effective public meetings with Taukei communities. This was very useful for me during the general election campaigns in 2001 and again in 2006. I am not a firebrand like Mr Butadroka, but I know how to communicate effectively in the language of the indigenous people. I learned much of that from him.

In my extensive travels I was always accompanied by one or two co-operative officers. Our job was to "close" the books of co-operative societies; prepare the accounts; hold annual meetings and supervise the distribution of dividends.

Often, we travelled by foot from one village to the next, carrying our travel bags and documents. There were few public roads in many provinces in those days and none in Lau and Lomaiviti. Road construction was just starting in Kadavu. Canoes were pressed into service to take us from island to island. Sometimes there was an outboard-powered punt available.

I liked sleeping in a *bure* with just a mat separating me from the sandy floor. Those long walks between villages, humping my travel bags and files were also good exercise. The meetings also taught me more about how to address groups. I added to my practical knowledge of village life, the daily routine of organizing food for a family, getting the children off to school, discussions in grog sessions in the evenings, preparing for Sunday church services, wedding celebrations, and many other activities. There was none of the grinding, desperate poverty of other developing countries.

Yes, money was often short, but there was food in the gardens, on the trees, and in the sea, and it was always possible to earn a few dollars. Village life had more than its share of happiness but without the amenities and services available in other places.

When a village co-operative had made a profit, we received a particularly warm welcome as we arrived to "close" the books. Pigs, goats and cattle would be slaughtered for a big celebration feast. Some people were sent out to fish; others prepared the food and organized the entertainment including traditional dances and singing. The Fijian attitude was such that even when there was no dividend the very act of closing the books was reason enough for a party! Anyway, my colleagues and I always joined in the fun. Next morning with bleary eyes, we would struggle along the path to the next village where the whole process would start again.

I understood how important it was for me, and my colleagues to stress that certain business principles and disciplines had to be followed. I did it in village after village, in meeting after meeting, and continued to preach the same message later in my career, and as a political leader. In its simplest form, what I said was that a business could not spend more than it made, or it would go broke. Profit therefore was the central objective. The income of a business should not be regarded as profit. Savings were important to provide capital to start a business and keep it going. Costs should be controlled at all times. This sounds pretty straightforward but to Fijians there were cultural issues to consider. Fijians are not brought up to be thrifty. They like to share and give things away rather than acquire and save.

Annual accounts for the co-operatives were presented in a simple format. In the profit and loss account, income was recorded on the right-hand side and expenses on the left. The difference was either profit or loss. I designed a new format for presenting accounts. It contained a section calculating in the profit and loss account the "cost of goods sold". Assets and liabilities were classified into current and fixed. Liabilities were categorised as current and long term. Share capital was set out separately. This new style of presentation was well received and became the standard for the department. Important ratios from profit and loss accounts and balance sheet were easily calculated for better understanding by officers and co-operative members.

Occasionally office holders from some societies tried some tricks in an attempt to give a more positive picture of performance. I remember very well one episode. After the accounts were prepared I noticed that the net profit appeared too high for the size of the co-op and closing stock looked to be excessive. I asked my assistant to check the number of large tins of biscuits in the corner of the co-operative store. Were they full or empty? My assistant soon discovered there was nothing inside the tins. The closing stock was therefore reduced, and the society made a loss rather than a profit. The secretary of the society was given a warning and got a lecture from members at the annual meeting.

I progressed well in the department and in 1976 was appointed registrar of co-operatives.

My years working in the co-operatives were professionally and personally rewarding. Looking back, I can see that it was crucial in fashioning my emerging vocation to serve the community and my attitudes towards life in general. It contributed to the almost obsessive interest I developed in furthering the welfare of rural communities; starting with Mavana. This obsession followed me right into prison.

## 14

# TO THE TOP OF THE PUBLIC SERVICE

B
ecause of their relatively small numbers there was a great demand in the public service for well-qualified, experienced Fijians with university degrees. In 1978 I was appointed deputy secretary for finance, which gave me a key role in managing government's financial affairs. In 1979 I rose further in the ranks when I became permanent secretary for commerce and industry. This gave me deeper knowledge and experience of the functions of the commercial and industrial sectors of the economy, the thinking of business people, the importance of investment and the need for the right environment for growth that creates employment. Without investment there is no employment.

The Public Service Commission, which operated independently, had wide responsibilities for the overall management and functioning of the entire civil service. It was in charge of appointments, remuneration, and discipline; and established regulations, rules and procedures under the Public Service Act.

The person holding the position of secretary to the Public Service Commission was regarded then as Fiji's most senior civil servant. In

1980 I was appointed to that role in a reshuffle of permanent secretaries. I was 39 years old.

I have to confess that the job of PSC permanent secretary was the most difficult I had encountered. Even with the delegation of powers to permanent secretaries in the ministries, I still had myriad tasks to perform. The PSC was Fiji's biggest employer with responsibility for around 22,000 civil servants. Naturally the human resource and personnel element was vital and sometimes involved sensitive issues. On more than one occasion, for example, I acted as unofficial marriage counselor! Although my qualification did not extend to this area, I managed to sort out (at least for a while) issues between marital antagonists.

One of the critical tasks of the PSC was the appointment of permanent secretaries who were essentially chief executive officers of government ministries. When there was a need for a reshuffle or new appointments, I would prepare a list of candidates for discussion with the PSC chair. After we reached agreement, we would seek a meeting with the prime minister for his approval. I stress that Ratu Mara never interfered with the operations of the PSC. It was obvious to me that he respected the independence of the PSC and other constitutional offices. This is a far cry from the current practices of the Bainimarama government which has politicised and tightly controlled these institutions.

The meetings with Ratu Mara were always short and to the point. Almost without exception, Ratu Mara endorsed our choices. I remember that on just two occasions he expressed some personal views on candidates.

During my service at the PSC I gained intimate knowledge about the workings of the vast bureaucratic machinery of the government. A crucial element of my duties was to deal with the public service trade unions, including negotiations on submissions from them on terms and conditions and disputes. During my tenure at the PSC, the relationship between the unions and the commission was generally cordial. There were one or two industrial actions, which were resolved amicably.

The union leaders were generally very able and well informed. The most formidable and skillful of them was Mr Mahendra Chaudhry, who was then leader of the Fiji Public Service Association (FPSA). We had quite a few duels.

Unfortunately for me, Mr Chaudhry often had statistical data on the issues at hand which was more reliable than the information I had from our official sources! He gained this advantage from his many contacts in the ministries and departments. This put me at something of a disadvantage. I had to negotiate very carefully to conceal the shortcomings in my own brief. Mr Chaudhry was to play a part in my political career as an often troublesome and determined opponent and occasionally as an ally.

Despite the challenges at the PSC I enjoyed my time there. The experience I gained was invaluable.

# 15

# BANKING FOR THE NATION

I n 1983 I had another big career move. I became the Fiji Development Bank's (FDB) first local managing director, succeeding Mr Lloyd Guthrie, an Australian. I was one of three or four applicants for the position, which had been publicly advertised.

At this stage I had served 23 years as a civil servant and had been appointed to the top position. I felt the time was right for me to move closer to the private sector. I was still only 42 years old. I had decided to apply for the position of managing director of the FDB because I was confident I was qualified for the job. I had a keen interest in the FDB's role and functions. I could see an opportunity to contribute to the development of this important institution and to the country as a whole.

Lyle Cupit, chairman of the bank, interviewed me in his office at his large Navua Farm, which he had purchased after serving successfully as managing director of the Carpenter Group of companies, one of Fiji's most important diversified commercial enterprises. Mr Cupit was a successful and astute businessman.

Although I had no direct commercial and banking experience, I was confident I could handle the role of FDB managing director. I was ready for the challenge. My B. Com degree in accounting provided a good professional platform. As part of the degree course I had completed units on company, commercial and trustee law. These would be useful tools in banking. My extensive experience in promoting the profitability and balance sheet stability of co- operative ventures was a great asset. I had gained knowledge of business and commerce from my role as permanent secretary for commerce and industry, especially through my detailed contact and liaison with the business sector on policy issues. I was sure I could quickly learn how to make sound assessments on loan applications.

In February 1983 I was appointed to the FDB position by the bank's board with the approval of the minister of finance. The FDB, which had evolved from the Agricultural and Industrial Loans Board, was pivotal to the drive to spur economic development. Its mandate and mission differed from that of normal commercial banks. The FDB was prepared to accept greater lending risks in the interests of establishing new industries and assisting farmers. It would go where commercial banks were reluctant to tread. A commercial bank might look at a proposed project and say, "this carries far too much risk for us". The FDB, on the other hand, was likely to take on the added risk if it felt the venture would add significantly to Fiji's economy. That is what development banking is about. Typically, the FDB would provide financial support until a business was able to survive on its own. Then we would move aside.

The FDB was funded from government grants and loans from various credit institutions. In turn it made its own advances to its customers. Traditionally its support was directed mainly to agriculture.

I settled in quickly. I liked the job and had a great management team. Staff loyalty and support was strong. It became apparent to me that the FDB needed to lift its public profile and image, develop its brand and do a better job of telling its story. So, we invested in a continuing campaign to achieve this. There was soon growing aware-ness of the bank, its role and services.

I made it my business to be familiar with the loan portfolios in the FDB offices in major towns. I also made sure I interacted with clients in their own environments to ensure I had a grasp of their specific local issues. At head office in Suva appraisal of applications for larger loans took up much of my time. These required board decisions. The FDB board at that time comprised people with a great deal of private sector experience. During my 14 years with the bank, Mr Cupit continued as board chairman. I learned a great deal from him.

The 1980s and 90s were a time of economic expansion in Fiji. Large industrial projects came online. Agriculture, forestry and fish-eries expanded too. Tourism was becoming increasingly important. Infrastructure diversification to cope with the growth also took place.

The board and the staff decided that the FDB was not going to be left behind. Our industrial and commercial loans began to account for a larger proportion of our business. This was good for the bank because these loans usually generated excellent profits. As the FDB's managing director, I often took a hands-on role in ventures of strategic importance to the country. Many of our clients were responding to a national policy of import substitution – making things in Fiji instead of simply importing them. This led to a prolifer-ation of new ventures. Through the bank, I had a critical role in estab-lishing the local television industry and commercial radio; manufacturing of building products such as roofing iron, blending fertilizer and numerous other significant enterprises.

Many of Fiji's outstanding local businesses saw benefits in seeking support from the FDB. We provided capital for these compa-nies for expansion and diversification in areas such as retailing, prop-erty development, manufacturing, timber production, fishing and tourism. This gave me an opportunity to work closely, often at board level, with some of Fiji's most gifted entrepreneurs including Mr Hari Punja, Mr Vinod Patel, Mr Bachu Patel, Mr Mac Patel, Mr Kanti Tappoo, Mr Mark Halabe and many more.

The FDB continued to focus on agriculture but this grew less rapidly than the other categories of loans. Fiji has always had great difficulty in reaching its full agricultural potential, mainly because of the need for farmers to shed traditional methods and switch to a more businesslike approach.

Sugar cane farming was central to our agricultural lending. We provided finance for many thousands of cane growers, thus assisting in keeping the wheels of Fiji's biggest industry moving. I acquired much knowledge about farms, harvesting and milling. This was invaluable later when the governments I led took major initiatives to reform the industry to meet changing conditions. Unfortunately, the military government, which ousted my SDL government by force, was too incompetent to follow through properly on the reforms and reorganisation. The farmers suffered as a consequence.

One of the FDB innovations I introduced was the restructuring of loans for large companies experiencing difficulties in certain aspects of their businesses. As a result, they were able to turn struggling ventures around; they became sound and successful.

Each of these projects involved a partnership. The FDB agreed to reorganize the client's loans in terms of repayments, interest charges, security requirements and other factors. In turn, the client was required to report frequently to the bank, provide critical management information and attend regular meetings between executives of both parties and ensure compliance with established operational procedures.

The overall aim of all this - today it's termed a 'workout' – was to turn the ailing enterprise around. This was done by putting it on a clear path forward, strengthening the balance sheet, ending losses through rigorous cost control, pursuing sales aggressively and finally achieving sustainable profitability. I am happy to say that there were more success stories under this scheme than failures.

One of the FDB's controversial policies was its special loans scheme to narrow the economic gap between the indigenous Fijians and the rest of the population. It was very obvious that Fiji could not achieve development in its fullest sense when a large ethnic grouping, the indigenes, were outside the economic mainstream.

The Fijian loans scheme was inaugurated by Ratu Sir Kamisese Mara's Alliance Party. During my term at the FDB we made further improvements to it. The Fijian portfolio grew rapidly. An indicator of its progress was the expanding membership of the indigenous Fijian Business Council. In 2001, when I became elected prime minister, I was chief guest at the council's annual meeting of that year. Just over 40 indigenous business owners and executives attended. The 2006 annual meeting where I was also chief guest had more than 160 delegates.

To broaden the scope of Fijian commercial participation, we brought in a scheme for making loans to purchase shares in profitable companies.

I was amazed and quite troubled at the reaction from some people especially to the purchase of shares in the successful invest-ment company Fijian Holdings Ltd. I will just say that this scheme was good for the bank and for those who borrowed under it. What was wrong with people making their money work for them in this way?

It was during this period that some critics began to pin the racist label on me. This was misconceived and unfounded. I abhor racism– the belief that someone is superior to another person because of their ethnicity. I never regretted having played a signifi-cant role in promoting the advancement of indigenous Fijians in business. This is not racism. I give more details elsewhere in these pages about affirmative action to accelerate Fijian economic partic-ipation.

To give a sense of perspective to this issue I often pointed out that total FDB loans under the Fijian scheme represented only about 10 per cent of the FDB's lending. The concessions granted were mainly in the form of reduced interest. The total value of this form of assistance was miniscule compared to the benefits in the millions given to many non-Fijian businesses as investment incentives which incorporated tax concessions, custom duty rebates, depreciation allowances, export incentives and many more.

When I left the bank in 1997, I could look back with a sense of some achievement and satisfaction. The bank was having a significant impact in enterprises such as the crucial sugar industry, other agricultural activities, in commerce and industry, forestry and fisheries, construction of high rise office buildings, establishment of village shops and marketplaces. I pay tribute to the talented and dedicated management team and staff who served with me, people like George Pickering, Umarji Musa, Vincent Yee, Isoa Kaloumaira, Tukana Bavoro, Anjna Deb and many others at all levels of management.

Our successes together kept the bank profitable every year during my term as managing director. Of course, the FDB like any bank had its share of bad projects; these are to be expected, specifically in development banking. The Eimcol store scheme based on an idea from Papua New Guinea was one of these. Several retail stores were bought by the FDB to be operated by specially trained managers. If they were successful they were granted a loan to purchase the store. It did not work well and the FDB had to sell off the stores and terminate the scheme, but ultimately FDB's loss was not substantial because of the good prices obtained from the sale of the store properties.

I still have encounters with former clients who remember vividly the circumstances in which I helped to launch them towards their entrepreneurial dreams. One of them, Mr Wah Sing, was a ginger farmer who diversified into processing and export. Then he sold the business and invested in real estate. He bought some land in Raiwai and transformed that into what became Garden City. He still operates a retail outlet there selling hardware and agricultural and related items.

In early 2016, I walked into Mr Wah Sing's Garden City shop to make some purchases. The former client greeted me warmly, and so did his wife. I asked how his business was going and he briefly mentioned how it had grown. As we talked other customers were attracted to the conversation. Soon there were about 10 of us standing there. The Garden City entrepreneur told everyone how he had applied to the FDB for a $40,000 loan to establish his ginger-processing factory. The application was rejected. Then he asked if he could put his case to me. He came into my office saying he was nervous but hopeful. I had studied his file, which was on my desk in front of me. As he sat down I told him that his project was sound, and I had approved his loan. He was very happy. Then he recollected that I asked him, "Are you sure you don't need more than $40,000?"

I had apparently said to him that the bank would be ready to assist further as his business grew. Frankly I had forgotten this particular part of the conversation. But the memory came back when he told the story to that group in his shop. I felt a quiet sense of accomplishment and happiness that my confidence as a banker in him had been repaid and, as a result, I had helped this hardworking entrepreneur and his family to fulfill their ambitions. He is a great Fiji success story.

From the FDB I moved to the Merchant Bank of Fiji (MBF). As with the FDB, I was the first local to become MBF's managing director. MBF began as a joint venture in the early 1990s between an Australian finance company and Fijian Holdings Ltd (FHL). By the time I went there it was a wholly owned subsidiary of FHL, primarily providing short-term credit for businesses for the purchase of plant and equipment, vehicles and heavy machinery. It also provided working capital. Security requirements were normally easier than those offered by the commercial banks. And decisions on loan applications were made quickly. The job was important and engrossing but sometimes I missed the diversified activities and excitement of the FDB[i].

# 16

## INTO THE FRAY

My first draft for this book focused on my 243 days in prison. In fact, that was its working title. But I finally decided that to place the prison term into context and to properly explain how I became a convict, I would have to write about some of the significant events of my political career. What I had started became a much larger project.

It was my leadership in politics that ultimately landed me in prison. My move into politics was not motivated by money. My position at Merchant Bank was well paid and the work was important. At just under 60 years of age, I was starting to plan for retirement in about five years time.

But as circumstances and events unfolded I became the unelected prime minister in the interim government following the George Speight coup of 2000. I went on to become elected prime minister after the general election in May 2001 and again after the general election in May 2006 until the military coup on 5<sup>th</sup> December 2006.

I had followed politics and political developments with interest but never envisaged taking an active role. Before the general election of 1992 I was approached by agents of Sitiveni Rabuka's Soqosoqo ni Vakavulewa ni Taukei (SVT) to consider standing as a candidate for that party. The prospect of becoming a minister after the election was mentioned. I declined on the grounds that I felt active politics was not my calling.

Just before the general elections of 1999, there was an unexpected turn of events that took me into my first political role. The parliament at that time had an upper chamber, the senate, which acted as a house of review and also possessed important veto powers to protect indigenous interests.

A senate seat allocated to the Great Council of Chiefs for Lau province was vacant. I was nominated, as was Adi Koila Nailatikau, a daughter of Fiji's president and the Lau high chief Ratu Sir Kamisese Mara, and Solomone Makasiale, a prominent Lauan. Our names were submitted for consideration to the Lau provincial council. I had received feedback that a large majority of council members would support me.

The meeting of the council to make the decision was held at the Civic Centre in Suva. No voting actually took place, but Ratu Sir Kamisese, chairman of the council, announced that I would represent Lau in the senate. So, I became Senator Laisenia Qarase.

During my relatively short stint in the upper house, I began to attract some national attention through my contributions to debates. I was also selected to head a senate committee to study the issue of indigenous involvement in commerce.

George Speight's disastrous takeover of parliament on 19th May 2000 became a central issue in my story. Speight was driven by extremist feelings of Fijian nationalism. His message to the country and the world was that he had acted to assert indigenous leadership and general preeminence.

The origins of Speight's takeover were always murky. The popular wisdom suggested that elements of the military leadership were behind the Speight coup and that he became the scapegoat when things went wrong. It was troubling that Bainimarama travelled to Europe a few days before Speight struck. His absence was a matter of concern to Ratu Sir Kamisese Mara, the president. According to reports from military sources, Bainimarama was aware of intelligence reports that something was brewing. Why then did he go away?

When he returned from his overseas visit the situation at the parliamentary complex was chaotic. It looked as though hundreds of coup supporters occupying the building and compound were supplied with food by the military. There was a large cache of arms and ammunition stored there. Who was authorising the delivery of the food? On whose orders were the armaments transferred from Queen Elizabeth barracks? These were some of the questions tenaciously pursued in a military board of inquiry. Bainimarama refused to give evidence to it.

Speight's holding of Prime minister Mahendra Chaudhry's government hostage and the associated turmoil which was spreading throughout Fiji, had brought the country to the edge of a precipice. There was fear and anxiety among the population, particularly in Suva and surrounding areas. Violence, anarchy and disorder were springing up and not only on Viti Levu. If Fiji could not pull itself out of this nightmarish situation, the consequences would be unthinkable.

Ratu Mara, meanwhile, had tried hard to hold the country together and to seek a resolution to the hostage standoff. His career came to an end in an extraordinary encounter with senior military figures on the naval vessel Kiro in Suva harbour. This was criticised by the RFMF Board of Inquiry as reported in these pages.

The president was whisked away from Government House on 28th May 2000 and taken to the Kiro, anchored in Suva harbour. There he met with Bainimarama; the then Commissioner of Police Isikia Savua, previously a senior military officer; former military commander Ratu Epeli Ganilau, who was also Ratu Mara's son in law; the 1987 coup leader Sitiveni Rabuka and Colonel Iowane

Naivalurua. Information filtered out that this delegation presented a *tabua* to Ratu Mara asking him to leave office as president.

I understand the reason they gave was that there was great risk to the president's life in view of the deteriorating security situation at the time. Ratu Mara reportedly said if he went, he would never return, and declared, "If the constitution goes, I go". He had correctly read the situation as a vote of no confidence in him. He stepped aside and later resigned. This great leader was taken to his home island of Lakeba in Lau to his village of Tubou. Speight had wanted him out of office. He got his wish as a result of the intervention by Bainimarama and those who went with him to the Kiro.

I thought the action by these senior military men was an act of insubordination towards their commander in chief. Many commentators, me included, have likened it to another coup. For the nation's security chiefs to say that they could not guarantee the security and safety of the president, with all the power they had was beyond comprehension. They were in charge of the nation's security and had trained soldiers, arms and ammunition. The episode on the Kiro was one of the fateful moments in Fiji's history.

The Kiro was in the news again when George Speight and his key accomplices were transported in it to Nukulau island, where they were initially imprisoned. Speight alleged that they had been assaulted and generally mistreated on the voyage to the island.

The Kiro met an ignominious end on 15th July 2016. It ran aground on Cakauyawa reef near Makuluva island, not far from the area of the Rewa delta. The defence minister at the time, Timoci Natuva, labeled the incident as "shameful news for the navy." He was quoted as saying that a ship equipped with modern technology such as a Global Positioning System (GPS), radar, gyrocompass, and sea charts should not run aground.

Eventually the navy abandoned attempts to remove the Kiro from the reef. Bainimarama as prime minister expressed the view that salvage attempts might have been a waste of time and resources. An inquiry into what happened apparently took place. At time of writing it had supposedly been completed but no details were made available for public information.

The Kiro was a rusting wreck damaging the reef, a blot on the environment and a marine hazard.

---

Bainimarama and his senior officers established a Military Council (MC) to deal with the governance of the country, as well as to resolve the hostage crisis unfolding at the parliament complex. I accepted an invitation to become the council's economic adviser. At that point I felt I might be able to make recommendations to counter the economic decline then setting in. One fine Sunday morning I arrived for a MC meeting at the Republic of Fiji Military Forces (RFMF) headquarters at Nabua, Suva. To my surprise I was asked to be prime minister in an interim administration. I was given the freedom to choose members of my own cabinet, but with the approval of the MC. Later, I learned that three other people had declined the offer to be prime minister. Perhaps they were wiser than me.

To this day I cannot fully explain why I said yes to the military. Maybe the dramatic circumstances of the moment, the crisis that enveloped the country, conspired to give me a sense that I could help Fiji through this ordeal. It was a fateful decision.

The Great Council of Chiefs (GCC) was summoned to meet in early July to decide on the form of government needed to rescue the situation. During the few weeks between May and July 2000 I was aware that several groups were interested in establishing an administration. I also learned from credible sources that Bainimarama had ambitions to rule the country for at least 10 years.

At a GCC meeting on or about the 4th July 2000, the President, Ratu Josefa Iloilovatu Uluivuda who had succeeded Ratu Mara, nominated me to be prime minister in a civilian interim administration. My nomination was approved unanimously. This mandate from the GCC made me more comfortable. The council was of high national importance. To many Fijians it represented a cherished symbol of their identity, their culture, their origins. It was said that the chiefs and the people were one. They could not be separated.

Throughout our modern history it had played a role in the affairs of the nation and had important constitutional powers. Its membership comprised chiefs from the 14 provinces, as well as the three paramount chiefs of the confederacies of Kubuna, Burebasaga, and Tovata. It could, therefore, be asserted that it represented all indigenous Fijians who comprised more than half the population.

Although other ethnic communities were not represented in the GCC, I was sure they would look to it to help resolve the political crisis and bring back the stability that was so desperately needed. In my view the population generally supported the GCC's actions.

The Cabinet I picked consisted of 18 ministers. I had invited several Indo-Fijians to join but there were no takers. I understood their position. All the ministers were credible and well-known, and mostly what I would term moderate. Many had already given outstanding service to Fiji in a political, professional or traditional capacity[ii].

We began the task of reassembling a fractured, weakened nation. First priority was restoration and maintenance of internal security. At that stage I had a commitment of support from Bainimarama and the Commissioner of Police, Isikia Savua. In one of my early broadcasts to the nation I was confident enough to give an assurance that the security situation was strong and stable. Media freedom continued, basic human rights were protected, and the existing 1997 constitution had continued as the supreme law. All this gave us a positive framework and foundation for elections.

Naturally some people were unhappy about the appointment of the interim government, but I sensed that most citizens just wanted us to get on with the job, restore confidence and get the country moving again through parliamentary government.

By late 2000 the historic Chandrika Prasad case was in our court system. Mr Prasad had challenged the legality of the civilian government that I led, as well as a Constitution Review Commission my government had established. In early March 2001, the high court in response to Mr Prasad's challenge decided that our government was illegal. Similarly, the Constitution Review Commission we had established was declared to be illegal. This was another crisis both for the interim government and for Fiji.

It was at about this time that the newly formed Assembly of Christian Churches in Fiji (ACCF) was becoming active. Its membership included the Methodist Church, the Seventh Day Adventist Church, Assemblies of God Church and the Pentecostal Church. It was a consultative forum, but in the circumstances then its focus became the promotion of reconciliation between different communities in our divided nation. I was very much in favour of this mission and began to meet regularly with ACCF leaders. I encouraged them to provide advice on crucial national issues. I also asked them to critically review various decrees and other legislations. The aim was to assist with improving the country's legislative framework.

On a fine evening in mid 2001 – I don't have the exact date - the ACCF staged a rally at Albert Park in Suva. It attracted a huge crowd. The objective was to further advance reconciliation as a vital requirement for our national rehabilitation. The then president, His Excellency Ratu Josefa Iloilovatu Uluivuda, made the opening address. I was also a main speaker. I decided it was the right time for me to make a Christian confession of my sins and any wrongdoings I might have committed against the people of Fiji during my public service career and in my role as interim prime minister. I asked for forgiveness. It was an emotional moment for me personally and I sensed that the crowd responded positively.

Later in the evening the rally reached a spiritual climax as the leaders of the church groups formed a circle around me and performed the ceremony of the laying on of hands[iii]. As they touched me and invoked God's blessing I experienced what can only be described as a warm current coursing through my body from head to toe. This was not my imagination. It was real. God's presence was strong that night. The main prayer focused on the need for peace in Fiji and a successful general election scheduled for August/September 2001. Rev. Poate told me afterwards that I would be the elected prime minister of Fiji come the general election.

# 17

# LACK OF LEADERSHIP AND CONFUSION

From 21$^{st}$ August 2000 through to 24$^{th}$ October 2000 the RFMF conducted a board of inquiry relating to the Speight group's occupation of parliament and the taking hostage of Prime minister Mahendra Chaudhry and members of his government. The aim of the inquiry was to record findings and opinions concerning the involvement of the RFMF's elite First Fiji Meridian Squadron (FFMS), also known as the Counter Revolutionary Warfare Unit (CRW). The president of the board was Lt. Col. J N Evans. The other members were Major A. Mohammed, Major T. Gucake, and Warrant Officer H. McComber.

Evidence was heard from 112 witnesses on many questions relating to the George Speight insurrection. The board produced a lengthy report which is available on the Internet http://www. truthforfiji.com/uploads/8/4/2/3/8423704/20120305- 1st_meridi-an_report_rfmf_opt2_small.pdf. The account that follows is extracted from it. I took the time to read through it because I am keenly interested in the role of the military in what happened. There is not much I wish to say about what I read, except that it is essential reading for anyone wishing to increase their understanding of the events I describe in this book. The report tells its own story. It is about lack of decisive and focused leadership, poor judgment, confused thinking, and sending the wrong signals. In other words, it is an indictment of the RFMF. However, to give credit where it is due, the RFMF did eventually manage to negotiate the freedom of the hostages after 56 days, bringing the immediate crisis to an end.

The inquiry faced a major obstacle. Commodore Bainimarama, obviously a key figure as leader of the military, did not appear before it and submit himself to questions. Its report simply said: "As to the commander RFMF's reaction to the events of May 19, the question cannot be answered because the board was not able to interview him."

The report said the FFMS was under the direct control of Commodore Bainimarama.

The RFMF, according to the report, stood firm in trying to resolve the crisis. The RFMF, it said, had never guaranteed its support to members of the First Fiji Meridian Squadron (FFMS). However certain decisions, actions and positions adopted by the RFMF were interpreted by the FFMS personnel involved and other RFMF personnel as indicating that the RFMF seemed to be in support. This came in the form of logistic and administrative support provided to the FFMS personnel in parliament by FFMS members who had remained in QEB.

The report said another indication were the numerous visits of all ranks of the RFMF to the complex. These visits were both official and casual, "but gave the wrong signals".

In its recommendations the BOI declared that the RFMF was held responsible for not totally stopping the support given to those at the parliamentary complex. It called for a much more accountable system to be implemented relevant to the relationship between FFMS and the commander of RFMF, i.e. transparency in the operability of the unit.

In his evidence, Lt. Serupepeli Dakai, an intelligence analyst, said after the 1999 election, intelligence briefs were given to the Commander of the end result of the election whereby the Labour government had a landslide victory and the continuous uprising of the indigenous Fijians. We have been giving the Commander continuous briefs of the end result as to what may eventuate considering the continuous uprising of the indigenous Fijians. We outlined to him that in the end it may result in a civilian coup or a military coup. That was the intelligence briefs that we were giving the Commander RFMF straight after the election. Whilst giving these briefs we envisaged that he and his Staff Officers would carry out preventative measures to stop the end state that we were giving him.

Lt. Dakai was quoted as saying that for one week there was no clear directive on what the army was going to do about the takeover.

"The army was letting the boys get their resupply from the camp. My belief was that the army was behind the takeover."

He went on to say that if the commander and his staff officers heeded the intelligence assessment reports ... and took a proactive stance or preventative measures, "all these things would not have happened including Pte Weleilakeba's death". (Private Joela Weleilakeba was ambushed in Naitasiri.)

Asked directly why he thought the incident of May 19 happened, the report quotes Lt. Dakai as responding: "because they did not heed the intelligence assessment reports".

Q: "Who do you mean?
A: "The commander RFMF and his staff."

The document mentions Bainimarama making a trip to Norway

just before the occupation of parliament. (This is the same trip that concerned the then president Ratu Sir Kamisese Mara.) Lt Dakai confirmed that Bainimarama had been briefed on the security situation in Fiji before his Norway visit.

In response to another question, Lt. Dakai said he and a colleague, Lt. Narawa, had indicated to Bainimarama the possibility of a military coup from disgruntled military officers and a civil coup.

"When Mr Narawa told him that there were disgruntled senior officers within the RFMF, he was insulted."

---

Q: "Insulted or angry?"

A: "Sorry he was angry. Actually he did not like us telling him that. I remember at one point in time he chased me out of his office.

Q: "During that brief?

A: "No, in another brief."

Q: "What were the words he uttered when he chased you out? What was the brief about resulting in you being chased out?"

A: "There was a meeting conducted in Raiwaqa/Raiwai area about the indigenous people. He actually called me up to his office. So after I briefed him then he said 'your brief is bullshit, you are wasting my time here, get out'. I took my leave."

Q: "What was said in the brief? Can you recall?

A: "It was a verbal brief. I told him the intentions of the indigenous Fijians."

---

Asked about information that the army was involved, Lt. Dakai according to the report, said: "Yes I heard. When I was in camp during that one week after the May 19 takeover, the RFMF was letting the resupply of everything from camp – weapons, rations and everything. So the word was going around that the RFMF was in support of the operation. That gave me the courage to stand up and walk across to try and give directions to those guys in parliament to try and bring about an amicable solution to the conflict and get out of there."

Lt. Penaia Baleinamau, a member of the FFMS, gave evidence about his experience of the takeover. He also confirmed that he was the person in command of the CRW (FFMS) when the events of 19th May occurred. He said the director of the unit was Major Ligairi.

(Major Ligairi, nicknamed Na Qase, the Old Man, was a pivotal figure in what transpired in parliament. He was a former member of the British SAS commandos. Major Ligairi was described in the BOI report as a legend within FFMS. There was even speculation among the people that he had magical powers. A journalist visited him in his office in the parliamentary compound during the hostage crisis. As they spoke the journalist was stunned when Major Ligairi pulled up his *sulu* to show a pistol strapped to one thigh and a knife to the other.)

The BOI report recommended that he be accountable for directing and ordering the involvement of FFMS personnel in the crisis and should be charged accordingly.

According to the BOI, members of the FFMS unit looked up to Major Ligairi as the "ever knowledgeable mentor whose decisions and directives were never questioned." The BOI report went on to say, however, that the RFMF must to an extent be grateful to Major Ligairi for his efforts in nurturing the FFMS unit from its inception in 1987. The report was critical of Bainimarama in the context of his relationship with Major Ligairi. It said he must take the blame for

being over awed by one man's past and giving that man so much control over a special unit that was highly trained and highly thought of.

Major Ligairi was described as the middle layer between commander RFMF and the unit in the tier of accountability. It was unfortunate, said the report, that Major Ligairi was given control of the unit despite his limitations. "His training and capability was that of a SNCO who had the limited capability of an operator and not a director and planner." This was stressed again later in the report, which said Major Ligairi was employed in a role where vision and strategic thought was required.

---

With his training he was an operator at the tactical level and very much lacked the capacity, nor did he have the requirements to operate at a level of a director. The then OC, Lt. Penaia Baleinamau, a very junior officer, did not have the characteristics or the experience to command such a unit. He was very much an operator and thinker at the tactical level. For a unit that was arguably elite, and answerable directly to the commander RFMF, it was very much lacking in leadership.

---

The board said the situation had changed from when the FFMS was set up in 1987, but the FFMS, its organization, operations, and accountability system were never reviewed. "It was still very much existing like a private army, answerable only to whoever the Comd RFMF was; whether Comd RFMF had any actual control over the unit could not be ascertained by the board. The events of 19th May had clearly highlighted the lack of a contingency plan, training and ability of the RFMF to deal with a national crisis such as that experienced on 19th May."

The episode on the naval ship Kiro leading to Ratu Sir Kamisese Mara vacating the presidency came in for criticism:

---

The RFMF in effect failed in its mission when it asked the president to step down and abrogated the constitution. The board is of the opinion that RFMF should now closely scrutinize its mission and roles and its ability to accomplish the same. The board does not intend to question the decision concerning the abrogation of the constitution and the 'removal' of His Excellency the president of Fiji and the government, because all this would have to be the subject of a national inquiry. RFMF should now reconsider its position in light of its assigned mission and roles. The board would like to indicate here that whoever gave the advice for the military to take the above two actions did so without considering the consequences of that action.

---

It said it heard from witnesses that a lot of confusion reigned within RFMF in the initial stages of 19th May events. Decisions were not timely, and actions were reactive rather than proactive. The board also highlighted that some very sound decisions were made resulting in the hostages being released with no loss of life within the complex itself.

The events of 19th May had taken the nation and the international community by surprise. The situation was undoubtedly one of a terrorist takeover by the very unit assigned the anti terrorist role. Whether or not a military option was viable remained open for scrutiny.

---

One fact for sure was that the bond within FFMS did not allow the option to use the rest of FFMS as an assault force. To use conventional forces in a role not trained for could have been disastrous. As stated earlier the conventional forces were not prepared for such a task.

Alternatively, RFMF or the leadership could have requested assistance from our military allies, resources and expertise could have been sought. In such a situation the 'key blue force negotiator' would be requested to play an important role. Fiji does not have a well-trained and qualified negotiator. The use of specialized forces could have been requested to assist in any way possible. Fiji forces are not equipped nor trained to handle complicated unconventional warfare situations and it would only be prudent to solicit the necessary support from our allies.

In his evidence Major Ligairi said he had been asked to come back to the RFMF after he had retired the previous year. "I am 60, the commander asked me to come back for six months this year. I told the commander, 'Frank, au sa qase (I am old).' He said, 'o iko *sega* ni qase (you are not old), so I accepted to come back. I just put myself there as advisor. I am not running the unit. This was my third week with the RFMF."

The Board of Inquiry wanted to know why Major Ligairi was recalled when he had gone past the retirement age. This was an issue that needed to be clarified by commander RFMF.

The board said it could not ascertain the role of director FFMS, which Major Ligairi held.

He definitely gave advice and was consulted on unit activities, the OC of the unit reported to him, and he should have been answerable directly to Comd RFMF. Whether any relevant briefing was given to Comd by director FFMS in the three weeks he was employed by RFMF could not be ascertained by the board.

Asked whether he had the impression that the RFMF was "supporting the whole thing?" Major Ligairi replied, "Yes I still think they are supporting me, but what I am saying now they do not agree with the way we did this. I expected at that time that the RFMF would not go against us."

He was asked whether some senior army officers from RFMF tried to use the situation to oust the current RFMF commander. "Do I believe? That question there I do not want to answer. I suspect but it is not that I believe, you know what I mean, I suspect that sort of thing." He spoke of a breakdown in communication, and then said, "all those things when you are an army officer, you know straight away that the leadership is wrong somewhere. I do not have to say it."

Lt. Baleinamau, when asked whether he was aware where the director got his directives, answered that his directive was from the commander. He described arriving at the parliamentary complex on the morning of May 19th where he saw Major Ligairi. Major Ligairi, according to the report, told him there had been a civilian takeover. Lt. Baleinamau said he had told Ligairi it would be better for them to brief the commander.

On a point of clarification, Lt. Baleinamau said that the commander he wanted to brief on 19th May was Col. Tuatoko. This was because Commodore Bainimarama was away at the time. Lt. Baleinamau spoke of meeting with Bainimarama when the commodore had returned from Norway.

---

I told him about everything that has happened. He asked me: 'Did you have any prior knowledge?'"

I answered: "No. The only thing I knew that we were going on an exercise and when we arrived there this thing has unfolded. That is why I told Na Qase that we had to go up and inform the main acting commander"

He spoke of presenting a *tabua* to the commander; the purpose was to tell him what has happened.

He told me to come to his house that night, so I went and had grog until 4 o'clock in the morning"

I think after three weeks he called me up again. He queried about my allegiance, I said 'I've already mentioned it because you have the tabua'. He said, 'you go home, don't come into camp, you stay home until I tell you to move ...'. On the day he arrived he spoke to those of us who were up there, and he said: 'I know that your bond is a very strong one'. He told the unit, 'if you want to go down, sign your leave and go down, the rest of you, if you want to stay here, you stay here.' "

At the time all this was going on there was a lot of public discussions about the weapons in the parliamentary complex. This issue comes up frequently in the BOI report. Lt. Baleinamau was questioned about some weapons being taken to parliament. He related how a Padre rang the barracks to say he saw the boys leaving and suspected weapons were being taken. Lt. Baleinamau saw that the armory was empty. He was asked whether he was given assurance about RFMF support and said: "the way things were going, it indicated to me that RFMF was supportive". He confirmed in evidence that one of his responsibilities was to gather or collate information from his "int. operatives". This was shared with the Old Man (Na Qase), the director. When Na Qase was not there, he shared information with Int at headquarters, usually once a month. He described Na Qase as a father figure to the men.

He said he was asked how he felt about his people who were already in custody:

he replied that he felt that he had been used without knowing the real thing that happened. He said no one knew what was going to happen."

At this time, I think, the unit, myself and the boys were just carrying orders from our superior. We did not know what was behind it and when it has happened, all of us were surprised. We were caught in the middle, but it was too late. I feel sorry for those guys in Nukulau and their families." (Nukulau is an island near the Rewa delta that was used for a time as a prison.)

---

He was asked when the field operatives last reported to him and he said he thought it was two weeks before (the takeover). They said that everything was just escalating and they said that the march (organized for May 19<sup>th</sup>) could get out of hand. This information was given to the director. (The march attracted a large crowd of mostly indigenous Fijians who delivered a petition to Government House.)

At one stage this was put to Lt Baleinamau:

---

What we are saying here, Mr Baleinamau, all records linking up to the 19<sup>th</sup> of May, rosters, weapons register, the duty officers' reports are all missing and to us it paints a picture that some people are trying to hide something. It seems that it is pointing towards you. You were seen when the time you were told to go on leave with the whole bunch of files in your vehicle. Lt. Baleinamau: Yes.

---

Later it was put to him that he was the link man with the RFMF.

Warrant Officer Class 1 Epineri Bainimoli who had been in the FFMS Unit said he went to observe the march. He was told that the Labour government had been taken over. He said he stayed in camp for the duration of the situation at the parliamentary complex. He could not remember whether it was the first week of June when he was told the Commander had asked him to take leave. He went straight home and stayed there until 30<sup>th</sup> of July when he was arrested by soldiers and brought to camp and put in a cell. He was told that his arrest was authorized "from the top".

He gave evidence of going to the complex to take rations. He said this had been approved by NatOps. He said he went once to the complex during the burial of Kolinio Tabua, a civilian who was shot.

At one stage he was reminded that the Board of Inquiry sat on behalf of the commander of the military forces. The BOI transcript says:

---

Before you took the rations down, there must be a request made to you. Who made that request for the rations? Did someone tell you to take it down?

WOC1 Bainimoli: We were thinking of the boys down at the complex and the ration. So our administrative officer made the request and the ration was approved from the top.

---

Witness SGT Iowane Waseroma later lost his life in the RFMF mutiny on 2nd November 2000. (He was among those beaten to death. There have been no legal findings on these crimes.) He said he had been recruited at FFMS, which was then known as CRW. He had been briefed by Mr Stevens after the commander told the unit that if they wanted to go on leave to remain outside the complex. He said he was confused about this brief because it was not clear. He had come back from Australia on a Friday and a Monday was briefed by Mr Stevens that the commander had said that if we had wanted to go on leave to go out and if not, to be inside. This directive was not clear. He said he was involved with the administration of those inside, the welfare of their families. He used to visit their families, their wives and children.

---

Their rations had to be taken inside and approval was given from the top for rations to be taken inside the parliamentary complex. That was my only involvement. I used to take rations inside and after one week I was told not to take any more rations inside or take the vehicle inside otherwise I will be arrested. That was the end of the matter and I stayed home until I was arrested.

---

He was asked about his appointment in the unit after he returned from Australia.

---

I only supplied rations at the time, there was no specific appointment because everything was in disarray.

---

In further evidence he said:

---

All I knew was that someone from the top had approved the ration and the role I played was only to escort the storeman.

---

He said he was arrested at home while he was asleep. He said he was detained for 17 days without any reason being given. He said to that date he still had not been told the reason for his arrest. SGT Waseroma was pressed again on the ration issue.

---

In your statement you said your rations came from the top; who was giving the rations from HQ?
SGT Waseroma: I have no idea.

---

Evidence was heard from Cpl Selesitino Kalounivale, a member of FFMS (CRW) (He was another one of those who died under questioning after the mutiny. But questions remain about the circumstances of his death. There is reason to believe, however, that on the day of the mutiny he was not on duty. Media reports mentioned his widow receiving workers compensation of $24,000. Radio New Zealand ran an item on 6th April 2006 quoting Magistrate Ajmal Khan as saying there was no evidence that Selesitino was a mutineer. But he was nevertheless beaten to death.)

In his evidence to the Board of Inquiry he said he was a driving supervisor and was attending a Red Cross course when the coup took place. He went to the parliamentary complex. He said there had not been a briefing or discussions about immunity adding,

---

I only knew that the things that we were doing, the army was backing us up.

What made you believe this?

We had rations coming from the army camp and the senior officers that were coming down ... they were more or less sympathizing with the course (cause).

---

He reported that in July he had been arrested at home because he was needed for questioning.

The late Col. S. U. Draunidalo, in his evidence, said he was a civil service divisional intelligence officer. He was required to gather and analyse all intelligence in the government. He said he did not know anything planned for the CRW to take place at parliament house. He said he had left the army but when the army advertised, he answered the call. When he came back to QEB, he was part of a Think Tank Group made up of Colonels.

---

We were trying to find out at that time our stance. The first meeting I attended, the commander said we support the cause. I'm a strategic thinker and operator too. When that comes across to me I know what it means to me. We were going to develop strategies that would enable that. I heard also, I do not know whether it was the commander or other officers who said, 'accept the method'. I did not say to anyone what I'm telling you now, I know of no other method. So my job being with the colonels in that group, there were quite heated arguments over it and what we were to do.

My view was ... we need to speak to all the stakeholders. It is no point not talking to the soldiers we are now trying to disown because of what they have done; they're part of the solution because they are made out to be the problems. We've done this work many times overseas, we speak to everyone. And right here at home we just seem to lose all those hard-earned experience. Where did they go? Quite disappointing in a way too. There was clearly, and this is my personal view, there was lack of leadership. We could not resolve that, a group of armed people, who were mainly our own guys. This was in the first week.

In the second week, when they started to allow in civilians, I knew clearly this was late. This thing was soon going to be out of their hands, it happened.

I would like to have this on record very clearly. The concept of the operation was 'no confrontation' and the strategy they developed they tightened up the noose. That cannot be logical. The soldiers could not be blamed, they did what they have to do because they were told ...... it was clear in my mind that whatever the concept, what were the strategy, I did not think at the time that the soldiers understood them clearly.

Col. Draunidalo said at one time he was promoted to go and negotiate on behalf of the army.

---

I had to go with the commander and Jerry Waqanisau. One meeting and that was the last meeting I attended.

Negotiation is a reconciliation process. If you go in there to throw your weight or to tell people, it can never be. The situation was not a war. It was a political situation and there were serious incidences that happened. The first one was wrong, what George Speight and his people did. What we did we have to answer, headquarters, RFMF, whether it was right or wrong and the subsequent actions that followed were in my personal view not right.

During the negotiation, we wanted to introduce a legally tight position. Who was right and who was wrong when I thought a pragmatic approach would have resolved this matter into its second or third week. So, in the other negotiation, I did not wish to participate.

---

In the evidence by Col. Alfred Tuatoko it was put to him that there were people who were still getting paid while they were involved in parliament, also rations were taken down and fuel. He was asked what the reason was for this.

---

The intent was for the safety of the hostages. The CRW people who were involved in the coup were directly responsible for the safety of the hostages. So commander RFMF decided that we continue to support them by providing them rations, providing them fuel, and the question of pay remains; that was on the understanding that when everything was over an inquiry would be conducted and then appropriate charges will be laid for individuals. But that was by no means a sign of condonement of what was going on. It was all for the safety of the hostages.

---

Lt. Col. T. Bukarau, legal adviser to those who had taken over parliament, and one of those in the parliamentary complex, mentioned in his evidence that there were allegations of treason, and investigations were being conducted by the police. He indicated that he might incriminate himself in answering questions. He said there were a lot of threats "between us and RFMF" in trying to curb the disturbances.

He was asked, "were you aware of instructions by commander RFMF for all army personnel to return to camp?"

Bukarau:

---

Is this about marching at 1500 hours on a certain date? We never received any instructions from commander. We only learned of the instructions between two and three when words were passed on from Suva city that everyone was vacating Suva city because the army were going to come in at three o'clock. It came in that form. After calling NATOPS then they said there was no such command.

Q: When commander put out the ultimatum, that all officers to return to camp did you hear anything like that?

A: There was no formal instruction from RFMF that came to the parliament complex despite numerous discussions with senior military officers from RFMF. A vehicle came to parliament with the instructions to take me and Vakalalabure to QEB. With just that instruction I was not prepared to go.

---

Later he was asked: "What was the view of the *vanua* for the army?"

---

A: There was elation in the *vanua* that the army was coming in to join in this thing.

Q: When you said to join in, what thing?

A: To complete the coup cycle. When the military stepped in to ask the president to step down, we assumed straight away that when that was done we were to hold hands in a joint effort to realize the objectives of the coup.

---

Lt. Col. Viliame Seruvakula, then commanding officer of the Third Infantry Battalion, said he had intelligence operators in the field since June 1999 straight after elections "because I felt then the political situation was not stable".

---

The operators kept on feeding me information from August and round about October the coup was becoming a reality. It was not until three weeks before May 19 that the coup was very close, a week before, it was imminent.

---

Lt. Col. Seruvakula referred to a suspicion of a 'mole' leaking information. This was later confirmed. "It was then we stopped informing headquarters through the Int. cell and we started going directly to the commander himself."

He went on to say that 24 hours before the commander left for Norway, he told him that the coup was in a week's time from that day.

He later referred to the situation in the camp as unstable.

Lt. Col. Seruvakula was asked whether he was aware of any

assurances given by RFMF towards the support of those persons that were in parliament.

---

A: When FFMS have taken the hostages they continued to take rations and I questioned that vigorously on the same afternoon as to why because I blocked it. I prevented them at the gate because during one of the rations runs, one MP5 was dug out of the pot of curry. I informed the headquarters that the carrier is not just a ration run, it is being used as a weapon carrier as well

I was told to just let it go because they were looking after the hostages, but the two officers Stevens and Tuivanuavou, kept on insisting right from the word go, no they were not protecting the hostages, they were part of George Speight's game plan. That went on for a while, every time we try and put a block, the block is lifted for some reason or another.

---

On severance of pay he was asked whether he was aware that the other members of the RFMF that were inside the parliament complex continued to be paid by the RFMF right up to the very end.

---

A: I do and I cannot understand why.

Lt. Col. Seruvakula said a very frustrating aspect of attempting to rectify the crisis was "the fact that we were being reactive right throughout instead of being proactive.

We were more or less doing our job with our hands tied behind our backs. We were told to do something but at the same time we were told to take it easy on these guys inside the complex.

---

He said a good number of officers were "sitting on the fence". This was unfortunate because it trickled down to the soldiers and created confusion amongst the troops. He believed that at some stage there were people just waiting to see who was going to come out as winner at the end of the week.

What he could not understand was that Baleinamau kept on going up to headquarters and then getting support.

---

Every time I got up and say something about Baleinamau for him to be stopped, I get a smack in the head and Baleinamau gets a kiss on the cheek, literally.

---

Lt. Col. Samuela Veileqe Raduva faced this question from the Board:

---

Is it not ironic Sir that we have used these CRW or FFMS soldiers for purposes like – they have done an illegal act and then we have used them for security purposes of the hostages, and in retrospective, we have come back and rearrested them and then we have subsequently charged them for treason?

---

He answered: "That is what I mean when I said initially that I do not really understand what is happening. I cannot match it."

His concluding statement was:

---

I just want to thank you gentlemen for having me here to try and put some clarification in what has happened. No one is the winner here, we are all losers. We have our families, people have lost their jobs and children have missed school, we are all losers.

---

Col. Ratu G. Kadavulevu told the Inquiry:

---

My position in 1987 has not changed. I stood against Rabuka in 1987. I stood against anything that is illegal. I told him my position and that was it. What I believe in 1987 I still believe in now.

---

According to the report, squadron members went into the parliamentary complex without rehearsals and appropriate training.

# 18

# MUTINY AT THE BARRACKS

O n 2nd November 2000 I returned from a Pacific Islands Forum meeting in Tarawa, Kiribati. On my arrival at Nadi I was unaware of serious trouble at the Queen Elizabeth Barracks, the FMF headquarters at Nabua, near Suva. I was taken to Suva on the main Queens Road. As we passed Navutulevu Village on the Coral Coast I saw a large military vehicle filled with soldiers parked on the roadside but did not attach much significance to it. Just before the police post at Deuba, Pacific Harbour, there was a roadblock. We stopped, The minister for Home Affairs, Ratu Talemo Ratakele, was there. He informed me that a mutiny was taking place at the Nabua Barracks and suggested I should return to the Nadi area for security reasons. There was no way I would do that when the country faced a deep crisis. I thanked Ratu Talemo for his briefing and told him I would be continuing on to Suva and would be grateful if he could make arrangements for an emergency cabinet meeting.

When I arrived at the new wing of government buildings at about 5.45pm, the ministers were gathered in the cabinet office. With them were the Commissioner of Police, Colonel Isikia Savua, and Colonel

Alfred Tuatoko, deputising for Bainimarama who was under protection at the naval base at Walu Bay. We received a full briefing about the events that had unfolded at the barracks and the situation at the time of the cabinet meeting. Some deaths were reported. Cabinet was asked to approve the necessary military action for ending the mutiny. We gave this approval and also rules of engagement based on the need for minimum casualties. Force was to be used only if absolutely necessary. The mutiny was suppressed a short time afterwards. It was clear that some actions went beyond the rules of engagement we had approved. These were to become the subject of investigations by the police.

Four of those resisting the uprising were killed. Four suspected mutineers were beaten to death. The beatings were brutal in the extreme and were being treated as murder. The perpetrators have never been brought to justice. During the mutiny there was an attempt to assassinate Commodore Bainimarama.

That evening I gave a televised address to the nation announcing that the mutiny had ended. I was able to give an assurance that the security situation was back to normal. I returned home to 18 Richards Road at about 10pm. It had been a long and trying day and I was tired and looked forward to a full rest.

This mutiny was another traumatic, agonising and dramatic occurrence for our suffering country. It had an enduring effect on the mind of Bainimarama. I don't believe his emotional scars ever healed.

## 19

# GOING TO THE PEOPLE

After the Prasad case decision, the question for my government was whether we should accept the pronouncement of our illegality and then take the country to a general election or continue to govern the country with presidential decrees. The return of the ousted prime minister, Mr Mahendra Chaudhry, was ruled out. Bainimarama was totally against the idea. Within cabinet, two or three of my colleagues favoured the continuation of the interim government.

As for me, the way forward was quite clear. We needed a democratically elected government. It would be the right thing to do. My view carried the day.

We decided to stage a general election for August/September 2001. This was a huge challenge. The country was still reeling from the effects of the anarchy caused by George Speight's insurrection and the bloody RFMF mutiny; electoral rolls had to be prepared and updated, the Office of the Supervisor of Election needed revitalising, and required adequate resources. Many other complex details had to be completed.

Those involved in the preparation from the supervisor of elections, to the electoral commissioners, staff of the Elections Office, the district commissioners, and sundry officials, rose to the occasion. My own role as PM was not to interfere in the elections or attempt to influence the electoral commission. I had to ensure the commission and others involved in the organization and operations of the elections had the resources to successfully conduct them. Cabinet, meanwhile, decided that we should contest as a group.

## Conflict of Interest

The ministerial role in elections was to become very controversial when Aiyaz Sayed-Khaiyum became minister for Elections prior to the 2014 poll which returned Fiji to parliamentary rule. There was an outcry about this based on the need for him to be detached from the electoral process. At the same time, he was a minister, he was also general secretary of the Fiji First party. He was criticized for having these dual roles. He reacted angrily.

On 8th May 2014, I made a statement stressing that he had a serious conflict of interest, which was not acceptable in a "free and fair election". Sayed-Khaiyum had argued that his position was no different from past practice.

When I was prime minister, I was also leader of the SDL party, but I was never minister for elections. I emphasized that since independence there has never been a minister for elections. The reason for this was that the Electoral Commission and the supervisor of elections must carry out their functions within the laws regulating their operations, with complete independence and without interference from the government in power. This golden rule had been broken for the first time by the Bainimarama- Sayed-Khaiyum regime when the attorney-general was appointed as minister for elections.

Sayed-Khaiyum at that point exercised the power of his portfolio as member of a government with no legal or popular mandate, no accountability and parliamentary oversight. In a parliamentary democracy all government agencies must come under a ministerial portfolio. Both the Electoral Commission and the office of the supervisor had always been part of the PM's portfolio.

I explained that, as prime minister, my role was two-fold in relation to these agencies. Firstly, I was expected to deal with their submissions for budgetary allocations and, secondly, I had a duty to respond to parliamentary questions. In no way did I influence or interfere in the work of the Electoral Commission or the supervisor of elections. The prime ministers who preceded me played a similar role.

In contrast to this legal and accountable role of an elected prime minister, both the regime's PM and the attorney general had been in complete control of the current election process.

***

THIS HAD INCLUDED THE FORMULATION OF THE ONEROUS POLITICAL PARTIES DECREE, THE ELECTORAL DECREE WITH ITS CONTROVERSIAL PROVISIONS, THE APPOINTMENT OF THE MEMBERS OF THE ELECTORAL COMMISSION AND OF THE SUPERVISOR OF ELECTIONS. THEY ALSO HAD CONTROL OF THE MEDIA RESULTING IN SELF-CENSORSHIP.

I CALLED FOR SAYED-KHAIYUM TO DO THE RIGHT THING AND STEP DOWN FROM THE POSITION OF MINISTER FOR ELECTIONS. INDEED, THERE SHOULD BE NO MINISTER FOR ELECTIONS.

GENERAL ELECTIONS MUST BE CARRIED OUT BY A TRULY INDEPENDENT ELECTORAL COMMISSION, AND SUPERVISOR FOR ELECTIONS.

***

By now I could see what was required to bring back confidence, bind and heal the country's wounds, lift the economy for the benefit of everyone, create jobs, and make space for commercial participation by the indigenous Fijians. Without this participation Fiji would never be a complete nation.

Although time was relatively short, we decided to form a new party, the *Soqosoqo Duavata ni Lewenivanua* (SDL), to rally our supporters. We already had the backing of many chiefs and were confident we would attract a good number of indigenous votes. We understood we were not likely to win much support from other communities. Someone I met with often told me it was virtually impossible to establish a party, develop a national base in just a few months, and then contest and win a general election under its banner. I thought he was wrong.

I led the SDL into the September 2001 election. When the results were in we were the largest party in parliament although short of an outright majority. This was the party result breakdown: SDL – 31 seats; Fiji Labour Party (FLP) – 27; Conservative Alliance/Matanitu Vanua (MV/CAMV) – six; New Labour Unity Party (NLUP) – two; National Federation Party (NFP) – one; United General Party (UGP) – one; and two independents. Interestingly George Speight was elected as a representative of CAMV but was unable to take his seat as he was in prison facing treason charges. He could not be prevented from contesting, as at that point he had no criminal record. Speight was ultimately found guilty of treason and sentenced to death. This penalty was commuted to life imprisonment by the Prerogative of Mercy Commission.

I moved quickly to form a government consisting of our own MPs, those from the Conservative Alliance Matanitu Vanua Party (CAMV) and two independents. With 36 members, our coalition had a majority. I was sworn in as the legal prime minister. I was very happy with the experience, knowledge and talents of my colleagues. I thought the cabinet team was one of the best-qualified line-ups since independence.

It had taken us just 16 months from the Speight coup of 19<sup>th</sup> May 2000 to return Fiji to parliamentary rule. Put another way, in six months from the Chandrika Prasad court case decision, we had restored legality and given the people an elected parliament. Without the support and co-operation of the people, we would not have been able to do this[iv].

Contrast our election achievement with the performance of the Bainimarama military government which succeeded us at the end of 2006. Initially he had promised through the Pacific Islands Forum (PIF) regional grouping to go to elections in 2009. He then reneged on this – leading to Fiji's suspension from the forum - and kept Fiji under the heel of the military for eight years. He was dragging his feet because he was reluctant to give up the power he had stolen, and he was acutely aware of the fate of George Speight.

---

# Only in Fiji

A FEW MONTHS AFTER THE 2001 POLL, I WENT TO MY HOME ISLAND VANUABALAVU IN THE GOVERNMENT SHIP MV TOVUTO. I INSPECTED SOME GOVERNMENT PROJECTS AND SPENT TWO DAYS AT MY HOME IN MAVANA VILLAGE.

AT 7.30AM ON A BEAUTIFUL SUNNY DAY, THE TOVUTO BEGAN ITS RETURN VOYAGE TO SUVA. WE WERE PASSING THROUGH A NARROW SHIP PASSAGE ON THE NORTHERN TIP OF THE ISLAND WHEN THE SHIP SLOWED DOWN. I STEPPED OUT OF MY CABIN TO FIND OUT WHY. STRAIGHT AHEAD, INSIDE THE REEF PASSAGE, I SAW A MAN STANDING IN AN OPEN FIBREGLASS LAUNCH WAVING

———

The waving man, bare chested and wearing a *sulu*, had with him a bundle of fish.

My security officers were mildly concerned about the situation and attempted to signal to the two men in the launch that they should move away. But instead they manoeuvred the launch alongside the Tovuto which was now almost at a standstill. I told the security people to let the man come on board to find out what they wanted.

I then realised I knew the person with the fish. His nickname was Tadeo and he had been my campaign manager on Vanuabalavu for the 2001 election. I greeted him. Tadeo, who looked visibly cold, told me he had been fishing whole night. He wanted to travel to Suva but had no money and hoped that I, as Prime Minister, would allow him onto the Tovuto for the voyage to the capital city. He said the only thing he had to cover his fare to Suva was his catch of fish.

The crew organised a hot breakfast for him and got him some clothing. Soon we were out of the passage and on course for Suva.

# 20

# SIR, MY CHIEF, FAREWELL

W e got right into the task of governance implementing the promises we made in our manifesto. There was much to do, and we had set our priorities. Time went by quickly.

On 18<sup>th</sup> April 2004, our nation lost Ratu Sir Kamisese Mara, our former president and prime minister who also had the traditional titles of Tui Nayau, Sau ni Vanua o Lau. He was 84.

His death was a defining moment for the nation he had led so well. Ratu Mara was truly the father of independent Fiji. His Catholic faith strengthened him while his intellect, education and traditional rank helped to propel him into politics.

Groomed for leadership by his uncle, Ratu Sukuna, he dominated national affairs in the period leading up to independence in 1970 and for many years afterwards. He was dedicated to peaceful co- existence among Fiji's diverse peoples. His multi-racial Alliance Party brought together a coalition of indigenes, Fiji Indians and minority groups of Europeans, part-Europeans, Chinese and others. His watchwords were tolerance, understanding and dialogue. Although he had many disagreements with those opposed to him, he was astute enough to seek out compromise and mutual accommodation when he felt this was feasible and necessary. Tall and imposing, he was also somewhat shy and not particularly good at social small talk. He possessed a sophisticated sense of humour, a sharp wit and an equally sharp tongue. I was one of those who more than once was at the receiving end of his temper.

Ratu Mara saw clearly that after the benign neglect of colonialism there was an urgent need to step up the pace of development. His governments gave special attention to the rural areas where most of the population lived. The concentration was on water supplies, power, jetties, health centres, hospital improvements, education and roads.

After much thought and planning, Ratu Mara and his ministers decided to proceed with the transformation of the Queens Road, a glorified gravel track between Suva and Nadi, into a sealed highway. This was at that stage the biggest project the government had taken on. It cost some $65 million, a very large price tag in those days.

But the jewel in the crown of development was the Monasavu Hydro Scheme. Its purpose was to reduce Fiji's dependency on expensive fuel oil – the kind needed for generating electricity. The price had risen alarmingly. The Fiji Electricity Authority, one of the worst hit organisations, was spending tens of millions of dollars on imported fuel and tariffs for electricity usage had to go up by large amounts to help cover the costs.

Various specialist reports on hydro potential pointed to the Nadrau Plateau near the centre of Viti Levu. It was there that the Monasavu dam and powerhouse would be built along with a transmission system linking in to the national grid.

Total capital expenditure of approximately $230 million would be needed. At the time Ratu Mara described this as a colossal sum, nearly equivalent to the government's entire budget. But the Cabinet decided to take the risk despite some private nervousness. Site works began in 1977 adjacent to the Monasavu waterfall and the scheme was inaugurated in 1983. Ratu Sir Kamisese felt Monasavu was one of his government's best decisions.

Ratu Mara's era saw big growth in tourism and manufacturing to replace imported products. The sugarcane crop grew substantially. The high chief had the major international role in the negotiations for and creation of the Lome Convention which led to preferential marketing arrangements for sugar exports from developing countries. He conceived and saw to the establishment of the pine industry to give the Fijians an improved stake in the economy.

Respected internationally, he was also the pivotal figure in setting up the South Pacific Forum which became the prime agency for encouraging co-operation among the island states of the region.

It was this that earned him the accolade in 2000 of Pacific Man of the Century by Islands Business magazine.

Ratu Mara's thoughts, doubts and fears as he prepared to head an unelected `interim administration after the 1987 coup are captured in his book, The Pacific Way: A Memoir. He said he had been asked on several occasions about the most difficult periods of the four and a half years of his interim government. He cited roadblocks instigated by fundamentalist members of the Methodist Church, to enforce their position on Sunday observance, as creating much worry and tension. He thought the psychological pressure associated with that crisis caused the first "mental blackout" he had ever suffered. This contributed to the deterioration in his health, which later included the insertion of a heart pacemaker. The torching of temples and mosques and politically-inspired boycotts of the sugar harvest were also testing episodes.

Ratu Mara said that through all these troubles he was sustained by a simple truth:

------

The majority of the population, to greater and lesser degrees, saw the interim administration as the country's best hope.

That is why stability prevailed and it also explains why the country is now on the verge of parliamentary government.

---

He said this in a long letter to the then Governor General, Ratu Sir Penaia Ganilau as he stepped down as head of the interim administration. I can never compare myself to Ratu Mara, but I identify with what he said in the letter.

In its conclusion, the high chief returned to his enduring message about the need for the people of Fiji to work together.

He said,

---

Despite my own unhappiness about the response to my policies of multi-racialism, there is only one way for this nation to go. We must all find a common path towards unity, a unity which transcends race and religion and recognizes that we are all sons and daughters of Fiji.

---

Other excerpts:

---

When you called me at Lomaloma in December 1987 and asked me to form an interim government to prepare the country for a return to parliamentary rule, I knew the task at hand would be onerous. Fiji had experienced the ordeal of two military coups. Society was fractured, the economy was tottering and the country had been ostracised by some of its oldest friends and allies. There was no parliament and no properly functioning political system. Even institutions of state, such as the judiciary, were seriously weakened, to the extent that the citizenry justifiably feared a breakdown in law and order. The business community was hit by a slump in sales and confidence, leading to reduced earnings and loss of jobs. There were worries about the army and its role and whether it would respond to civilian control.

Nationalism, racialism and extremism were on the rise and, for the first time, religion was becoming a central factor in politics. We saw the face of intolerance. We heard the voice of bigotry and fundamentalism. Religion mixed with politics had produced a deadly effect in other countries. Was Fiji now threatened with the same danger?

I was aware, too, that if I was to accept appointment as head of an unelected government there would be vigorous and angry opposition. I would be portrayed as yet another third world tyrant, intent on suppressing the masses and consolidating power for power's sake. There were numerous people, here and overseas, who were saying the country was finished, that it was headed into an irreversible decline leading straight to the rubbish heap of history. Would it be my fate to preside over the inevitable? Would I be attempting the impossible? How did one restore a country and its people when society was close to collapse? How did one turn Fiji away from anarchy and back to order and stability? Would a government hold, or was the political tightrope simply too narrow?

Thoughts about all those questions came to mind, and I can tell you now that I was filled with trepidation. I did not relish the assignment. It was true that I had ample experience of government and leadership – but that had been within the context of a recognized and legally established framework. We had a constitution, organised politics, a legislature and the other functioning accoutrements of a nation-state.

The prospect before me now was desolate indeed – like heading into a storm in a leaky craft, with only a handful of crew members and no navigation aids.

But, as I reflected, I could not deny that I had been

brought up in a tradition of public service and leadership. I had always been taught that I had obligations to the people and to Fiji. A sense of duty and loyalty had been instilled into me as part of my upbringing as a chief and this had sustained me many times during my long political career. I recognized, too, that the Fijian chiefly system – that centuries-old order of authority and social organisation – was intact and that within it, lay strength and stability. The whole nation could draw on this for the process of reconstruction and renewal. I was certainly reacting to its influence when I responded to your call. You spoke to me as a fellow chief, with all the authority and prestige of the Tui Cakau. That weighed heavily in my thinking.

I took comfort from the fact that most of Fiji's people were peace-loving and tolerant and that many, many citizens from all our communities had asked me to come back into government. Finally I acknowledged, in all humility, that after serving so long as head of government I was perhaps the person best qualified to provide national leadership in this time of crisis.

There were two priorities, as I saw it. First we had to repair the economy and then we had to ensure Fiji had a new constitution. If the economic tailspin continued the people would suffer further. Jobs and money would be even scarcer, creating social instability which could lead to chaos and violence. An army without pay was also a potential source of civil unrest and upheaval. So I felt we had to initially help keep bread on the tables and then address the issue of formulating a constitution that would return the country to parliamentary rule.

In the absence of a parliament, the main forum for decision-making would be cabinet, the collective grouping of ministers who would decide policy, take executive decisions and then make sure they were implemented by the civil service. Laws would be enacted by Presidential decree.

---

Describing his approach to recruiting ministers. Ratu Mara said he had to strike a balance between the different centres of power including the military, extremists and the moderates, and the traditional confederacies.

He added:

---

It was obvious that if the majority of the population was against the administration there would be little chance of us accomplishing our objectives. I appealed directly to the people for their understanding, making it clear I had taken on the biggest challenge I had ever faced in my career. There was despair in the community – especially among the unemployed – and I pledged to do what I would to make work available again, and to promote harmony and confidence. Thankfully the broad mass of the people gave us their endorsement in what one media commentator called a "groundswell of goodwill". Special expressions of support came from important groups and numerous individuals. The dissenters had their say too – as they would throughout our tenure of office. They were determined, well-organised and outspoken.

---

He described how his government had to move quickly to identify the best ways of attaining and sustaining growth and increasing employment. It launched a number of successful initiatives. One of these was a decision to work closely with EIE, a Japanese company, to develop Denarau Island at Nadi into an integrated resort with hotels, villas and many amenities. Denarau today is a thriving hub of the tourism industry. It represented a scale of private investment new to Fiji and the southwest Pacific and is a testament to Ratu Mara's determination and vision.

He reported a rise in employment and a decline in the unemployment rate. In 1989 Fiji achieved economic growth of almost 12 percent – one of the best in the world. Average growth from 1988 to 1991 was four percent.

Ratu Mara stressed that the coups had served to concentrate attention on many issues affecting the Fijian people. "One of the most pressing of these was the need for greater Fijian involvement in all sectors of the economy. Fijians were feeling more and more insecure about their economic position which saw them virtually excluded from key sectors of commerce and business. My previous governments had adopted a number of measures to accelerate Fijian economic progress, but we now decided to devote greater resources to this.

---

We adopted a nine-point plan relating, among other things, to finance, investment, incentives and savings. A $20 million loan was made available to Fijian Holdings Ltd, an investment company formed in 1984 and supported by the Fijian provinces.

Fijian Holdings was able to acquire significant additional shareholdings in established companies, thus enhancing its rate of return. Fijians were encouraged to invest in the Unit Trust of Fiji – and by the end of 1991 about 58 per cent of the unit holders in the trust were Fijian organisations or individuals. The Fiji Development Bank continued its role as a vehicle for identifying and initially assisting Fijian entrepreneurs. For the three years from 1989 loans amounting to $45.4 million were approved for 3,532 Fijians.

All this, and other aspects of the government's policy, gave new impetus to Fijian economic progress."

Ratu Mara added, however,

there is no quick or easy answer on this issue and our strategy must be for sure and steady advancement over the longer term. If our people are misled into believing that economic manna will simply fall from heaven because there is a Fijian government, then those responsible will have to answer to the country when the truth becomes evident.

In a major speech, to Pacific Islanders in Auckland in July 1999, Ratu Mara shared some more insights into the enduring question of the relationship of indigenous Fijians, and indeed most Pacific peoples, to modern economic and commercial practices. He spoke of the fundamental challenges posed by attitudes to money:

A lot of would-be island entrepreneurs still tend to forget that business and money go hand in hand. I've noticed with Fijians that they might have a perfectly good plan for business, but when it comes to the money side, they often start to get vague and illogical. Priorities get confused. When the loan money is approved, for instance, a Pajero might appear in the driveway instead of a more modest vehicle suitable for a small business.

Money, as we all know, will too often trickle through an islander's fingers like water. There never seems to be enough of it, but when it is plentiful it is usually given away, in the time-honoured manner of our culture. People spend more than they should and often on the wrong things. Then the debts mount. And financial ruin looms.

The fact remains, though, that frugality is not in our nature.

---

He went on to make that basic point that business is about returning a profit, spending less than you earn, controlling costs and using cashflow wisely.

---

So any Pacific islander aspiring to own and operate a business had to have a clear appreciation of these fundamentals. There are choices to be made. Much discipline and patience is required and some cultural and social adjustment.

---

I have included details about Ratu Mara's achievements and his thoughts because there is a tendency by those in power now to dismiss and downplay the performance of all previous governments. The message they convey is that only they know how to manage and develop the country despite the growing and glaring evidence of their many failures.

At the state funeral of Ratu Mara on that morning of 30th April 2004, the duty fell to me as prime minister to deliver the national eulogy for the great chief. I was nervous because of the overwhelming emotion and significance of the moment. I was conscious too of my own lower ranking in the Fijian traditional system. Was I worthy to speak on this historic and sorrowful occasion? I remember doing some final editing to my text, and getting a second opinion on it, just minutes before I left my office for Albert Park.

Here are parts of what I said:
*I, a commoner, from the Tui Nayau's ancestral realm, must come here to utter words so difficult to find about his death. I can*

*only bow my head in humility and wonder why I was destined to do this.*

I went on to say I would do my best for his wife, Ro Lady Lala and the family, for Ratu Sir Kamisese's people, for my own paramount chief and for Fiji. I quoted from some parts of the famous song Ciri Koto, written by Ratu Mara about the thoughts of home of a young Fijian soldier helping to keep peace in the Middle East:

*"Don't cry for me, my beloved Fiji I give my life*

*So, you will be recognized ... My beloved land, land of life ...*

*I am far away yet I dream of my islands ... It always brings me back to my home Land I love, Land of Life"*

I then added:

*"Yes, Fiji was the land he loved, with every fibre of his being. It was his Land of Life. And so it is for us."*

*"That is what he wanted; that we should feel everything he felt about Fiji and that the land of life would hold us all to her breast and unite us in peace and happiness.*

*"We think of the sacrifices he made and the price he paid to further his heartfelt belief in the coming together of our different communities in the quest for nationhood. Hear what he said about this and remember it, for it will be our hope and national salvation.*

*Towards the end of his career, he said that despite his own unhappiness about the response to his policies on multiracialism, there was only one way for this nation to go. We had to find a common path towards unity, a unity which transcends race and religion and recognizing that we are all sons and daughters of Fiji. That was the centre of his belief, that's what he leaves us. That is what we must cherish and live by to honour his memory."*

I spoke of the tamarind tree not far from my own village, Mavana.

*"One day a group of us sat with the Tui Nayau under that tree in that beautiful place and listened to a story he told. He said the tamarind had been planted there with his umbilical cord after his birth in accordance with tradition. The tree has grown tall with deep roots.*

*Its spreading branches give shade and it bears much fruit. It overlooks the sea, which the Tui Nayau so loved.*

*"Like his tamarind tree, the Tui Nayau's roots are implanted in this country. He grew tall and strong and produced much fruit for Fiji. We sheltered in his shade. We will always feel close to him at that tree by the sea. When it dies, our clan will plant another for the spirit of the Tui Nayau."*

I ended my eulogy with the words, *"Sir, my Chief, farewell"*.

Several years later, a branch of the tree snapped off and fell unexpectedly to the ground. That was the beginning of the end. The tree gradually withered away. But Fiji should never let his legacy wither.

# 21

# BEGINNINGS OF A DISASTER

The relationship between Bainimarama and the interim civilian government I led was positive. This continued for the two years 2001-2002 of the first SDL–led government. But the military commander had issues with some members of parliament from the Conservative Alliance Matanitu Vanua Party. He thought they had been involved with the Speight group. I've already mentioned my suspicion that the military itself had a key role in Speight's takeover. The origins of the uprising remain shadowy to this day.

Bainimarama was also expressing concern over the pace of investigations into the Speight insurrection. The red flags were starting to go up about Bainimarama not only among ministers and our MPs. There was a growing realisation in some sectors of the public service that he was aggressive, difficult, rude and unpleasant to deal with.

This is captured well in a letter from Dr Nacanieli Goneyali, when he was permanent secretary at Government House in 2003. I knew Dr Goneyali as a quiet and gentlemanly type. He wrote to the permanent secretary for home affairs (Waqanisau) on April 7th to complain about Bainimarama's conduct during a visit to the President, His Excellency Ratu Josefa Iloilo. The subject of the visit was a controversy over some general court martial findings and sentences.

Dr Goneyali stated that he was very "annoyed and frustrated regarding the unprofessional, rude, unrespectable behaviour" of Bainimarama. Bainimarama had emphasized that he did not want the permanent secretary in his meeting with the president. Dr Goneyali argued there was a need for him to be beside the president all the time in all meetings "because of the present state of his mind." On arrival at the office Bainimarama went straight in to see Ratu Iloilo. Dr Goneyali joined the meeting. But as soon as he sat down Bainimarama "ordered me with a high-pitched voice that I should go outside."

I replied that I was not going to go outside and after some exchange of words he mentioned, and I quote: 'I do not care whether His Excellency will remember what we discussed or not.'

Dr Goneyali withdrew from the discussion after a request from the president.

Later, he said he,

felt sorry for His Excellency because he could see he was disturbed and distressed by what was happening, a situation which I always do not allow His Excellency to reach because of the danger of him getting another heart attack.

His Excellency felt sick after this meeting that he had to go home and rest because of the severe headache. He did not come back to work in the afternoon.

Dr Goneyali stated that Bainimarama had no respect for the Office of the President.

---

> He was sitting with his right leg flexed over his left knee and both of his arms were fully extended laterally over the sofa at ninety degrees. There is obviously something wrong with this man, as no respectable Fijian will ever behave in this manner in the President's Office.

---

He added that the president later admitted he could not remember anything discussed with Bainimarama.

The relationship between my government and Bainimarama soured further from 2003 and continued to worsen up to the general election of 2006 and afterwards. The military leader had become vocal in his dislike of some parliamentarians from the Conservative Alliance Matanitu Vanua Party. He pressed us about the 2000 coup, again alleging that police investigations were not moving quickly enough. I was surprised at this. By the end of 2005 the Fiji Police Force had completed about 3,000 investigations with some 800 prosecutions.

(About the same time the International Criminal Court was initiating investigations into the Rwanda genocide in Africa. Those investigations were extremely slow with very few prosecutions. By comparison, our independent police force and independent judiciary did extremely well, even if the circumstances and context for the two investigations were drastically different.)

# 22

# TO THE POLLS AGAIN

B ainimarama's open hostility to the government and relentless efforts to discredit my leadership and government policies led to more uncertainty and further damaged national confidence. We were getting on with the reconstruction of the country and the economy; his aggression and threats served as a distraction.

At one point we decided to reassign him, with the offer of a diplomatic posting overseas. At first, he seemed interested, but finally declined. We nominated him for a UN peacekeeping position; he did not make the grade owing to lack of relevant experience.

In early 2006, I announced the next general election would be held in May. By this time Bainimarama's dislike of the SDL–led government and me as its leader was all-consuming.

The timing of the election was earlier than the constitution required. But in view of the ongoing attacks on my government from Bainimarama and the consequential damage to the confidence we had worked so hard to achieve, I felt a new mandate could assist us in maintaining our path towards peace and stability .

Bainimarama led a vigorous political campaign against the SDL

Party, illegally using soldiers and public funds. This was in direct contravention of the 1997 constitution, the provisions of the Finance Management Act and other legislation. He openly supported the Fiji Labour Party, again ignoring the rule about the non-political role of the army. He had effectively removed the institution from civilian control. It was operating outside the law. He was now very much the politician, but backed by force.

Commander Bainimarama spoke out in strong terms about the Qoliqoli Bill that was in circulation at the time. The Bill's purpose was to return traditional fishing grounds to customary owners while also protecting the interests of the general public and commercial operators. There was much controversy and very intense debate about the issue. It was democracy in action. I travelled widely to make the case for the legislation and to counter those who saw it as something akin to the end of the world.

The need we saw was to resolve a grievance the Fijians had carried since just after the signing of the Deed of Cession. There is an expression which describes the rather relaxed Fijian attitude towards the dictates of a clock or a watch. It is called "Fiji time". The Qoliqoli delay of 124 years was stretching "Fiji time" beyond its limits. The Fijians should surely be rewarded for their patience.

Resolving the qoliqoli question would help to lay a secure foundation for the future. We believed it would strengthen the investment climate by removing misunderstanding and improving cooperation between qoliqoli owners and other groups especially some tourism industry operators.

Our proposed bill echoed a call of the 1997 constitution, Fiji's supreme law, for a more equitable sharing of economic and commercial power. It fulfilled the constitution's requirements for parliament to have regard to the customs, traditions, usages, values and aspirations of the indigenous people. Customary fishing rights related directly to this.

Previous governments had intended to take the same course of action that we proposed. They too saw that a historical wrong and anomaly had to be corrected. But for whatever reasons this was not done. Perhaps it went into the too hard basket.

The determined opposition to the Bill was mainly from those worried about possible implications for investment and tourism. They feared it might adversely affect the use of foreshore areas for development, water sports and associated recreational activities.

We tried very hard to allay this apprehension through dialogue and consultation, but misunderstandings, misconceptions and misrepresentations persisted.

As I remember, Bainimarama predicted the Bill would take the Fijians back to the age of cannibalism!

He was supported in particular by two wealthy hotel owners who helped to fund the New Alliance Party led by Ratu Epeli Gani-lau, a former army commander and son of Ratu Penaia Ganilau, who gave Fiji distinguished service for many years. Ratu Epeli's New Alliance would unsuccessfully challenge the SDL in the upcoming election.

I was amazed at the complete about-turn by Bainimarama on the Qoliqoli Bill and other indigenous issues. Prior to my appointment on or about the 4th July 2000, when I became prime minister in an unelected interim civilian government, Bainimarama invited me to address officers of the RFMF.

My remarks to them were based on what became known as the "Blueprint" for indigenous Fijian development. It consisted of about 40 recommendations, including the Qoliqoli Bill, the establishment of a Land Claims Tribunal and the transfer of ownership of State Schedule A and B lands to original indigenous Fijian owners. The Blueprint was the outcome of the work of a Senate Committee that I chaired. Its brief was to examine the reasons why indigenous Fijians lagged so far behind in the economic and business sectors and make recommendations.

On the day of the Speight coup, the committee was holding its last meeting at Vunisea, Kadavu. Because of the severe crisis that gripped the country, and its aftermath, we were not able to compile our committee report. But we did formulate and agree on several policy recommendations which were adapted for the Blueprint.

The meeting with officers of the RFMF held at Bainimarama's invitation took place in their Mess Hall. It was packed. I am pretty sure that not only the officers were present. Additionally, scores of soldiers stood outside. I wanted to make a good presentation, because in my view much of Fiji's future for the long term depended on the country's ability to bring the indigenous people into the commercial and economic mainstream. At the end of my comments, there was huge applause led by Bainimarama. For a moment I thought the roof was going to fall in!

So, when Bainimarama later started to attack the Qoliqoli Bill and other proposals in the Blueprint. I was surprised and disturbed. The prime army cheerleader for the Blueprint, which included the Qoliqoli Bill, had become its bitterest opponent. It raised questions about his credibility and reliability.

I still remember a prominent business executive saying that he thought the qoliqoli legislation was a smokescreen aimed at satisfying a small group of agitators. There spoke the voice of ignorance. The same person has been appointed to senior positions as a director by the current Bainimarama government.

The purpose of the Qoliqoli Bill was to transfer legal ownership of qoliqoli back to the Fijians from the state. Under existing laws, the Fijians only had rights of usage. This did not permit them to receive the full benefit from these traditional resources, especially in view of their increasing commercial utilisation by others. The proprietary ownership to be vested in the indigenous owners included the soil under the water, and the seabed and reefs within the customary fishing areas.

At the time when I was meeting with all the stakeholders and addressing public meetings on the legislation, I stressed that appropriate and adequate safeguards would be included to ensure public access and protection of the interests of investors. It would not affect or interfere with the legal interests already conferred or that might be acquired according to law within customary fisheries areas. However, renewal of such legal rights would be done under the legislation. There would be navigational rights under common law, and the right to free passage recognized by international law.

I spoke about the introduction of appropriate management, supervisory and enforcement systems governing the issuing and use of licences, permits and fees for commercial usage such as fishing and other water sports. The law would also contain measures to ensure conservation and sustainable harvesting of marine life and resources which had always been a source of food and livelihoods.

It was, I said, about meeting the requirements of the present generation without compromising the ability of those who followed to meet their own needs.

To a certain extent I, and my colleagues in government, appreciated the caution from tourism operators about the proposed changes. Change is often difficult, especially when it is marked by a lack of understanding of cultural and historical facts. What I found harder to understand was why there should be reluctance to acknowledge the right of the indigenous people to freely reap a commercial benefit from ownership of one of their natural resources.

Put another way, if someone had an asset used by others for a profit and did not receive a fair share of that, the person would be subject to a denial of rights. It would be natural for him or her to want an equitable share of the return from that asset. What is wrong with that? It was the same with the traditional foreshore fisheries rights areas. If a commercial gain was derived from them by others, it was only fair and just that the owners should also equitably benefit.

The historical background is critical for understanding the context of this issue which created so much bitter controversy and was used by the military as partial justification for their illegal takeover of our government.

When the Fijian chiefs ceded Fiji to Queen Victoria in 1874, ownership of their land and reefs was very much on their minds. They were concerned that cession should not alter their proprietary rights over land, rivers, mangroves, swamps and fishing grounds. It was said that the Fijians clung tenaciously to their fishing rights. They attached as much importance to their reefs as to their land. There is no doubt that the chiefs felt the reefs would be returned to them in the same way as their lands.

There was in fact an assurance from Queen Victoria that the Fijians would not be deprived of any rights they had enjoyed under custom.

Sir William Des Voeux's statement to the Council of Chiefs at Nailaga, Ba, in September 1881, explained Queen Victoria's position clearly.

Sir William said:

---

I now return to the Queen's letter, and I have to tell you, with regard to your representation of the subject of the reefs, that the matter will be carefully investigated, and it is Her Majesty's desire, that neither you, nor your people, should be deprived of any rights in those reefs, which you have enjoyed under your own laws and customs; and I may tell you, on my own part, that measures will be taken for securing to each *mataqali*, the reefs which properly belong to it, exactly in the same way the rest of their land will be secure to them.

---

Earlier, after a meeting at Bau, the chiefs had written to Her Majesty in these terms:

---

We are anxious, because it has the appearance as though our rights over, and ownership of our reefs were passing away from us...they have belonged to the several tribes, from all past times, down to the present

---

Again, it is clear that the chiefs were exerting their ownership rights over reefs and foreshore that had customarily belonged to them from time immemorial. The Queen's intentions to protect their rights were clear.

Unfortunately, colonial government officials of later times acted in defiance of the wishes and the pledge of Her Majesty. They chose to apply the British common law principle whereby the crown owned all the foreshore and reefs in Fiji. This was not consistent with the custom and customary rights of the indigenous community. It did not fulfill the legitimate wishes of the chiefs and the people as acknowledged by Queen Victoria.

The years passed but the fishing rights grievance did not go away. There was some progress when it was decided in 1941 to inquire into and establish the boundaries and ownership of customary fishing areas. Lingering discontent continued; the Fijians maintained their stance on ownership rather than just usage. Disputes increased about the usage and benefits from the qoliqoli.

In May 1978, the Council of Chiefs resolved that a committee be appointed to consider the issue. One of the members of that committee was Ratu Josefa Iloilo who, at the time we introduced the Qoliqoli Bill, was the president of Fiji. Our then Attorney General and Minister for Justice, the late Qoriniasi Bale, was also a member. The committee recommended that the government should be requested to produce new legislation to declare definitively that the reefs and the foreshores belonged to the Fijians on a proprietary basis.

In 1982, the GCC concluded again that the existing laws were not in line with the undertakings given to the Fijians. It decided to ask the government of the day to amend and enact legislation. The Fijian Affairs Board requested the Native Fisheries Commission to complete the task of determining which rights were held by each yavusa or vanua.

Our interim government of 2000 made a commitment to proceed with the legislation that was reflected in the manifesto of the SDL.

Authorisation to complete the draft form of the bill was given by cabinet in September 2003. Initial drafts of the bill had been considered by cabinet and its legislation committee on a number of occasions. Ownership and boundaries of individual fishing areas were determined. Completion of registration would be the responsibility of a customary fisheries commission to be established. This new commission would be responsible for all customary as well as commercial use of fisheries resources within customary fisheries areas.

I told parliament that after the bill was passed, the legislation would come into effect on a date gazetted by the minister. This took into account the need to prepare for promulgation of regulations, bylaws and orders to help implement the Bill, including effective enforcement and management. I emphasised we were keeping an open mind on the possibility of excluding certain provisions if there were sufficiently persuasive reasons for doing this.

I said the draft legislation had received overwhelming support from qoliqoli owners and we pledged not to let them down. We also committed to protect the interests of the general public and the tourism industry.

I have no regrets about our decision to enact the qoliqoli legislation. There was a sound historical, moral and ethical case for this. There was no reason to fear the proposed law. It was undone by emotion, unfounded suspicion, and manipulation by the army led by a man who would stop at nothing to discredit our government and who would finally overthrow it at the point of a gun.

We were extremely responsible, open and democratic in the way we handled this issue. But the will of Bainimarama and his army, backed by certain political and commercial interests, ensured that the indigenous people were once again denied part of their birthright.

# ARMY RESISTANCE FROM WITHIN

Within the RFMF, Bainimarama did not have things all his own way. For a while his actions and treasonous intent had met with opposition from right-thinking members of the army's officer corps. A number of those who crossed him by speaking up in favour of the army sticking to its legal role, detached from politics, were removed by Bainimarama. They gave him advice he did not want to hear about his obsession to remove or overthrow a duly elected government.

So, he simply employed his legal authority to hire and fire. He thus ultimately strengthened his position by surrounding himself with those who were more inclined to accept what he was intending to do. Documents available publicly online show that as early as 2003, he was planning a takeover; treason was brewing in his mind.

I now refer to some of these documents because they add further context and depth to the picture that emerges of the RFMF, its internal tensions and leadership issues.

A statement by Colonel Alfred Tuatoko, which is on the Internet http://www.truthforfiji.com/uploads/8/4/2/3/8423704/

col_tuatoko_statement- combined.pdf, is instructive and revealing. It cost him his job.

Dated 11th March 2004 and witnessed by Lt. Col. S.V. Raduva and Commander (N) T.T. Koroi, it is an account of a meeting that took place on Tuesday, 16th December 2003. This was attended by a number of senior officers. According to the colonel. Bainimarama took over the meeting and advised of his intent to remove the current government. He indicated that some NGOs and diplomats were supporting him. He gave instructions for plans to be drawn up for the government's removal. He wanted a briefing on 21st December when he returned from Labasa. He ended the meeting by telling those present to hurry up with the plan.

Col. Tuatoko's statement continues:

---

After the Comd left the meeting we decided that we would not draw up plans for the military takeover as this was a criminal and treasonous act. However the staff of HQ RFMF would draw up an advice for Comd RFMF advising him against his intention to remove the government.

---

But Col. Tuatoko makes it clear that Commodore Bainimarama was very much focused on a coup.

---

On Thursday 18 December during Comd's scheduled conference he reiterated his intent to remove the government of the day, save HE the President, and that we were to continue and draw up plans for the takeover of government. He added that he did not want anybody sitting on the fence and if anyone does not agree with his intention, is to leave. At the end of this meeting Comd personally interviewed several officers. These officers are Col. Kadavulevu, Col Tuatoko,

Capt (N) Teleni, LTCOL Raduva and Comdrs Koroi and Natuva.

In my interview with Comd he stated that he would forcefully remove the present government if his term as Comd RFMF was not renewed.

---

(He was aware that my government was looking at the possibility of ending his contract.) Col. Tuatoko's statement continued:

---

I advised him that such an act was illegal and amounted to treason. I advised him that there are legal ways to settle his disagreement with government and that he must follow that legal path. Comd said that doing so would take too much time. He said that removing the government may be legally wrong but was morally correct. He also said that he must remain as Comd because there was no one who could be Comd and pursue the May 2000 prosecutions as he is doing.

I told him that the issue regarding the renewal of his term was a matter between him and government. He should not use the institution as a means of renewing his term. Comd did not accept this and asked where I stood regarding his intention to remove government. I told him that I could not support him on such an illegal and treasonable act. Comd then directed that I keep out of the planning activities. My interview thus ended.

Following the individual interviews we spoke amongst ourselves and except for Comdr Natuva whom I did not speak to, we all had advised

Comd that his intention was illegal and treasonable and that each of us did not support the Comd in such an activity. Col. GK then advised us that we must provide Comd with a written advice in order to convince him not to carry out his intent. The advice should be ready for Comd before 31 Dec. the advice was actually tendered to the Comd in early Jan 01.

On 19 December 2003 at the WOs & SGTs Mess, in his address to the officers and senior non-commissioned officers, he said that 2004 will be a difficult year and our individual loyalty to him (Commander RFMF) will be put to the test.

On the afternoon of Monday 12 January, COS HQ RFMF called a meeting of the HQ RFMF staff and advised that he had been relieved of his appointment and told to go (on) leave because of the advice that was tendered to Comd advising him against his intent to remove the government. Comd also advised him that all officers who formed or contributed to the advice are to also go on leave.

Comd RFMF called a conference on Tuesday 13 January 04 and amongst other things advised the conference that we should not be shaken by the ongoing saga over the renewal or otherwise of his term as Comd RFMF. He also advised the conference that he had relieved Col Kadavulevu of the COS HQ RFMF appointment and has nominated LTCOL Baledrokadroka as COS because he was disappointed with the written advice he received. He also directed that all the officers who formed the advice and all officers at both SHQ and LFC who did not support him on the path he was taking the RFMF, to stick to their principles, take all outstanding leave and when their leave was finished, that they do the honourable thing and resign from the RFMF. He also mentioned that he was only testing us in the interviews and that he would not force anyone to resign.

On Thurs 15 Jan I received a posting order showing amongst other changes that LTCOL J Pickering had assumed my appointment of DSC & FD.

---

On 5th of January 2004, Colonel George Kadavulevu, RFMF

chief of staff, wrote formally to Bainimarama with advice http://
www.truthforfiji.com/uploads/8/4/2/3/8423704/
col_g_kadavulevus_advice- opt.pdf which he said represented a
professional, legal and moral stand that the RFMF had been
supporting all along. He hoped good sense would prevail.

Col. Kadavulevu's arguments are sound and well put. They
represent a persuasive case for Bainimarama to call a halt to what he
was intending to do. Bainimarama rejected them. Col. Kadavulevu
was relieved of his appointment.

Here are some extracts from his advice, which also underlines the
feelings of the senior officers:

---

The saying that 'the military is the last bastion of law and
order' not only holds true in any democratic society but has a
much deeper meaning and standing. It connotes that the
military recognizes the supremacy of civilian rule and that it
is committed to upholding constitutional rule. The RFMF
represents this in Fiji. What is unfortunate is that the
reputation of the RFMF as a professional institution that
upholds the rule of law has been tainted after the events of
1987 and 2000. What is reassuring however is that the
RFMF continues to pursue the persecution of those military
personnel involved in the 2000 coup. This is what is
sustaining our (RFMF) reputation as a professional military
institution.

The on-going confrontation between you as Commander
RFMF and the government is unfortunate and is causing
concern and some anxiety amongst the local and international
communities. This is especially so when this confrontation is
being aired openly in the press. Such differences should be
resolved professionally and in a professional manner between
you as Commander and the Minister for Home Affairs and
Immigration. The matters under dispute (the prosecution of

the 2000 coup perpetrators, your contract and investigations into the actions of the RFMF during the May 2000 incidents) are nothing that is out of the ordinary. The differences in opinion over the issues under dispute can always be resolved through negotiation based on the principles of transparency and fairness.

Your recent utterances at your conferences of 16 and 18 December are of deep concern to us (officers). We feel that your intentions are contrary to all that is stated above. Besides we feel that the interests of the RFMF and the nation have been overridden by your personal wishes. First and foremost the issues under dispute, especially the renewal of your contract, are matters to be resolved between you and the government. The RFMF as an institution cannot and must not be dragged into the dispute as a means for its resolution.

Secondly, please bear in mind the oath of allegiance that we all swore to when we first enlisted into the RFMF. The officers are standing by this oath. You have interviewed some of the officers personally. They have all individually given advice on the matter and as requested by you they have shown their standing regarding your intention. These officers' views and stance must be respected. These officers have taken both a legal and moral stand which is contrary to yours. This does not mean they are disloyal to you, they are only exercising their right as professional military officers in what they believe in – 'to discharge their duty according to law'. Should you persist with your intention then this same privilege you gave to these officers must be extended to all ranks of the RFMF.

Thirdly the situation which you are bringing to bear on the RFMF, and the nation for that matter, cannot be compared to the incidents of 1987 and 2000. Under the circumstances there is no way in which you can justify your intent and impending action. On the other hand the consequences of such action would only be catastrophic for Fiji. The despair and suffering will be unbearable and longer lasting than that experienced after 1987 and 2000. Whatever your feelings are about the issues under dispute, there is no other avenue open to you but to resolve the issues through legal means.

We must all recognize the fact that the RFMF is the 'final guarantor of law' and our actions must therefore confer accordingly. Any attempt to create a supposedly national crisis so as to influence government action is considered unprofessional and falls within the elements of conspiracy and contempt. I strongly recommend to you that you make a bold stand as Commander of the RFMF and go back to government and seek redress on the issues under dispute through the professional approach of negotiation and dialogue. There is no other way. To do otherwise is tantamount to conspiracy and treason.

I mentioned to you in our interview that I would provide you with a written advice. I have shared this paper with the senior officers of this Headquarters and they are in agreement with the contents. I urge you to please take heed of this advice and place the interests of the RFMF, the nation and its people before your own personal feelings and interests.

May God bless us all.

---

The following was handwritten to the chief executive officer in the Ministry of Home Affairs on 19 January 2004 by Lt. Col. Samuela Veileqe Raduva.

## AN OFFENCE ABOUT TO BE COMMITTED

1. It is the duty of every Officer and soldier of the Republic of Fiji Military Forces (RFMF), in accordance with RFMF Standing Orders Volume One Part XXI Section I para 21.4 "to notice and to repress or report any negligence or impropriety of conduct on the part of officers and soldiers".

2. I was interviewed by the Commander RFMF, Commodore Josaia Voreqe Bainimarama in his office at Headquarter RFMF on Thursday 18 December 2003, with regards to my position, in relation to his intent he discussed during his conference that day. As I sat down, he told me that there are people in government, who are trying to destabilize our country and also there are civil servants, who want him removed. He told me that he had made himself clear at the conference and at other previous conferences of his intention to remove government. I told him that his intention against government is clear to me. He went on to tell me, that the military must not only carry out what is legal, it must also carry out what is moral. And, since government is trying to remove him as Commander, by not extending his contract, he will remove government using the military. Then he asked me where I stood with his intent.

3. I told him, that I shall never support him if he wants to remove government. Further, I advised him that he ought to be upright, as God is in control of everything and that he had done with by putting the soldiers, who were guilty of offences relating to the events of 19 May 2000 in prison. And then I told him, that what he is intending to do, is exactly the same thing the soldiers involved in May 2000, are in gaol for. I told him he must not do it, since the weak and the poor will be more disadvantaged and that our country will spiral down into chaos and despair.

4. He told me that he will get support from the non government organisations, international communities and the diplomatic corps. And that, some officers are formulating contingency plans, for his intent.

5. I made it very clear to him, that removing the government unlawfully is wrong and I shall not be party to it and that I shall never support him, but the institution.

6. He then told me, not to be involved with the planning team and to keep clear.

7. Reporting the Commander RFMF, for an offence is not easy. But as he had openly discussed, in his conferences and now has interviewed me in his office, asking of my position towards his intent to remove government using the military, his action is improper, and to me, in my professional opinion, he is in the province of impropriety of conduct and ought to be reported.

8. I am doing my duty to RFMF and my country in reporting this impropriety of conduct, by Commodore Bainimarama; fully aware of the consequences he might take against me and my family. But, I am calm as I report this offence to you, as a superior officer and especially when Commodore Bainimarama, by all indications is serious in carrying out his intention.

Indication of his seriousness

9. At the annual end of the year Officers and Warrant Officers and Senior Non Commission Officers (WOs and SNCOs) get together at the Sergeants Mess; Commodore Bainimarama told us that 2004 will be a difficult year and that our individual loyalty to him, will be put to the test. In his reciprocal speech, a Warrant Officer Class One stated "na *vanua* o lako kina keimami na lako kina, na *vanua* o mate kina keimami na mate kina" (we will go wherever you go, wherever you die, we will die).

10. Recent visitors for Commodore Bainimarama to HQ

RFMF included a senior legal officer and a senior official of a NGO.

11. In December 2003, contrary to proper procedures RFMF purchased large quantities of: uniforms (greens and boots), beddings and eating utensils. The total RFMF over expenditure in 2003 is $21 million and after taking into account the unbudgeted expenditure on: COLA, assistance for Cyclone Ami, etc, our over expenditure is about $12 million. Included in the over expenditure is the unpaid expenditure of $2.0 million.

12. At the Commander's conference on 14 January 04, he immediately referred to the RFMF Chief of Staff's (COS) advice to him, on his intent (copy attach). He was disappointed with the advice, and stated that he had relieved his COS, and that all senior officers involved in the advice, were to take all their outstanding leave (copy of directive attach). He

further stated that since those officers do not support him on the path he is going to take RFMF through, they must do the honourable thing and resign, as individual leave expires. He further stated, he only tested us in his interview and that he will not put pressure on us to resign.

13. I submit to you this report of an offence about to be committed by Commodore Bainimarama with much concern for RFMF and my will to remain professional, with my conduct.

---

Lieutenant Colonel Filipo Tarakinikini became the face of the RFMF as its articulate spokesperson.

On 27th February 2002 he wrote a letter of resignation to Bainimarama, copy to my office. He stated that the ethics and moral values of the RFMF had become "hardly recognisable".

"We have clearly lost the high moral ground. There is no way that the nation can go forward towards national reconciliation and the enduring peace and security that all citizens aspire to until the RFMF regains that high moral ground."

Lt. Col. Tarakinikini recalled that Bainimarama had said a full public commission of inquiry into the RFMF and its failures prior to and during the May 2000 coup was irrelevant.

---

It appears to me therefore that your agenda against me is a personal one and that the investigation presently conducted in RFMF by you is a discriminatory and selective means to frame and purge those professional officers, including myself, who question your command ethics. The Regimental Fund that you are refusing to allow the Auditor General to look into is only an example.

God only knows the efforts of some senior officers and I to regain the confidence of the nation in RFMF and to press on for the safe release of the hostages during the darkest hours of the crisis. Even when you agree to a power-sharing deal with George Speight and his group, another senior officer and myself during the officers meeting the next morning refused to surrender the nation and told you to call off your agreement. Having faced much more difficult operational situations overseas we were confident we would find a way out, and we did at Muanikau.

Our sole purpose was to free the national leaders who were held hostage so that they could once again fulfill their role to the people. Once released it was up to them as the people's elected representatives to explore the way forward for the nation. Our job as their servants is to be accountable to them, as our political masters and the law. That is what democracy is all about.

Unfortunately, during the crisis and even now there exists in the RFMF a dearth of strategic understanding and lack of moral courage to accept the reality of what happened and draw the right lessons for the future. Instead some continue to exploit the public feeling of insecurity brought on by the May 2000 crisis and its aftermath to justify immature vanities and cover up abuse and excesses to the continuing detriment of the Force and the country's recovery and progress.

---

Lt. Col. Tarakinikini quoted the adage: "There are no bad Regiments only bad officers". This, he said, was a universal truth. "I trust RFMF officers now and in generations to come will not forget, deny or shirk their responsibilities to this truth."

---

Ratu Jone Madraiwiwi, Fiji's vice president, stepped forward as a prospective peacemaker as relationships between our government and Bainimarama continue to worsen, and the army intensified its campaign against the government. Ratu Joni was a skilled mediator, an articulate intellectual, a lawyer and a high-ranking chief with the title of Roko Tui Bau.

Bainimarama and I were invited to meet with him at his office at Government House, on or about 16th February 2006. I was aware that the police were investigating some of his actions and comments. He was, meanwhile, discrediting the SDL government publicly, and urging citizens not to vote for us at the May election. Again he had authorized the illegal use of public funds and military personnel.

Ratu Joni's purpose was to help narrow the differences between the two sides and create the conditions for an agreement. But before the meeting began, Bainimarama set the scene for what was to follow.

He placed a voice-recorder on the table before us and said he would be recording the conversation.

To me it sounded like a demand. Bainimarama then regurgitated his list of wild allegations which was growing longer and longer. His voice was not normal. He spoke in a very high-pitched tone. He called me a liar and uttered other abusive comments and appeared to be trying to prevent me speaking. I maintained my composure and asked him to offer some proof for his allegations. But he just ignored this. He was following a permanent collision course with the government. It was more than evident that he did not want to end the crisis.

Ratu Joni's initiative for mediation was frustrated by Bainimarama's behaviour. I felt sorry for the vice president. Bainimarama failed to accord him the respect he deserved as a high chief and as the holder of the second highest public office in the land. Ratu Joni thanked me afterwards for exercising restraint and patience in the face of the tirade from Bainimarama.

I heard on good authority that Bainimarama later in the afternoon called his officers together and played the record of the meeting to them. My source told me there was loud applause when Bainimarama called me a liar and other names. I imagine the beer and spirits must have flowed freely at the officers' mess that evening – at public expense of course.

# 24

# ANOTHER VICTORY FOR SDL

The support for the SDL party going into the 2006 general election was encouraging. I was confident the party would capture enough seats to govern.

The SDL succeeded with a majority of one. The Fiji Labour Party came in as runner-up. To me the outcome demonstrated that the allegations against us were not accepted by the public.

Bainimarama was beside himself, a man obsessed. After the close of the poll, he was personally telephoning two independents, Robin Irwin, and Joji Konrote, (who was later Bainimarama's pick for President) to persuade them not to give us their support. He failed. Both of them joined us.

We convened a meeting of SDL parliamentarians where it was agreed I lead the party again as prime minister in the next government. I thanked my colleagues for their confidence.

Just like their leader Bainimarama and his colleagues, elements of the military were not happy with the election outcome and I received reports that they were attempting to delay the swearing-in of my government. It failed simply because the SDL party had the numbers and the president was, therefore, required under the constitution to proceed with the swearing in.

I told our successful candidates I would proceed to government House to advise the president that the SDL was in a position to form a government. I also announced that I intended to establish the first multi-party cabinet in accordance with the provisions of the 1997 constitution.

To me the multi party cabinet concept as enshrined in the constitution was problematic; it had never appealed to me. I could see the possibility of significant problems emerging with an enforced political union. My preference had always been for a voluntary coming together of like-minded parties and individuals.

However, the constitution was the supreme law and I had to try to make it work.

After the 2001 poll, I had attempted to reach a constitutional cabinet accord with the Fiji Labour Party, which was then the second biggest party in parliament. This did not succeed because of disagreements over what I perceived to be certain conditions set down by the FLP. This led to court action that went against the SDL. My subsequent offer of ministerial portfolios was rejected by the FLP. I did not agree with the claim that the positions I offered were of no consequence.

We were now faced with the need after the 2006 elections to once more conform with the constitution's multi party provisions. Our discussions were ultimately favourable although there was initially some difficulty about the consultation aspect.

After I was duly appointed prime minister by the president, the legal procedures were followed for the commissioning of our SDL ministers and colleagues from the FLP. Mr Chaudhry, leader of the FLP, declined to accept a ministerial position. But this did not stand in the way of the birth of the first multi party cabinet as determined by the constitution[v].

There was very good support from many sections of the community for this new form of national multi racial accommodation. I held the view that the effort to form a multi party cabinet was not only meant to fulfill the constitution. It had become clear that the public approved of the elected leaders from our different ethnic communities joining hands in Cabinet. The people of Fiji expected the two major political parties to agree to work together.

Even Bainimarama joined in the acclamation! The army's spokesperson, Captain Neumi Leweni, described the cabinet as the way forward for Fiji. It created a good symbol of peace for everyone. The military was all for it. The enthusiastic endorsement from the military was deceitful in the extreme in view of the treasonous plans that had already formed in Bainimarama's mind. It wasn't long before he would brutally knock Fiji off the course it had embarked on for a secure, united and prosperous future. The symbol of peace for everyone was smashed.

As the ministers settled in to their portfolios the cabinet functioned well. I was very pleased with the contributions of FLP members. There was a spirit of co-operation and a willingness to tackle thorny issues through give and take in the interests of all. One of our first initiatives was to establish a cabinet sub committee to identify areas of difference between the SDL and FLP manifestos and then to resolve these through compromise. Frankly we were surprised to discover how much common ground we had. The differences, mainly related to the longstanding land lease issue, affirmative action and policies on some other issues.

When Bainimarama unleashed the army, the sub committee was already getting to grips with the main sticking points on leases and establishing a framework for agreement. Ten years on his government has been unable to find an answer.

# 25

# FURY AND THREATS INCREASE

Bainimarama's relentless anti-government vendetta, his public statements and apparent intentions to commit treason naturally attracted the attention of the police. Investigations started under the supervision of Police Commissioner Andrew Hughes. The allegations facing Bainimarama included two intended takeovers of government and one of sedition. The investigations also covered suspicions of Bainimarama's involvement in the deaths of Counter Revolutionary Warfare (CRW) soldiers in 2000 at the time of the mutiny against him at the Queen Elizabeth barracks.

The interview process dragged on and on, due mainly to Bainimarama's unavailability for pre-arranged meetings with the investigating officers. He was also usually accompanied by a large group of bodyguards. In addition, attempts to acquire documents and other evidential materials were blocked and frustrated.

Bainimarama was demanding the police drop their enquiries into the accusations against him and other senior military officers. This meant he was attempting to evade the law. I understand the laying of charges was imminent just before his coup. Bainimarama had no legal way out of the problems he had created for himself. The only way he could avoid prosecution was to take illegal action by seizing our government.

Josefa Vosanibola, who served as minister for Home Affairs from December, 2004, was uniquely qualified to comment on Bainimarama's behaviour and activities during this period. His portfolio gave him constitutional, legal and political responsibility for the RFMF.

I n selecting him, I had given Mr Vosanibola the job of improving the strained relations between the RFMF and my government. Mr Vosanibola had a steady hand; had been a senior public servant, including permanent secretary at Government House and had many contacts in ministries and departments.

He described some of his experiences and frustrations in dealing with Bainimarama in a sworn affidavit prepared later for the court action we were to take after the coup against the RFMF, Bainimarama, the State and the Attorney General.

I include here summaries of parts of the content of the Vosanibola document. It is a compelling and disturbing read underscoring some of Bainimarama's bizarre behaviour. Mr Vosanibola had regularly briefed me and cabinet but his affidavit had much value because it was a detailed cohesive story of Bainimarama's persistence and aggressive insubordination. Mr Vosanibola deposed that the contents of the affidavit were based on his personal knowledge, information received by him as a minister, as a member of various cabinet subcommittees and a member of parliament. He had also received information from official advisers.

Mr Vosanibola recalled that following the attempt on his life in the attempted mutiny by rebel soldiers in his own Counter Revolutionary Warfare (CRW) Unit on November 22nd 2000 Bainimarama declared his commitment to bring all those implicated in the George Speight Coup and the mutiny to justice. Bainimarama's frequent outbursts about this commitment became "so intense that many began to interpret his public statements as amounting to an obsession for revenge instead of just pursuing justice."

Mr Vosanibola related how Bainimarama showed his strong opposition against the return to power of Mahendra Chaudhry's Fiji Labour Party government. Bainimarama regarded this possibility as a "serious threat to national security."

The affidavit identified as a central issue, Bainimarama's perception that my government was supportive of those implicated in the Speight Coup and was interfering with and delaying investigations. He was wrong about that. There were assurances by the Commissioner of Police that this was wholly incorrect, baseless and unjustified; and was misconceived as explained by a government statement issued at the end of 2003.

We did not interfere in the judiciary when Mr Speight was sentenced to death for treason; that sentence was later commuted to life imprisonment by the Prerogative of Mercy Commission. A large number of those involved with Speight were dealt with by the courts during our time in office.)

Bainimarama, according to Mr Vosanibola, constantly ignored police explanations that the investigations were progressing well without any interference whatsoever from government. Mr Vosanibola laid out a list of Bainimarama grievances against our government which, he said varied over time, depending on which issues attracted his attention. He spoke of the threat Bainimarama made to the Cabinet Sub Committee on National Security (NCS) at an April 2003 meeting that he "intended to come down and complete what he started in 2000" if our government interfered with the Speight coup investigations.

He refused to respect or heed the president's decision to reduce the severity of penalties imposed on soldiers convicted of mutiny and related offences at the Labasa military camp shortly after the Speight coup. The president considered, on advice from the then minister for home affairs, that these sentences appeared grossly incompatible with sentences earlier meted out by a Military Court Martial for soldiers convicted of identical offences during the QEB mutiny.

There were further eruptions from Bainimarama against the government's delay in ratifying the Immunity Decree he initially promulgated in 2000 under his assumed executive authority. He purported to grant immunity to loyal soldiers for their actions that may otherwise have amounted to criminal or civil wrongs during and following the Speight coup.

He was angry about the government's proposal to introduce legislation for the promotion of reconciliation, tolerance and unity among victims and victimisers in the Speight coup. He believed this was an attempt to free or frustrate the conviction of those implicated or of those already imprisoned.

There was more anger against our proposal to introduce qoliqoli (customary fishing areas) legislation (described at length elsewhere in this book), and the proposed inquiry into long-standing claims by native landowners in connection with their original ownership of native land that they had lost through alleged fraudulent or dubious means.

There were issues about the marginalizing or forcing out of the RFMF some senior military officers who did not support, and had advised against, Bainimarama's constant threats and plan to take over a lawfully elected government; this was unconstitutional and illegal.

According to Mr Vosanibola's affidavit, Bainimarama had a belief bordering on an obsession that the Qarase government must be removed unless it submitted to his various demands. He also had spoken out publicly against the investigation of himself or soldiers in the RFMF accused of criminal conduct outside the boundaries of lawful military orders.

The former minister outlined how Bainimarama became more aggressive about certain political policies of the government despite wide local and international condemnation of his deliberate involvement of the RFMF in politics and government policies. He was quoted frequently as reminding government and the nation that he brought stability after the Speight coup and also brought the Qarase government into existence. He frequently threatened that he would "take out" this government if it ignored his wishes and views.

Mr Vosanibola stated that Bainimarama constantly ignored government's invitations to discuss the issues he was raising with his minister or the ministry, instead of in the media.

He openly refused to comply with directions to him by Mr Vosanibola, myself and even the vice president. He publicly declared that he didn't recognize the minister's power of control over him or the RFMF. He began to accuse our government of being generally corrupt and incompetent and he intended to take it over.

M r Vosanibola detailed government's responses to Bainimarama's outbursts:

- • That neither the RFMF nor its leadership had any role in forming policies of any government and that Bainimarama's public criticism of these was very misconceived and highly improper;
- • His continuing insubordinate conduct and open defiance against his minister, the prime minister and the vice president were constitutionally inexcusable and contrary not only to law but to official protocol and plain cultural decency.
- • His public threats to take over government were completely unjustified, irrational and harmful to Fiji's political and socio- economic stability, development and growth and attracted severe condemnation from sectors of the public as well as the international community;

Bainimarama was free to follow proper channels to air his grievances through lawful channels employed by all other organs of government.

- • Bainimarama's claims that he put the government in power, and by implication, he could and would also take it out of power if it did not perform in accordance with his expectations. This represented a very serious misconception since the government was voted into power by the people through general elections held in accordance with the constitution and the Electoral Act.

- • His threats to take over government, if it did not withdraw certain legislative proposals, which involved wide consultations among members of the public, including representations from the RFMF, were totally contrary and inconsistent with the constitution and the rule of law and democracy.

- • His frequent allegations about corruption were already a main concern of the Qarase government, which constantly issued warnings to both public officials and the private sector that allegations of this kind ought to be reported to the police at once for investigation and prosecution according to law.

- • His public outbursts and threats were increasingly the most recognized threat to national security.

M r Vosanibola told of his plans for encouraging dialogue between the RFMF leadership and the government leadership. Bainimarama seemed to be in a calmer mood when he went to Mr Vosanibola's office in January 2005 in response to an invitation from the new minister. There was discussion about improving working relationships, meeting regularly to discuss issues instead of through the media. It was agreed that the minister of finance and Mr

Vosanibola would visit the Queen Elizabeth Barracks, with other ministers, to gain an understanding of working conditions of the soldiers, with a view to improving these.

Mr Vosanibola related visits to the RFMF Strategic Command Centre at Berkley Crescent and the QEB, on two separate occasions; he was accompanied by other ministers. Bainimarama did not, however, visit him or request meetings about any of his complaints. But he was part of a joint military and police team making submissions against the proposed promotion of Reconciliation, Tolerance and Unity Bill.

Any hope of a permanent improvement was quickly dashed. Mr Vosanibola's affidavit said:

---

I quickly realized that both the Qarase government and I ... were faced with a virtually insurmountable task because it increasingly appeared ... that Bainimarama was virtually committed to his mission to take over government when he could find the right excuse and the right time to do it.

---

The minister said that initially he issued polite and later stern reminders to Bainimarama to refrain from public outbursts. But Bainimarama "continued with his hostile and often arrogant public outbursts and confrontational posturing against the Qarase government". Mr Vosanibola then detailed an entirely new list of issues and grievances which Bainimarama introduced. These included the:

- • Relocation of the RFMF commander to government buildings close to the minister, to allow the commander and not the CEO for the ministry of home affairs or anyone else to advise the minister and government on security and military operational matters.

- • The unilateral withdrawal by Bainimarama of security details normally provided by the RFMF to the prime minister.
- • Bainimarama's concern of plans to remove or suspend him as commander.

Mr Vosanibola referred to Bainimarama's 'fury' over being reported to the police and over police investigation against him. He also mentioned threats by Bainimarama to kill the CEO home affairs.

He said there were rumours of growing tension within the RFMF over the suspension or termination of senior officers who did not agree with Bainimarama. Mentioned as well in the affidavit were threats by soldiers to certain prominent government office holders allegedly with the knowledge of, or at the direction of, Bainimarama. There was also a tendency by Bainimarama to bypass the minister and refer policy issues directly to the president. There were concerns about his unlawful removal of Ratu Sir Kamisese Mara as president. It was at this time that the minister's approach changed. He felt government's responsibility should be more about finding an effective way of avoiding Bainimarama's determined effort to take over the government.

He has concluded that further dialogue with Bainimarama "would be pointless as he was only interested in this government submitting to his demands".

Mr Vosanibola deposed: "Increasingly during late 2005 and 2006, Bainimarama and his loyal followers within the RFMF were no longer camouflaging their threats to take over government. They started issuing non-negotiable demands to the prime minister ... These demands were deliberately designed with the knowledge that government would not be able to comply with them lawfully; and this was to give Bainimarama the excuse to take over government on the ground that these demands were not met."

Mr Vosanibola's view was that the only way in which Bainimarama's obsession to overthrow the government was to discipline him. I agreed with that. He related how his earlier advice to establish a Commission of Inquiry into the impasse arising out of these difficulties with the RFMF and its leadership was stopped by the president after what was believed to be the result of pressure from Bainimarama.

Mr Vosanibola then went on to advocate something that might appear to be unusual, but in the circumstances, was understandable. It indicated graphically the minister's considered view about Bainimarama's state of mind. His affidavit said: "My subsequent advice to send Bainimarama on leave with full pay to enable him to undergo trauma counseling was not acted on by Government House."

I'm sure it was the first time such a recommendation had been made by the relevant minister about a Commander of the RFMF. He was to return to it, in the affidavit, two paragraphs later.

The minister declared that, as a result of "escalating indications" towards the end of 2006, Bainimarama had virtually committed himself and the RFMF to take over government almost at any cost. He had no option but to recommend that Bainimarama be disciplined. He recommended and advised the president under Section 112 (2) of the 1997 constitution to suspend Bainimarama while investigation into his seditious statements and threats were fully, fairly and properly investigated. The president approved this course of action but reportedly countermanded it under pressure from Bainimarama.

Minister Vosanibola placed on record that the moody, arrogant and disrespectful attitude exhibited by Bainimarama could have been controlled and the takeover of government avoided through a firm decision by the president to discipline him effectively. This would include various sanctions ranging from sending him on leave with full pay for trauma counseling, suspension, termination of contract or dismissal.

Mr Vosanibola expressed "with the greatest respect" the firm belief of his ministry and himself that the firm decision anticipated from Government House did not come as the president and the vice president constantly preferred a "softer approach".

That regretfully also reflected my own assessment. Having said that, I think in retrospect, my government's reaction to Bainimarama was probably too cautious and careful.

In his final affidavit statements, the minister said he was firmly of the view that without Bainimarama's leadership there would be no coup in Fiji and it was not necessary to overthrow a lawfully elected government to remedy his grievances. He concluded that,

Bainimarama already had a fixation from as early as 2002, which simply gathered intensity in later years, to take over the Qarase government when he considered the time was right and there was, in his mind, a good excuse to do so. He deposed that in the weeks leading up to the coup, there was relative peace and calm in the country; the only threat to national security ... was the fixation in the minds of Bainimarama himself and some of his followers ... that they must take over government.

He had been advised by the police that Bainimarama was due to be arrested for offences related to his constant threats to take over government.

W hat of the threat to kill the late Mr Jeremaia Waqanisau, CEO for Home Affairs and a former RFMF Colonel? In a typed statement Mr Waqanisau described an epic confrontation with Bainimarama in the Office of the then minister of Home Affairs, Mr Joketani

Cokanasiga, on 12th January 2004. This was at a time when Mr Cokanasiga was increasingly aligning himself with Bainimarama. His bias towards the commander became so evident that I had to remove him from his portfolio.

In his statement Mr Waqanisau, who was then chief executive officer at the Ministry of Home Affairs, provided further evidence of Bainimarama's tendency to succumb to explosive rages. He recounted how he was briefing the minister about a release that had been published in the *Fiji Times*. It was then that Bainimarama, accompanied by armed bodyguards, entered the minister's office without knocking.

At the top of his voice he started accusing me of trying to raise an army to fight against RFMF. Bainimarama continued to accuse me, pointing close to my nose and saying that I was on the radio that morning, which I denied. I then remembered my interview with FM96 some two weeks ago answering their questions in relation to the recommendation of the Defence Review on counter terrorism. I asked Bainimarama to take a seat so we could discuss the truth of the matter. Bainimarama replied that he had no interest in discussing anything with me.

Bainimarama further said had it not been for the minister, I would have been dead already and next time the military comes back to finish what they started he would personally lead the military to town and would make sure that I would be the first to die. At that point I told Bainimarama that when he comes down next, he should come alone, without his weapon and without his armed bodyguards and then try to kill me. He became very furious and challenged me to a fight by taking off his web belt (with his weapon) and posing for a fight, saying that he was not scared of me and that he was ready to fight me. I told him I did not want to fight him and that he should go away. At this point the minister was trying to restrain him by holding him back and eventually pushed him out of the door.

---

This requires no comment from me. The statement says all that is necessary about the person we were dealing with.

---

Bainimarama's destabilisation activities attracted comment from international figures.

The 1996 Nobel Peace Prize Winner, Dr Jose Ramos-Horta, visited Fiji when he was foreign minister of East Timor, which had a traumatic transition to independence. He was a key figure in his country's struggle for independence from Indonesia. Dr Ramos-Horta had first hand knowledge of the devastation caused by the Indonesian army.

In an interview on *Fiji One* he gave some very forthright comments about the role an army should play. He said that Fiji was better off than most islands in the Pacific and many countries in the ACP group. It was important, he said, that political leaders in Fiji and the military elite did not take steps that could undermine Fiji's prestige. That prestige had been undermined in the past when force was used against a constitutionally elected government or to impose someone's views.

He was talking as a friend, as someone from a country that had suffered like few others. He would caution anyone against falling into the temptation of pulling out his gun whenever there was a slight or major disagreement on policies. He said he was surprised, "that certain forces in this country seem to talk a bit too much".

In Timor Leste, which had only been independent for three and a half years, the military did not offer opinions on politics. "They do not opinionate, they do not interfere, even if we have internal chaos." The East Timor army were not allowed to intervene, let alone offer a political opinion.

Dr Ramos-Horta said the country's soldiers had spent 24 years in the jungle, but they were quite disciplined and sensitive about the role they had to play in the country, which was to protect it against external aggression.

He praised the late Ratu Joni Madraiwiwi, who was then acting president. He found the late Ratu Joni to be a most humble and charming person. He complemented the foreign affairs minister Kaliopate Tavola. Fiji, he said, was fortunate to have many highly intelligent people. He had words of commendation for Fiji's military for its tremendous professionalism in peacekeeping. He was sure

they were able to sit down and calm their own people. He had a special message for those considering violent intervention.

---

In East Timor some people had been indicted for crimes against humanity and war crimes. It was necessary for those who took part in the violence to have the courage and humility to confess ... accept ... responsibilities and apologise to the victims. Those who were victimized should walk halfway and forgive ... But first and foremost, those involved in the violence, one way or another ... tell the whole story. Why they did it?

Dr Ramos-Horta spoke of looking at root causes ... the failings, not only of individuals, but of institutions ... The weakness of the institutions could be changed to prevent conflict from occurring again. He urged dialogue and more

dialogue ... listening to everyone's views ... this, would in the
end, result in a solution to any dispute.

---

This distinguished and courageous visitor, who spoke from bitter
experience, could not have been more direct but his message was
ignored by Bainimarama and his officers who were intent on seizing
an elected government by force of arms.

# 26

# "COUP WOULD NOT SOLVE ANYTHING"

Rumours continued to spread during 2006 of a military take-over. There were denials by the military. In fact, acting military commander Esala Teleni in October had assured me in a private meeting that there was no intention to seize government. He was quite clear about this.

The assurance was false, as were other military denials that a takeover was planned.

The late Michael Green, the New Zealand ambassador at the time, gives in his book 'Persona Non-Grata' an account of a conversation with Bainimarama during a one-on-one lunch at the ambassador's residence in Suva on 22nd July 2006. Some of the conversation revolved around the controversial Reconciliation, Truth and Unity (RTU) Bill. Mr Green asked if the RFMF was the only effective force against the Bill, did this explain the talks of coups or other actions against the government? "Bainimarama was evasive," wrote Mr Green.

According to Mr Green, Bainimarama said a coup would not solve anything other than the immediate problem posed by the Bill. It might make many of Fiji's problems worse. He stated the army did not want to run the country. It would give that job to the president. Mr Green, in response, said this assumed that the president at the time was sympathetic to the RFMF view. "I went on to say that the talk of coups had been noted in other countries, including New Zealand, and have not been well received. There were potentially damaging consequences for our bilateral relations and especially for defence co-operation, only recently re-established and about to be showcased in a major exercise. I could not see how the RFMF's cause would benefit from cancellation of the exercise and other planned co-operative activities. Moreover, things he was reported to have said did not accord with New Zealand's view of civil-military relations.

Even taking Fiji's different circumstances into account, we could not accept the concept of civil-military relations implied in his warnings to the government. The commander said he understood and added that other relationships important to the RFMF, not only the New Zealand link, would be jeopardized."

So here was Bainimarama making it plain that he believed a coup would not solve anything other than the immediate problem posed by the RTU Bill. (He was choosing to ignore that we were receptive to making changes to the draft legislation. Another example of bad faith on his part.)

His reported comment that a coup might make Fiji's problems worse was double talk. As far back as December 2003 he had disclosed to his officers his intention to remove the government. He had been warned that the consequences of that would be catastrophic for Fiji, but he had persisted with his coup plans and had got rid of senior officers who would not back his treasonous intent.

Bainimarama had also kept up his mission of disruption, destabilization and agitation. He had an extensive list of allegations against the SDL government. There were five initially but then it just kept growing. It went up to nine and then to eleven on the day of the coup. After the coup the allegations increased further to about twenty-five. The ever-expanding grievances were given as the reasons for the military take-over. It is still not clear to many Fiji citizens what the central purpose of the coup was. I had the impression Bainimarama and the officers closest to him were manufacturing the grounds for it as they went along.

The expanding master list included corruption, racism, nepotism, bad governance, slow investigations into the 2000 coup and much more. As mentioned, no evidence was provided in support. Taking into account the events leading up to the coup, it became clear that the military leadership was bent on removing the SDL government come what may.

---

I n October 2006, we were considering suspending Bainimarama when he returned from a visit to the Middle East. Our thinking was that Lt Col Meli Saubulinayau, would be appointed commander on an acting basis. All this was verbal. There was a leak, however, and Saubulinayau declined.

Bainimarama was not happy with an initiative I took to involve the Great Council of Chiefs (GCC) in the general effort to resolve the stalemate between the government and the military through proper dialogue. In November 2006, I attended a GCC meeting in Suva to provide the members with any clarifications they needed on the government's position. The GCC deliberated at length. They then appointed a mediation committee responsible for approaching Bainimarama and the military to facilitate dialogue with me, and my government. Bainimarama's response was that this was a waste of time and money.

Later he was reported to have said that he would not participate in any mediation, unless the army's list of written demands were met. It was at this point that he made his notorious comment that chiefs "should go and sit under a mango tree and drink home brew".

# 27

# NEW ZEALAND'S LAST MINUTE TRY AT PEACE-MAKING

A s the crisis deepened our neighbour, New Zealand stepped forward with a dramatic eleventh-hour initiative to mediate. They wished to do all they could to turn Fiji away from the path that Bainimarama was following. They knew that coups were always destructive; they disrupted international relations, created huge legal problems, led to abuse of human rights and created economic distress. The New Zealanders, therefore, proposed a meeting between Bainimarama and me in Wellington. It was to be another landmark in the fateful saga of Bainimarama's planned coup. But the military commander refused to enter into the spirit of reconciliation, thereby making a mockery of the New Zealand intervention. At the same time, he also managed to insult the New Zealand head of state.

On 29ᵗʰ November 2006, a New Zealand Air Force aircraft used for VIP travel flew into Nadi to take me to New Zealand. Bainimarama was already there on a family visit. Travelling with me were Joji Kotobalavu, my permanent secretary; Sakiasi Ditoka, private secretary; and two security officers. Also, on the plane was our commissioner of police, Mr Hughes, who was bound for New Zealand on police business connected with investigations into Bainimarama's behaviour in Fiji. Two of his senior officers had travelled ahead of Mr Hughes. They were continuing with the investigations against Bainimarama. My understanding is that the police had been waiting for an opportunity to question Bainimarama on a sedition charge but were unable to do so because of the commander's heavily armed personal security detail.

Mr Hughes asked to take some leave at the end of his New Zealand trip. This was granted, and he later left for his home in Australia. I discovered that Mr Hughes had been threatened by the army and so had his family. They had been evacuated to Australia before the Wellington meeting. Mr Hughes eventually stated in a media interview that the military had plotted to kidnap his family and hold them to ransom.

He felt that he was becoming part of the problem, not part of the solution. He was also concerned that the police would stand up to the military and get seriously hurt.

There was another sidelight to the situation. Commissioner Hughes had reportedly made a private call to his New Zealand counterpart urging him to arrest Bainimarama while he was visiting New Zealand. But the New Zealand government finally decided not to take this action for a variety of reasons. I was not aware of or informed about the call Mr Hughes made to his New Zealand counterpart.

It was later disclosed that the US ambassador to Fiji, Larry Dinger, had reported to Washington in a cable released by Wikileaks that "being passive with bullies only encourages them. An arrest abroad might be the only way to enforce a criminal charge and remove the Bainimarama thorn".

In Wellington I had a brief meeting with Helen Clark the then prime minister who expressed neighbourly concern and reiterated the desire of her government to be helpful in any attempt to resolve the conflict. She had arranged for Winston Peters, her foreign affairs minister, to chair the discussion between Commodore Bainimarama and me.

I was well prepared for the meeting, which took place at Government House.

Beforehand, Bainimarama and me were to have an audience with His Excellency, the Governor-General of New Zealand, Mr Anand Satyanand, a former citizen of Fiji. I arrived at Government House a few minutes early.

Right at the appointed time, Mr Satyanand entered the room and greeted me warmly. I responded courteously and then we had a bit of a *"talanoa"*, expecting Bainimarama to arrive soon. But he kept us waiting for 45 minutes. I felt embarrassed about this and apologised to His Excellency. Mr Satyanand was gracious and kind. He understood my predicament and tried to make me feel at ease.

When Bainimarama finally came, Mr Satyanand greeted him warmly and wished us well in our deliberation. I don't believe Bainimarama apologized for coming late.

I mention this incident to illustrate how Bainimarama seemed to attach little importance to common courtesies. When a country's governor general makes a special effort to meet with you as part of a peacemaking initiative you at least have a basic responsibility to be punctual.

At the meeting venue, Mr Peters was accompanied by a senior official from his ministry who was to take notes. Bainimarama and I sat on opposite sides of the table. The atmosphere was tense. Mr Peters skillfully opened up space to allow for discussion.

We went through the allegations made by Bainimarama against the SDL government. There were nine at the time. On each allegation I explained government's position, including the relevant provisions of the law. For example, Bainimarama wanted the termination of the appointment of the commissioner of police Andrew Hughes. I explained that the appointment of the Commissioner of Police was the responsibility of the Constitutional Offices Commission. If the issue was referred to the Commission and the relevant provisions of the law followed, then I had no reason to object to that. But as prime minister, I had no legal authority to terminate the appointment of the Commissioner and would not do so.

Bainimarama's responses to my explanations were brief and curt. It was clear to me he was still in "command" mode. There was no reasonable discussion. It appeared it was either his way or no way. The gap between Bainimarama and me was obviously wide.

To his credit, Mr Peters attempted to find some common ground. I thought that towards the end of the meeting there was a clear understanding that each allegation would be dealt with quickly but within the provisions of the law. That was reflected in the minutes of the discussion which Bainimarama did not question.

As part of the New Zealand diplomatic effort, Mr Peters was good enough to propose assistance to Fiji in some particular areas of development. I mentioned the need to accelerate our efforts in providing low cost housing. His response was positive and there was a real opportunity for some action by the New Zealand government. I made a note to follow this up as early as possible. But, of course, the military takeover took place and that was the end of that. Many low-income workers lost an opportunity to occupy affordable housing because Bainimarama was set on conducting his coup.

On 30th November 2006, I issued a statement in Fiji on the outcome of the Wellington discussions. I realized not long afterwards I was too optimistic in my approach and too accommodating; I made a number of concessions to Bainimarama as a show of good faith. This meant nothing to him. One concession was to temporarily hold action on the Reconciliation, Tolerance and Unity Bill and the Qoliqoli Bill and the proposed Land Claims Tribunal. New Zealand offered to assist with an independent review of the Reconciliation and Qoliqoli Bills. If the Bills were found to be legal and constitutionally unsound, they would be automatically suspended. If the review found to the contrary, the government would enter into renewed consultation with the RFMF and other interested parties. My statement noted that international precedence around issues such as indigenous land ownership and reform typically required lengthy consultation and inclusive processes to ensure broad-based consensus. Such an approach would be equally appropriate for Fiji.

On the investigations against Bainimarama and the RFMF, I explained that we would not interfere with authorities such as the solicitor-general, the DPP and the police. However, if we received advice from these authorities that the disputed investigations should be suspended, we would be prepared to follow that. This, again, was a substantial concession in response to Bainimarama's aggressive insistence that investigations against him should be dropped.

In a follow up letter to Bainimarama, I stressed the importance of establishing a peaceful path for resolving differences. I mentioned that the leaders of the Pacific Islands Forum, of which Fiji was a founding member, had adopted the Biketawa Declaration. This bound all forum governments to the principles of the rule of law, democratic government, peaceful resolution of differences and disputes, and a rejection of the use of force and extra constitutional means to resolve a political situation. It was important for him to understand these forum governing principles. In the event he fundamentally ignored them, and his military government was eventually suspended from the forum.

I told him that the tension and instability the current situation was creating was not only undermining the people's confidence in their future; it was also seriously damaging the economy. The downturn in the critically important tourism industry was a direct consequence of the current position. I urged him and the military to commit themselves to the dialogue we had started. I asked him to make a public statement that the military had no plans to resort to the use of force or to act outside the law. He never did.

I committed to advance the dialogue process and confirmed that Mrs Clark and Mr Peters had indicated their willingness to continue to assist Fiji in the role of mediator. I commend the New Zealand government for their efforts in the spirit of regional neighbourliness to avert Fiji 's impending calamity.

The arguments I put to Bainimarama in my letter were to no avail. He was fixated on his treasonous coup plan even though he knew what the consequences would be.

---

As part of its warm up for seizing the government, the RFMF unleashed a dose of psychological warfare on the evening of my return from Wellington. It appeared to be aimed directly at the citizens of Suva. The army conducted what looked like a night warfare exercise with flares soaring high over the harbor, lighting up the landscape. Soldiers were reportedly seen in Suva. Residents observed, with alarm, this show of force from their own military. The RFMF tried to pass it off as a preparation against foreign intervention, as Australian naval ships were stationed off the coast in readiness to evacuate their nationals if this became necessary.

But I am sure most of the populace saw this display of military aggression as a warning to them. Watch out, be careful, we're armed and ready.

On 1st December 2006 the military leadership openly rejected the public statement I had made, and Fiji was headed straight for long years of oppressive army rule. As a government we had learned the hard way of the difficulties of reining in a rogue military commander, rebellious officers and soldiers. They had the guns; we didn't.

I have often been asked why our government did not organize mass street protests to confront the military. In my estimation that would have probably led to the shooting of innocent civilians and we wanted to avoid a bloodbath at all costs. Bainimarama's state of mind was unpredictable; I was pretty certain he would use force to get his way if he thought this was necessary. My thinking was reinforced when Bainimarama gave a specific and ominous warning in an Australian Broadcastiong Corporation (ABC) interview broadcast on 2nd November. He declared that I (meaning me, L Qarase) had put the military in a situation "where there's going to be bloodshed and violence". This was because I couldn't get my way. I was refusing to agree to his "requests", I would not resign and had called for a meeting of the Council Chiefs.

This was sufficient reason to kill or wound people. He was like an angry child – but with the capacity to inflict lethal injury. Even peaceful protests might have been enough to trigger him off. I do not believe in violence. There was no way I would take action that would likely have left the streets littered with the dead.

Our government remained united, even though we could sense that power would soon be taken from us by treason. On December 4th a group of SDL backbenchers managed to meet in the government members' office to draft what they called a Deed of Commitment. It is a unique document, a piece of history and a testament to the courage and loyalty of the signatories. They knew they were in danger and were prepared to stand against it. They anticipated cruel persecution and "persuasion" to force them to sign false

declarations recanting their loyalty to my government. But they made it clear that the deed represented the truth; any other signed statement by any of them should be discarded.

Their forebodings came to pass. Some parliamentarians were literally hunted down. Those picked up, and some who voluntarily went to military premises, were subjected to severe intimidation and humiliating treatment by senior officers who were either armed or accompanied by armed soldiers. Many felt compelled to leave Suva and go into hiding.

The Deed of Commitment acknowledged Fiji was in crisis due to the continuing stand off between the elected government and the military. The end to the impasse was uncertain.

The deed said that in the circumstances it was necessary for the signatories as members of parliament to declare their support to the prime minister, the elected SDL government and the rule of law. They declared their "abiding support for and promise always, during this crisis, to uphold democracy and the rule of law". They gave their support also to the cabinet and the constitution. There were further professions of "individual and personal support" for me as prime minister.

The deed went on to say that through rumour or otherwise it might appear they had deviated from the support they had expressed. But this could only happen by fraud or duress.

It stated that they would rely "on this provision (the deed) only as evidence of our commitment of support to the prime minister, the cabinet, parliament and the constitution".

It added: "In the event that we are forced to sign by duress any other document, or our signatures (are) forged, this commitment shall override such illegal act."[vi]

I pay my tribute to them all, and to my other colleagues, who did not flinch under the threat of force.

I was proud of them and grateful at the time for their support and I am proud of them and grateful today. At least two of them – Joji Banuve and Mataiasi Ragigia - have passed on. I have not forgotten them.

---

While the Deed of Commitment was being drafted, discussed and then signed, Bainimarama and his soldiers were ramping up the pressure in readiness for taking over the government and the country. The RFMF unlawfully seized weapons from the police armoury at Nasova and erected checkpoints in some parts of Suva. They had me firmly in their sights. A barricade across the Sawani- Serea road was an attempt to stop me from returning from Viria village in Naitasiri where I had attended a provincial council meeting. I took the opportunity to update the council members on the unfolding drama in Suva and the erection of roadblocks to isolate me. There was a stunned silence as delegates absorbed the information about the army's moves against their prime minister. I avoided the Sawani-Serea blockade by travelling to the capital city by helicopter.

## 28

# SLOW STRANGULATIONS

By November 2006 Fiji was gripped by nervousness and uncertainty. The nation watched as Bainimarama's army became more and more aggressive and threatening.

On the morning of December 5th, the day the RFMF finally did its deed, I had not gone to the office but remained at 18 Richards Road, Suva, the prime minister's residence. The RFMF had begun to slowly strangle the government of the people. Checkpoints had been set up throughout the city. Before 8am the government offices complex was surrounded by fully-armed soldiers. Army personnel seized vehicles used by ministers. At some point in this confusing and tension filled day I was told by my security personnel that they had been informed by the army that I was under house arrest. Despite this however, I managed to issue a public statement explaining my government's position on the crisis. I had a duty to do whatever I could to tell the people about the armed insurrection and what it meant. The statement was to be my last to the nation as the legal occupier of the office of prime minister. I was beleaguered, under arrest, threatened by soldiers but I would not be stopped from doing my duty while I still could.

. . .

Τ his is what I said:

Fellow citizens, bula vinaka and greetings to you all. I am still here, your prime minister.

As you will have heard from the news media and seen on television, serious developments are taking place in Suva. The Fiji Military Forces have seized control of all government vehicles assigned to ministers. These include my own official vehicle. They have mounted road checkpoints throughout the city. They have taken the keys to the Office of the Prime minister in Government Buildings. It is clear that their intention is to bring to a standstill the functioning of my elected government.

This morning, I had intended to convene a special meeting of our country's Multi-party Cabinet. This was to specifically consider the new demands of the Military Commander, as conveyed to the president and Vice president.

These new demands included the extension of the Commander's contract of appointment to the year 2012, even though his current five year contract has another two years to run.

Another development this morning was the meeting by our president with the Military Commander. I understand the president will publicly announce the outcome of that meeting.

However, in earlier contacts with me, the president had wanted me either to totally accept the demands of the Military, or to resign as prime minister.

I want to inform you all, the people of Fiji, that as your elected prime minister, I have absolutely refused to bend these demands. Both courses of actions would be contrary to the supreme law of our country, and that of Fiji's constitution.

As your prime minister, I stand firmly in support and defence of our constitution, and of the rule of law and parliamentary democracy in Fiji.

Any Military takeover of the elected government would be unlaw-

*ful*, and those responsible would bear the consequences, as no one is above the law.

Worse still, the consequences of Fiji's economy would be catastrophic. Already, we are seeing innocent people being laid off their jobs. Investments are being put on hold.

A development that should be of concern to us all is the decision by the Emperor Gold Mining Company at Vatukoula to close its operations. This means that 1750 innocent workers would lose their jobs, and just imagine the suffering this would bring to their families.

I appeal to the military and to all those solders who are loyal and who remain faithful to their oath of office. It is not too late to draw back from the brink of disaster with which our country is now faced.

Already, the New Zealand government has announced several sanctions against Fiji. The stoppage of all military assistance to Fiji. A ban on travel to NZ by senior military staff and their families. New Zealand will also call on the Commonwealth to place Fiji on its Commonwealth Action Group agenda. This could mean the expulsion of Fiji from the Commonwealth of Nations. Other countries are expected to follow what New Zealand has done.

To you, the citizens of Fiji, let me assure you, categorically, that under no circumstances will I resign as prime minister, or give advice to His Excellency to dissolve parliament. There is no reason whatsoever, for me to do so.

I am the democratically-elected prime minister, appointed in accordance with the constitution, and the general elections in May gave my party a clear majority in parliament.

The functions of law and order, as exercised by the police, are intact. There is no outbreak of civil disorder. The public are coming out openly expressing their support for the maintenance of the rule of law and parliamentary democracy.

I am much heartened by the expressions of support the government is receiving from right across the community. I make particular mention of the overwhelming backing from the vanua which is standing against any threat to our democratically-elected government.

*The vanua does not want an unlawful seizure of power. The emphatic message I am receiving is in favour of the rule of law, parliamentary democracy, and the preservation of order by the Police.*

*As I have said, any forcible takeover of government and parliament would be a breach of our constitution.*

*Anyone who is a party to the illegal overthrow of the government would be guilty of an act of treason. This is the most serious offence against the State, punishable by life imprisonment.*

*I ask those considering such a course to think very, very carefully about what they would be doing.*

*I issue the same warning to anyone contemplating accepting an appointment in an illegal administration.*

*The constitution would remain in place, as would all the laws of our country. People who might try to usurp power would, therefore, be answerable to the constitution and to criminal laws.*

*The law has a long reach. There is no escape from it, especially when evidence is readily available.*

*The Military leadership has been citing the Doctrine of Necessity to justify intervention by His Excellency the President. They claim it is necessary for His Excellency to dismiss the government, dissolve parliament and appoint an interim Administration.*

*The Doctrine of Necessity is totally irrelevant to the present circumstances. It simply does not apply.*

*What we are witnessing instead is an orchestrated attempt to try to destabilize the country and justify a Military takeover of government and our country.*

*I ask members of the Military to consider the consequences not only for themselves, but also for their families and relatives.*

*Are you prepared to break the law, sacrifice your freedom, and condemn your families to suffer, only so that the Commander can get his contract extended to 2012?*

*Are you prepared to put our country at the risk of sanctions and boycotts, and withdrawal of vital aid? I ask every soldier to think very carefully about the legal consequences of taking part in an illegal takeover of government. In the ultimate, it will be their own families who will suffer from any unlawful action they take now.*

*Ladies and gentlemen, it is still not too late to save our country. There is still time for every section of our society to make their voices known. I appeal to you to come out and express your support for the rule of law and democracy in Fiji, and say no to an unlawful takeover of our country by the military.*

*In this late hour, it is never too late to speak out with one voice, to save our country from economic calamity and ruin.*

*May God bless you all".*

---

Soon after the news of the coup broke, my cabinet colleagues, senior ministers of the Methodist Church and hundreds of supporters had gathered by 18 Richards Road, and in the house and compound. A choir formed quickly by the roadside and soon the sound of hymns filled the air. A large shed beside the residence was filled with colleagues from the multi-party cabinet, senior Methodist ministers and many other sympathisers. The kava began to flow as we discussed the consequences of what was happening. I received updates from the security detail.

By late afternoon, the RFMF had extended its grip to other urban centres. A contingent of armed soldiers came home to disperse the crowd at Richards Road and took away the prime minister's official vehicle.

At about 6pm Bainimarama, in his military fatigues and looking rather cocky, made his way to a podium at the Queen Elizabeth barracks and explained to a gathering of local and international press that the army had taken over executive authority in the country. His rambling, badly written speech was full of misinformation and outright lies and untruths. Extracts follow with my comments.

He said the government and all those empowered to make decisions in Fiji's constitutional democracy "are unable to make these decisions to save our people from destruction". Bainimarama urged citizens to maintain the peace; the military and police were working together to ensure calm and that the people did not take advantage of the situation and break the law.

The country was at peace. The army was breaking the law.

He tried to paint a picture of the RFMF raising issues with my government "in all fairness and sincerity". But the army's concerns were "apparently ... never accepted in true spirit."

Whatever that meant. He made no mention of his aggressive and angry behaviour; the insults; his refusal to enter into genuine dialogue; his ever-changing demands.

He made the outlandish claim that I had already conducted a "silent coup" through "bribery, corruption and introduction of controversial bills." He never provided any proof for his corruption allegations – because there was nothing to back them - and obviously did not understand that governments everywhere sponsor legislation that is controversial. It is the norm.

He claimed that the RFMF throughout the impasse had wanted to solve it constitutionally, legally and expeditiously. The RFMF, he said, could have carried out unconstitutional and illegal activities but had not done so and will not do so.

All of this was untrue.

He went on to say that the RFMF believed in the rule of law and would adhere to the constitution. More importantly it believed in the adherence to the spirit of the law and constitution.

All untrue.

Bainimarama spoke of the president's constitutional prerogative to dismiss the prime minister in exceptional circumstances.

As commander of the RFMF, under the legal doctrine of necessity, he would step into the shoes of the president who had been blocked from exercising his constitutional powers.

The constitutional prerogative was finally rejected by the Fiji Court of Appeal. How had the president been blocked from exercising his powers?

Bainimarama said special steps were required to preserve the constitution and maintain the integrity of the state.

He and the army were working outside the constitution and damaging the integrity of the state.

He spoke of acting under the legal doctrine of necessity and said once more he was stepping into the shoes of the president who had been blocked by some, including the vice president, from exercising his constitutional prerogative to dismiss the prime minister in exceptional circumstances.

Bainimarama himself then purported to dismiss me.

He went through the motions of appointing Dr Jona Baravilala Senilagakali, an army doctor, as caretaker prime minister.

He had no power to do this.

Dr Senilagakali was to advise Bainimarama to dissolve parliament. Following this an announcement would be made on forming of an interim government to manage the affairs of the country.

None of this was permissible under the constitution. It was not long before Senilagakali went off script. He said publicly that he recognized the unlawfulness of what Bainimarama and the army had done. This at a time when Bainimarama was saying the army had acted within the constitution.

Bainimarama gave an undertaking that all the rights of the citizens of Fiji would be protected.

Their rights were comprehensively breached.

---

During the evening, Bainimarama himself sent a mobile 'phone message to my security personnel at my residence threatening to physically harm me.

My private secretary, Sakiasi Ditoka, informed me that His Excellency the President, Ratu Josefa Iloilovatu Uluivuda who had succeeded Ratu Mara as president, had summoned me to Government House at 7pm. Five minutes before this my security officers and

I were at the back gate. There were armed soldiers everywhere. Mr Ditoka told them that His Excellency was expecting me at 7pm. Apparently there was no instruction to the guards who told us they could not let us through. After some discussion, we returned to the PM's residence. About 30 minutes later we were advised that His Excellency was ready to meet me. I asked Mr Ditoka to advise Government House that I would not come because I believed my personal security could not be guaranteed due to the presence of heavily armed soldiers. Bizarrely the military cited my refusal to meet with the president as a breakdown in governance. It was given as one of their reasons for the coup.

Later I learned that Bainimarama himself was waiting for me at Government House with the president. I received information that Bainimarama intended to "force" me to resign as prime minister.

By 10pm many of those who gathered at the shed at home had left for the night. I told those remaining that I was tired and would like to take some rest. Before leaving Mr Ditoka briefed me about a number of further abusive calls he received from the RFMF head-quarters. The calls came from the top echelon of the military. They used unspeakable language and threatened to ship me to the prison at Nukulau Island the following morning. According to Mr Ditoka the callers sounded heavily intoxicated. In the background was the sound of music and celebration. It was party time at the barracks.

# 29

# MIRACLE OF THE CHECKPOINTS

L eba and I were unsettled and could not sleep. At about 3 o'clock there was a knock on our bedroom door. It was the officer-in-charge of my security detail. He asked us to pack a few clothes into a travel bag as we were to leave for Vanuabalavu in two minutes, via Nausori Airport. There was intelligence that the military was serious about taking me to the Nukulau Island prison where George Speight and his accomplices were held. I asked whether there was a better option than escaping to Lau and was told immediate evacuation to Mavana was the best course in light of the very threatening circumstances.

Our journey out of Suva to Vanuabalavu and then to the village is the stuff of fiction. But it went beyond that. It was marked by what Leba and I saw as some of the miracles mentioned in the title of this book.

As we stepped outside we saw a police car with flashing roof lights. We were ushered into the back seat. Obviously, some in the senior ranks of the police force had a plan in place to free us from house arrest and get us to the comparative safety of the village in Lau.

Leba wore a floral dress while I was in a sulu with a *bula* shirt.

Leba packed just one or two items for each of us. There was always sufficient clothing at our home in Mavana because of our frequent visits.

It was very dark. The lights around our house had been switched off. There were two people in the front of the vehicle, the driver, and Mr Ditoka. The driver was a police officer in civilian clothing. Afterwards I wondered why he was not in uniform?

Mr. Ditoka was in disguise. He wore a senior police officer's cap with a light blue police shirt. A four-wheel drive containing two of the regular security personnel waited behind. The small convoy left 18 Richards Road and disappeared into the night with our car's roof lights on.

Within minutes we were at the roundabout at the Knollys Street junction. This was the first immediate danger zone. There was a military checkpoint here with armed soldiers. The soldiers waved at us as we passed slowly by. It would not have been prudent to accelerate. We were through and clear. I was number one on the military leader's enemies' list, and yet, with Leba, had just slipped through a critical part of the RFMF control cordon.

How did that happen?

We travelled through Toorak and up past Tamavua village where there were more armed military. Again, the soldiers waved us on without incident, and we moved on.

How did that happen?

We picked up speed and travelled over the ridge through Colo-i-Suva, then down into Sawani and to the Waila flatlands leading to the bridge over the Rewa River.

As we came closer to Waila Housing Estate near Davuilevu, Mr Ditoka told me we would make a short stop at a home nearby. We arrived and were taken straight in. It was medium sized concrete and timber house. The lounge was small and tidy. We sat on the floor.

The man of the house was a SDL parliamentarian. He and his wife had prepared hot coffee and tea and warm, crispy pancakes. My parliamentary colleague conducted a short devotion before we tucked into the pancakes and enjoyed a coffee. Conversation was limited and mostly concerned with what had happened and the adverse impact this would have. We instinctly kept our voices low as we did not want to attract attention from outside.

It was daybreak on 6th December. Two or three people were walking along the road, probably to a bus stop or to the shops for bread. Very shortly we said goodbye to our hosts, got into our vehicles and headed for Nausori Airport.

The sun was already up. That increased the danger. As we neared the Rewa bridge, I saw many soldiers with weapons stationed on both sides. It was the largest checkpoint of them all. I thought we would not get through undetected. But for whatever reasons, Leba and I felt composed. As we drove through the barrier onto the bridge, soldiers waved at us. We waved back.

Surely, they must have recognised us? They did not.

Exactly the same thing happened at the other end of the bridge. We went straight through.

More waves; one or two smiles.

How had we got through? What was going on?

Maybe at all the checkpoints the soldiers noticed who we were but were sympathisers and let us pass. The odds were against that. Ditoka's disguise then must have been enough to get us through? But why had none of the soldiers asked for the vehicle windows to be wound down so they could have a closer look inside?

I believe we were protected by Divine intervention that morning. I cannot think of any other explanation for what happened. Glory be to God! He gave those soldiers a vision problem that lasted long enough for us to pass through unnoticed.

As we passed Nausori, Mr Ditoka told us we were not going to the airport terminal, but to the nearby hangar. When we arrived a security officer, who must have been part of the escape plan, opened the gate, and we drove straight into the hangar. A Twin Otter was ready to take us to Vanuabalavu. I was introduced to the two pilots and we got into our seats. With us were

Mr Ditoka, and the two security people from the second vehicle.

The pilots learned they were to go to Vanuabalavu only a few minutes before take-off. The Twin Otter taxied past the terminal building towards the Nausori end of the runway. Because the aircraft was not carrying a heavy load we turned around for take off well before we reached the normal starting point on the runway. We took off, into a beautiful morning with a clear sky. It was just before six o'clock. I looked down to the terminal area and noticed vehicles travelling to and fro. They had a military appearance.

The flight to Vanuabalavu was smooth and the weather fine all the way. We touched down at Vanuabalavu airstrip at 7am. Not a soul on the island was aware of the unscheduled flight. I thanked the two pilots who were airborne again for Nausori airport within minutes. Sakiasi Ditoka did not go with them. He stayed in the village for a while with the two security officers who had returned with us. We waited at the airstrip for transport to the village. A passing truck picked us up and we arrived at Mavana at 7.30am.

I later learned that the police officer who drove us to Nausori was taken to the RFMF military camp in Nabua where he was assaulted. He eventually escaped to his home island of Kadavu. Years later I met him in Suva and thanked him once more for his courage, and loyalty. I also learned that the two pilots were taken to the camp. I do not know what happened to them there.

I pay tribute to the two security officers who stayed with us at Mavana.They too were men of courage. Sakiasi Ditoka earned our special thanks for his daring and boldness and his refusal to be intimidated by thuggery and threats.

---

The villagers of Mavana were surprised to see us. A shed quickly went up beside my house and soon it was full of people who wanted to know about the circumstances of our arrival back home. Within minutes I received a call for an interview from Mr Masimeke Latianara, a senior newscaster, at the Fiji Broadcasting Commission. He was surprised when I told him that I had just arrived at Mavana. I gave him an interview and then spent the whole day receiving delegations from villages on Vanuabalavu.

At some point I made a media statement telling overseas reporters that the government the military wanted to set up would be totally illegal and that they had raped our constitution. There were

international protests. Helen Clark, for instance, said what was happening in Fiji was an outrage. Britain announced it was suspending military aid.

# PART II

## 30

---

## EXILE

Everyone wanted to know what was going on. I had to spend a lot of time explaining the upheaval. As new groups of villagers kept arriving, I jokingly said it would have been better if I had simply recorded our story on tape and then played it to all those keen to listen!

There was plenty of kava and food to share. The mood of the islanders was relaxed but curious. They wanted to know what had happened and why and were disappointed that once again another illegal takeover of government had occurred and that I was the victim along with the rest of the country.

We spent nine months at Mavana. It was a time of personal renewal, reflection and strategising.

Leba and I quickly adjusted to the rhythms of village life, occupying the comfortable home that we had built in 1986. It is named Naivaka, after Leba's family landholding in Dravuwalu village, Totoya, Lau.

I suppose some people who were always ready to think the worst of me, might have questioned how we could afford to build the Mavana house. I had also been asked on a number of occasions why I built an executive home in the village? My reply was that we might retire to Mavana at some point. In strictly commercial terms, the Mavana house was a questionable investment. If something similar had been built in Namadi Heights in Suva, it might have fetched a rental income of between $2,000 to $3,000 a month. But I wasn't acting to make a capital gain and I have never regretted building Naivaka.

It is our haven for Mavana holidays. We spent many Christmas breaks there with our children and try to spend an additional two or three weeks in the residence during the rest of the year.

When I retired from the civil service at age 45, I opted for a reduced pension and a gratuity – a lump sum payment. It was this that financed the home. It was designed by a registered architect and consisted of a master bedroom, two smaller bedrooms with a common shower and toilet; a kitchen, dining room, lounge, storeroom and verandah overlooking the ocean just meters away. The construction materials, with the addition of freight costs from Suva, cost about $50,000 at that time. A retired carpenter, a fellow villager, took on the task of supervising construction using concrete blocks, timber and clip-lock roofing iron. With another $10,000 I built a concrete 18,000-gallon water tank. The completed house was painted white inside and outside with a blue roof. The final cost was about $60,000. It was built to last. In 30 years Naivaka had survived a number of severe cyclones, including Winston in February 2016.

Our modest home at 6 Moti Street, Samabula in Suva, was the first residence we owned. It was here that Leba and I raised our children. We had to sell two other heavily mortgaged properties to clear a mortgage on 6 Moti Street. It was relatively close to central Suva, the CWM hospital and Suva Grammar School, where all our six children were educated.

During the first days at Mavana, we began to think about what we should do from this point on. We felt that an early return to Suva was not an option. We were still getting threatening anonymous calls. Some of the callers mentioned they were from the Queen Elizabeth barracks. I recognized one voice in particular. In fact I will never forget it. All the calls were couched in foul language and invariably included a threat to kill me.

There was an unpleasant surprise in early 2007 when two police officers from Suva came to interview me. They focused on a conversation I had with the prime minister of Australia, John Howard; my role as chairman of the Native Land Trust Board; and my part in some share transactions as a director of Fijian Holdings Limited. I responded briefly to the questions raised by the two police officers and they left. It was the beginning of the regime's campaign to put me behind bars.

I regularly received calls from friends and relatives, SDL party officials, and kept up to date with international affairs. There were frequent inquiries coming in from international media asking for my comments on developments in what was now the South Pacific's first full-fledged military dictatorship. I did not hesitate to speak out strongly when this was necessary. The military were angered when I was quoted in news reports. This did not fit their agenda. They just wanted me to vanish from the scene.

In late January 2007 I had a message that an Eminent Persons' Group (EPG) formed by the Pacific Islands Forum (PIF) wished to meet with me. I was more than happy to do this.

Since the Bainimarama coup, the situation in Fiji had regularly appeared on the agenda. We were clearly in breach of the Biketawa Declaration, which set out principles and procedures to be applied by the forum when any member country was beset by problems such as afflicted Fiji.

Fiji was to become a regular forum agenda item. Fast forwarding, I note that the communiqué from the 40th forum held at Cairns from

5th-6th August 2009, strongly condemned the actions of the Baini-marama Sayed-Khaiyum regime. It mentioned a severe deterioration in basic liberties and democratic institutions, the abrogation of the constitution, imposition of media controls, restrictions on freedom of assembly and the ongoing erosion of the traditional pillars of Fijian civil society, including the churches and chiefs. The forum leaders deplored the recent detention of church leaders. Deep concern was expressed at the rejection by the regime of calls by the Common-wealth for elections and leaders called on Fiji to re-engage on dialogue for an earlier return to democracy.

Back in December 2006, a meeting of forum foreign ministers had agreed that an Eminent Persons Group (EPG) would meet all the parties to the then impasse between my government and the mili-tary and to make recommendations for a way forward. When Baini-marama conducted his coup new terms of reference were drafted for a visit, which was now scheduled to happen with a trip to Mavana on the agenda for the EPG.

The members of the EPG were Sato Kilman, Deputy Prime minister and Foreign Affairs minister of Vanuatu as Chair, Faumuina Liuga, Samoa's minister for Natural Resources and Environment; Sir Arnold Amet, retired Chief Justice of Papua New Guinea and General Peter Gosgrove, retired Chief of the Australian Defence Force.

They were to have discussions in Fiji with a wide range of stake-holders including the president, vice president, the interim prime minister, members of the interim government, the Great Council of Chiefs, myself as the ousted prime minister, members of my govern-ment and other MPs, the suspended chief justice; other members of the judiciary; the Fiji Human Rights Commission; the business community; representatives of NGOs, churches, the media; Suva-based forum representatives; and forum representatives and foreign government diplomats representing countries that normally engaged in dialogue with the forum.

The EPG's mission was clearly a credibility test for Bainimarama

- Sayed-Khaiyum. Based on misconceived advice they were insisting that what they did was legal. In later years Sayed-Khaiyum character-ized it as simply a "change of government". A big hurdle was for them to justify to the EPG their argument that they acted on 5$^{th}$ December 2006 in accordance with the doctrine of necessity. Would the EPG accept this? Presumably Bainimarama and Sayed-Khaiyum thought they would. I doubted very much that the EPG could be persuaded by the regime's implausible arguments for what they had done to Fiji.

Bainimarama and his accomplices had tried to paint a picture of Fiji on the brink of destruction. The reality when they seized power was that Fiji was at peace, a new multi party Cabinet was working well and had broad multi racial support; institutions of state were functioning; and investment was continuing, although at a reduced rate because of the uncertainty caused by the military. Yes, we had introduced controversial legislation and this was at the centre of a vigorous and impassioned debate. This was actually democracy in its purest sense.

The only crisis was created by the military itself with its constant aggressive threats and grandstanding against the elected government. What necessity then could be invoked to validate the takeover? Another major test was for the regime to show that it had won the broad acquiescence of the population.

At Mavana we got ready for the EPG. They came by chartered aircraft and travelled from the airstrip in a twin cab to Mavana. The village had been a hive of activity since early morning preparing for the visitors. A group of women were getting morning tea ready, some of the men were preparing a lovo lunch. Other residents waited patiently for the arrival of the VIPs.

I met them and took them to our community hall where our men and women were ready to conduct a short ceremony of welcome. Fine mats were laid out as seating for the guests. We offered a sevu-sevu (presentation of kava root as part of a welcome), followed by a qaloqalovi (equivalent to freedom of the village). This was followed by yaqona, and then garlanding before morning tea.

Our discussions would be held at the hillside home of the Rev. Josateki Koroi, who had agreed for the meeting to be held there. (Rev Koroi passed away in 2014. His house was virtually destroyed in Cyclone Winston.) The home overlooked the village and the sea, with a good view of Avea island close by and Cikobia in the distance. We sat around a coffee table relaxed and ready to talk.

The EPG members asked me many questions, which I answered to the best of my ability. I stressed issues and points I felt were important. The questions and answers lasted for about 90 minutes. After that we had lunch, mostly comprising seafood, lots of homegrown vegetables and fruits and including fresh coconut juice. Time was short and the group had to leave by 3pm. I was happy that they came and confident that they had listened carefully to what I had to say.

Bainimarama and Sayed-Khaiyum and their supporters employed all the propaganda and persuasion they could muster to influence the EPG. But it was to no avail. None of their arguments worked.

The EPG members were not taken in. They flatly rejected what they considered to be the illegal overthrow of a democratically elected government and were critical of the military regime.

The EPG report was comprehensive. Its members had asked the right questions. The report gave valuable background and context. I agreed with the majority of its content. I noted however that the report made the mistake of asserting that my government had included blanket amnesty in the Reconciliation, Tolerance and Unity (RTU) Bill. There was no such proposal. There was no guarantee that amnesty would be granted to an applicant. We had eventually agreed to withdraw the amnesty section in its entirety. I mention this because of all the disinformation and misrepresentations promoted by the military and other opponents of the bill. Clearly those who persistently promoted this inaccuracy had some success. The EPG report accepted that the 2006 elections, which gave us a second term, were credible. Bainimarama had argued that they were rigged.

The EPG found that the interim government had entrenched

itself gradually and it appeared that many citizens had accepted with varying degrees of enthusiasm or reluctance, the reality of what had happened. It also noted reports that human rights abuse had been perpetrated by the military against the critics of the Commander and the RFMF.

It understood that another factor influencing the military's decision to take over the government was that in late 2006, under Commissioner Andrew Hughes police had been conducting investigations against Commander Bainimarama relating to sedition and his alleged role in the deaths of four Counter Revolutionary Warfare (CRW) soldiers in 2000.

The EPG referred to the "significant justification" offered by the military for its actions of 5$^{th}$ December stemming from the belief that my government was engaged in widespread corruption.

Its report said: "While the EPG did not discount this possibility, it noted that only anecdotal evidence of this was provided during the visit and it also noted the view expressed by some groups that allegations of corruption were not of themselves, sufficient ground to move against a democratically elected government. I told the EPG that our government would welcome the establishment of a Commission of Enquiry into allegations of corruption, but we saw no need to link this to an election timetable. I add here that we were very concerned about reports of mismanagement and abuse of certain funds by the military, which had been resisting attempts to audit and investigate.

Crucially the EPG reported that while some people agreed with the commander's claim that his actions were justified under the doctrine of necessity, the majority of those with whom its members spoke were not convinced that the extra constitutional actions of the Commander (and subsequently the president) could be upheld on this ground.

"The legal difficulty arises in particular because the actions taken were in fulfillment of threats to the public order made by the RFMF itself, a situation which excludes the applicability of the necessity doctrine. The EPG understands that the prevailing legal view is therefore that the Commander's action in seizing power on 5$^{th}$ December was illegal."

In the conclusion of its report, the EPG said following its discussion and analysis of legal precedence and in relation to the doctrine of necessity, it was persuaded by the majority view that the RFMF's takeover of government was unlawful.

Based on this view, the immediate next step would be to reconvene parliament and restore constitutional government drawn from the elected parliament. The EPG believed, however, that this was unlikely to occur. There was acceptance that the regime had established day-to-day control, but the EPG report added that the military statement that it enjoyed widespread support was not supported by the majority of individuals and organisations consulted.

The interim government appeared firm in its intention not to hold an election for a protracted period (up to five years). Some members of the interim government said the election preparation would take at least three years. The EPG thought this was excessive and said the majority of people with whom it spoke preferred an earlier return to parliamentary government. The report questioned the requirement for an ongoing state of emergency and the disturbing number of human rights abuses.

EPG members noted that during their visit, soldiers remained in place at checkpoints throughout Suva and they understood there were numerous cases of citizens being denied their constitutional rights. This was through subjection to intimidation, harassment and physical abuse at the Queen Elizabeth Barracks.

The EPG report understood that an atmosphere had been created in which people felt unable to express their views; members of the media had been subjected to threats and intimidation in situations where stories unsympathetic to the interim government's position had been run. Citizens were reluctant to speak with the media for fear of retributive acts against them and their families. This has led to some self-censorship by the media. EPG members heard conflicting opinions on the support for the interim government and my government. Their report said: "While many in the community are reticent about expressing their opinion publicly, support for the ousted government among indigenous Fijians reportedly remains strong while the interim government seems to have gained support among other communities."

The report said the continuing independent functioning of the judiciary had been compromised by the manner in which the chief justice was requested to take leave and then suspended, and an acting chief justice appointed. The Court of Appeal and Supreme Court might not be able to function beyond September and there was the prospect of non-resident judges refusing to sit. Ample comment was made that due process under the constitution had not been applied in the termination of contracts of public office holders. The integrity of the Fiji Human Rights Commission was in question as a result of internal disputes and some politicization.

In its recommendations, the report included a call for the RFMF to return to the barracks and for Commander Bainimarama to vacate the position of prime minister. A civilian should be appointed to that post. The state of emergency should be lifted. The interim government should restrict its activities to matters necessary to meet the basic requirements of the community. It should uphold the 1997 constitution and Fiji's domestic and international obligations. It should stop all interference with the judiciary and accountable institutions and the Chief Justice should be reinstated to office, citizens should be free to seek legal redress in the Courts in relation to Bainimarama's coup and events following December 5. The EPG was firm in calling for a commitment "without delay" for a timetable for holding a national election which should be between 18 months and two years, if not sooner. The report asked the forum to call on the interim government and the RFMF to immediately stop human rights abuses.

So, in summary this group of experienced leaders representing the preeminent regional organization had slapped down the Bainimarama military government's justifications for their actions. It could see no justification for the coup and the so-called clean up campaign.

My time in the village gave me an opportunity to think about a number of things including the Fiji Labour Party (FLP) and its leader Mahendra Chaudhry. They were a major stakeholder as a partner in the multi-party Cabinet which had been so well received by the people. But there were tensions and complications due mainly to the decision of the FLP leader, Mr Mahendra Chaudhry, to stay out of the ministerial line-up. Mr Chaudhry is a complex person with an agile mind and shrewd political instincts. He was a principal archi-tect of the Peoples' Coalition victory over Ratu Mara's Alliance Party in 1987 and became minister of Finance and Economic Planning in the coalition government. But the Coalition lost power after about a month when Sitiveni Rabuka staged Fiji's first coup.

Mr Chaudhry achieved a major success in the 1999 election when Labour again came into government and he became Fiji's first Indo- Fijian prime minister.

When George Speight struck in 2000 Mr Chaudhry was a coup casualty again and endured the considerable ordeal of being held hostage with many of his parliamentary colleagues. He was physi-cally abused.

As Fiji stood at the brink of another army rebellion, Mr Chaudhry remained a significant political player with the ability to disrupt the operations of the Cabinet.

He and I had confronted each other many times in industrial relations negotiations and politically. We managed to preserve civility in our personal relations but when the gloves were off we both fought hard to protect our fundamental political positions. The FLP always stood by strong democratic principles and values and was a vocal advocate for parliamentary government, the rule of law, freedom of association and the media and basic human rights. It saw its constituency as ordinary citizens, the poor and disadvantaged, the workers and cane farmers. After the take-over of governments in 1987 and 2000, the FLP campaigned for a return to parliamentary democracy. I am aware, from a first hand account that Mr Chaudhry suspected Bainimarama had an involvement in the ousting of his government by George Speight.

Despite this, I detected a pro-Bainimarama sentiment among certain senior members of the FLP even though Labour and SDL were in the multi-party Cabinet together and it was functioning well. Mrs Jokapeci Koroi, the FLP president, was making statements against SDL and even appeared to suggest the removal of our government by a coup. I received intelligence reports that Mr Chaudhry and some of his supporters had meetings with Bainimarama.

During the Budget meeting of parliament in November of 2006 Bainimarama had a discussion in the Office of the Leader of the Opposition at the parliamentary complex. I was an accidental eyewitness while I was having a coffee in the PM's office at parliament. I saw Bainimarama and an entourage walk into Mr Chaudhry's office right under my nose, so to speak. A number of questions went through my mind. What government business would a military commander have with the Leader of the

Opposition? Was the minister responsible for the military aware of the visit? Was the impending take-over of government discussed? I, and my colleagues, will probably never know the full story. But the visit certainly stirred suspicions.

I learned that a few days before the coup, the FLP had removed non-government furniture and equipment from its parliamentary office. Later I received another intelligence report that the FLP had submitted 40 unverified allegations against our government to the military commander.

To me all this was enough to create a strong perception that Mr Chaudhry and a group of his senior people were supportive of Bainimarama's treason. The acceptance by Mr Chaudhry and another senior member of his party, Mr Poseci Bune, of ministerial portfolios in Bainimarama's military regime, tended to support my belief. Both of them eventually found themselves on the outer and lost their portfolios.

I was surprised that the FLP had done a complete turnaround on its basic democratic beliefs by teaming up with Bainimarama and his military government.

Afterwards Chaudhry and I were able to bridge our differences and work jointly on occasions in the interests of getting the nation back on track. I have a copy of a letter to Bainimarama we both signed as the leaders of the political parties which won 67 out of the 71 seats in the 2006 elections. We warned him about the precarious state of the nation, including increasing unemployment, the need to salvage the sugar industry, loss of skills and strained relations with international partners leading to a reduction in aid. It was time, we said, to leave the past behind and look to a future of promise for the people, irrespective of race, colour or creed. The letter was copied to the Military Council that was then playing a role in Fiji's governance. There was no reply.

Chaudhry and I, along with Opposition Leader Mick Beddoes, came together to make submissions to a Pacific Islands Forum delegation in Suva.

---

L eba and I quickly assumed our role again as village leaders. This was not difficult; the village was in my blood and I had been heavily involved in its development throughout my working life. Leba joined with the village women's group, and organised regular meetings where a number of projects were agreed and implemented. One of them was making mats and handicrafts for traditional gatherings and social occasions such as weddings. Soon there was a good stock of these items which became a useful resource for the village. Leba worked with the women to assist in improving the village environment. She also set up a prayer group which met regularly.

To support our livelihood, I set up a plantation of staple rootcrops and vegetables. Two other projects were on my mind. I was determined to establish the largest yam garden on Mavana and indeed the whole of Vanuabalavu. I was keen to transform Mavana into one of the cleanest and tidiest villages in Fiji. After all cleanliness is next to Godliness.

At the first village meeting of 2007, we decided to move forward with the beautification scheme. For months I led a team of men clearing the perimeter of the village. I said I wished to see this happening fortnightly using lawnmowers and brush cutters rather than the usual cane knives. Slowly and surely, we worked our way from one end of the village to the other, a distance of between 300 to 400 meters. All the weeds and unwanted plants were removed to allow for a new covering of grass. By the end of March, the task was finished and we continue to this day using brush cutters to keep the area tidy.

I remember God's creation of the universe and the earth as recorded in the book of Genesis. At the end of each day of creation, God saw what He had done and was pleased. Our men of Mavana also saw what they had done daily in creating a new look village and were pleased. We took on the challenge of encouraging the beautification of individual compounds. Leba and I kept our place well groomed with our lawn mower and planted new plants around the house.

The villagers were reminded constantly about keeping their surroundings clean. With the use of lawn mowers and brush cutters, the appearance of the village improved tremendously. Greenery and flowers, surrounded by stones painted white, were planted on both sides of the public road that runs through the village.

I had long been interested in the planting of yams (uvi). It is traditionally a prestigious crop reflective of our culture and way of life. Lauan men are often judged by the volume and size of the yams they cultivate. If I were to establish the largest yam garden on Vanuabalavu, I would need an area that could contain about 2,000 plants. First, I asked for permission from my clan to use three or four acres of our communal land. After receiving this, I began to collect sufficient cuttings for planting material. Some came from relatives and friends.

I also bought some. I hired ten young men, paid weekly, to clear the thick bush and small trees from the area allocated for the project. About six others looking for some cash income joined the group. I didn't really need them but employed them anyway, which wasn't a very efficient way of operating.

Preparing a yam garden and planting in the Lauan way is laborious. It took about a week to clear the area. The waste was left to dry and then burnt. Then we had to move burnt tree stumps, roots and other waste material. In another week, we began digging holes for the yams. For the large variety (*uvi balavu*) the depth of each hole must equal the length of a heavy duty garden fork or spade. The diameter was about 24 inches. Each hole would be refilled with soil and a mound was built on top of it. For planting a small hole is scooped out by hand at the top of the mound, the yam cutting placed inside the hole and then covered with soil. One of our elders suggested to me that before planting, I should face the sun, say a short prayer requesting blessings and then complete the task. I followed his advice.

Altogether we planted 1,000 long variety yams and 1,000 short variety (*uvi* leka). The preparation for *uvi* leka is much easier. You just have to turn the top soil a few times with a garden fork, and then place the planting material in it.

The normal time to plant is between April and June. Harvesting takes place between March and June.

By 1$^{st}$ September 2007, the date we decided to return to Suva, the yam garden was looking great. I was certain I would get a good harvest in April-June next year. In fact, we came back for the occasion. The harvest was huge. A 20' x 16' shed beside our house was filled to capacity. Photos of heaps of yams appeared in the Internet. I decided that the crop was not a commercial project. We gave away lots of yams to relatives and friends and kept some for our domestic consumption and reserved planting material for 2008. With just one exception, I established a garden annually from 2007. Every year has seen good harvests and I was happy to see that other villagers were motivated to improve their own crops after observing what I had done.

The Mavana exile gave me space to consider what action to take in response to Bainimarama's coup. I decided that although I had reservations about the integrity of the regime court system I would launch a legal challenge through the High Court. I felt that not all the judges would necessarily be compromised in a military dictatorship. Some would preserve their impartiality. It was the luck of the draw. I thought it was important for the nation, and for me and my colleagues, to take the legal option. It was the right thing to do, no matter the difficulties. It would also be a test for the legal system and for the rule of law the regime claimed to support.

I consulted some of my political associates by 'phone and invited them to be part of the proposed action. The response was overwhelming. Those who were finally named as first plaintiffs were Ratu Naiqama Lalabalavu, a Cabinet minister who also held the high chiefly title of *Tui Cakau*; Ro Teimumu Vuikaba Kepa, of Lomanikoro village, Rewa, Cabinet minister and also a high chief, as *Roko Tui Dreketi*; Ratu Suliano Matanitobua, a Minister of State with the chiefly rank of *Tui Namosi*, and Josefa Vosanibola, a Cabinet minister. Second plaintiffs were named as Ratu Apenisa Kalokalo Loki of Tamavua village, near Suva, a politician; and Peceli Kinivuwai, Suva, SDL national director.

My difficulties began straight away. I had to explain in the affidavit that Air Fiji, the local airline, appeared to be reluctant to take me to Suva where I would have access to the legal amenities and support I would require. I believed that the airline had been warned by Bainimarama and the RFMF not to offer me a seat. My access to lawyers was difficult and it was not possible to find a Commissioner for Oaths prepared to come to Vanuabalavu to have my affidavit properly sworn. Commissioners who were approached feared reprisals by Bainimarama and the military. My affidavit had to be declared before a local Justice of Peace and delivered to my lawyers by facsimile.

There was another hurdle in engaging solicitors. Four or five local legal firms declined to accept the brief as they feared a hostile reaction from the regime. Eventually, Mr Tevita Fa of Fa & Company agreed to represent us. Qoriniasi Bale, my former Attorney General, who had returned to private practice and was high on Bainimarama's enemies list, assisted discreetly.

Mr Fa soon paid a price for his courage. He was subject to constant harassment and intimidation and then his residence and private vehicle were torched. I understand these crimes were supposed to be investigated. But nothing happened. Such was the state of law and order Bainimarama had pledged to uphold.

I had set the legal wheels in motion. My detailed affidavit was completed and the other plaintiffs were preparing theirs. Things would pick up speed when I got back to Suva.

About a week before we were to return to Viti Levu, the telephone threats began again. I received them on most mornings. I recognized the same voice that had been so persistent after we had arrived back at Mavana. I have no doubt that the caller is still a senior officer in our security forces.

This time I was told my throat would be slashed on arrival at Nausori airport. When we got off the plane at Nausori, on 1st September 2007 after nine months in the village, there was a heavy presence of military and police. But nothing happened.

With my throat intact, we drove straight home to the Moti Street house. I am sure spying eyes kept us under surveillance. Bainimarama was so agitated about my return that he declared another state of emergency.

# 31

# AN UNBELIEVABLE DECISION

I discovered at the SDL office in the capital that the party had tried to maintain some level of service to members and the public. This was difficult because of lack of funds but supporters appreciated the SDL listening to their worries and concerns and helping out whenever it could. The party's national director, Mr Peceli Kinivuwai, refused to be intimidated by the military. They saw him as a thorn in their side. Every time he said something publicly, or met with supporters, the army became nervous and clearly felt threatened. Mr Kinivuwai was taken up to the military camp nearly

20 times. He was verbally abused and physically attacked on a number of occasions. He was warned that if the military found it necessary to bring him in again, he would leave in a "body bag". This brave man finally settled in Australia. It was not surprising that in his affidavit for the planned court action, he talked of the "reign of terror" imposed by Bainimarama and the Army. That's exactly what it was.

Other officials and supporters of the SDL party and deposed SDL parliamentarians were pursued, harassed and assaulted. At least two former Cabinet ministers suffered serious injuries when they were attacked by military personnel. They too started new lives in Australia.

I was to become more familiar with the Bainimarama dictatorship's thuggery and violence and have included a number of cases in this book.

Getting ready for the court challenge, known as Qarase and Others vs Bainimarama and Others, became a daily preoccupation. We listed Josaia Voreqe Bainimarama, Commander of the Republic of Fiji Military Forces, as the first defendant. The RFMF, second defendant; the State of the Republic of the Fiji Islands, third defendant; and the Attorney General of the interim regime as fourth defendant.

Securing the services of eminent counsel to represent us in a case of such historical importance to Fiji, and which would also attract international notice, was a substantial challenge. We knew the regime would spare no expense in their use of public funds to retain top legal talent. The professional charges for us would be very high and the SDL did not have much money.

Qoriniasi Bale, my former attorney general, identified the Australian, Nye Perram, as a possibility for handling my case. Mr Perram, a rising legal star, was practising as a senior counsel (SC) in Sydney. He was also a member of the New South Wales Bar Council. Later, at the age of just 39, he became a judge of the Federal Court of Australia. Qoriniasi explained our straitened circumstances and suggested that Mr Perram might like to consider taking a brief from us pro bono (free of charge). To his credit, and with our gratitude, Mr Perram agreed. He was to be praised in the legal profession for his work on our behalf.

Qoriniasi also succeeded in persuading the New South Wales barrister Ms Rachel Pepper to be part of our legal representation pro bono. She went on to become a judge of the NSW Land and Environment Court. She was recognised as an author, teacher and community advocate and served as an associate to High Court Justice Michael McHugh. Tevita Fa, of Fa & Company, who had faced persecution for taking our case, became the local member of our court team.

Our lawyers were up against Guy Reynolds, QC, and QC Gerard McCoy for the defence.

The high court bench to deliberate on the case consisted of the Acting Chief Justice, Mr Anthony Gates, UK born, formerly Deputy Director of Public Prosecutions, practising lawyer, magistrate and then a High Court Judge; Mr John Byrne, an experienced Australian judge, who had been involved in many notable cases and Mr Davendra Pathik, a well-known figure in Fiji, formerly in private practice, appointed as a magistrate and then a judge. He later taught law at the University of Fiji.

We had some concerns over perceptions that all three were pro-regime. The International Bar Association Human Rights Institute (IBAHRI), in a March 2009 rule of law report on Fiji, said Mr Gates had become Acting Chief Justice "as a direct result of the military take-over" while Mr Byrne was reappointed to the bench following the coup. He was, therefore, a military appointee. The IBAHRI declared it had significant concerns about the impartiality of the bench and felt the Acting Chief Justice and Justice Byrne should have recused themselves from our case.

On 20th February 2007, in our first court move, we had issued an originating summons seeking from the court 12 declarations, chief of which was that the removal of the prime minister and ministers by force of arms was unconstitutional and unlawful. There were considerable delays and postponements from both sides in the pre- trial hearings.

The trial proper was held in the court room which was formerly the seat of parliament in the colonial era government buildings in Suva. It started on March 5th 2008 and continued till the 20th with judgment delivered on October 9th 2008. The chamber was usually filled with spectators, many of them supporters of the SDL. I spent considerable time giving evidence and being cross examined. Bainimarama did not appear.

The core of the defendants' case was that the president had acted lawfully by using "prerogative" powers inherited from British history which enabled him to act in an emergency for the public good.

The background to my evidence was the affidavit I had sworn about what had happened. Much of it is covered in this book but I will include some parts of it for the record. I deposed that the:

- • Removal of the democratically elected and constitutionally appointed prime minister, his Cabinet ... and members of parliament by the first and second defendants by force of arms ... was unconstitutional and unlawful;
- • Usurpation of executive authority and power by the first defendant ... was unconstitutional and unlawful;
- • Decisions and actions taken by the first defendant in the purported exercise of executive authority were unlawful and unconstitutional, null, void and of no effect. The decisions and actions included the dissolution of parliament, the dismissal of senior officials, the dismissal or termination of senior executives of statutory boards, the dismissal of members of statutory boards and boards of some government commercial companies, the suspension of the Chief Justice and the placing of the Chief Magistrate on forced indefinite leave.
- • Appointment of the first interim prime minister, Dr Jona Senilagakali and appointments by him of various persons to senior positions were unlawful and unconstitutional;
- • Appointment by the president of the second interim prime minister and other persons as members of the Cabinet of the interim government was unconstitutional;
- • Declaration by the first defendant of a state of emergency effective from December 5$^{th}$, 2006 and the

subsequent promulgation of emergency regulations were
contrary to law and the constitution;

- • First named plaintiff remained the lawful and
  constitutional prime minister and the members of his
  Cabinet, other ministers and his government remained
  the lawful government;
- • Promulgation by the unlawful interim government to
  grant immunity to the first and second defendants and
  any person proven to have been accessory before or after
  their treasonous acts was contrary to law and null, void
  and of no effect.

The affidavit said I initiated discussions to involve the Great
Council of Chiefs (GCC) in the general effort to encourage
the first and second defendants on the one hand and the government
on the other to try to resolve the stalemate between them.

I deposed the GCC appointed a mediation committee to
approach the first and second defendants to engage in a meaningful
dialogue with me and my government. However the first defendant
said publicly that the GCC committee was a waste of time and
money.

On 22nd November the first defendant was reported as saying
that the GCC committee members and their consultants "should go
and sit under a mango tree and drink homebrew". He stated that he
would not participate in any mediation talks unless the list of written
demands signed by Captain Teleni were met.

The affidavit stated that like most members of the public, I was
aware of the determined efforts of the first and second defendants
"since 2003 to find a good excuse and time to overthrow my government". I added that like the majority of people, I had only been able
to speculate about his real motives for his obsession.

I stated that the 2006 general election was probably the best opportunity for the voters in Fiji to judge for themselves the allegations constantly and publicly mounted by the first defendant against my leadership and the manner in which my government was managing the affairs of the country. I was happy and willing to ask the people "to decide through the democratic process, prescribed in our laws and constitution, whether or not we were suitable leaders of the country".

I declared that the elections were clear and the people had made their decision. I therefore sincerely believe that the outcome of the 2006 general elections also demonstrated in sufficiently clear and democratic terms that the allegations and efforts publicly orchestrated by the first defendant and his political supporters and instigators to discredit the SDL party and my government were not accepted by the public and the voters.

Despite the mandate given to me and my party to lead the country for a further five years, the first defendant remained determined to overthrow my leadership and my government. The first defendant remained relentless in his efforts to discredit my leadership and government and its policies at every opportunity available to him.

The affidavit said the determination of the first defendant to overthrow my government had been further illustrated in days

following the coup to remove through indefinite leave, termination or other disciplinary means, a number of very senior officers in the RFMF; invariably they gave him advice he did not want to hear in relation to his obsession with removing or overthrowing the duly elected government.

The events which had occurred and others continuing to unfold illustrated clearly the extent by which the first defendant was prepared to ignore the rule of law, the democratic system prescribed by the constitution, the principles of good governance and the protections guaranteed under the constitution, to achieve his unlawful purposes by gaining and retaining power at any cost.

I deposed that after he declared a state of emergency and dissolve parliament on the advice of the interim prime minister, the first defendant publicly added "there is no point in debating the legality or otherwise of our actions, Qarase and his cronies are not coming back".

I listed the groups and organisations that had expressed disapproval of the overthrowing of the democratically elected government. These included Fiji's churches, non-government organisations, the GCC, the Fiji Law Society, and the Human Rights Commission. International condemnation had been expressed by the governments of New Zealand, Australia, the US, Samoa, and Papua New Guinea (to name a few); along with organisations such as the Commonwealth, the Pacific Islands Forum, the Melanesian Spearhead Group, African Caribbean Heads of State, the European Union, the United Nations and International Commission of Jurists.

I stressed that there was no civil unrest or chaos, or uncontrollable crisis to justify military intervention or removal of government. On the contrary, it had been the acts and constant bullying tactics of the first and second defendants over recent years that had always caused anxiety among the people. The first and second defendants had been creating a crisis themselves to justify their intervention and unlawful overthrow of the government.

I declared that I sincerely believed that the first and second defendants were simply taking advantage of a necessity of their own making and that the coup was instigated by them over issues that could and should have been resolved by lawful and democratic processes prescribed under the constitution and other laws in Fiji. The first and second defendants had instead turned this situation into a source of absolute power and authority for themselves.

I mentioned that after the coup the first and second defendants had published advertisements inviting applications for positions of ministers in their interim regime (Probably they thought this was a democratic way of assembling a government. It was certainly the first time that people in Fiji could apply, through advertisements, to become ministers. It may have been a world's first for that matter. The talk at the time was some resourceful taxi drivers and market vendors threw their hats into the ring for consideration as Cabinet members.)

My deposition noted that I was not aware whether responses to these advertisements were taken into account in the selection of ministers in the interim regime. The Cabinet line up that eventuated was mostly persons defeated in the 2006 general elections; members of the Fiji Labour Party including its leader Mahendra Chaudhry and deputy leader, Poseci Bune. I mentioned that a state minister in my government contacted me indicating that he wanted to resign from the SDL so he could consider an offer to serve as an interim regime minister. He stressed to me his personal reasons for wishing to accept an appointment. I left it to him on the understanding that he fully understood the possible implications of the decision. He was subsequently appointed. At least he had the courtesy to mention to me his intentions in advance.

I made the point that the second defendants were the only ones effectively armed in Fiji

---

yet its members continued to parade their arms in public "virtually daring any unarmed member of the public to defy their existence and it is difficult in these circumstances for the people not to be obedient.

---

I spent considerable time giving evidence and being cross examined. Bainimarama did not submit himself to cross examination.

One specific issue I was questioned on related to the army's obsession that I had favoured an armed invasion to restore order and that I had inquired about the possibility of Australian troops coming in.

The context for this was the Pacific Islands Forum Biketawa Declaration. I was among regional leaders who approved the declaration in October 2000. One of its aims was to provide regional support for any PIF member gripped by crisis. The Solomon Islands had benefitted from the Biketawa provisions when a Regional Assistance Mission (RAMSI) was formed and sent in 2003 to help restore stability and peace in that country following internal strife. Every PIF nation, including Fiji, participated in RAMSI. Bainimarama was fully aware of its intent and purpose and the circumstances under which it would go onto the regional agenda.

The court was packed on October 9$^{th}$ when the judgment was delivered. As I had observed during the proceedings it looked to me as though the judges were not paying much attention to the case we, the plaintiffs, put. I had the impression that the bench was not focused on the military takeover and the illegality of that. It appeared to be focused on justifying the ratification by the president, of Bainimarama's actions in seizing government, using prerogative powers.

The judgment expounded at some length on the nature of prerogative powers from ancient times to the present. It even touched on the Magna Carta and the Stuart Kings.

An *Extraordinary Fiji Gazette Notice* was cited, which declared:

The primary objective of the interim Military government is to take the country towards good governance, rid us of corruption and bad practices and at the same time provide the well being of Fiji and its people at the earliest possible opportunity.

The normal day-to-day affairs of the country were to continue as usual.

(There had been a military takeover, Fiji was ruled by a military junta, fear was abroad, and people were being taken to the barracks. How then could the affairs of the country continue as usual?)

In the discussion about prerogative Lord Denning was quoted as stating that it was a discretionary power to be exercised by the executive government for the public good in cases where the law had made no provision.

The judgment stated that the prerogative, as part of the common law of Fiji, sat happily with statute law. Oliver Cromwell came into the High Court's thinking as its judgment reached a crucial point in building up to its final decisions. It said the president had assessed that Fiji was at a crossroads and had reached a grave crisis. The Bainimarama take-over was characterized as a "military intervention" occurring at the end of a long tunnel of "civil strife". It seemed to me in referring to "civil strife" the Court must have been referring to Bainimarama's insubordination and refusal to bow to civilian control. There had been no civil strife according to the accepted definition of the phrase.

The judgment pondered on what the result might have been if the president had returned to the status quo and declared that when he had the freedom to act again as president on 4th January he had to act swiftly and decisively.

Then came the Cromwell thinking:

---

Cromwell, though a usurper himself, percipiently observed of the urgency of such a moment: 'If nothing should be done but what is according to law, the throat of the nation might be cut while we send for someone to make a law.'

---

From this the court appeared to draw some of the justification for what was done by Bainimarama and the military.

The court found that exceptional circumstances did exist, not provided for by the constitution and that the stability of the state was endangered. It said: "We also find that no other course of action was reasonably available and that such action as taken by the president was reasonably necessary in the interests of peace, order and good government. Rather than impairing the just rights of citizens, we conclude that the president's actions were designed to protect a wide variety of competing rights from displacement by avoiding conflagration."

The court said the constitution remained intact. The government existed in the interim by way of direct presidential rule with His Excellency by a prime minister and cabinet of ministers. The court then declared that our originating summons was dismissed. The court found that the president's decisions to ratify the dismissal of the prime minister and his ministers, to appoint Dr Senilagakali as caretaker prime minister, and the dissolving of parliament were "valid and lawful acts in exercise of the prerogative powers of the head of state to act for the public good in a crisis."

It found that the president's decision to rule directly pending elections was valid and lawful as was his decision to promulgate legislation and to grant immunity.

We had lost. The usurpers had won.

There was complete silence during the reading of the judgment. When Justice Gates finished, I looked around and saw utter disbelief on many faces including those of prominent local lawyers, civil

servants and other citizens. Some of those present had what I can only describe as expressions of satisfaction and relief. They must have been soldiers and opponents of the SDL. Members of the media rushed out of court with note pads, mobile phones and personal computers. All of them wanted to be first to communicate the news to the public.

Asked for my reaction by journalists, one of the comments I made was that most people would be stunned, including myself.

It is quite an unbelievable decision. I'm extremely disappointed ... It is a ridiculous situation. It will encourage future coups. I think the impartiality of our judiciary is completely gone.

Mick Beddoes, who had been Leader of the Opposition, said the judgment "legitimizes treason as a means of changing governments in Fiji which only serves to encourage more coups". Mr Beddoes felt the decision exposed the judiciary as being no longer independent.

Professor George Williams from the University of New South Wales echoed some of what Mr Beddoes said. The decision, in his view, was at odds with the most important principles of the rule of law. It would not only provide encouragement to further coups in Fiji, and elsewhere in the Pacific, but undermine the rule of law by providing unfettered power to the president that placed him above the clear provisions of the Fiji constitution.

# 32

# VICTORY! AND THEN CRUCIFIXION

The decision to appeal was easy. We felt the high court judgment was so faulty and divorced from reality that an appeal must have a very good chance of succeeding. There was a quick consultation with our solicitors, Fa and Company.

The appeal documents were prepared and an application filed with the Fiji Court of Appeal. The application was approved and a hearing set for 6th, 7th and 8th of April, 2009.

Unfortunately, Nye Perram, our lead counsel in the high court case, was not available to take on the appeal. He had been elevated as a judge to the Federal Court of Australia. But Qoriniasi Bale managed to secure the pro bono services of another eminent Australian lawyer, Bret Walker SC the former head of the NSW Bar Association. Ms Pepper agreed to continue to represent us, again free of charge.

On Bainimarama's side was one of Britain's most costly lawyers, Richard Gordon, QC.

Three well-known Australian jurists, Randall Powell, Ian Lloyd and Francis Douglas, presided at the Court of Appeal hearing. They delivered their judgment on April 9th 2009 in the same court room. Again the court was packed.

Messrs Powell, Lloyd and Douglas demolished the high court decision precisely and methodically. To them the constitution was all. Prerogative powers Bainimarama had relied on did not apply. They said that clearly the constitution "intended to delineate as precisely as possible the circumstances in which the president could dismiss the prime minister." Section 109 laid these out: The president may not dismiss a prime minister unless a government failed to get, or lost the confidence of, the House of Representatives and the prime minister did not resign or get a dissolution of parliament. The right of the president to do anything otherwise than on advice was strictly limited.

Then the judgment began to move to the heart of the matter. It asked

---

why does a matter of national security call for the dismissal of a prime minister and his ministers and the dissolution of parliament? Under the constitution it is he and his Cabinet who have the responsibility to lead the country through a crisis and to advise the president in relation thereto.

It is entirely unclear to us why the first thing called for in a time of national emergency is the dismissal of the prime minister and his government.

---

Then the knockout blow:

---

This, we consider, exposes the real flaw in the argument for the respondents. It exposes the fact that what has occurred in this case and previous cases is simply a military coup or an unlawful usurpation of power.

In their outline of the facts and circumstances of the case, the judges said the RFMF took control of the streets of Suva on 5 December 2006 and the commander assumed the executive authority of the State. This conduct was not engaged in at the time with the sanction of the president. The Commander then purported to exercise presidential powers and appoint Dr Senilagakali as care-taker prime minister to advise the dissolution of parliament.

The appeal judges described the other events and actions that had occurred, adding "none of what was done in the circumstances ... was, in our opinion, sanctioned by the constitution."

They pointed out:

Throughout the period when these events occurred Mr Qarase retained and had not lost the confidence of the House of Representatives, so no power on the part of the president, or the Commander of the RFMF on behalf of the president, existed to dismiss the prime minister.

Their judgment said the respondents' position was that the Court had a duty, in granting any relief, to minimize the adverse public consequences and to take account of the risk of social upheaval and disruption if I was, in effect, restored to power, even for a limited period. It added: 1

Yet in response to a question from the Court senior counsel for the respondents said that he had been unable to obtain instructions from the respondents as to the earliest date an election could be held.

We are naturally concerned that no responsive answer

was given to this enquiry and are unpersuaded that the undertaking itself would lead to chaos. Our concerns are more those of dealing with the practical reality facing the Court after a period of unconstitutional government.

---

In the opinion of the judges the only appropriate course at the present time was for elections to be held that enable Fiji to get a fresh start.

They also said there was a very real question whether I remained the prime minister, notwithstanding that I had not formally resigned. They were fortified by public statements of both the president and the Commander that the mandate of the interim government was to uphold the Fiji constitution and that it was anticipated to take the people smoothly to the next elections.

As judges they could only express the hope that the people of Fiji would again have the freedom of choice of their parliamentary representatives that was enshrined for them in the Fiji constitution. In their declarations and orders the judges declared as unlawful acts under the Fiji constitution:

- • The assumption of executive authority and the declaration of a state of emergergency by Bainimarama;
- • My dismissal from office and the appointment of Dr Senilagakali;
- • The order by Bainimarama that parliament be dissolved;
- • The appointment by the president of Bainimarama as prime minister and of other persons as his ministers.
- • The judges declared that it would be lawful for the president to appoint a caretaker prime minister to advise a dissolution of parliament and the issuance of writs for an election.

So, there it was. The attempt by Bainimarama and Sayed-Khaiyum to legally justify their seizure of government was rejected. What we had known all along was officially confirmed. They had committed a coup. A coup is a crime and was not permitted under the constitution.

The Court of Appeal decision was a huge relief to me, and many thousands of citizens. The judges had reached the right decision in the interests of justice, the people and the country. We were to be freed from military rule founded on treason.

There was jubilation amongst our supporters in the court and in workplaces, homes and villages throughout the country. But some people were cautious and doubted that Bainimarama-Sayed-Khaiyum would actually vacate office. They were right.

That evening Bainimarama went on television, indicating that he would be returning to the barracks while warning that there would be no toleration of breaches of the peace. However, he made a comment that gave a clue to how he and his accomplices would deal with the instructions of the appeal judges. He said the ruling of the court and its refusal to grant a stay pending an appeal, meant in practical terms that Fiji effectively did not have a prime minister or ministers. In other words, he said, there was no government in place. That would be the excuse they used for what happened next. Bainimarama, Sayed-Khaiyum and others went into frantic night time discussions to plot an escape route. This was on the eve of Easter weekend.

I was coming out of church next morning when I heard that the president had allegedly tossed out the constitution, appointed himself head of state, assumed all government power and sacked the judiciary. The next day he subsequently reappointed Bainimarama prime minister.

To me it was as though the country had been crucified on Good Friday.

The actions of the president, clearly orchestrated by Bainimarama- Sayed-Khaiyum, showed their continued intention to rule the country illegally. Their professed commitment to the constitution was tossed aside the moment the law worked against them. It was all a facade.

The appeal justices harshly condemned the Bainimarama-Sayed Khaiyum regime. They emphasised that Fiji had not been left without a government. They had given instructions for the appointment of a caretaker prime minister. Obviously, this could not be done on day one and might take time to implement. Bainimarama and Co would have to stay in place until that happened.

Justice Ian Lloyd spoke on *Radio Australia* of

quite malicious misinformation" spread by Bainimarama and the president "to enable them to abrogate the constitution and run the country as a military regime, a dictatorship that they want.

He said the judges had deliberately sought to avoid a power vacuum.

We had the option in the judgment of making orders which would have seen Mr Qarase restored as prime minister. But we actually gave a third way – that is the appointment of an independent person to advise the president to call elections.

And we also stressed ... that the judgment did not in any way invalidate legislation ... So again it was just used as an excuse by the military to do what they've done.

We obviously anticipated there might be problems – I don't think any of us anticipated that Bainimarama would take the judgment well and I don't think the ramifications were out of our mind," he said. "But I don't think we quite thought that Bainimarama would go to this extreme. I don't think any of us thought things would go that far and certainly go that far that quickly, that the country would suddenly be overtaken by an illegal military regime."

According to the Radio Australia report, Justice Lloyd said it was clear to him that Commodore Bainimarama was behind the president's actions. "One can only assume that from the pace of what has occurred in the past few days, the president simply, from my observation, would not have been the one making these decisions," he said.

Clearly he would have been acting on advice and the advice could only have come from Bainimarama. I don't think one can say other than sensibly – he is the puppet and Bainimarama is the puppet master.

Justice Douglas also denied that their decision had created a power vacuum, "It is no more a vacuum than the hiatus that exists between one government going out of power prior to elections and another one coming in," he said.

You've still got the functioning executive, you've still got the courts, all of whom are bound to uphold the constitution. (The sacking of the courts) Is not us creating a vacuum – it's Bainimarama creating a vacuum."

There was a strong reaction from New Zealand. The then foreign Affairs minister, Murray McCully said: "We have effectively got a self-appointed dictator. It's now a very much less predictable place than it was.

Stephen Smith, Australian Foreign minister at the time, said Bainimarama had turned Fiji into a military state by "suspending freedom of speech and undermining the well-being of its citizens."

Bainimarama quickly introduced more repression, posting censors in newsrooms and roadblocks in the capital's streets. The *Fiji Times* published its Sunday and Monday editions with several blank pages to indicate where censorship had occurred. The *Fiji One* TV News

refused to broadcast its nightly news bulletin on Sunday. The president of the Fiji Law Society, Dorsami Naidu, was detained, and the Courts were closed.

Fiji was now firmly in the grip of tyranny.

# 33

# ABUSE AND TORTURE

I recount here details of what happened to some of the other citizens known to me who were picked up by the military. I know there is a tendency for some members of the public to prefer that instances of abuse and torture should be allowed to simply fade away into history. Why bring them up again years afterwards and put them in the public spotlight? Isn't it better just to forget all about them? No, it isn't. Those who perpetrate such uncivilized and cruel behaviour and cause such suffering must be held accountable. They've committed serious crimes, and those crimes must be dealt with by a fair and impartial system of criminal justice. If they are allowed impunity, justice is not served and those affected will be left to nurse their sorrow without any form of closure. There must be public pressure on the security forces until all members have a deep-rooted understanding that thuggery and illegal violence have no place in our country.

The attorney general is dismissive of accusations of violent crimes by the army and police from Amnesty International and other institutions. They are biased and selective, he says. He usually resorts

to sweeping rejections of wrongdoing and denials of any state sanctioned policy of torture.

Unfortunately for Sayed-Khaiyum, Brigadier-General Mosese
Tikoitoga, a handpicked successor to Bainimarama as FMF commander, has a different story. He reportedly admitted in an interview in
an Australian newspaper that citizens had been beaten and tortured
by the military regime. "I wouldn't deny that these things happened,"
he was quoted as saying. He then claimed a lot of the victims were

> trying to instigate violence ... If you let them continue to have
> a voice, you create a potentially dangerous environment. So it
> was the lesser of two evils.

The people of Fiji know the truth about innocent people who
were "taken" to the barracks for special treatment. Brigadier-General
Tikoitoga did not last as head of the army. He was sent to Ethiopia as
ambassador amid speculation that he had presented criticism of
Sayed-Khaiyum to Bainimarama.

In their campaign of incarceration and mistreatment, the military
cast their net widely. Here are some accounts of what happened to
victims:

# Ulai Taoi

I know Ulai Taoi. He is a great champion of the cause of advancing
the role of Fijians in commerce and is a former president of the
Fiji Indigenous Business Council which is now a much-weakened
institution. This is an edited and shortened version of his account of
what happened to him when he was "taken to the barracks" and

detained for 24 hours on Friday, 11<sup>th</sup> May 2007. He was assaulted by a group of soldiers; threatened, subjected to abusive language, forced to sleep naked on the floor of his cell and deprived of sleep. His ordeal was reported on Radio New Zealand. He told the RNZ journalist that he felt he had to speak out so that people would know what was happening, He said he had forgiven those who had abused him.

Ulai wrote that he received a call at 12.50pm on May 11 from someone claiming to be Pita Driti, one of Bainimarama's senior officers. He had a leading role in the coup. Later he fell foul of Bainimarama and ended up in prison for allegedly planning to remove the dictator from power. He had a particular problem about Aiyaz Sayed Khaiyum's role in the dictatorship.

According to Ulai this first conversation with Driti was full of abuse and threats. Driti apparently claimed that Ulai's company was the originator of a certain blogsite on the Internet. Ulai reportedly said he had no idea about this blogsite. He then told Driti that he was not afraid of the army officer's threats. If Driti really was a man, they could meet somewhere one to one to square things. The phone went dead.

Ulai reported that he asked his office administrator to trace the call because he thought it might have been a prank. But, again, the same voice answered. There was, said Ulai, a tirade of abusive language. Ulai repeated his willingness to meet with the caller face-to-face to fix things. Driti, if it was him, said he was in Nadi and would deal with this matter when he returned to Suva. Ulai said he looked forward to meeting him.

Ulai said an hour later a tall man in civilian dress came to his office and asked for him. The visitor, who was well-built, had not shaved. He suggested that Ulai should go to the army camp for questioning and directed him to a rental car waiting downstairs. He gave instructions for Ulai to leave his mobile phone in the office.

When they reached the Queen Elizabeth barracks soldiers removed from his pocket a $20 note and some coins, a handkerchief and notebook. He was shown into a cell beside the gate. Guards took his photo. Ulai said he realized he was truly confined and his thoughts were for his wife and children. A guard asked him to take a call which was from the person who had said he was Pita Driti. He indicated he would see Ulai when he returned to Suva.

After a while, a tall officer appeared at the cell door with a sergeant and a corporal. He figured the tall officer was Lt-Col Ului Mara (Commanding Officer Fiji Infantry Regiment). He recognized his face from newspaper photos. The Lt-Col was a son of the former president, Ratu Sir Kamisese Mara, and was a strong supporter of Commodore Bainimarama. He too was devoured by the Bainimarama upheaval. After being implicated with Pita Driti in a plot to allegedly remove the Bainimarama military government, Lt Col Mara made a dramatic escape to Tonga in a Tongan naval ship and was given sanctuary by his relative the late King of Tonga, King George Tupou IV. At the end of 2016 he was still living in exile in the Kingdom. To his credit he did issue a media statement from Tonga that he was prepared to be accountable for his actions.

In his account of his experience at the barracks, Ulai said Lt Col Mara asked what he was doing there and asked why he had challenged his senior officer, presumably Pita Driti. According to Ulai "abusive gutter language" started.

Ulai said Lt Col Mara then asked what he had contributed to his province and the nation. Ulai responded that he was from Vanuavatu in Lau and ran a business employing 10 people.

He mentioned he was president of the Fiji Indigenous Business Council with 152 member companies. He did not disclose that during the time of my SDL government he had been a member of several statutory boards.

Ulai reported that Lieutenant Colonel Mara gave instructions for Ulai's clothes to be removed, except for his under wear.

---

I peeled off my shirt and pants, handed them to the guards

and sat on the bare floor ... I began to think and pray for God's deliverance as it was close to the Sabbath ... however, deliverance did not come.

After a while the same regimental sergeant major arrived and questioned me about my political views and my answering his boss which I assumed to be Lt Col Ului Mara.

After 10 minutes a masked officer, a fair bloke with one pip, which I noticed, rushed to my cell door and warned me 'O na veka bogi ni kua ni boko na icina, raica o na veka.' (You will shit tonight once the light is turned off.) He disappeared as soon as he uttered those threatening words.

I figured from those words that this is a tactic to break, intimidate, cow and create fear in the victim. I also weighed that given my situation retaliating will not be possible. However, their punches will be calculated and targeted at spots to cause less visibility. I began to psyche myself mentally and physically should it come to this worse scenario.

After 10 minutes, I was visited by a person in civilian clothes. He dragged a chair into my room and referred to me as Mr Taoi. He was polite ... this was Lt Col Kolinisau, if I am correct, from Rewa.

He mentioned that my laptop and mobile 'phone had been picked up by his people from my office. They suspected that my company was the originator of this new blog website that was cursing the army and flashing a lot of misinformation. He spoke politely and lifted my hope in such a situation. I said that because my laptop was locked, I can allow them into it for viewing once it is brought to me. He left after about 10 minutes.

The sergeant in charge of the guardhouse was a polite person. He brought me my mattress, offered me a meal which I refused as I had to condition my body for the night.

Under a heading, Terror at Night, Ulai wrote that at a time he thought was between 9pm and 10pm, he heard shuffling and a whisper to turn off the light. What happened next was an illustration of the kind of physical torment and humiliation that countless victims suffered.

"I knew that this was it," Ulai wrote.

---

The private in charge unlocked my cell gate together with the same masked officer that had warned me earlier in the day, only this time the uniform had changed; he had on green t-shirt and trousers like black training pants, with a black balaclava slightly above his eyebrows.

He pushed me into the working area and threw my pants at me as I was still in my underwear. I figured there were six to eight soldiers wearing similar work-out uniforms. They started throwing punches just as I got my right leg into my pants. I buckled but I knew I had to remain standing to refrain (sic) the kicks. One of the soldiers ... pushed me outside and continued punching. They made me hop on my left leg while kicking and throwing punches. I dropped onto the ground but got up again to save the kicks, bruising my left knee and below my forearm. They stopped when a van, maybe a Pajero, maroon in colour I think, flashed its light from in front of the road and drove past. This gave me time to take in some quick breaths and steady myself. They then pushed me into my cell and sat me down, and by this time I was dazed but well aware of what was happening around me. I recognized this fair officer again, the officer in charge of this group, he squeezed my mouth, cursed and threw punches into my face causing a cut on my right lower lip. However, I knew these punches were calculated to limit marks and scars. They left as soon as they finished with me. The incident must have taken about 20-30 minutes.

I received a gash on my lower right lip, bruise under my forearm, bruise on my left knee and bruise on my right lower cheek. I continuously have pain in my lower right back, I guess the result of a kidney punch.

As soon as this group left, the private in charge requested my pants. I dropped my pants and gave it to him. I laid on my mattress in my underwear all night. The interrogation did not end. This time by another private officer.

I also overheard 'phone conversations that Pita Driti ... will be delayed ... and should arrive on Saturday afternoon. This was my greatest concern as I was on his turf, having challenged him to a fair fight.

---

Every now and then, said Ulai, the soldier-private would stand in front of his cell door and ask questions about members of the Fiji Indigenous Business Council. Ulai felt that based on common origins, if he told the soldier everything, he would assist him.

---

I told him I was a Christian and will tell him the truth ... He was accompanied by another soldier who swore at me and threatened to punch me up. From the body language of the private in charge I felt he was not at all serious but just trying to intimidate me. He then asked me for the list of FIBC members and suggested one of us was operating this blogspot website. I willingly gave him 30 of our members and told him they were honest people. I could furnish more names once he provided me with my laptop.

Once he stood in front of my cell and commanded me to crouch...with my hands on my ears for five minutes. I did this.

I told him that I will seek forgiveness and surrender but will only tell them the truth as there was nothing to hide."

Towards the early morning, Private 'Waimaro' requested

the names, company names and 'phone numbers of the board members of the Fiji Indigenous Business Council. I obliged and said that with my laptop I can provide...... a full list of FIBC members.

He ordered me to do 20 press-ups which I did. I was offered a cup of tea and bread which I accepted. However, I barely ate as my mind was on meeting Driti. I continued to drink water.

Between 7-8 in the morning, an older person in civilian clothes and army boots rushed to my door. He cursed me and threatened to punch me, He ordered that I take off my underwear and threw it out the window. He also removed the mattress I was sitting on. I...sat down naked on the floor. Sometime later, another soldier about the same age .... rushed to the cell door and cursed me. He threatened to punch me.

---

Ulai reported that twenty minutes later, three MPs (military police) stood in front of his door stating that it wasn't appropriate to reply to commanding officers.

The senior person spoke softly in the Lauan language. One asked him if he knew Sikeli who worked for Colonial (an insurance company).

A soldier told Ulai he was a Chinese, not a Fijian. Another appeared and asked whether Ulai was related to me (Qarase). He revisited questions asked by the other soldiers.

---

What was the significance of the blue ribbon I wore on my shirt pocket? How was FIBC associated with SDL? Do we agree with the current situation, and so forth?

---

Again Ulai was ordered to squat and pull his ears.

About 12am I think, I requested my underwear. This was handed to me indirectly, hanging from the window ledge. I laid down on the bare floor using my water bottle as my pillow.

Close to 2pm, said Ulai, his cell door opened while he was still lying down. Col Pita Driti in full uniform entered. He was accompanied by a major, bodyguard and driver.

Ulai stated that he and Driti shook hands. Driti was apologetic for what happened.

I also was apologetic for what I may have caused and asked his forgiveness. He crouched low and sat cross-legged in the other corner opposite me. He ordered his officers to disappear, and my clothes was brought to me. I was overwhelmed by this gesture and sobbed to know that my prayer was answered, and GOD was real. I also was overwhelmed to realize that in any human being is respect and dignity.

We sat talking for about five minutes about the situation. He raised his concerns and why I was brought up for questioning. I also shared with him our concerns as FIBC members. After which I requested we have a word of prayer. He obliged and I prayed ... we shook hands again and left the cell. I requested my laptop and mobile 'phone and he arranged to have it delivered to me in the evening. Col Driti asked how I was going home, and I said I did not have transport. He offered to have his people drop me in his official car. I arrived home safely at 2.30pm.

# L osena Tubanavau Salabula

L osena was a minister of State in the prime minister's office. She was a quiet and effective performer. She was taken to the barracks on 8<sup>th</sup> May 2007 between 9.20-10am. She had asked an army officer if someone from the SDL office could accompany her. Mrs Marica Karikaritu, secretary of the SDL women's wing, was permitted to go with her. But she was not allowed to be there when Losena had to face Lt-Col Ului Mara. Another officer was reportedly with Lt-Col Mara. A statement issued on Losena's behalf said she was ordered just to listen to Lt. Col. Mara and say nothing. But she was to relay a message to me and to Ro Teimumu Vuikaba Kepa, minister for Education in my government, who held the very high chiefly position of Roko Tui Dreketi. Ro Teimumu was also the aunt of Lt. Col. Mara.

T he main points of the message she was to convey were that:

- • The SDL Party would never come back to power.
- • The army was not worried about the repercussions of their actions on EU aid of $350 million for the sugar industry. (The aid was cancelled because of the coup and its aftermath). Lt- Col Mara said the army wanted to clean-up.
- • Losena was to tell me to stop making statements from Mavana village.
- • Ro Teimumu Vuikaba Kepa should not say too much.
- • The army was lenient towards the deposed SDL

parliamentarians, but it could throw us all into Naboro prison.

- • The army could come to a SDL parliamentarian's house anytime, even in the middle of the night, if it wished to, to pick up someone.
- • The army was fully informed of what was going on in the SDL office.
- • He did not want to see or speak to Losena again. Next time it would be a different story.
- • The court case against the military by the SDL was a waste of time.

Losena was also interviewed by Radio New Zealand. She said her trip to the barracks had created a lasting impression on her. She said she had felt very intimidated. "I was there with two huge men and I know very well they have the guns with them."

*Radio New Zealand* called me for a comment about the treatment of Mr Taoi and Ms Salabula. I said I would continue to make public comments adding that freedom of expression was guaranteed under the constitution which the army said it was upholding. I would continue saying what needed to be said. I had a duty to express my views and to speak the truth. I expressed my extreme disappointment because we had been assured by interim Attorney General, Mr Aiyaz-Khaiyum, that people would no longer be rounded up by the military and taken up to the barracks. The radio station recalled that in March, Bainimarama had stated that the military would not condone the use of force and was responsive to public views on the abuse of human rights. It also reported that in an earlier statement, Commodore Bainimarama had said all cases of human right abuse would be independently investigated by the Police.

I said what was happening meant the military government and the military could not be trusted. Ms Salabula was quoted by Radio

New Zealand as saying there was no point in reporting the incident involving her to the police because they were in collusion with the military.

# R o Teimumu Vuikaba Kepa

R o Teimumu Vuikaba Kepa, the aunt of Roko Ului Mara, holds one of Fiji's highest chiefly titles. She is addressed as Marama Bale na Roko Tui Dreketi. Her authority extends throughout Rewa province and the Burebasaga confederacy. The military decided to move against her for her offer on behalf of Rewa to host the 2009 Methodist conference. At that point the military had the Methodist Church in its sights.

Ro Teimumu gave an account of what happened in a speech to the Social Democratic Liberal Party (SODELPA).

In mid 2009, 16 policemen took me from my home in the dead of night. I was first placed in a cell at the Central Police Station and later moved to another cell. This one was at the Queen Elizabeth Barracks. My transgression was to offer, on behalf of Rewa, to host that year's Methodist Conference. This was supposedly against the law. But I refused to withdraw the invitation to the Church. That was why I ended up in a cell.

A youngish soldier came to interrogate me. I could tell he was not very experienced. I asked him what he was doing, and what kind of legacy he wanted to leave to Fiji and his children? He did not answer, but hung his head. I then said to

him, "Young man, I am going to pray for you." His answer
was, "Don't pray for me. Pray for Fiji."

---

Ro Teimumu then asked the assembled delegates to pray for "that
confused soldier, that he may be freed from his shame and receive
enlightenment".

# S am Speight Jnr aka Samisoni Tikoinasau

S am Speight Jnr aka Samisoni Tikoinasau held ministerial
positions in my governments. He is the elder brother of George
Speight who led the insurrection which toppled Mr Chaudhry's
government in

May 2000. His son, Henry Speight, is a famed rugby league star
in Australia. Mr Speight (snr) was a victim of military thuggery. He
had to wear neck brace for the injuries he received and went to
Australia for urgent medical attention. He is still in Australia.

Mr Tikoinasau was detained at the Queen Elizabeth barracks
during February 2011 and was beaten repeatedly until he lost
consciousness. Amnesty International reported that the military
continually denied knowledge of Tikoinasau's whereabouts to his
wife and family members during his three days detention.

Amnesty reported that human rights activists who visited the
barracks to obtain more information on Mr Tikoinasau, said the military threatened them and warned them to keep quiet, or they themselves would be beaten.

.  .  .

In a statement Mr Tikoinasau said he was at our SDL head office on Monday, 21st February, when a group of men in civilian clothes arrived and ordered me to get into a waiting utility vehicle. He reported being locked into a concrete cell at the barracks. The cell had a thin dirty sponge mattress with no pillow or cover. The walls of the cell were also dirty. A soldier asked about him about a certain DVD and threatened him.

The next day, according to his statement, Mr Tikoinasau was kept locked up with virtually no meals and without a shower. He said at around 3am on 23rd February he was awakened by loud shouting and boots to his head.

---

I was ordered to crawl on my stomach along the narrow corridor towards the guardroom. As I was crawling, severe verbal abuse and kicks were directed at me until I was lying on the floor (on my stomach) of the guardroom proper. These men numbered five or six in total with a few of them wearing scarves to conceal their faces.

They then proceeded to interrogate me about the existence of a certain DVD containing material that was, in their view, critical of the military regime. I acknowledged the existence of the DVD, and they continued to exert more pressure in the form of torture tactics in their effort to ascertain the source of the DVD and to whom I had passed the disc on to.

As I was lying on the concrete floor, hot water was poured beside my hips and legs to intimidate me and there was the continued use of an M16 rifle butt on my back and head. There was no let up in the torrent of abuse and the threats to kill me. I was at one stage made to sit on a chair where I was slapped and punched.

I was made to lay my hands on a table where they

proceeded to bend all of my fingers and thumbs backwards to almost breaking point, resulting in excruciating pain. With the blows to my face and head, I experienced moments of dizziness. As part of this assault one of them had armed himself with a chair and threatened to smash it on me. I was then dragged outside the guardhouse onto the road and ordered to run along the road in the camp, and then to run onto a field, which I presumed to be a parade ground. The soldier ordering me to do this was in possession of an iron rod barricade shaped as an X.

As I returned to the guardroom, I received more blows and swears and abuse of a very violent nature. An extremely disturbing and humiliating element of the violent treatment that I was receiving was the incident where I was on the cement floor lying face down receiving blows on my back and head and my head being stepped on by a boot. The soldier whom I identified as Penioni Naliva (reportedly closely associated with Bainimarama) was armed with a M16 rifle and I was shocked when I felt the metal barrel of the gun forcing my shorts down from the hip exposing my buttocks and to my horror he attempted to force the point of the gun into my rear end. I immediately turned over and asked him what was he trying to do and to which he responded by swearing and confirming his intentions. I struggled to my feet and was further assaulted. I heard one of the assailants cautioning the others to be careful that I did not incur any visible injury. I interpreted this as their efforts in trying to conceal the physical abuse that was being inflicted upon me.

The assault and interrogation seemed to last forever and the swear words used in the Fijian language were of the most degrading imaginable. This continued until I was ordered to go back to the cell and they left.

A military police on duty came to see how I was and

apologized for the treatment that I had received, I asked him what the time was and was told it was around 0420hrs.

During the course of Wednesday the 23$^{rd}$ I was not given any medical treatment and I did not eat anything ... my face was swollen and bruised with swelling on my fingers that were subject to bending. I had very

severe and sharp head pains to my neck, back and body. There was also swelling sustained to my head.

At around 2230hrs on Wednesday evening the military police on duty informed me that they had been advised that I was to be released. One of the men who had been part of the beatings and interrogation appeared and warned me not to engage or try and do anything to oppose the regime and that next time I would be taken out of the camp in a coffin. He swore at me and told me to find my own way home.

I walked out of the military camp and made my way slowly to the main road being careful to try and avoid traffic coming out of the camp in case they changed their mind to have me re-detained. My family picked me up from the lower Mead Road and from there I asked to be taken to the hospital in Suva. There was no resident doctor however I was attended to briefly by a contracted intern who gave me a pain killing injection. I left the hospital at around 0130 hrs in a disorientated state and was taken to Nadi airport to catch a flight to Australia for further medical treatment and to avoid further illegal persecution.

---

In a note to his report, Mr Tikoinasau said:

---

The two soldiers who were identifiable to me out of the six who were responsible for the beatings, interrogation and abuse were one Penioni Naliva and Siwatibau Rabuka. I was informed by sources within the military camp that these soldiers are part of a special Hit Squad acting under the direct orders of Frank Bainimarama.

---

In its statement on the treatment of Samisoni Tikoinasau, Amnesty International also mentioned the reported detention and beating of several trade unionists and politicians in the preceding week. This indicated to Amnesty that the human rights situation in Fiji was worsening.

The organization added:

---

Speight's detention and torture followed the recent arrest of a number of trade unionists and politicians who were also threatened and beaten by military officers at the Queen Elizabeth Barracks. Those who were beaten up include trade unionists Felix Anthony and Maika Namudu and two politicians. They have subsequently been released, but there are continuing fears for their safety.

Amnesty International is gravely concerned for the safety of activists and government critics as another crackdown begins in the country.

---

Mesake Koroi, a genial and relaxed character, is one of Fiji's best- known journalists. He has worked for leading media outlets including the *Fiji Times* and had a senior position in the now defunct *Daily Post*. I know him very well because we are related, and he is my traditional spokesperson (*matanivanua*). What follows is his account of his experience at the Queen Elizabeth barracks. The then

Major Sitiveni Qiliho (now Brigadier General and Commissioner of Police) features in Mesake's encounter with the military.

# M esake Koroi

---

When my wife Maria called me at work on that Saturday afternoon ... I was at work at the *Daily Post* newspaper. Maria was quite hysterical. Amid her sobbing and crying out, I picked up the message that a twin cab filled with armed soldiers was looking for me. I advised her to calm down and said I would be coming home immediately. The atmosphere at home was tense. The family had not expected to see me. They thought the soldiers would have apprehended me as I was driving back from the Post.

My wife relayed the order that I was to report to Colonel Roko Ului Mara at the military camp at 8am sharp. I wondered why Colonel Mara wanted to see me. Here was I, a very insignificant person being sought out by the most powerful group in Fiji. Why me? I asked myself. I must be really important. Maria had earlier warned me not to make light of the matter, "These men are armed. They could mean trouble."

Perhaps they wanted to hire me as their public relations officer. Their general PR was very bad, and they needed to dramatically improve it to lift their image after their treasonous act.

During the weekend I focussed on the possibility that I might be in uniform on Monday morning. I remembered my experience during my military cadet training at school where the instructor constantly reminded us that in the army "you are trained to become a dog. You kill first before you think." I made up my mind, then and there, that I would not be a good soldier. I couldn't kill a fly, let alone a fellow human being.

By Monday morning my feelings were mixed. Doubt was beginning to rise in my mind. Our office driver, Api Mataitoga, himself a military reservist, arrived at 7 to collect me. I sought his opinion. He smiled and said, "Let's wait and see who meets us at the gate."

At 8 sharp we were there. Api reported to those on duty that I had arrived to see Colonel Roko Ului Mara. We were told to wait. As I sat in the car, Api tapped my knee whispering, "Oh, oh, here's trouble. You'd better have your wits about you. Don't talk unless you are told to."

Marching towards us was Major Qiliho. Standing beside our vehicle, he bent down, adjusting a hand pistol strapped to his leg. A shiver ran down my spine. Api's next words calmed me. "That's intimidation. He's trying to scare you and show who's in control."

Before I could further collect my thoughts, Qiliho yelled at me, "You follow me!"

I hopped out of the car and did as he had asked. Api indicated he would wait for me.

I was taken to a conference room. It had a large table with chairs around it. I was ordered to sit down. Qiliho sat directly opposite me. He removed his pistol, cocked it, and placed it on the table facing me. He didn't say a word. Neither did I. We just stared at each other. I began to think and then surprisingly I began to form a plan. He was no bigger than me, perhaps slightly taller, but I was sure I could handle him. I thought I could just stand up, grab the pistol, lift the table, and push it over Qiliho. Then I would hold him in captivity just like in the movies, but this was no movie, this was real.

As my mind was drifting, the door burst open. A man in full uniform with all his decorations stood there. Qiliho sprang to his feet, and so did I, spontaneously, out of fear I suppose.

"Sit down," the new arrival barked. "I'm Colonel Driti. Col. Mara is not able to meet you. He asked me to talk to you instead."

I must have said something aloud, unwittingly, because I was told in no uncertain terms that I should shut up and speak only when I was told to.

Driti continued: "We know everything about you. Who is this man Qurukutu, who is a regular correspondent in your newspaper? He's been rubbishing us in almost all his utterances. He even referred to us as "kutu sebe" (bed bugs). You are a grandfather, think of your children and grandchildren. We've taken over government and are prepared to die for our action ... we do not want to kill, unless we have to, you included. How dare you smuggle Qarase's grandchildren out of Suva? Your paper has been rubbishing the army. You don't know how powerful we are? You are a small person like Qurukutu. Why are you trying to put a spanner in the works? I tell you that will not work. The only thing saving your skin now is because I feel sorry for you. That's a warning to you, overstep the mark and we'll come after you."

As Driti continued with this verbal attack, I was reminded of the famous words of Shakespeare, 'the pen is mightier than the sword'. Only this time, the sword seemed to be mightier than the pen.

I tried to speak out but was sworn at and told to shut up. Qiliho, my escort, moved from the other side of the table and grabbed my neck, trying to choke me. I was in pain and if he had continued for much longer, I could have been a goner. He only let go when Driti intervened. This changed the mood of the meeting. For the first time, I saw the human side of Driti.

He ordered the maniac to leave me alone, and to fetch some tea.

This was the first of 13 encounters with the military leading to the final closure of the *Daily Post*. A week after my encounter at the barracks, what appeared to be a military "goon squad" entered my compound at Vuci Road, Nausori, and smashed my car and that of my daughter. It was around 3am. I was awakened by what I thought was a car travelling on the road with a punctured tyre. But the thumping sound appeared to be stationary. I put on the porch light and saw a number of men running away from my driveway towards the main road where they boarded a moving vehicle and sped off towards Nausori.

I looked at the remains of my car and my daughter's vehicle. They were complete write offs. The Nausori police came to investigate, but I've yet to hear from them; nor have I been compensated for my loss.

Perhaps my most humiliating experience with the army was when a group of armed soldiers came to my office at Vatuwaqa and arrested me. It was about 9 in the morning and I was farewelling a friend. As he left, a giant of a man in military uniform, armed to the teeth, stood at the door and announced that I was to be escorted to the camp. The *Daily Post* employees had just been settling into their work routines, but the unexpected military presence attracted a lot of attention and the workers came to see what was happening. As I walked down the staircase, some of the female staff were crying. The best I could do was to wave at them and assure them that I would be back on Friday to sign the pay cheques.

At the camp, I was pushed into a concrete cellblock and locked up. I was given a dirty mattress and a bottle of water. At midday, a plate of food arrived, I wasn't hungry, so I didn't eat. Instead I drifted off to sleep. I was rudely awakened when some drips of water landed on my face. A man, obviously returning from a road run, was leaning over me. I tried to sit up. My unwelcome visitor punched my face and banged my head against the concrete hall, I saw a thousand stars. The road runner said he was going to beat me up and kill me, if he had to. He pressed my neck against the wall as if to choke me.

Using all my strength I stood up and pushed him aside ready to fight him off. I found myself giving him a piece of my mind, which somehow checked his aggression. Amazingly he accused me of trying to create trouble for the army, by staging a hunger strike. This was because I had not eaten lunch! He punched me in the belly, telling me that I would be fixed up in the night. My body would be cut into pieces, which will be placed in a body bag and dropped off at my home. When he left, I sat there staring at the blank wall. I noticed a column of ants, busily digging into the untouched food on my plate, carrying it away. To keep my mind off the possibility of the night time threat, I decided to count how many ants were busy taking the food. There were about 2,500 of them. I thought it's a pity that they were running around free, while innocent humans were locked up and subjected to all kinds of torture.

When I was released, I wrote about my experience in the *Daily Post*. The article was published in a book titled '20 years on', examining how Fiji had performed 20 years after the first coup.

Surprisingly I really slept well that night. I awoke at daylight to the familiar voices of my wife and daughter talking to the guards. They had brought me a change of clothing. It was a relief to hear their voices and naturally I was relieved that the night squad did not come to put me in a body bag.

An hour later a guard told me that a vehicle was waiting to take me home. I told him that I wanted to be dropped at the office as it was Friday and I had to find ten thousand dollars to pay my staff. He just laughed and wished me well. As I walked towards the van, he asked me what I had done. I told him I hadn't the slightest idea. He shook his head and said, "I'm sure you have better things to do than being locked up for no reason at all".

I had many other experiences with the military, but I think it would be absurd and plain stupidity for me to write about them.

---

Fiji-born Ballu Khan is a New Zealand citizen. He had business interests in Fiji.

## Ballu Khan

Mr Khan was apprehended near Delainavesi and beaten savagely amidst allegations of an assassination plot against Bainimarama. He suffered a broken jaw and broken ribs, and was having trouble speaking. New Zealand Prime minister Helen Clark said she was "absolutely appalled" about what had happened. She said the New Zealand High Commission had been prevented from seeing Mr Khan, and he was also unable to get proper hospital care, while he was kept in detention. When the High Commission staff did get to see him, he had difficulty talking because his face had been so beaten up.

Ms Clark said Mr Khan had been surrounded by guards at night. One of the guards had taken part in the assault on him. Ms Clark said all this was "absolutely terrifying and no person should be treated like this".

Later, in a TV interview in New Zealand, Mr Khan described members of the Bainimarama regime as thugs.

---

F ather Kevin Barr is a well-known advocate for social justice concentrating on the need for increased wages to offset poverty. He writes here about what happened to him when a letter he signed appeared in a newspaper letters column. This account is available online.

## A SURPRISING DAY IN MY LIFE - Father Kevin Barr

---

On the 8th January 2013 The *Fiji Sun* published a short letter I had sent in to them. The letter noted that a change was to be expected in the Fiji Flag to represent changed realities in Fiji.

With tongue in cheek, I asked: "Is the rumour true that the Union Jack is going to be replaced with a small version of the Chinese flag to show that our old allegiance to Britain is being replaced with a new allegiance to China?"

On the morning of the 10th January I was at my desk at the PCN Office when the phone rang and someone who said he was a Colonel in the prime minister's Office asked if this was my number. I said it was and he hung up. A few minutes later I received a call from the prime minister. I greeted him and wished him a happy New Year. Then in a very angry voice he said that I should apologise to the people of Fiji for my letter concerning the Fijian flag in the newspaper. I said that I thought it expressed a real concern with a touch of joking humour.

The PM said it was irresponsible coming from a recognised leader in the community. He stated he was not a Catholic but a Methodist. He then called me "a fucked-up priest" and said I had become anti-government. He said he used to try and help me but would do so no longer. I said I would be prepared to come and speak with him. Instead he repeated I was a "fucked up priest", threw in a few swear words, told me to go back to where I came from and put down the phone. His tone was angry and really over the top.

Our Director (Semiti Qalowasa) and Assistant Director (Savu Tawake) were in the room and were able to pick up most of the angry statements of the prime minister. They were rather shocked and remarked that the words about China must have hit a sore spot.

A few minutes later there was a text message on the phone from the prime minister which read: "I think you owe the people of Fiji an apology for your childish comments. You give all Catholic priests a bad name. ". It seemed more of a calm message. I replied saying I was sorry if he was upset by my letter and I apologise. However, many people were concerned about the influx of Chinese into Fiji. I said I would always be happy to meet with you and discuss issues. I am not anti- government but disappointed with some developments.

I was about to go to lunch when another texted message arrived saying: "Fuck U arsehole. Stay well away from me." I texted back: "Thankyou Sir for the nice words. If you want me to apologise I will do as you wish."

As I was having lunch another text arrived: "Start saying your goodbyes Father Kevin James Barr, Australian national, work permit as a missionary, expiry date for permit 31/12/2013." I did not reply. Then came the final text: "Go and be a missionary in China".

I laughed as there was a touch of humour there.

When I returned home about 4.15 there was an

apologetic call from the Ministry of Housing saying they had been directed by government to withdraw my membership as a Member of the Housing Authority and Public Rental Board and that a letter would soon be delivered to me on that issue. In some ways I was expecting this vindictive reaction. I also suspect that others apart from the PM were involved. The Land Force Commander is noted for his coarse language and the AG for his vindictiveness.

What surprised me was not only the coarse language used by the prime minister but his over-the-top angry and uncontrolled reaction. I have heard that he has treated others in a similar way and aims to intimidate.

Those who heard of the above exchanges were shocked and very concerned that the prime minister could act in this way. They were also concerned for me. I do not intend to be intimidated.

I am writing this account of events for the records of Archbishop Mataca and the Australian High Commission in case there are further repercussions. I may also share it with a few close friends.

(Fr Kevin J. Barr)

---

Kenneth Zinck is usually the life and soul of any party he goes to. He likes to sing and play the guitar, and was always cheering on the Fiji team at the annual Hong Kong Sevens rugby tournament. He is also dedicated to trade unionism and to the needs of the common people. Kenneth was minister for Labour, Industrial Relations and Productivity in my government following the 2001 elections.

. . .

# K enneth Zinck

A fter a relative of Bainimarama heard Mr Zinck making derogatory comments about the military leader in a Suva social club, he was arrested by soldiers. He claimed to have been subjected to degrading treatment at the main barracks, including being forced to run around the grounds and jump over drains, with soldiers carrying automatic weapons chasing after him. He was then allegedly made to stand under a spotlight, with soldiers standing beside him, warning him not to make further statements against Bainimarama.

Mr Zinck, however, continued to speak out and write critical letters to the newspapers. He said he was taken twice more to the barracks and had again been abused. Finally he escaped from Suva after a hectic car chase through the streets. He gained entry to Australia where he lives in exile. A regime's spokesman had said there was no truth to what Mr Zinck has been saying.

---

D r Brij Lal is a prominent Fiji academic, author and historian. He was one of the commissioners who conducted the research and consultations for the 1997 constitution and authored a report which formed the basis for the drafting of the document. It was unanimously passed by parliament and the Great Council of Chiefs. Professor Lal was a victim of military abuse, although he did not suffer direct physical mistreatment. However he was deported to Australia, where he works, because he is regarded in Fiji as some kind of "security risk" and remains there in exile with his wife Padma, who is also an accomplished Fiji-born academic. She is the sister of the economist, commentator and writer Dr Wadan Narsey. The government consistently refuses to lift the ban on their return.

Bainimarama and Sayed-Khaiyum simply do not like the couple, and therefore they should not be allowed in the country. What about their rights to live in the place where they were born?

# Dr Brij Lal

The scholar was kept in detention on 4th November 2009 at the QEB Barracks while he awaited deportation to Australia. Colonel Qiliho was his main abuser. Qiliho reportedly spat at him; during his interrogation Dr Lal's reading glasses were somehow broken. The interrogation, he said, was very unpleasant, marked by intense verbal abuse, foul language and explosive anger. He confirmed there was no actual physical abuse, but added that he wouldn't wish the experience he had endured on his worst enemy. He had been detained in a cell for three hours and told that some of his comments about the expulsion of the Australian ambassador James Batley were unacceptable to the military, and were inciting people. He had to leave the country within 24 hours. He said it was scary being driven in a military truck, surrounded by soldiers without knowing where he was going and how long he would be in detention. He felt uncertainty and anxiety. Professor Lal declared he had no regrets for statements he made about coups and it was absurd for him to be considered a security risk. He felt there was something vindictive and personal about what had happened. Meanwhile he's still in exile while Bainimarama claims that Fiji is some sort of model democracy.

# Laisa Vulakoro

Laisa Vulakoro is one of Fiji's most loved singers. She is known as the Queen of Vude for her regular performances of a distinctive rhythmic form of Fijian popular music. She is so accomplished that a writer described her as "Fiji's first living national treasure".

Laisa survived a serious cancer attack and subsequently campaigned to raise funds for cancer victims. She famously shaved off all her hair in solidarity with cancer patients who undergo chemotherapy.

Shortly after the 2006 coup, Laisa wrote a poem expressing her anger and anguish at what had happened. It was published – I think in the Fiji Times. For this peaceful form of protest, Laisa was taken in by the military at night and abused, tormented and humiliated. The experience was so traumatic that she left Fiji for a while to recover.

This is the poem that led to her ordeal:

*Fiji my beloved Fiji*
*You are so precious to me*
*You are the beautiful song that I sing*
*I sing with pride that "you are the way the*
*    world should be"*
*But something has happened to my heart It*
*    has been torn apart*
*My beautiful song is lost to me Oh! Dear God*
*    what are we?*
*Everywhere I turn I see helmets and guns Our*
*    leaders are removed and ordered to run*
*What will our future hold?*

*Where had my freedom gone?*
*Fiji my beloved Fiji*
*I feel so very very sad*
*Watching this coup culture striking our land*
    *Is this a dream or all part of the plan?*
*In the name of a cause they think is just*
*No more than hunger for the power they lust*
    *They tell me they care at the point of a*
    *gun Oh! My beautiful song what has it*
    *become?*
*What song shall I sing to the world right now?*
    *My beautiful melody taken from me*
*Oh where art thou Democracy?*
*What hope have I left for my beloved Fiji?*

# 34

# AMNESTY REPORT: "BEATING JUSTICE"

The regime's terrible record on human rights came under a very harsh spotlight in 2016 when the renowned global human rights organization Amnesty International published a report entitled *'Beating Justice. How Fiji's Security Forces Get Away With Torture'* Significant extracts from this were published locally. The Bainimarama-Sayed-Khaiyum government rejected the report. Sayed Khaiyum later spoke out strongly in parliament against it. He also told the 18th Attorney General's conference that the report was "very flawed." He said it related to past events and "we are saying we need to move forward." That was the best he could do.

Anyone reading the report should be guided by the main facts of what occurred. In light of this the government's denunciation is shallow and unconvincing. The Amnesty report stated that weak institutions, inconsistent leadership, lack of independent oversight, a failure to investigate complaints, interference with justice and legal immunities, undermined attempts to hold officers accountable and created a climate of impunity.

According to the report:

It is difficult to tell how pervasive torture and other ill treatment is in Fiji as information is not publicly available, is actively hidden or dismissed by government and people are afraid to report such abuses.

However in recent years, there have been a number of high-profile torture cases and deaths in custody that highlights the gaps in the investigation and prosecution of such crimes. There is clearly a lack of accountability, especially where the military is involved. Worse than inaction, there has been active protection of some of those accused in these cases.

The report highlights the infamous case of Iowane Benedito and another man. What happened to them was filmed. The film found its way onto youtube and was viewed throughout the world.

Amnesty reported that the film showed security officers (some in uniform) beating and sexually assaulting a half-naked man on the back of a utility truck. The man's hands were cuffed behind his back. Another man was being dragged along the ground by a dog while the assailants could be heard laughing. It was later confirmed by the authorities that this footage shows Iowane Benedito and another person being beaten after they escaped from prison while on remand in late 2012. Like thousands of people here and elsewhere I viewed the youtube film. The level of torture used was extremely savage. One of the main attackers appeared to be trying to break the bones in Benedito's ankle with what looked like a short metal bar. To me this indicated that he might have had specialised training in torture.

Amnesty went on to say it was not clear whether the authorities took any steps to investigate this incident before 2014. It was nearly two years later when the then police commissioner Ben Groenewald ordered the reopening of this investigation.

Commissioner Groenewald told amnesty he reviewed the police

investigation file and saw a statement withdrawing the complaint purportedly signed by Benedito. He believed this document to be false or forged. The case was then reopened in 2014 and properly investigated.

In October 2015 three police officers and two military officers were charged with offences related to Benedito's assault and were still awaiting trial. One of the accused, said Amnesty, was Pita Matairavula who was identified as a former bodyguard of prime minister Bainimarama.

Amnesty was critical of the official reaction to what it called "these brutal acts of torture" when they came to light. It said the government was unequivocally in support of its security officers. It went on to quote from a comment made by Bainimarama which was widely publicized in Fiji and overseas.

This is what he said:

---

At the end of the day I will stick by my men, by the police officers or anyone else that might be named in this investigation .... We cannot discard them just because they have done their duties in looking after the security of this nation and making sure we sleep peacefully at night.

---

So he is saying here that barbaric torture is acceptable as part of law enforcement.

Naturally, Amnesty was critical of Bainimarama's statement: "Such responses from the highest level of government make it difficult to believe there will be genuine accountability in such cases."

Amnesty said that initially the military refused to cooperate with the police over Pita Matairavula. Commissioner Groenewald made damning comments about the attitude of the military to the investigations. He reportedly told Amnesty that Matairavula, whom his officers had attempted to arrest in relation to the Benedito case and in another horrific episode involving Vilikesa Soko, was tipped off about his pending arrest and harboured by the Fiji military. He has, however, now appeared before the courts in relation to these charges.

Groenewald, said amnesty, also noted that when he ordered the suspension of three police officers in connection with Benedito's torture case, all three were immediately recruited into the military by Lt Col Sitiveni Qiliho, who was then Land Force Commander. Qiliho has stated that he felt the officers had been 'abandoned' by the police. Following intervention by the Director of Public Prosecutions, Qiliho later agreed to suspend these officers pending the outcome of the court proceedings.

Amnesty described as alarming the recruitment of men charged with torture into positions where they may commit further abuses. Amnesty noted that Groenewald said he resigned as police commissioner because of this incident. He lodged a formal complaint with the police on 16th February 2016 alleging obstruction of justice by the military.

However, at the time of writing the amnesty report, Groenewald's complaint did not appear to have been investigated by the police. Qiliho was appointed as Police Commissioner after Groenewald's resignation although the Leader of the Opposition, Ro Teimumu Vuikaba Kepa, opposed his appointment.

Amnesty recalled that around the same time as Benedito's torture in 2012, it received medical reports and testimony regarding five other escaped prisoners who were severely beaten when they were arrested. One of them had to have his leg amputated. The organization wrote to Bainimarama about these cases but said it never received a reply.

In the case involving Vilikesa Soko, amnesty related that Soko died from injuries sustained during his arrest. It said the trial judge held that there was evidence that Soko and another accused, Senijeli Boila, had chillies crushed and rubbed on their face and anuses, were hit with sticks and kicked, and that Soko was raped with a stick. A leaked autopsy report revealed that Soko – who was 30 – died as a result of a blood clot on his lung after suffering multiple traumatic injuries including to his rectum and penis.

The amnesty report said in late 2015, over a year after Soko's death, four police officers were arrested and charged with rape, sexual assault and perverting the course of justice. Initial charges of manslaughter were laid but later dropped. By February 2016 a total of eight police officers and one military officer had been charged. All were convicted and sentenced for rape and sexual assault. Pita Matairavula, the military man and former Bainimarama bodyguard, got the heaviest sentence – nine years. Soko's father said he felt the sentences were lenient.

Interestingly two men found guilty of cultivating marijuana were sentenced to 18 and 19 years in prison respectively in January 2017. The severity of these sentences in comparison to those for the brutal death of Vilikesa Soko raises the issue of fairness and equity in the administration of justice.

Amnesty pointed out that apart from Matairavula, a police officer sentenced in Soko's death had also been charged in the Benedito case. The organisation said that had these officers been promptly independently and impartially investigated for their role in Benedito's torture and held accountable through a court of law, Soko's death may have been avoided.

The death of 19-year-old Sakiusa Rabaka from Votualevu, Nadi, is highlighted by Amnesty. It reports that he was killed after he was assaulted by eight military officers and one police officer, at the Black Rock military site in Nadi, in January 2007. The trial judge referred to Rabaka's "degrading and inhumane treatment at the hands of the accused officers". He was stripped, physically and sexually assaulted and subjected to military exercises resulting in severe brain trauma that eventually led to his death.

Here is an extract from the judgment delivered in the Rabaka court case (date of hearing and sentence - Tuesday 17<sup>th</sup> March, 2009):

---

After the deceased was released from custody, he suffered
from severe headaches and vomiting. His body was bruised.
He started having fits. According to medical evidence, the
deceased had an increased pressure in the brain as a result of
fluid such as blood occupying the space in the brain. A CT
scan revealed that the deceased was slightly bleeding between
the two hemispheres of the brain. Albeit the deceased was
conscious and alert in the hospital, his symptoms increased.
Headaches, vomiting and fits increased. A substantial amount
of blood was drained out from the brain after a surgery.
Subsequently, the victim died due to intensive blood clots
inside and outside surface of the brain. The medical evidence
was that the injury was more likely to have been caused by
forceful blunt trauma to the head.

---

Further background to the case was that the military officers
involved were arrested at Nadi Airport as they were about to be
deployed on a UN peacekeeping mission by the RFMF. Amnesty
said this would in affect have avoided accountability of those
involved.

---

While this attempt was thwarted by an eleventh-hour court
injunction, the conviction was undermined by the early
release of officers involved just three weeks into their
sentences.

In March 2009, nine security officers were each
sentenced to an average four years in prison after a lengthy six
weeks trial. Shortly after their sentences were handed down
on 10<sup>th</sup> April 2009, the military government purported to
abrogate the 1997 constitution, dismissed all judicial officers
and imposed strict emergency regulations. Within less than a

month of their conviction, all nine officers were released on a compulsory supervision order.

---

The Amnesty report is critical of Commander Francis Kean (brother- in-law of the prime minister) serving as the Commissioner of Corrections. The report refers to concerns about his suitability for the role, because he is a military officer, "he has a criminal record ... and had made statements in support of corporal punishment, which would amount to torture".

The report goes on:

---

Commander Kean is the current Commissioner of Corrections, after being appointed in March 2016. There are concerns about his suitability for the role, in line with the Minimum Standards Rules, because he is a military officer, he has a criminal record for violent offences and he has made statements in support of corporal punishment, which would amount to torture.

In December 2006, Francis Kean beat John Whippy to death at a wedding. He was initially charged with murder, but pleaded guilty to manslaughter. The court, in sentencing Kean, found there were aggravating factors because Kean punched the victim more than once, including after he was lying on the ground.

Justice Winter said, 'Your serious loss of self-control also aggravates this crime... Kicking this man when he was down demonstrates to me that this was an attack of considerable ferocity. You lost your temper. You resorted to violence. You had to be dragged away from your victim.'

He was sentenced to 18 months in prison. Kean returned to his position as Commander of the Navy immediately after his release from prison in early 2009. In 2011, he was appointed as Acting permanent secretary to the Department of Works, in addition to retaining his position as Commander. Kean was appointed as Commissioner of Corrections on 5 March 2016. He retains his military title.

Kean has not resigned from the military and it is not clear that even if he did so, that he would be able to independently manage prisons administration outside a military command. His closeness to the military and his past criminal record casts a shadow on his appointment, undermining public faith in the Corrections Service.

In addition, Kean has recently spoken in support of Introducing corporal punishment of prisoners. Corporal punishment, which includes flogging, caning, and whipping ... is prohibited by international laws as it violates the absolute prohibition of torture and other cruel, inhuman and degrading treatment or punishment. Prolonged solitary confinement may also violate the absolute prohibition of torture and other ill- treatment.

---

The government, says Amnesty, should appoint a civilian to manage the prisons.

The report provides brief details about what happened to Nimilote Verebasaga who died aged 41, after being assaulted in custody on 5th January 2007. "Verebasaga was assaulted as he was made to crawl on the ground at a military camp. The post mortem report revealed that he died as a result of serious injuries to his vital organs due to the assault. Maika Vuniwawa, a military officer, was convicted of manslaughter on 7th April 2009 and sentenced to three years imprisoned. He was released on 7th May 2009, just a few weeks after being sentenced.

In his rebuttal of the Amnesty report, Mr Sayed-Khaiyum stressed that his government has ratified the United Nation's Convention Against Torture. The ratification, however, contains limitations which indicate, in my view, a continuing ambivalence on torture by Bainimarama. It's almost as though there was hesitation on his part in accepting the convention.

Amnesty stressed that Fiji had "carved out huge chunks" of the convention before ratifying it. Fiji's ratification had a reservation on the definition of torture. Fiji wouldn't owe victims anything if it broke the rules. Meaning it did not agree to be bound by the right for torture victims to obtain redress and to fair and adequate compensation. International scrutiny would be restricted.

Specifically, Fiji did not recognize the competence of the UN Committee Against Torture to conduct confidential inquiries, to receive communications by individuals alleging torture and to receive communications from other States about Fiji's failure to fulfill its obligations. Fiji also did not recognize the jurisdiction of the International Court of Justice.

There is an interesting comment attributed by Amnesty to the attorney general that his government made reservations to various accountability mechanisms because

---

we do not have the level of maturity in our society for people to use that complaints process in good faith to bring legitimate complaints, it would be politically motivated.

---

My personal sense of this is that there will be a number of motivations which might be driven by a continuing sense of grief, injustice and, yes, politics as well. What is wrong with that? Someone might be politically opposed to torture. What is immature about that? It was typical of Mr Sayed- Khaiyum's arrogance that he has decided that we the people do not have the judgment to express grievances in a responsible manner about abuse of our human rights.

Amnesty International dismissed Mr Sayed-Khaiyum's comment. It said: "This explanation is unsatisfactory – the appropriate way to dispute the merits and motivation of individual complaints against the government should be through the complaints process itself, not through the use of a blanket reservation.

---

Because of the absolute prohibition on torture under international law, the attempted reservations by the Fiji government are meaningless in practice. However, it conveys the message that the Fiji government will not only be the sole arbiter of what constitutes torture domestically but also decide when and how people will be held responsible, if at all.

A more likely explanation for Fiji's wide-reaching reservations to the CAT is to avoid scrutiny and accountability measures, which could conflict with the vast constitutional immunities enjoyed by military, police and government officials for abuses committed prior to October 2014.

While ratification of the CAT is a positive step, removing the widespread reservations is crucial to making it more than a symbolic gesture.

---

Amnesty says the Fiji government must ensure that the definition of the offence of torture is in line with international law and that immunities do not undermine the absolute prohibition on the use of torture and prevent victims from accessing justice.

It points out in its report a serious contradiction. Fiji's constitution, it says, contains the right to freedom from torture and other forms of cruel, inhumane or degrading treatment or punishment. However, the constitution also grants extensive criminal and civil immunity to the military, police and other government officials for violations committed between 5th December 2006 and the first sitting of the first parliament elected after the constitution started on 6<sup>th</sup> October 2014.

Said the report:

---

It also continues previous immunities granted under the Limitation of Liability for Past Political Events Decree 2010, which includes immunity for past acts by government officials, including by the military during the 2000 coup and subsequent mutiny (from 19 May 2000 until September 2001) and immunities under the previous 1990 constitution, which related to the 1987 military coup.

---

The report says the immunities have become an integral part of Fiji's coup culture.

---

The immunity protects perpetrators from any civil or criminal liability whatsoever and is made unconditional and irrevocable. In effect, for more than eight of the past 14 years, there is a black hole in Fiji's legal protection against torture and other ill-treatment. Fijians who have suffered torture or other-ill-treatment as recently as two years ago are constitutionally barred from ever seeking redress and perpetrators face no prospect of ever being held to account.

The protection of human rights and civil liberties are sacrificed in the interests of a superficial and subjective notion of 'peace and national security'. Immunity is granted under the pretense of protecting select persons from liability during loosely defined 'political events' such as

the unconstitutional overthrow of an elected government, however it merely entrenches the lack of accountability for human rights violations by the police and security forces.

There can be no justification for torture and other ill-treatment. The prohibition against torture and other ill-treatment under international law is absolute. All states have an obligation not only to prevent and prohibit violations of customary international law, but also to provide victims with access to justice, rehabilitation and other forms of reparations.

These immunities continue to violate the obligation under international law to provide redress to victims of human rights abuses. They also send a destructive message to the people of Fiji – that in certain circumstances and at certain times, anything goes. It is a message that still resonates throughout Fiji.

# More repression; end of SDL

As the years passed the dictatorship maintained and even tightened its grip on the country; people were afraid to speak out; there was constant fear of being "taken to the barracks". Although censors were eventually removed from newsrooms, media coverage was constrained and self- censorship evident. The screws were turned again when the so-called Media Industry Development Decree (MIDA) was introduced. This draconian legislation criminalises journalism and provides for prison sentences for those who offend. At the time of writing it was still in force.

The political rights of citizens and the freedom of political parties were further restricted with the promulgation of the Political Parties Decree in 2012. My attention focused on one particular aspect. Under the decree a citizen/voter who has served a prison term of 12 months or more cannot hold an official position in any political party.

Under the 2013 Bainimarama-Khaiyum constitution a citizen who has served 12 months or more in prison is not allowed to be a candidate in a general election. A person caught under these laws is punished twice – by imprisonment and then by restricting that person's political rights for eight years after the person's release from prison. I have a suspicion these laws were made to remove me from politics.

WHILE IN PRISON, I HAD BEEN IN CONTACT WITH THE LATE MATAIASI RAGIGIA WHO WAS HOLDING THE FORT FOR THE SDL AFTER THE CRUELLY ABUSED MR PECELI KINIVUWAI LEFT FIJI FOR AUSTRALIA. HOWEVER, MR RAGIGIA DIED IN LATE 2012. BY THIS TIME THE POLITICAL PARTIES DECREE WAS IN FORCE. AN OFFICIAL OF THE SDL PARTY CONTACTED ME BY PHONE AT KOROVOU TO SAY IT MIGHT BE NECESSARY TO FORM A NEW PARTY AND WIND UP THE SDL. ONE OF THE REASONS GIVEN WAS THAT, UNDER THE NEW LAW, THE NAME OF ANY PARTY MUST NOT BE IN THE INDIGENOUS FIJIAN LANGUAGE. I THOUGHT THIS WAS AN EXTRAORDINARY INSULT TO THE INDIGENOUS COMMUNITY. BUT THAT IS THE LAW, AS IT STANDS NOW.

I SUGGESTED THAT A CHANGE IN NAME WOULD BE SIMPLE AND THAT THE PARTY COULD REMAIN THE SAME IN ALL OTHER RESPECTS. HOWEVER, THE SDL ELDERS DECIDED TO FORM A NEW PARTY WITH A NEW CONSTITUTION. THE SOCIAL DEMOCRATIC LIBERAL PARTY (SODELPA) THEREFORE CAME INTO BEING. THE SDL WAS THEN DISSOLVED AND WOUND-UP. THIS WAS DISTRESSING FOR ME POLITICALLY SINCE I WAS ONE OF THE FOUNDERS OF SDL. IT HAD BECOME A HOUSEHOLD NAME, PARTICULARLY AMONG THE INDIGENOUS FIJIAN POPULATION. IT WAS A POWERFUL AND POPULAR BRAND.

ALTHOUGH THE PROMULGATION OF THE POLITICAL PARTIES DECREE AUTOMATICALLY DISQUALIFIED ME FROM ANY OFFICIAL POSITION IN SODELPA DUE TO MY IMPRISONMENT, I REMAINED A MEMBER AND SUPPORTER OF THE PARTY. HOWEVER,

SOME RELATIVELY RECENT DEVELOPMENTS ARE MATTERS OF CONCERN TO MANY SUPPORTERS. SODELPA ADOPTED A NEW CONSTITUTION IN LATE 2015. THIS CHANGED THE STRUCTURE OF THE PARTY SIGNIFICANTLY. THREE SENIOR POSITIONS WERE VESTED WITH EXECUTIVE AUTHORITY: THE PRESIDENT OF THE PARTY; THE PARTY LEADER AND THE PARLIAMENTARY LEADER/LEADER OF OPPOSITION. IN ADDITION, THE GENERAL SECRETARY HAD WIDE POWERS. I BELIEVE THIS STRUCTURE WILL LEAD TO DISUNITY AND DIVIDED LOYALTIES.

THE PARTY LEADERSHIP MAY LIKE TO CONSIDER WHAT THE SCRIPTURES SAY ABOUT SERVING TWO OR MORE MASTERS.

> MATHEW 6: 24 - "NO ONE CAN SERVE TWO MASTERS.
> EITHER HE WILL HATE THE ONE AND LOVE THE OTHER, OR HE WILL BE DEVOTED TO THE ONE AND DESPISE THE OTHER."

THE WORD OF GOD IS ALWAYS THE TRUTH. WE SHOULD LEARN FROM IT AND APPLY ITS WISDOM IN OUR DAILY LIVES.

# 35

# CURIOUS CASE OF THE PEOPLE'S CHARTER

In September 2007 the Bainimarama-Khaiyum regime launched an initiative that was supposed to be the salvation of Fiji. It was called the People's Charter. The italics in this account of the charter are mine.

It was to be a miraculous document that would right all the country's wrongs, heal our divisions, provide a sound foundation for national unity, ensure good governance, create economic progress with many new jobs, revitalise education, health and social services and generally make Fiji into some kind of utopia. Poverty, for instance, was to be virtually wiped out by 2015! That was a very severe miscalculation. Ask the people who are still gripped by poverty.

The ideas and policies it contained would be so marvelous that political parties in the future would have no need for manifestos! The charter would be everyone's manifesto! This would all be achieved within the 1997 constitution, which was recognized as Fiji's highest law. It did not seem to occur to those actively working on the charter that in a democratic context political parties offer their own platforms and policies. That's how democracy works.

There are differing versions of how this strange project originated. But despite all the rhetoric about democratic ideals, honesty and openness, in the end it was just a military-regime propaganda effort to gain some form of legitimacy both in Fiji and internationally. In fact Commodore Bainimarama even got to promote it at a session of the United Nations general assembly. He tried to sell it in the region to the Pacific Islands Forum. He didn't get very far with the forum. The strong Bainimarama critic Tuilaepa Sailele Malielegaoi, Prime Minister of Samoa, dismissed the charter as "utter rubbish". "He's trying to replace Fiji's constitution with that People's Claptrap or whatever it is."

Bainimarama's thinking and that of his colleagues seem to be that the international community would be so impressed by this enlightened document it would stop pressuring the government to put Fiji's house in order and get back to democratic elections. The adoption of the charter would somehow offset or even completely neutralize the act of treason of the 2006 coup. That appeared to be the reasoning.

Large amounts of taxpayers' dollars were spent on it - never fully accounted for of course - and consultants were brought in. One of them, a former permanent secretary, John Samy, who was a central figure in the scheme, disclosed that he was being paid $14,000 a month before tax. Meetings were held all over the place to justify the claim that the charter somehow gave voice to the concerns of the people.

The foreword to the charter grandly declared that its overall objective was to rebuild Fiji into a non-racial, culturally vibrant and united, well-governed, truly democratic nation; a nation that seeks progress and prosperity through merit-based equality of opportunity and peace.

It all came to nothing and these days hardly ever gets mentioned. It was clear that the charter would always struggle to gain legitimacy. To me it was just window-dressing, an attempt to divert attention away from the military coup. My party, the SDL, felt the same way and refused to be part of the process. So did a number of other leading organisations and well-known citizens. For the SDL's part, however, we did keep the door open for dialogue. But Commodore Bainimarama has difficulty with the concept of exchanging ideas and differing view points to arrive at a middle ground. He never did respond positively to our overtures. In fact, his attitude to me appeared to be that I should never be allowed to contest another election.

The military did not help their cause when they gave the impression that the charter would be a means of maintaining control. In fact, Lt. Col. Mosese Tikoitoga saw the charter in the context of "forcing people to change their mindset".

He wanted to see leadership by the "right people with right minds". If you didn't agree with the military presumably, your mind wouldn't be right.

The work of compiling the charter was supposed to be independent. But it was never going to be possible to overcome the perception that it was driven by the military and their regime. In fact, Commodore Bainimarama specifically undermined the claim of independence when he went on record as saying that the charter was part of the military's "clean up" campaign.

Remarkably the authors of the charter appeared to believe it would be binding on future governments. This was completely undemocratic and authoritarian. There was a mention of a timeframe of 15 to 20 years for the measures in the charter to become an established part of Fiji's national life.

The final document was signed off by Commodore Bainimarama, who was co-chair of something aligned with the charter called the *National Council for Building a Better Fiji* (NCBBF) along with the late Archbishop Petero Mataca. Interestingly the charter contained proposals for affirmative action which was a pillar of my governments. But after the People's Charter faded from the landscape, Bainimarama-Khaiyum dropped affirmative action completely. I sensed that was a manifestation of Mr Khaiyum's increasing power.

The charter placed emphasis on the constitution. In fact, its first affirmation was that the constitution was supreme and provided the framework for the conduct of government and the people. The aim was to strengthen it. However, this crucial part of the charter was simply abandoned and ignored when on 10<sup>th</sup> April 2009 the military regime purported to abrogate it. (Judge Anthony Gates had famously declared that it was indestructible, and it was not possible for any man to tear it up. The constitution remained in place, he said, until amended by parliament.)

So, with their attempt to abrogate it, the military government was also sabotaging their own People's Charter. In time the constitution which they had used as a foundation for the charter was branded by Bainimarama as no good for Fiji. The moral of this story was that the constitution was there to be exploited or dumped depending on the circumstances. Although its promoters claim the charter was the will of the people, the facts did not support this. There was no secret ballot, citizens were expected to sign their support in the presence of civil servants and even military officers.

At first there was an attempt to claim the charter was endorsed by some 90 percent of the adult population. Then someone must have realized that this was way beyond reason. So finally, the figure of 64.2 percent was decided upon. I'm not sure how the 0.2 percent came into it.

Archbishop Mataca and Mr Samy finally parted ways with Baini-marama-Khaiyum. They saw what had been evident. The regime was not serious about the charter. It was there to serve their convenience.

To the credit of the Archbishop and Mr Samy they were forth-right in expressing their disappointment and concern about the behaviour of the government. They wrote to Bainimarama in November 2011, complaining that his administration had signaled that it had drifted away "from the spirit and key principles" of the charter and that it had betrayed the people of Fiji on its most solemn promises. They were now merely playing lip-service to it and instead of practicing transparent and accountable government, had adopted the might- of-the-military approach to rule in Fiji.

---

# S our lemon

A rchbishop Mataca did try to set up a channel of communication between Bainimarama and me. In this effort to start dialogue to end the crisis gripping the nation, the Archbishop was joined by Rev. Laisiasa Ratabacaca, President of the Methodist Church. I decided to be as optimistic as possible but of course I was familiar with Bainimarama's confrontational approach. His performance in Wellington was still fresh in my mind. I arrived on time at the parliament office for the first meeting. Both the church leaders were waiting. I seem to remember that Bainimarama and I shook hands and we greeted the Archbishop and Rev. Ratabacaca with respect. After sharing a short prayer, Archbishop Mataca explained that the purpose of the meeting was to find common ground and a way to peace. Bainimarama ran true to form. He recited his list of reasons for the military take-over. I had to again remind him politely that the take-over was illegal and an act of treason. It was clear from Bainimarama's demeanour and tone, that there would be no resolution. We were poles apart. For him it was still a case of "my way or no way".

There was a brief respite when morning tea was served. We were given a choice of ordinary tea or lemon tea made with lemon leaves. I opted for lemon tea. In a media briefing afterwards I mentioned this. This got special mention in media reports. It was probably seen as lemon tea diplomacy.

I was grateful to Archbishop Mataca and Rev. Ratabacaca for their efforts.

According to the Archbishop and Mr Samy, people across Fiji society were becoming increasingly disillusioned. The current environment in Fiji, they said, was highly controlled and there was a growing sense of fear among the populace. The interim government had adopted a "strong-fisted" unilateralist approach increasingly alienating the very people that could be playing an active role in building broad-based consensus.

They were critical of the abrogation of the 1997 constitution, introduction of public emergency regulations, restrictions on the media and on basic freedoms and rights, handling of pension funding issues, and imposition of the Essential Industries Decree.

A recent announcement that the new constitution making process would not start till late 2012 had further heightened speculation that Bainimarama was not genuine about a general election being held at the latest by September 2014.

The Archbishop and Mr Samy commented on emerging issues

---

such as a few cabinet ministers holding multiple portfolios, especially you and the attorney general, resulting in whispers... that both of you are being paid exorbitant salaries ... payment of salaries of all ministers being administered outside the government through a contractual arrangement involving a close relative of the AG.

---

(This was through the accounting services of Ms Nur Bano Ali, Sayed-Khaiyum's aunt. The full details of this arrangement were still secret at the time of writing.)

The Archbishop and Mr Samy said Bainimarama's failure to address these had fuelled "the growing perception that you, your ministers and the Military Council are now enjoying power and the benefits associated with it that you will not relinquish it voluntarily; that power has corrupted you all".

They proposed a sweeping list of changes and even attached a draft address to the nation outlining this. Of course, nothing happened. The Archbishop and Mr Samy simply discovered that their agenda was not, after all, the agenda of Bainimarama, his government and the military. It was never evident to me why they and many other people, felt they had a shared common mission with the military dictator and his officers.

On the fifth anniversary of the coup, Mr Samy expressed his disillusionment in a *Radio Australia* interview about what he had seen in Fiji. He said he was aghast at how Fiji's infrastructure had deteriorated rather than improved.

So the People's Charter about which Commodore Bainimarama and the military had been so obsessive went on to the ash heap of history. We will never know the full cost of it to the people of Fiji.

# 36

# FULL MOON AND THE FORUM

It was after he reneged on a commitment to hold elections in 2009 that the Pacific Islands Forum (PIF) suspended the Bainimarama Sayed-Khaiyum government from membership. Bainimarama publicly doubted whether the forum would go ahead with suspension. It was beyond the forum's mandate, he said, to suspend a member nation. Those comments showed how out of touch he was with the mood of the forum and the purpose of the Biketawa Declaration. He had completely misjudged the leaders.

There was a continuing refrain from him at this stage that it was Australia and New Zealand that should be removed from the forum for putting undue pressure on the Pacific Islands. This was not "how we operate in the Pacific", he was quoted as saying. (In fact, his behaviour was an object lesson in how the Pacific does not operate.)

Some forum leaders were becoming openly disillusioned with Bainimarama. Sir Michael Somare, then Papua New Guinea Prime minister, and a regional elder statesman, warned that he was running out of patience. The long-serving prime minister of Samoa, Tuilaepa Sailele Malielegaoi, emerged as an extremely outspoken critic. He did not pull his punches. I had met Tuilaepa at forum meetings and at Commonwealth conferences. He struck me as a no- nonsense person who did not mince his words when he wanted to make a point. Bainimarama's deeds and words brought out the fighting Samoan in him. He was merciless and cutting in his denunciations.

When Bainimarama grouped Samoa with Australia and New Zealand as a source of pressure for Fiji to return to democracy, Tuilaepa in media interviews lectured Bainimarama about his responsibility to comply with the principles on which the forum was established. I quote here from various media accounts including Radio Australia, and Savali Newspaper/Pacnews.

Prime Minister Tuilaepa questioned Bainimarama's state of mind, saying 'he might have been drunk or it may have been a full moon' when he made the comments about Samoa and pressure against Fiji. He thought Bainimarama was quite ignorant of the democratic processes that all forum leaders ought to observe.

"I think he is trying to find some stupid clowns to hide behind his own failure to honour his commitment" (to hold elections.) He flatly accused Bainimarama of lying to the forum. He said Bainimarama sent his "young attorney general", to a leaders' summit in Port Moresby and he "lied through his teeth". Bainimarama and his guns, he said, controlled the road to democracy in Fiji.

---

The last time I looked neither the United Nations nor the Commonwealth have a fund to prop up unelected dictators and coup- installed military regimes.

---

Tuilaepa disclosed that he was receiving communications from NGOs and individuals in Fiji asking him to speak out on Fiji.

Tuilaepa was asked again what he thought of Bainimarama's claims about Samoa, Australia and New Zealand ganging up on Fiji. The Samoan PM suggested Bainimarama had been misquoted by the media.

What he may actually have meant was that the maturity of Samoa's leadership is on par with that of New Zealand and Australia. That's obviously what he meant. Therefore given that seniority he should be keen to absorb my tit-for-tat.

Bainimarama had recently pronounced defiantly that: "no one's going to force us what to do here. We've already decided what's going to happen". What did the Samoan PM think of this? "Well no one is forcing Fiji to do anything," replied Tuilaepa.

The forum is simply asking what his (Bainimarama's) plans for Fiji's road back to democracy are in accordance with the principles of democratic government the forum was established upon. May I also remind the Fiji interim prime minister that Fiji is a founding member of the forum. One of the forum's founding fathers was none other than Fiji's Ratu Sir Kamisese Mara, a distinguished and respected leader whose principles of democratic government the forum stood for in its formative years.

Tuilaepa added that the forum continued to be misled by untruths told by Bainimarama and his representatives. He recalled that at the forum meeting in Nuku'alofa in 2007, Bainimarama told leaders that the general elections in Fiji would be in March 2009.

Again during the recent leaders' summit in Port Moresby, his handpicked attorney general during his presentation to the leaders provided a roadmap for elections which led the forum to set out in its communiqué of the 1st of May a timetable and elections in Fiji by the end of the year. That is the basis of the communiqué that was issued following the meeting. It was based on the Fiji attorney general's presentation to the forum. Now Bainimarama and his attorney general are singing a different tune. Not only did Bainimarama lie to the forum, but also sent his attorney general to lie to the forum leaders. How is the forum to believe these two proven liars?

---

Bainimarama was claiming at this stage that the continuing travel bans by New Zealand and Australia on those associated with the military regime were "counter productive to a return to democracy". Prime Minister Tuilaepa did not agree:

---

Only Bainimarama and his guns control the road to democracy in Fiji. Only Bainimarama controls Fiji's return to democratic rule, not the travel bans.

---

He added that he believed Bainimarama had a problem comprehending the issues involved. He went on to say that Bainimarama "has an awful lot to say for someone who surrounds himself with armed soldiers."

Referring to various media reports, Prime Minister Tuilaepa said that Bainimarama had quietly claimed for himself "back pay of $200,000". "That's stealing money," said Tuilaepa. "And yet he had been telling everybody he needs to clean up Fiji of corruption. I think it's a classic case of do as I say and not as I do." (Bainimarama reportedly eventually repaid the money).

The Samoan PM went even further. He responded to the appointment by Bainimarama of former navy commander Esala Teleni, as commissioner of police, and accusations against Teleni of bringing in religiously contentious policies relating to Hindu and Muslim police officers (see box at the end of this chapter). "That's what mad men who appoint themselves to office do," said Tuilaepa. "They appoint other mad men to positions of power."

# Teleni and his police crusade for souls

Esala Teleni was the central figure in one of the many strange episodes of the Bainimarama military regime. As a senior figure in the military, he was appointed Commissioner of Police although he had no police experience. In 2009 he launched a Christian crusade to fight crime and other social ills. The Commissioner's personal commitment to Christ, whom he called "my Jesus", appeared to form the principle thrust of his national policing efforts. As I remember even the police telephonist had to respond to calls with the appropriate religious greeting. The Commissioner's religious fervour began to express itself publicly when police officers in uniform were required to perform daytime Christian dances accompanied by inspiring music. One of the problems with this was that these routines were taking place when the dancing officers were supposed to be carrying out the standard police work, which is at the centre of any law enforcement effort. But to Teleni, this was all about using spiritual guidance to reduce crime, especially among young people.

There was another problem. Hindu and Muslim police officers felt that they were being evangelized. An article in the Sydney Morning Herald described how rank-and-file and senior officers were stunned to be ordered to attend a carpark preaching rally. Hindu and Muslim officers had to attend too. Teleni got wind that they were unhappy and castigated them in public. It looked as though they would face the sack if they didn't fall into line. Luckily Teleni did not last long as Commissioner of Police. Bainimarama could presumably see that he was an embarrassment and removed him from the position.

Tuilaepa spoke about suppression of dissent and the media in Fiji. "It's a sign of inexperience," he said.

---

A sign of weakness. Every good government needs alternative views to discern its policies. You cannot surround yourself with yes men and expect a yes public to everything you do. You can't forcibly take over the reigns of government and expect people to just shut up. That's stupid ... Those actions are reminiscent of Stalin, Mussolini and Hitler. Well where are they now? And how are they remembered?

---

He asked a question that many people in Fiji think about but are cautious about expressing. Why does Fiji need an army? With pointed sarcasm he said:

---

Perhaps Bainimarama fears a combined canoe attack from Tuvalu and Kiribati, its closest members. That must be it ... This is a region known for friendly people and its pristine environment – a paradise on earth. Having a (interim) prime minister dressed up in army beret and full military guard is a bit ridiculous.

---

The PM said he had been told that Bainimarama was part Samoan and had a Samoan grandmother.

---

I'm tempted to go down to the Lands and Titles Courts and look up his family genealogy in Samoa. Then I'll send for his family matai (chief) in Samoa and tell him to reprimand his long lost descendant in Fiji to give him (Bainimarama) severe censure for being cheeky, being ill-disciplined and having no manners.

---

Never had a prime minister from the region been given such severe tongue lashings to another Pacific PM.

There is another interlude, this one with an especially humorous twist that I feel belongs in my story. It is an excerpt from a book, Palemia (prime minister), by Tuilaepa published in 2017. He described being part of a forum group that went to see Bainimarama. The Fiji dictator was accompanied by Ratu Epeli Nailatikau, then serving as Bainimarama's foreign minister, and the ever-present Sayed-Khaiyum.

Tuilaepa wrote: "Bainimarama told us there was so much corruption he had to stamp out and 'only after stamping it out, we will go back to the barracks'". Tuilaepa said the Australian foreign minister, who was with the forum group, replied: 'Bainimarama, if you are going to wipe out corruption and then you go back to the barracks, it means you will be here for eternity.'

Everybody laughed.

---

Bainimarama said: 'Oh, the chiefs of Fiji are a pack of crooks. The same thing with the leaders of religion. They are telling people not to vote for me. That's it, all the Ratus are crooks.'

'We all looked at Ratu Epeli.

'Then Baini looked at us all looking at Ratu Epeli sitting next to him and he realized what he had said.

Then he said, 'Except for Ratu Epeli'.

---

Tuilaepa said they told Bainimarama that the Pacific leaders were not fools and that "what he was saying was stupid".

---

Announcing Fiji's suspension from the forum on 2nd May 2009, the Chair, Toke Talagi of Niue, said Commodore Bainimarama had failed to return Fiji to democratic governance in an acceptable timeframe. The suspension, he said, was timely given the recent disturbing deterioration of the political, legal and human rights situation in Fiji since 10th April 2009. Mr Talagi said the military regime had confirmed particularly through its recent actions that it rejected fundamental forum obligations and core principles as outlined in the Biketawa Declaration.

"A regime which displays such a total disregard of basic human rights, democracy and freedom has no place in the Pacific Islands Forum," he said.

The forum decision involved implementation of two specific targeted measures taken in accordance with the Biketawa Declaration. Bainimarama, his ministers and officials were suspended from taking part in all forum meetings and events. The military regime was not to benefit directly from forum regional co-operation initiatives or any new financial or technical assistance, unless it was for helping with the restoration of democracy.

---

That was not to be the end of the story. The Melanesian Spearhead Group (MSG) – whose membership includes Papua New Guinea, Solomon Islands, Vanuatu, the Kanak FLNKS from New Caledonia, and Fiji - came into play. I was never much of a fan of the MSG.

In my view it fragmented regional co-operation. The Pacific

Islands Forum had done a good job in fully representing the interests of the region.

Still angered by what he thought was his unjust treatment by the forum, Bainimarama set his sights on becoming head of the MSG thus creating a platform to hit back at the premier regional grouping.

Although MSG members in the forum had supported the decision to suspend Fiji, they had a different approach in their own deliberations. At its meeting in Fiji in March 2011 the members made Bainimarama their chair! Like many other people I felt the MSG, in taking this action, had tarnished its reputation. It had clearly compromised its ideals. As with the forum, the MSG has a set of standards and rules. These strongly affirm the universal nature of democratic principles; consistent with this the MSG espouses a firm commitment to fundamental freedoms, human rights, including indigenous rights, and political engagement based on inclusive dialogue. It stands by the rule of law, judicial independence transparency and accountability.

To me it was bizarre that the MSG had agreed to be guided in their deliberations by the South Pacific's first enduring dictator. The MSG never did adequately explain why it had endorsed as its chair someone who came to power through an act of treason and had rejected the precepts and beliefs that define the organisation.

Bainimarama began to promote the MSG as the main regional grouping. He appeared to base this claim on the population size and larger economies of Fiji and PNG. They were the biggest and therefore they should be the leaders. That was the logic in his scheme of things. This would relegate the smaller states to a secondary position. In the forum all countries were equal, irrespective of size. Bainimarama thought the MSG was more

dynamic and progressive. The forum would remain "irrelevant and useless". He made much of Melanesian brotherhood and solidarity. These were the binding traits that would keep the MSG united and forward looking.

It was not long before Bainimarama was seeing himself as the potential leader of the entire region. He didn't say it exactly, but I had the clear impression that this was his aim. He made some remarks at a Pacific Community Conference in Suva in 2013 in which he lectured the region for what he saw as its many shortcomings. I think he was telling the Pacific nations that he had the answers. He condemned many of the development policies of Pacific Community member nations, accusing them, and by extension their governments, of being half-hearted, sporadic, and inadequate. He reprimanded them for their lack of "resolve" and urged them to take a new approach to seeking solutions.

It was significant that Dr Jimmie Rodgers, retiring director of the Pacific Community, was not buying into the dictator's claim to be regional leader. In one of his conference statements he described PNG and New Caledonia as the super powers of the Pacific. This was a rebuke for Bainimarama.

Ratu Inoke Kubuabola, when he was responsible for Foreign Affairs, echoed his leader's Pacific Community lecture by accusing Pacific countries of delaying important decisions.

This was all very strange stuff coming from Bainimarama and Kubuabola, representing a regime based on treason, a lack of legitimacy, and known for poor governance, abuse of human rights and oppression of its people. Professor Yash Ghai had remarked that dictators have a great capacity for self-deception. It was very much in evidence as Bainimarama began to see himself as the dictator who would become leader of the region.

PNG, however, wasn't buying into his delusions. Peter O'Neill, the PNG prime minister, made it clear that he and his country did not think that the Pacific Islands Forum was of no use. The PNG government, he said, remained loyal to the PIF. Mr O'Neill took Bainimarama on directly. He was quoted as saying: "We must make sure that we don't forget that we all live in the same region and Australia and New Zealand are very much part of that region." He and his government were obviously not going to be part of Bainimarama's vendetta against the two developed neighbours.

Mr O'Neill reinforced his credentials as a "big man" in the region when he offered Fiji a large amount of aid money to assist with the Fiji elections which the forum had been pushing for. Fiji accepted the offer but I wonder what was going through Bainimarama's mind at the time.

Melanesian solidarity in the MSG began to falter. Some of the FLNKS representatives from New Caledonia were not happy about Bainimarama's involvement with the MSG. A newspaper article in June 2014 in the *Fiji Sun* contained details which hinted at internal stress. It said Fiji was not represented at an MSG summit meeting in PNG. Fiji had requested that the meeting be delayed because of commitments by Bainimarama and his minister for Foreign Affairs and International Cooperation, Ratu Inoke Kubuabola. The meeting went ahead.

The MSG became seriously divided over the issue of member-ship for the territory of West Papua. This was taken over by Indonesia in 1969 after a sham act of free choice following the with-drawal of the Dutch colonial power. After initially giving a warm welcome to a West Papua delegation in Suva, Bainimarama then began to distance himself from full MSG membership for the Papuans. He was clearly influenced by diplomatic pressure from Indonesia. He betrayed and abandoned his Papuan Melanesian brothers.

Vanuatu, meanwhile, broke ranks with the MSG over the organi-sation's capitulation to Indonesia on West Papua. It has stood loyally by the oppressed peoples of West Papua. Vanuatu did something very odd and illogical in March 2012 when Bainimarama was installed as the chief of Malampa, one of the largest provinces in the country. There was great inconsistency in this decision. Bainimarama thanked the chiefs and government of Vanuatu for his appointment. In Fiji, Bainimarama was committed to sidelining and diminishing the role of Fiji's traditional leaders and had spoken out regularly against the chiefly system and the Great Council of Chiefs. And yet he did not hesitate to accept appointment as a chief in Vanuatu, which also has its own Council of Chiefs. More hypocrisy.

Fiji became involved in a long standoff with the Solomon Islands, an MSG member, in an aviation dispute. A Solomon Island official accused the Fiji government of "bully boy" tactics and "pulling out the big stick to belt us around the head".

All was not well with the MSG operations generally. There were reports that it was experiencing financial difficulties

When Bainimarama's government was allowed to take its place again in the Pacific Islands Forum following Fiji's election in 2014, he continued to protest about the membership of Australia and New Zealand. He has so far refused to attend forum leaders' meetings but is happy to take aid and technical assistance from the two developed neighbours.

He succeeded, however, in establishing a regional organization called the Pacific Islands Development Forum (PIDF). Although he denied it, this was to counter the role and influence of the Pacific Islands Forum and Australia and New Zealand. It duplicates functions of the forum and stands as a testament to one man's ego and desire for revenge. Frankly I have doubts whether it will survive for the long term.

# 37

# "RULE OF LAW NO LONGER OPERATES"

Like many citizens I was very dubious about the judiciary. The normal safeguards for an independent judiciary were no longer in place. Soldiers who had committed treason were ultimately in charge of all the mechanisms of the state including the courts and appointments of judges and magistrates. The legally appointed chief justice had been forced out of office by the military and constitution processes were not followed in the appointment of an acting chief justice. Later the entire bench of the Court of Appeal resigned.

A team from the International Bar Association Human Rights Institute (IBAHRI) which had planned a visit to consider the state of the law and the judiciary in Fiji, was refused entry. One member was turned away at Nadi International Airport. Also, a UN rapporteur had been denied access.

I made a statement at the time that if Sayed-Khaiyum had nothing to hide, there was no harm in allowing the IBAHRI's visit. I said that Sayed-Khaiyum's claim of independence of the judiciary was a big joke. I urged Sayed-Khaiyum to swallow his pride and allow the team to come. Sayed-Khaiyum had good reason to be cautious about the visit in light of what was happening in Fiji. Eventually, the regime relented and an IBAHRI delegation conducted a fact-finding mission.

The International Bar Association (IBA) is the world's largest lawyers' representative organization. In 1995 the IBA established the International Bar Association Human Rights Institute with Nelson Mandela as honorary president.

The IBAHRI came to Fiji from December 8th to 13th, 2008. In a carefully worded report published in March 2009, the IBAHRI concluded that the rule of law in Fiji had been steadily deteriorating. It said that constitutional limitations and rights appeared to have been disregarded.

Fiji's "coup culture" was a serious concern for the international community, for the impact it had on individuals in Fiji and its "destabilizing effects" throughout the region.

The report said: "Unlike previous coups, the interim regime appears to have successfully infiltrated every aspect of the justice and political system, which will make any future attempt to restore the rule of law extremely difficult."

It condemned the efforts of the regime to prevent the IBAHRI delegation from visiting Fiji as "entirely unacceptable." It was particularly critical of Sayed-Khaiyum. "The IBAHRI remains deeply concerned by the responses of the attorney-general and the implications that his actions have for the present and future state of Fiji's justice system."

It said it was disturbed by "inaccurate and misleading comments" by the interim attorney general and at least two judges, claiming that three independent review missions had found no executive interference in the judiciary. This had been shown to be false.

The regime, it said, had attacked members of the judiciary and the legal profession who had attempted to defend human rights and the justice system.

The report said the suspension of Chief Justice Fatiaki, should be condemned by all supporters of the rule of law, particularly given that all charges were eventually dropped, and a large settlement payment made. It expressed extreme concern about reports of physical threats and attacks against judges perceived to have been independent from the regime. It understood that in August 2007, Justice Gordon Ward's home was burned down while he was out of the country. The IBAHRI had received reports that there was no conclusion to any investigations into the fire although there was reported circumstantial evidence that it was arson. Reports had been received about the sabotage of Justice Gerard Winter's car involving removal of mechanical components that could have resulted in a serious accident.

There had been reports as well that Justice Conventry had been followed by military officers after he made a ruling awarding $20,000 in costs against the interim attorney general.

There were concerns about a number of judges appointed or promoted following the December 2006 coup who had heard cases relating to the constitutionality of their own appointments.

The IBAHRI found an apparent lack of public confidence in the judiciary. It was disturbed by reports that in the immediate aftermath of the coup, the military brought certain lawyers to the barracks and physically abused and threatened them.

---

In November 2011, a UK lawyer, Nigel Dodds, conducted a secret investigation of Fiji's legal system while on a private visit. He was an important figure because he was chair of the UK's Law Society Charity. This was set up by the Law Society of England and Wales to fund and provide expertise to organisations whose work is related to the law and the legal profession with a view to furthering law and justice.

Mr Dodds concluded that the rule of law no longer operated; and that the independence of the judiciary could not be relied on. He felt that the competence and independence of the prosecution services had been reduced to an unacceptable level. Government controls and restrictions made it virtually impossible for an independent legal profession to function appropriately. Mr Dodds asserted there was no peaceful and lawful way to challenge government decisions. He noted that judges dismissed in April 2009 were given no reasons, no notice and no compensation for loss of office. "It was apparent", said Mr Dodds, "that their sin was to comply with an oath of office and act independently ... It was difficult to conceive of a more obvious attack on judicial independence".

Judges from Sri Lanka, said Mr Dodds, were recruited on short term

renewable contracts. He observed that, in their position, maintaining independence from government must be difficult. The judge who heard my case was Sri Lankan.

In 2011 government refused to permit the Fiji Law Society to hold its annual general meeting. As if symbolising the overturning of the rule of law, the Fiji Law Society offices in Gordon Street in Suva were gutted in an arson attack. The culprits have never been brought to justice.

I think the reader will understand why I felt I would not get a fair hearing in the legal actions brought against me by the Bainimarama dictatorship.

Another harshly critical analysist of the legal environment came from Justice William Marshall, who had been appointed as a judge. His contract was not renewed. He went online to give the circumstances of his dismissal and his petitioning of the prime minister and his military council for the dismissal of the attorney general. Justice Marshall accused the AG of running censorship and untrue propaganda. He claimed that the AG completed the removal of judiciary independence in Fiji in April 2012. The judges, he said, no longer did their duty and no longer served the people of Fiji.

They do what they believe the attorney general would wish them to do. In many cases this is specifically explained to them by or on behalf of the attorney general.

# 38

# FLABBERGASTED

Criminal Case No. (HAC) 26 of 2009 related to my involvement in some NLTB decisions. I was charged with abuse of office in connection with my position as chairman of the board. Later the charge was amended by FICAC to one of fraudulent conversion of several hundred thousand dollars. I was flabbergasted. I could not believe it. I never used one cent of NLTB money for my personal use. In fact, during my term as chairman of the board, I declined to accept any director's fees payable for the position. I thought someone in FICAC must be utterly stupid to come up with such a charge.

Criminal Case HAC. 27 of 2009 was about my participation in some share transactions relating to Fijian Holdings Limited (FHL). The transactions took place in 1992. The charges against me were laid in 2009, some seventeen years afterwards. In 1992 I was financial advisor to the Fijian Affairs Board as well as advisor to the Great Council of Chiefs. I was also a director of FHL.

Three companies, namely Q-Ten Investments Limited, Mavana Investments Limited and Cicia Plantations Co-operative Society Limited were allotted and issued with shares in FHL. Q-Ten was my family company while Mavana Investments was the village company. I had no financial interest in Cicia Plantations Co- operative but helped in its establishment. From time to time I also offered advice on investment opportunities that might interest the co-operative share-holders.

For the offence of abuse of office, it was alleged that I had applied for shares on behalf of the three companies. In addition, it was also alleged that I facilitated the approval of the allotment and issuance of shares to these companies – a total of six counts. Three other counts referred to discharge of duty with respect to property in which "he has a private interest", whatever that means. It was also alleged that I did not declare my interest in these companies when their applications for shares were considered by the Board of FHL.

I did declare my interest, but this was not recorded in the minutes of the relevant meetings of the FHL board. On the six counts of abuse of office all I can say is that I was very familiar with the provisions of the Companies Act. I also had a thorough knowledge and understanding of the Memorandum and Articles of Association of FHL. I am certain that my actions did not breach the Companies Act nor FHL's Memorandum and Articles of Association.

# 39

# BIRTH AND SUCCESS OF FIJIAN HOLDINGS

F ijian Holdings Limited (FHL) is the flagship for indigenous investment. It has become one of Fiji's great commercial success stories. With total assets of around $475 million in 2016 and consistently good profits and dividends, it has interests in many commercial sectors.

FHL was the initiative of the first prime minister of Fiji, the late Ratu Sir Kamisese Mara. It was incorporated in 1984 with the endorsement of the Great Council of Chiefs (GCC). The principal purpose was "to accelerate the participation of indigenous Fijians in the commercial sector and in doing so, enhance their socio- economic standing". In my capacity as financial advisor to the Fijian Affairs Board, I had the privilege of presenting the case for the establishment of FHL at a meeting of the GCC held at the New Town Hall, Suva, in 1984. At the time I held the position of managing director of the Fiji Development Bank. Mr Lyle Cupit, chairman of the Bank, was appointed first chairman of FHL. He was an accomplished former chief executive of the Carpenter Group of Companies, one of Fiji's largest commercial concerns.

After incorporation of FHL, I was involved in explaining to

provincial councils the intended aim of FHL and its virtues and advantages for the long-term future of the indigenous Fijian community. All the 14 provincial councils supported the concept of FHL. Each council was asked to subscribe for 50,000 $1 shares. Both the Fijian Affairs Board (FAB) and the Native Land Trust Board (NLTB) were also asked to subscribe.

As first chairman of FHL, Mr Cupit was assisted by a very good team of directors, including the late Josefata Kamikamica, the late Berenado Vunibobo, prominent businessmen, Gerald Barrack, and Joe Mar, and Ratu Jone Kubuabola. Mr Sitiveni Weleilakeba became the first chief executive officer of the company in about 1991/1992.

The subscriptions of $50,000 by each provincial council, even with additional shares from the FAB and NLTB, did not provide enough capital. FHL did not, therefore, make much progress from 1984 to 1987.

After the military coup in 1987 and in my capacity as financial advisor to the FAB, I presented a paper to the board recommending an interest-free loan of $40 million from government to FHL to accelerate the expansion of the company's portfolio of investments. The paper was a product of the Fijian Initiative, a group of young indigenous executives who were concerned about the lack of indigenous involvement in the economy. The FAB endorsed the paper, which was later presented to Cabinet for decision. The Cabinet approved an interest-free loan of $20 million, instead of the $40 million requested.

The concept for FHL was based on a study into the operations of the National Investment Corporation (NIC) of Malaysia. I was asked to carry this out in 1985, by the then minister of Finance, the late Mosese Qionibaravi. The NIC of Malaysia was granted an interest-free loan of US$200 million from the government of Malaysia. In addition, the government permitted the purchase by the NIC of shares in profitable companies and certain government enterprises. These purchases were made at cost and not at valuation. The government of Malaysia also established a National Unit Trust for the

Bhumiputra (indigenous Malay) community with substantial concessions/assistance.

All these initiatives propelled the NIC forward. It became a significant player in the Malaysian economy, and a great success for the shareholders and the Bhumiputra community generally. Like the indigenous Fijians they had lagged in economic participation.

The injection of $20 million into FHL, together with Mr Cupit's leadership of a competent, professional board of directors, also transformed FHL. It became a major player in the economy.

On receipt of the interest-free loan the company moved quickly to acquire substantial investments in the share capital of some profitable companies and other assets. Initial investments included shares in Carlton Brewery (Fiji) Limited, Carpenters Properties Limited, Merchant Bank of Fiji Limited, Fiji Industries Limited, Basic Industries Limited, Blue Lagoon Cruises Limited and more. Again, I was privileged to have been involved in the discussions and appraisal of some of these projects led by Mr Cupit who had a keen eye for good investments.

As managing director of the Fiji Development Bank, I had already amassed a lot of experience in starting, sustaining and expanding businesses as part of an overall thrust to strengthen the economy. But I took my knowledge to a new level by observing closely how Mr Cupit analysed investment proposals and made decisions on them. FHL was converted into a public company in 1991/92. I can say without fear of contradiction that FHL has enabled indigenous Fijians to acquire a bigger stake in commercial investments. That is good for Fiji.

Its A class shares are available for purchase by individuals and Fijian privately-owned enterprises. They are funded from their own resources. The Class B shares are held by the Fijian Affairs Board, the Native Land Trust Board and provincial councils. These were funded from the $20 million interest free loan from the government to FAB. Initially Class B shares received a lower rate of dividend. But later both classes of shares received the same rate of return. So they now rank equally in every respect. FHL has been dogged by allegations that its shareholder structure is not fair. In fact, shareholdings are spread widely throughout Fijian society and include *tikina* councils and companies, village funds, and many individuals. FHL shares are traded on the South Pacific Stock Exchange. They earn attractive dividends and there is a ready market for them.

As I write there are worrying signs relating to government interference in the operations of the company and its board appointments.

I am pretty sure that since 2007 some senior executives of FHL and its subsidiaries have achieved their positions through government intervention and normal recruitment procedures have been bypassed. Also, some senior executives and board members have been removed. It is my belief that these problems have arisen from the misuse of powers conferred on the minister for Fijian affairs and prime minister under the FHL Articles of Association. Under these Articles directors representing Class B shareholders were appointed on the nomination of the minister for Fijian Affairs with the approval of the prime minister. The holders of these positions are one and the same person, Bainimarama. He was approving his own nominations!

There may have been justification for these provisions in the Articles when the initial loan of $20 million from government to capitalize FHL was still in place, but the loan has been fully repaid. There should, therefore, be no more government involvement in the operations of FHL and the appointment of directors. I advocate introduction of amendments to the Articles to remove the powers of the minister for Fijian Affairs and the prime minister in appointing directors representing Class B shareholders. Furthermore, Class B shares were created only for the purpose of differentiating dividend payments. Now that dividend rates are the same, there is no need for two classes of shares. All shareholders should appoint directors without involvement of outside parties. I also suggest that new Articles of Association should be prepared for FHL and adopted without delay. They should be designed to govern FHL without intervention from outside. If these suggestions, or something similar, are not acted on, FHL will continue to be a political football.

I am aware that many shareholders are worried about trends in the company's board appointments and operations. They have every reason to be concerned.

# 40

# TRIAL, JUDGMENT, AND SENTENCE

In early 2008, I was taken in for questioning by officers of the Fiji Independent Commission Against Corruption (FICAC). (I argue that FICAC cannot be independent because it is headed by an army officer who was part of the Bainimarama coup.) I was interviewed about my role in some 2004 NLTB investment decisions made during my term in office as prime minister and also as chairman of NLTB. I was also questioned about some share transactions when I was a director of Fijian Holdings Limited. The share transactions were approved by the Board of FHL in 1992, 17 years ago. The investigations ultimately led to my conviction, sentence and imprisonment on 3$^{rd}$ August 2012.

The trial relating to *High Court Case* No. HAC. 27 of 2009, FICAC vs Laisenia Qarase (FHL Case) took place over two weeks. The summing up was given on 30$^{th}$ July 2012 and the judgment was on 31$^{st}$ July. The sentence was handed down on 3$^{rd}$ August.

Counsel for the prosecution (FICAC) were Mr M. Blanchflower, Ms E. Yang and Ms. Sanmogam. Counsel for the accused (that was me) were Ms Tupou Draunidalo and Ms Silika Waqabitu. I believe Mr Blanchflower was a QC – a kind of super lawyer - and both he and Ms. E. Yang were hired from Hong Kong by FICAC. The judge for the case was Mr Priyantha Feranando, a Sri Lankan national.

The drama that unfolded on Sunday, 4th July, before the start of the trial the next day was extraordinary. From 2009, to one day before the trial, Mr Qoriniasi Bale was my lawyer. He had agreed to take on my case. As time passed I noticed that Mr Bale's health was not good. He was often sick. One day I politely suggested that he might like to consider someone else taking the case. He rejected this and re-affirmed his commitment.

Sometime later Mr Bale mentioned to me that he might have to withdraw from the case, because he was too close to me. He had served as attorney general in my SDL government.

We both came from Vanuabalavu and attended QVS together. I was taken by surprise at his comment. I wished that he had mentioned this to me in the first place. So I could have searched for another lawyer. But then Mr Bale said he would consider the matter further and let me know soon. At our next meeting he re-affirmed he would continue with the case.

I was not particularly happy. Time was running out, the trial was approaching. I noticed too that the level of our preparation was not good. All we had at the time were bundles of documents submitted by FICAC and from our side. We had not discussed the strategies that the defence would take and other options that would help our case.

On Sunday, just 24 hours before the trial began, the unthinkable happened. Mr Bale asked me for a meeting in his office. We met at about 10am and he told me that he would not be able to represent me. I was shocked but, in truth, not too surprised. He looked frail and I knew the trial would place a heavy burden on him physically.

So here I was on the day before the trial was to start and I had no lawyer! I rang around urgently to look for someone willing to take on the case in this emergency situation. One practitioner responded positively but did not turn up at a proposed meeting later that afternoon. By then I managed to contact Ms Tupou Draunidalo, who was willing to represent me.

Ms Draunidalo is a rising lawyer and an able and courageous politician. I knew her parents well. Her father, the late Col. Savenaca Draunidalo, was a career soldier. He later entered politics and contested the 2001 general election under the SDL ticket. He was a minister in the SDL government I led in 2001 and again after the general election of 2006. Ms. Tupou Draunidalo's mother was Adi Kuini, a high chief of Navosa, and also a highly regarded national politician and leader.

Ms Draunidalo was briefed on the case by Mr Bale on the Sunday evening before the trial was to begin the next morning, 5th July 2012.

She was also given volumes of files containing all documentations regarding both the FHL and NLTB cases. Ms Waqabitu assisted Ms Draunidalo. During the next few days I was impressed with the speed with which Ms. Draunidalo was able to grasp the facts and many other details of the two cases against me. I felt confident and looked forward to the rest of the trial. My confidence was further boosted by the manner Ms. Draunidalo presented the defence case. She remained cool, calm and collected. Her evaluation contrasted with the almost unintelligible English of the judge.

I wish to reiterate that I was extremely grateful to Ms Draunidalo for her willingness to become my lawyer at such short notice. It was also an act of courage. The case was high profile, controversial and public attention was focussed on it. Ms Draunidalo and Ms Waqabitu worked tirelessly under extreme pressure to prepare my defence. It was an astonishing, almost superhuman effort.

The introduction of the case by the prosecution lawyer, Mr Blanchflower, gave a good idea of the prosecution strategy. My lawyers and I held several discussions in between hearings on matters that might assist in our preparation.

The prosecution had arranged for quite a number of witnesses but only a few were called to provide evidence. The first witness for the prosecution was the late Mr Meli Bainimarama, a brother of the prime minister. He was permanent secretary for Fijian Affairs from 1991–1993 and from 1999 to 2008. He confirmed that I was appointed financial advisor to the Fijian Affairs Board (FAB) in March 1979. In this position I was also advisor to the Great Council of Chiefs (GCC) on financial matters. It was also confirmed that I was appointed a director of FHL by the minister for Fijian affairs.

The decision to sell FHL class A shares to tikinas, companies and individuals was confirmed by various letters from FHL, FAB and GCC. FHL was a private company on incorporation and remained so for some time. Class B shares were reserved for FAB and provincial councils and were not available for sale to companies and individuals.

The next prosecution witness was Mr Sitiveni T. Weleilakeba, a close friend. It is an understatement to say that his role in the trial strained our friendship. Mr Weleilakeba was appointed company secretary of FHL in 1987. In February 1992 he was appointed chief executive officer. Mr Weleilakeba was a key state witness. In return for his evidence, charges against him relating to FHL were dropped by the State. Mr Weleilakeba confirmed that when he was appointed company secretary I was already a director of FHL.

Giving evidence Mr Weleilakeba said that I was appointed a director of FHL as a result of my role as financial advisor to FAB. This statement was false. The truth is that the Chairman of FHL, the late Mr Lyle Cupit, recommended my appointment as a director based on my knowledge and experience in commerce, economics, financial matters and other attributes. My appointment had nothing to do with my role as financial advisor to FAB. It was also said that I represented class B shareholders. This statement is correct, but it ignores the fact that all directors represent all shareholders and not just one section of them.

Mr Weleilakeba gave evidence on procedures at FHL board meetings and, in particular, on declaration of interests by directors in matters under discussion. The minutes of relevant board meetings where the application, allotment, and issuance of shares to Q-Ten Investments, Cicia Plantations Co-operative, and Mavana Investments did not record any declarations of my interest in these companies. Furthermore, I did not raise the issue at subsequent board meetings when the minutes were confirmed.

All of this does not mean that I did not declare my interest. I am certain in my mind that I made declarations in relation to the three companies when the question of application for shares, allotment and issuance came before the board for decision. I am also clear in my mind that I declared my interests to the chairman who told me not to leave the meeting room, but that I should remain silent and not vote. It is unfortunate that Mr Cupit, who knew of my declarations, had passed away by the time of the trial.

There was no way that I could "win" this debate. My declarations were not recorded in the minutes of board meetings. But the issue, in my view, was given far too much significance. In the Companies Act failure to declare an interest, if proven, meant a fine of up to a mere $1,000.00 and not imprisonment.

Mr Weleilakeba also gave evidence on the questions of application for shares, allotment and issuance of shares. The evidence was detailed. The information and documents submitted to directors on these matters were also detailed.

Mr Timoci Vesikula was the next witness. He was minister for Fijian Affairs from June 1992 to October 1993. He confirmed that when he became minister I was already the financial advisor to FAB and GCC, as well as a director of FHL.

Mr Vesikula said that he was "scared" when he found out that about 80 percent of Class A shares were owned by Fijian owned companies and that only 20 per cent were owned by the provincial councils, NLTB and FAB. (The fact of the matter is that these institutions did not apply for additional shares at the relevant times. Whether or not to invest in shares is a matter of choice. These institutions chose not to invest more in FHL at certain points.)

Mr Vesikula also said that he could not find my declaration of interest in the files of FAB and GCC. Of course, they wouldn't be there. Why should they be?

Mr Isireli Mokunitulevu was chairman of the board of directors of Cicia Plantations Co-operative Society Limited (CPCS). He gave evidence on my involvement with CPCS. He confirmed that I was advisor to the co-operative, particularly on matters relating to investments. He said that I was never paid any form of remuneration for my services. His statements were essentially factually correct. Mr Adriu Ledua Ratumaiyale, member of Cicia Plantation Co-operative Society, made statements that were also factually correct. In my view, the evidence given by the two witnesses from CPCS did not prejudice the defence case.

Mr Epeli U. Racule, senior operational risk and compliance officer of the Westpac Banking Corporation, essentially confirmed that I was one of the signatories to CPCS's Westpac bank account.

Mr Abhi Ram, Acting Registrar of Companies, confirmed some information about Q-Ten Investments contained in the company's files with the Registrar of Companies.

Last witness for the prosecution was Mr Salimoni D. T. Karusi, senior legal officer for the Fiji Development Bank. A significant statement by Mr Karusi was that when Mavana Investments loan application came before the FDB board for decision I declared my interest and that I was also a director of FHL. Also, when the loan application for Q-Ten Investments was submitted for FDB board decision the board paper format disclosed my interest in the company.

My defence team called several witnesses. The first was Mr Usaia R. Ravono, the operational officer audit at Westpac Bank. He said that, in his view, the documents referred to did not show any fraudulent activities in the bank account of Cicia Plantations Co-operative. The next witness, Mr Bai Tikoikoro, a shareholder in the co-operative, confirmed I was advisor to Cicia and that I never received any payment for my services.

Mr Navitalai Cakacaka, general manager business risk services, Fiji Development Bank (FDB), explained the FDB's subsidised special loan scheme. The scheme was available to all and many who applied for shares in FHL did so under the scheme which was widely advertised. Mr Cakacaka said that if a director of FDB had an interest in a board matter that director would not take part in the discussion and would not vote on the issue. He confirmed that I was managing director of FDB at the time. Q-Ten's loan application would be considered by the board, because I was involved. The board paper disclosed my interest in the company. It would not normally have gone to the board but did so because I was involved. Mr Naulumatua Josateki Koroi, a shareholder in Mavana Investments, recalled a Mavana Village meeting where a proposal to invest in FHL was discussed. I was present at the meeting. He confirmed that Q-Ten was a shareholder in Mavana Investments.

There was no limitation on Mavana villagers to own shares. If you had the money you could buy shares. The next witness was Mr Josua Toa, a Mavana villager and shareholder in Mavana Investments. He confirmed that I was advisor to Mavana Investments and had encouraged villagers to invest in the company. The last defence witness was Mr Josaia Bainivalu Mar, a director of FHL and a widely experienced business executive. He was living in England and gave evidence via video conference. Mr Mar explained some procedures at board meetings. He stated that his responsibility would be to shareholders. He never thought that his responsibility included being custodian of Fijian business investments. He had no special duty to provincial and *tikina* councils or FAB or Fijians. He said the Memorandum and Articles of Association of FHL did not require a director to carry a fiduciary duty to the indigenous Fijian people.

Mr Mar's family company, Nabuadua, had also purchased shares in FHL. He had declared his interest at the relevant board meeting. He was concerned that his declaration was not recorded in the minutes. He could not recall whether I had declared my interests when the applications for shares for Q-Ten, Mavana Investments, and Cicia Plantations Co-operative came before the board. However, this did not mean that I did not declare my interests. Mr Mar said he did not doubt my integrity.

In his closing address the prosecution counsel said that the four elements of abuse of office had been proved beyond reasonable doubt. The four elements are:

1) The accused was employed in the public service.

2) He did an arbitrary act.

3) He acted in abuse of the authority of his office; and

4) The act was prejudicial to the rights of another person, in this case the provincial and *tikina* councils, FAB and all other indigenous Fijian people.

My defence counsel of course argued that not all the four elements were proved beyond reasonable doubt.

If only one of the four elements were not proved beyond reasonable doubt, then the prosecution case must fail. I thought that Ms Draunidalo's submission was soundly based and was optimistic that the judgment would be in my favour.

Judge Priyantha Fernando delivered his judgment on 31st July 2012. Fifteen minutes before the court sat the courtroom was packed. My wife Leba, Rev. Josateki Koroi, a cousin, Mesake Koroi, a relative and my *matanivanua* (spokesman), other relatives, friends and supporters were present. There was silence in the court room, all were anxious to hear the judgment. As the judge entered we all stood up at the command of the court clerk. I stood at the dock. I did not feel nervous.

Judge Fernando opened a brown envelope and started to read his judgment. He said that the assessors had taken 2½ hours to deliberate. Half way through the judgment I was certain the court would find me guilty. The opinion of the assessors was unanimous that I was guilty of six counts of abuse of office punishable under section 111 of the penal code cap. 17 and three counts of "discharge of duty with respect to property in which he had a private interest" punishable under Section 109 of the Penal Code.

The Judge was satisfied:

(a) that the prosecution has proved all the elements of the offence of abuse of office in counts 1-6 beyond reasonable doubt.

(b) that the prosecution has proved all the elements of the offence of discharge of duty with respect to property in which he has a private interest in counts No, 7-9 beyond reasonable doubt.

(c) that I abused my office for the purpose of gain.

(d) that the assessors' opinions were supported by the evidence addressed at the trial.

(e) that he agreed with the assessors that I was guilty of a felony in counts 1-6 and that I was guilty of the offences in counts No.7-9 as charged.

The judge accordingly convicted me of a felony on counts 1-6 and convicted me on counts 7-9. After delivering his judgment Judge Fernando quickly left the court room.

I could not discern the mood that prevailed. There was probably a feeling of surprise, a bit of quiet anger, and a bit of disbelief. In any case the judge had delivered his judgment and that was it. I shook hands with Ms. Draunidalo and Ms. Waqabitu, my loyal and able lawyers, and then we left for home.

In between the judgment and the sentence, the high court sat to hear submissions on mitigating factors. Ratu Joni Madraiwiwi, vice-president of Fiji during my term as prime minister, and Rev. Josateki Koroi, my relative and former president of the Methodist Church in Fiji made submissions on my character and other attributes. Ro Teimumu Vuikaba Kepa, Roko Tui Dreketi and Rev. Poate Mata, also submitted written submissions in mitigation. Dr. Ami Chandra, our family doctor, gave a submission on the state of my health.

---

S entencing by the high court was scheduled to take place at 11.45am on Friday 3$^{rd}$ August 2012. I arrived at the court house about 11.30am. Leba accompanied me and some close relatives. Outside the court house there was a large crowd of sympathisers and well wishers. A police cordon left some space at the entrance. Leba and I were quickly whisked into the building. I had time to turn to the crowd, waved to them, and acknowledged their support. They were singing hymns.

Inside the court house the atmosphere was tense and quiet. Rev. Koroi, Mesake Koroi and other relatives were there and many more friends and supporters. The place was packed. At 11.45am the judge, Mr Fernando, walked in.

I had taken my seat at the dock. I stood up to listen to the judge. Again I felt relaxed and at peace. I was ready for whatever the sentence was going to be. The judge began to read. Mid-way in his delivery I felt certain I was going to prison.

The judge said that he had taken into account all the mitigating factors submitted by my defence counsel. The sentence was as follows:

a) Counts 1-6 - 12 months imprisonment.

b) Counts 7-9 - 6 months imprisonment.

c) The sentences in counts 1-9 were to run concurrently.

d) Therefore, the sentence I had to serve was 12 months imprisonment.

The outcome was a surprise to many. There was a feeling that a prison sentence was too harsh and that a suspended sentence would have been appropriate. That was not to be. I was led away by two police officers. I was now a prisoner.

# 41

# KOROVOU GOAL

S uva gaol, known later as Korovou prison, was established around 1887. Its thick white washed-walls – in more recent times decorated with art work - still front the main road at Walu Bay leading into the capital city's main industrial area. According to the files of the Fiji Society, the earliest official record dealing with Suva gaol was in 1887 when the Prison Service took over the duty of burials in the Old Suva Cemetery.

The gaol was initially composed of a collection of huts behind a reed fence and the road first stopped at the foot of Old Hospital Hill. A track along the beach led to the gaol and the cemetery and ended at the Tamavua river. One of the special duties of a prison warder in those early days was to escort hospital sisters into Suva and back after dark.

It was not until about 1912-13 that any serious attempt was made to provide more substantial accommodation. Then, under the direction of Mr Amie Ragg, the present main building with 171 cells was erected. This was one of the first, if not the very first, ferro- concrete building in Fiji. The present front walls were constructed from coral rock. With the advent of the Fiji Brick Company, which manufactured bricks from a clay deposit at Lami, the rear wall and other gaol buildings were constructed, including the hospital and one officer's quarters. They were built with prison labour under the direction of a Mr Marr who was a prison officer and a master brick layer.

Suva gaol has housed a number of notorious criminals at various times including a Belgian who was said to be the last pirate in the Pacific. He was defended by a then young barrister who had recently set up a practice, the late Sir Henry Scott. The Belgian was imprisoned in what is now the female section of the prison and then later transferred to Bathurst prison in Australia. He was released after some years, when he returned to his native country.

The ferro-concrete buildings mentioned above have been declared unsafe for occupation. I believe they are now part of the National Trust of Fiji.

One of the gaol's notorious buildings is on a hillside above the kitchen area. This was the location of the gallows used to dispatch those sentenced to death when capital punishment was in force. A former Fiji hangman, originally from the UK, once told the Fiji Times that every convict he had executed went to his death "like a man".

I had no occasion to visit the gallows buildings. But in December 2012 Rev Laisiasa Ratabacaca became a fellow inmate. He was assigned with a few other prisoners to clean up the building. They did a good job of it. Apparently, the basic apparatus used for hanging is still there. There was talk that the facility might be used for Bible studies. I thought this was a brilliant idea; the light of the Bible shining on this place of death.

Throughout my imprisonment I could sense a desire for Bible knowledge and spiritual growth among many inmates. The clear evidence for this was the many small groups who would gather at Rev. Ratabacaca's cell, or at other available space for Bible studies.

If the gallows building did not become the Bible centre, I thought that instead it might be reserved for certain high-profile prisoners who should become permanent residents of Korovou, sooner rather than later.

# 42

## 'GOD BE WITH YOU'

I was led away for my journey to Korovou by two police officers. I had little time to say goodbye to Rev. Koroi, other relatives and supporters. Our granddaughter, Fane, was very emotional. She cried, hugged me and would not let go. Leba accompanied me downstairs and then out through the backdoor to a police vehicle. I kissed her goodbye. Holding back her emotions, she whispered: "God be with you".

I sat on the back seat of the police vehicle with a police officer beside me. At the front was the driver and another police officer. A police motorcycle drove ahead of us as an escort. I was not handcuffed.

As we moved away, I waved to Leba. I was to see her again before the day was out.

We left from the back way to avoid the large crowd at the front of the building. We travelled up MacGregor Road and on to Rewa Street at around 100km per hour. There was a fair amount of traffic on the road as it was lunch hour. The police officer in the front was communicating with headquarters telling them our position at certain intervals. I could not understand why we were travelling at such high speed. I did not think anyone would consider an ambush or hijack.

Before we reached the Samabula junction our vehicle almost overturned as we passed a bus travelling in the same direction. It could have been the end for the four of us.

From Samabula we travelled down Edinburgh Drive, then into Walu Bay. The police motorcycle came to an abrupt stop at the entrance to Korovou prison. As we did the same, the driver lurched forward and fell, but fortunately escaped serious injury.

It was about 1pm. Still wearing a dark suit with red tie, I was interviewed in the interview/meeting room which had one table and two chairs. A prison officer entered, sat down and invited me to be seated on the other chair. Two other officers were standing by as witnesses to what was said.

The interviewing officer, who was in his late 40s or 50s, looked familiar. It took me just a few seconds to recall that I had met him at a social function for villagers from Vanuavatu. He was related to my wife Leba, whose mother was a Vanuavatu native. It is said that baldness in middle age is a characteristic of Vanuavatu men. The officer had lost most of his hair. A tavale (brother-in-law) of mine once told me that baldness is a sign of wisdom and intelligence. As I came to know more and more people from Vanuavatu I concluded that its community had a high proportion of well educated young men and women. Maybe there was some truth in what my "tavale" told me.

The bald person in the interview room started to ask me questions, recording my answers in a very large notebook. He asked my name, date of birth, my village, *tikina*, province and educational background. Then he asked my occupation. I replied: "I am the constitutional prime minister of Fiji."

The officer hesitated and looked at me. His pen did not move. I took pity on him and rephrased my response, telling him I was a retired politician. His hesitation ended and he began to write again.

After the interview I was taken to another room for the usual prison haircut. I asked the barber, who was a prisoner, not to cut my hair too short. He never said a word. He kept moving the electric hair clipper from one side of my head to the other. It was all over in less than a minute.

Another prisoner was waiting to give me my prison uniform, a pair of orange shorts and a shirt. I was given only one pair instead of the regulation three, since there was a shortage. The uniform issued to me was not new. It was old, dirty and smelling of body odour, and whatever else.

I changed into this soiled uniform and was told to leave my suit in an open locker for collection by family members. I wore that obnoxious uniform for three days before someone thought to give me clean shorts and a shirt.

Leba was my first visitor that afternoon. I was called to the OC (officer in charge) to be briefed on the prison rules. Leba was there too with Rev. Gonerau, the Prison Chaplain, from the Methodist Church. She had been allowed in to collect my civilian clothes and to bring some of my immediate requirements for personal use such as toiletries, a pair of flip-flops and a suit for pending court hearings.

My wife was seeing me for the first time in an orange convict's uniform – stinking and filthy – with my hair cut short. I did not know what was going on in her mind. Whether it was surprise, curiosity, sadness about my plight, she certainly did not show it. She was calm and collected. Leba's spiritual life was much stronger than mine. I believe this was why she was handling our ordeal with courage, grace and strength. After the meeting with Leba, I kissed her goodbye and she left.

It was made plain to me that, although I was a former prime minister, the prison authorities were not going to treat me differently from other inmates. I did not expect to be.

# 43

# ON THE DOUBLE FOR TWO ROTI

The rest of the day went quickly. At 4pm the inmates in Makosoi, the area where I was to stay, were called for the routine parade before dinner. Led by a prison officer we marched on-the-double to the dining hall. One by one we received our dinner on aluminium plates, the same kind used by curry shops along Suva's Cumming Street 30–40 years ago. Dinner was two *roti*, a few pieces of baigan, Chinese cabbage and a cup of tea. We had to eat quickly so that other waiting inmates could use the same dining tables. We had to wash our plates before marching back to Makosoi. It was noticeable that the kitchen and dining hall were in very poor condition. Tabletops were dirty. I was surprised to see some inmates putting bread on dirty tables.

At 5pm we had to move into our cells which were then locked up. There were three of us in the 16' x 8' concrete block structure with a corrugated iron roof that would be my home for the next nine months. The existing inmates, one from Tailevu, one from Bua, were kind enough to offer me the bottom bunk. There were no steps to the top bunk. You had to haul yourself up. My considerate fellow boarders knew this would have been difficult for me, with my creaky 71-old limbs. The Tailevu prisoner volunteered to sleep on the floor on his mattress.

The lights went out at 8pm. It had been a long and tiring day, which probably explained why I slept well even though I was still wearing that unwashed uniform. We were never offered sulus or pyjamas for sleeping. We went to bed in the same shorts and shirts we had worn all day.

Our cell, painted off-white, was part of a dormitory with several separate units. The door comprised a number of iron bars a few inches apart. It was secured with a heavy-duty lock located outside the bars. Although the door represented a typical image of prison, the bars did have the merit of letting the air circulate freely; this was very welcome on hot, humid days and nights. On the left just past the door was a small cupboard with two compartments. It was used for storing items such as fruit, biscuits and papers. On the right- hand side was a small metal table, fixed to the wall and a metal stool, secured to the concrete floor. The table was only big enough for one person writing or reading a book. Immediately behind it was the two-tier bunk with a metal frame and base.

At the back of the cell the floor was raised about six inches in an area about 8' x 6'. This had a flush toilet on one side and a shower on the other. The door to the toilet/shower was only a few feet high so there was little privacy. At the back of the cell was a small window with iron bars. It was reasonably comfortable for two prisoners, but three were a crowd.

I got on well with my companions. The Tailevu native was in his late 40s. He did a lot of Bible study and could recite verses of scripture with ease. He was always respectful to me. Addressing the prison officers, he tended to be forthright and direct. Sometimes I saw flashes of temper, but they were never directed at me. He was in for life. The circumstances which led to his sentence were known to me. They were tragic and terrible. Out of deference and respect for this man who shared my life so closely for all those months I decided not to disclose the details in this book. He welcomed me when I was a stranger in a strange place, gave up his bed for me and was courteous and considerate. I think he has made his peace with God. I am sure he has sought forgiveness, but his mental suffering over what he did must still be very great. (Others, too, would be suffering for the crime he committed.)

My Bua colleague was serving a sentence for robbery with violence. Not long before I was released I helped him prepare an application for a Fiji Development Bank loan for his brother who had leased some of his *mataqali* land. He wanted to use it for an agricultural project. I do not know whether the application was successful.

When they were allowed to, many inmates visited me in the cell to say hello and to offer to assist if I needed help. Some volunteered to wash my uniform while others said they would be happy to bring my food to the cell so that I did not have to go to the dining hall.

I sincerely thanked them all but said I had attended two boarding schools and therefore would have no problem looking after myself, even in prison.

The prison officers were polite and respectful, their dealings with me strictly within the rules. Ocassionally, however, some wanted to have their photographs taken with me.

---

Sunday, 5th August, started with no water in the taps. There was a problem in the system somewhere. By 9am there was still no water, and a planned combined church service was cancelled. The Commissioner of Prisons, a military man, visited later in the morning and called in at my cell to welcome me. We talked briefly about prison routine and then he left to complete his rounds. Later in the day new security measures were put in place. We were kept in our cells except during meal times. This turn of events was received with great disappointment by the prisoners. I wondered whether my presence at Korovou was a factor in this?

From Monday 6th to Sunday 12th August, routine activities were the order of the week. Breakfast each day was half a loaf of bread and a cup of tea. Lunch was the same. Dinner consisted mainly of *roti* or rice with curry tinned fish and vegetable (mainly *bele*). Sometimes I had toast for breakfast. My two cellmates were very good at making this. The process involved cutting half a loaf in half again, lengthwise, and then exposing the inside to an open fire near the kitchen. It was more like roast bread.

Members of the Methodist Church held their church service at the Prison Chapel. The service on Sunday, 12th August, was conducted by Ratu Apenisa Dakuna from the Centenary Church. Members of other denominations held their devotions in separate allocated places.

I recollect that on Sunday, 19th August 2012 I was pleasantly surprised when Rev. Kalivati Rokisi, minister from the Vanuabalavu division of the Methodist Church, arrived to deliver the sermon for

the Methodists. He was accompanied by one of his church elders and a certain Suliasi from the Centenary Church in Suva.

After the service, as we walked past Mokosoi, I stopped and said

—

---

Talatala, this is where I have to leave you. I am sorry I can't invite you for lunch! My loloma to the people of Vanuabalavu and thank you for the message in Church. Ni sa moce.

---

On Thursday, 23rd August 2012 I received my first letter from overseas. It had a Canadian postmark, was unsigned and addressed me by my first name. Its content was hostile and written in broken English and the Fijian language. The writer complained about the allocation of government scholarships during my term as prime minister. He also complained about native land leases. It appeared that his lease in the Labasa area was not renewed. He protested about the Qoliqoli Bill and accused me of being a corrupt person and claimed I stole money from FHL. Half the contents, which were hand-written, were swear words directed at me. It is a pity the writer did not give his name and postal address. I would have liked to reply to him with the truth.

# 44

# GETTING TO KNOW THE SYSTEM

I noticed that some inmates had extra bedding items such as pillow cases, bed sheets and blankets. I discovered that the prison supply of one thin foam mattress, two bed sheets, one pillow, one pillow case and one blanket, could be supplemented from home. My cellmates suggested that I should apply for approval for some of these items to be brought in. I did so and was given approval for one bed sheet, one pillow, one blanket and one pillow case. My standard of living had increased slightly.

On Sunday 12th August, Alipate, our cellmate who was in for robbery with violence, was moved to another cell. The Tailevu prisoner was able to take back his bunk, and no one had to sleep on the floor. Again a slight improvement in living conditions.

On Monday, 13th August, I washed my uniform for the first time. It was a fine day and all was dry by mid-day. There was no iron provided so I did what every other inmate did. I folded my uniform neatly and placed it under my pillow. It looked pretty good the following morning. I followed the same routine each time I washed my uniforms.

On Tuesday, 14th August, the allocation board met to decide on my work placement. The board consisted of senior officers from head office and the prison. It was confirmed that I would remain at Korovou. I was assigned to work in the office.

My first day was fairly normal. Another inmate who had been working there for some time informed me that office hours were from 8am to 11am and then 2pm to 4pm. The lunch break was fairly long. A much more relaxed schedule than I followed in my job as PM and as a civil servant and banker! But then the work was not as demanding.

I was introduced to the prison officers who worked in the office. Normally there were two officers, the officer-in-charge and his assistant.

All prisoners, those convicted and those on remand, had to report to the office. Here, their personal details were recorded in a large register by the two officers. Personal details included their names, educational background, crimes, their provinces, religion, length of imprisonment and so on. Afterwards the prisoners would be issued with their uniforms, bedding and then moved to their assigned dormitories.

My closest inmate neighbour appeared to be between 50-60 years of age. He occupied the prison cell next to mine. We had an easy relationship. He was an ex-school teacher, spoke well, and was polite and respectful. He knew the prison office system very well. Part of our work was to transfer some of the information recorded in the main registers to special registers for particular purposes. It was routine work but it did mean time passed by more quickly than other-wise. We were diligent in our duties. All the registers under our care were updated every time additional information came in.

My work in the office at Korovou was purely clerical and occu-pied a large part of my term in prison. I was able to meet many people from all walks of life: prison officers; fellow inmates; and members of the public during their visits to meet relatives in prison. As always they greeted and treated me with deference. I also met many cler-gymen who offered words of encouragement and hope. I thank God for their kindness. I do not know what has happened to my fellow inmate who worked with me in the office. He had applied for early release because of illness. He was sickly. He suffered from serious heart problems and diabetes. I thank him for his companionship. I hope he is now a free person.

There was a large information board fixed on a wall. It contained the names of convicted prisoners, their provinces, and religion. The information was recorded on small strips of vanguard sheet, about two inches long and ½ inch width. The strips were then fixed on to the board. I suppose the purpose of the board was to allow officers to get basic information at a glance. When I started on this task I found the information completely outdated because no one was assigned to maintain it. It took me some time to bring it up to date. I made sure to keep it that way.

The office consisted of only two rooms, crowded with registers, files and equipment. There were two computers, quite often under-utilized or not used at all, because of a lack of computer operators. It is one of the reasons why various registers were maintained manually. The office reflected the sub-standard conditions of the whole prison complex.

Part of our job was to clean the office before work each morning. My neighbour inmate tried his best to prevent me sweeping the floor. Out of respect I suppose. I told him that it was okay for me to use the broom. I reminded him that I attended two boarding schools, where many manual tasks were carried out by students. To beat him I used to try and get into the office first, grab the broom and get on with the job. After a while my neighbour got used to this and the idea that there was nothing extraordinary about sweeping a dirty floor.

The two officers who worked there also felt awkward and uncom-fortable seeing me sweeping the floor and cleaning up. I suspect they were coming to terms with an ex-prime minister as a prisoner doing the type of work assigned to me. After a while, they too got used to their former prime minister working for them doing manual jobs in the Korovou office. Or at least they appeared to accept it.

The office area and the adjacent meeting/visitors' room was often dirty and dusty. One of the reasons was the heavy traffic in and out of the area. Scores of prisoners would pass through the area daily on their way to work outside the prison complex, and on their return. Dozens of prison officers passed through. Then during visiting hours scores of visitors would be there. With such a high volume of pedestrian traffic it was not surprising that dust and dirt accumulated quickly. It was often necessary for my fellow inmate and I to sweep the area twice or even more each day.

# 45

# UNACCEPTABLE CONDITIONS

After a couple of weeks as a prisoner I was eager to take a closer look at Korovou's amenities. During a sports afternoon, and accompanied by a senior inmate, I inspected the dining hall, kitchen, and food preparation area. The dining hall is an old open building with walls about two or three metres from the floor. The wooden dining tables with benches looked old. There were about 12 tables, six on either side of the hall. The tables could accommodate a few dozen prisoners at a time. There were a few sittings during each meal. Tabletops did not look clean at any time. A thin layer of dirt appeared to cover them all.

The kitchen was very old, constructed of timber and corrugated roofing iron. There are two service counters, one for serving bread and the other for serving tea, dhal soup, rice and evening meals. There is also a large wood fireplace where some food items are prepared. Firewood is scattered over the open space. During rainy days the roofs in this area leaked, and with water running from the slopes, the ground around the fireplace became muddy.

There is no question that the conditions of the kitchen, food preparation area, and the dining hall were well below acceptable standards. In my view the current facilities should be dismantled and replaced by new and modern facilities.

There was serious overcrowding at Korovou during my time there. I inspected two dormitories that accommodated remand prisoners. They were overcrowded. Each of them had about 40-60 prisoners instead of the normal 30. About 30 had beds and the remainder slept on the floor. At one end of the building were two or three water taps for showers and one common toilet. The conditions of the buildings were poor.

The bedding in each of the dormitories was very bad. Foam mattresses had holes in them and so did the covers. Blankets were in a similar condition. Bedding was infested with bugs and in spite of regular cleaning by prisoners, the insects thrived.

(They were real blood suckers and we had to search for them all the time. Sometimes there were spots of my own blood on the sheets.) I did not visit the three or four other dormitories. I was given to understand that the conditions were similar.

Makosoi Wing was different. There were about a dozen cells at Makosoi, each with two to six beds. Makosoi was also overcrowded, with some cells accommodating five or six instead of four. The cell I stayed in had two beds and for periods of time there would be three of us there. But Makosoi generally provided a better standard of accommodation. It was generally clean and each cell had a shower and toilet at one end of the room.

The prison's infirmary or health clinic was part of the office complex. The condition of the complex, with the exception of the health clinic, was below standard. The building leaked badly during rainy days, even in the office area.

I have not visited the prisons at Naboro, as well as at Lautoka and Labasa. But I believe that the facilities at those centres are more or less the same as at Korovou. The conditions I experienced reflect neglect by all previous governments including the current one.

Successive governments simply have not devoted sufficient resources for much needed capital works at these centres. I must, obviously, take some of the blame for this. To upgrade and modernize our prisons would require massive capital works over a period of time. It will require proper planning by the government and commitment to transform our prison services.

My work with the office files gave me a special insight into the types of crimes committed in our society. Predominating were sexual offences, aggravated robberies with violence, thefts, violence against women and children, domestic violence, and assaults.

As expected, movements within the prison compound were severely restricted and closely supervised. Contacts among inmates were only possible during meal times, on work assignments, and in visiting hours. At other times we were locked up within our cells/dormitories or kept confined in limited areas.

I mostly met prisoners very briefly, on the way to or from the dining hall. Now and then some would introduce themselves as from Vanuabalavu or relatives of people that I worked with in the public service or in politics.

At Makosoi the story was different. There was more interaction because we lived in the same confined space. The cells were adjacent to each other. We could talk to one another when not locked up. I came to know quite a few of the other prisoners. I learned that the occupants of Makosoi were senior inmates, serving long sentences, some in excess of 10 years. But they had behaved well and moving to Makosoi was some kind of reward for good behaviour.

I discovered a high level of political awareness among the inmates. I discerned strong support for the SDL party, as well as dislike for the military dictatorship. They were concerned about the suppression of basic human rights; restrictions on the media and of political rights; interference in religious activities; the dismantling of indigenous Fijian institutions; and the heavy hand of our security forces. They were also concerned about the prospect of a new constitution that lacked proper public consultation and involvement.

A father and son were among the Makosoi inmates. One day the father asked me if I could write a letter to the high court requesting a review of their sentence. Their story as I understood it was that they were serving a long prison term for assault on a police officer causing grievous bodily harm. At the time the duo were drinking homebrew. Afterwards they walked home and were stopped by a police officer. They were rather noisy but had not at that stage done any harm. The police officer cautioned them. The son then picked up a piece of metal and struck the officer on the head causing serious injury. He was taken in by other officers nearby. The father tried to argue with them and he was taken in as well. Unknown to the police officers the son had been in and out of St. Giles hospital. He was mentally retarded.

The father gave me a copy of the transcript of their trial. What struck me was the brief reference by the judge to the son's mental history. He was obviously not mentally sound at all. He was not assigned work. He would spend each day simply walking around the confined area at Makosoi. He would speak to himself and now and then made odd gestures. The father would remain near him all the time in case he went completely off the rails.

I felt sorry for them. The father had written to the authorities about their case. No one appeared concerned. A number of questions came to mind. Did the duo get a fair trial? Why was the son at Korovou and not at St. Giles hospital for the mentally handicapped, given his psychological state?

Another prisoner in his 40s was serving a life sentence for murder. He was assigned to work at the prison's mechanical workshop. He was an outstanding mechanic. With a few other similarly skilled convicts he would strip a car engine to pieces and put it together again fully repaired and cleaned. The prison department must have saved a lot of money because of the special abilities of these inmates.

Quite often, while waiting for breakfast, I would quote to this prisoner, and others around us, a verse of scripture, from I Thessalonians 5: 16-18:

> "Rejoice always; pray without ceasing; in
> everything give thanks for this is the will
> of God for you in Christ Jesus."

The Fijian version says:

> "Reki tikoga; masu tikoga ka kua ni mudu; ia
> na vakavinavinaka ena vuku ni veika
> keceqa, ni sa loma ni Kalou oqo vei
> kemudou, ena vuku i Karisito Jisu."

This verse became very popular. I was happy to see the smiles as we greeted each other with it before we started each day.

One day a young man in his mid-twenties asked if I could help in preparing a submission to support his appeal against sentence. He gave me a hand-written submission for my review and comments. He could not afford a lawyer and wanted to fight his own case.

I was amazed at the quality of his presentation. The English was excellent with short sentences, and good grammar. The arguments were logical. The young man had attended USP but dropped out because of financial difficulties.

I told him I was impressed with what he had prepared. I could not do any better. I advised him to try to resume his studies and perhaps study law on his release. What a tragedy that a young man of such talent had ended up in jail.

About six cells from mine were five inmates from Vanuabalavu. On some evenings they would sing traditional "*polotu*" songs, peculiar to Lau, before evening prayers. It was always good to hear them. One Saturday morning I visited them to talk about the Vanuabalavu Day Festival to be held in October. All of them had been in prison for some time. They didn't seem to be interested in the festival. I suggested that we might have some Vanuabalavu meetings to consider whether we could assist the fundraising.

# 46

# AFRICAN GIANTS AND OTHER STORIES

One day, while I was returning from the dining hall, a remand prisoner was coming from the opposite direction. There were other prisoners with him. As they came near he called out my name – "Mr Qarase, Mr Qarase. Run! Run! Run! The African giants are coming! Run! Run! They are big! The other prisoners quickly grabbed him and pulled him away. I was told he was mentally unstable. I wondered why he was at Korovou and not at St. Giles hospital just up the hill from the prison complex.

I did not see any African giants.

Further down from my cell was another man in his late 60s or early 70s. This was Franz Von Hapsburg, a remand prisoner, who had been in prison for months. He used to boast of his ancestry, claiming he was a direct descendent of the last Austrian Emperor. He said he was a cousin of Queen Elizabeth II of England. We all called him Frank.

Frank must have travelled widely. He had a good knowledge of many countries in Europe, Asia, the Americas, the West Indies and the Pacific island region. He had also spent quite some time in India and spoke Hindi fluently. He was fond of the Pacific islands. I was told he held passports from two or three island countries.

Frank read a lot of books. He would complete reading one or two daily since he was not assigned any work and had the entire day to himself. He was very knowledgeable about issues such as economics, politics, international relations and so on. He was a good conversationist, but it was always difficult keeping up with him.

Although Frank had spent a considerable part of his life among coloured people, I could detect an occasional element of racist superiority in his comments. But he got on well with fellow inmates. He was of course deeply frustrated and disappointed with the delays in his court case. It was called up for hearing a few times during 2012/2013. I was told that he was likely to be deported. The problem was that he had no valid travel documents to any country. After my release I was told that Frank finally managed to acquire documents that enabled him to travel to Canada. I would not be surprised if he once again appears on our shores.

---

What struck me was the wide variation in penalties imposed by the courts for similar offenses. The variations appeared in the sentences for all crimes committed, including murders, sexual violations, domestic violence, robberies, violence against women and children and so on. Admittedly, crimes were committed under different circumstances and this may explain the variation in penalties. However there must be established rules that guide the courts in passing sentences. If these rules are followed then the penalties imposed for similar offenses committed under similar circumstances should be basically the same.

I came across a case which I considered outrageous. The prisoner concerned committed incest and rape. He was tried in a magistrates court, found guilty and sentenced to imprisonment for eight years.

He was to serve his sentence through imprisonment from Friday evening to Sunday evening every weekend. He was free during week days. In other words he could be employed for wages from Monday to Friday and then relaxed in prison during weekends, with no work, but with free board and lodging. I thought that serious cases such as rape were never tried in the magistrates court but in the high court. I believe the prosecution had appealed the magistrates court decision.

In my opinion a review of the rules relating to penalties/sentences for all types of offences is overdue. There is a need to ensure consistencies, fairness and integrity on these matters.

# 47

# WHAT WAS I DOING HERE?

One afternoon, as I was reading in my cell, there was a commotion in the outside passage. It sounded like two people arguing heatedly. It seemed there were a few spectators as well. Some of them were laughing and they appeared to be cheering on those having the row. There were more verbal exchanges between the two combatants before they calmed down.

I stepped out of my cell and asked what the commotion was about. Another inmate explained that apparently there was "love in the air". The two were arguing over another inmate who was the common object of their affection.

One day a young lad of 17 joined us at Makosoi. He was a remand prisoner and had been at the juvenile centre at the Domain, Suva. Apparently, he and two other juveniles broke the rules and were then transferred to Korovou.

The day he was admitted his elderly much loved aunt visited him. On seeing her, the lad completely broke down and cried his heart out. During the following few days some of us at Makosoi tried to cheer him up and he responded positively.

One day I asked the youngster why he was in prison. He told me he was charged with sexual assault and attempted rape of a woman in her 20s. He related his version of the circumstances which led him to prison. He was on an outer island drinking homebrew with some friends, including the woman. He said they were all intoxicated. He and the woman were involved in some kind of intimacy in one corner of the *bure*. An older married man watched the two jealously from another corner. Apparently he wanted to be with the woman too.

This jealous observer later reported the two to a local police officer, who was his good friend. The young man was charged with sexual assault and attempted rape and placed on remand awaiting trial. According to the lad the woman was not medically examined.

The accused, of course, had pleaded not guilty to the charge. I tried to encourage him and told him that based on his account there did not appear to be a case to answer. I advised him to get a lawyer or ask the Legal Aid Commission for assistance.

As the weeks passed I came to know the background of many more inmates at Makosoi and in the wider prison. One memory stands out. During a pre-breakfast parade I stood in the back row; two other rows of prisoners were in front of me. Among those on the front row, I could see two who had committed murders; two serious sex offenders; and three jailed for aggravated robbery with violence. And then I observed in the second row, two others who had committed sex crimes; two domestic violence perpetrators; and three prisoners guilty of robbery with violence. In the back row, where I stood, the same sort of picture emerged. There were child molesters, murderers, rapists and so on.

I began to think I did not really belong here. Why was I standing on parade with such a collection of criminals? What had brought me to this? But I accepted that I had no choice in the matter. My situation was what it was. And the sensible course was to make the best of it, learn from the experience, and get on well with all inmates.

Saturdays were for laundry and clean-up. Soon after breakfast you would see inmates busy washing their clothes and putting them out on the lines. Soon these would be full and many prisoners would have to wait until they were clear. The lines were a riot of colour with the orange-colored uniforms dominating. Other lines had off- white bed sheets, white or off-white pillow cases, brown bath towels, and mixed colour mattress covers.

Based on my experience at RKS and QVS I had no problem washing my own clothes. But you never stop learning. I found a new way of doing this chore. In my cell there was a plastic bucket, courtesy of FMF biscuits (the owner of the biscuit company would be one of my visitors). There was also a piece of two-inch plastic pipe about half my height. These two items, the bucket and the pipe, were used for washing clothes.

All you had to do was drop your dirty apparel into the bucket, pour in some water and mix in washing powder; take the bucket outside and start pounding the clothes with the piece of plastic pipe. Continue for about 30 minutes and then rinse with clean water. Your clothes would then be cleaner than if you had used a washing machine! And this washing technique was good exercise.

Our cells would be turned upside down for a good clean out. Bedding, mattresses, clothes and other items would go through a thorough process of cleaning and then be placed in the sun. The rooms would be scrubbed with soapy water and then left to dry. We washed the metal frames of the beds with soapy hot water.

One of the objectives of this was to ensure that the ever-present bed bugs (Kutunitana) were eradicated. This was not possible of course but, at least the population was kept under reasonable control. My blood was still on the sheets.

I also learned another new skill in prison – how to trap flies. Another inmate in the adjacent cell showed us an effective way of reducing the fly population. It was close to Christmas 2012, the usual season for flies around Fiji. A colleague used an empty tea cup for his demonstration. It was filled with water up to just below the brim, and then topped up with soap lather. This lather would be built up and it looked like a half circle on top of the cup.

The flies were attracted by this and once they landed on the lather they were caught and could not escape. The demonstration used three cups. After a few minutes there were up to 10 flies dead in each of the three traps.

It was an odd feature of Korovou that I never encountered a mosquito.

———————

I n prison, rules and regulations are the order of each day, 24 hours a day. Wake-up calls, breakfast, work, lunch, dinner and lights out are strictly regulated.

I was impressed with the general response and attitude of prisoners to all this control. I often wondered if this disciplined life was followed when a prisoner left prison. Of course, not all the prisoners follow the rules. In a population of 200-300 inmates, you can expect infringements.

A surprise search on 25$^{th}$ September 2012 found many contraband items. Following this, some tight security measures were imposed. One of these was the use of metal detectors adjacent to the entrance to the prison. All those who entered, both prisoners and visitors, were subject to this check. Contraband items were found and confiscated. Marijuana, cigarettes and *suki* (Fijian tobacco) were also discovered and confiscated. In a nearby room three or four security officers conducted further searches.

For this purpose, there was a large mirror on the floor of the room. Prisoners/visitors caught with banned items were taken to this room to be strip-searched. Some prisoners/visitors who behaved in a suspicious manner were taken to the room also.

Each suspect would be required to strip to his/her underwear and then be searched. In some cases, they were required to strip naked and then told to squat over the mirror. Female visitors were dealt with by female officers.

In many instances more banned items were found which the electronic metal detectors had failed to identify. These items included cigarettes, marijuana, *suki* and even mobile phones. At least two women were caught with banned items under these strip- checks.

Quite a few items were confiscated including mobile phones, radios- and a few television sets! There were many pieces of clothing and bedding, including uniforms, mattresses, and pillows. These were in excess of the numbers officially issued to prisoners.

As a consequence of these surprise searches the commissioner of prisons and senior officers talked to us on Monday 1st October 2012. The message was short and clear. More stringent security

arrangements were put in place immediately and visits were reduced significantly. Each prisoner was allowed only three visitors every two weeks, confined to immediate family members. Tighter security was also a reflection of a break-out at Naboro prison during the last few days.

Early on Monday, 15th October 2012 at about 4am the alarm went off. This was followed immediately by a lot of noise. There was some shouting and the sound of heavy boots running to and fro. In the morning I learned that four remand prisoners were caught trying to cut through their cell bars. The four were transferred to the maximum-security prison at Naboro.

On Sunday 2nd December 2012 all prisoners at Korovou were told to gather at the dining hall at 2.30pm where the supervisor would speak to us. It was a full house when the supervisor and some officers arrived. The supervisor told us that no contraband items should be brought into prison. He advised against attempts to escape. Those caught breaking the rules could expect to be treated appropriately with the probability of an extension of their stay in prison. He thanked those prisoners who followed the rules strictly.

Despite these warnings at about 3pm the alarm went off. It was a sure sign there was a serious breach of security. The supervisor looked around. We all looked around. Prison guards were running to the location of the security breach. The assembly dispersed and we returned to our dormitories.

Later I learned the flap was caused by four prisoners trying to escape. One of them managed to get away. The daring daylight bid for freedom became headline news the next day. On the night of 18ᵗʰ December 2012 four more prisoners were caught with mobile phones. They were transferred to Naboro.

It was towards the end of 2012, that Rev. Ratabacaca, an ex military man, came in for a two-year sentence. He was accommodated at Makosoi. Soon he began to conduct Bible studies for small groups. The groups grew quickly in size. After a few weeks the studies stopped. I learned later that the instruction came from higher authorities.

This controversial talatala was head of the Christian Mission of Fiji (CMF), a movement gaining ground throughout the country. Rev. Ratabacaca was an effective preacher of the Word. On many occasions his sermons were critical of the military dictatorship's policies, which were inconsistent with the Scriptures. Allegations were laid against him and he was subsequently imprisoned for alleged sexual offences. Before and during his trial there were unsubstantiated stories that the charges against Rev. Ratabacaca were a frame up to remove him from his growing flock of followers. Korovou prison houses a mixture of people who reflect the real world. There were inmates who reformed themselves in prison and came out responsible citizens. There were those who accepted Jesus Christ as our Lord and Saviour, and later became pastors and preachers. But there were those who did not change. Sooner or later they were back in a cell for similar or more serious offenses.

# 48

# CHRIST WITHIN KOROVOU

Methodism was drummed into me from my childhood. It was the main denomination of Mavana Village where I was baptized into the Methodist Church soon after I was born in February 1941. By parental instruction I attended church and Sunday School regularly. The option of skipping a service was unthinkable. At RKS and QVS worship on Sunday morning was compulsory.

The core of my religious belief is that God, Jehovah, is the creator of the universe and mankind. I believe Jesus Christ is the Son of God and that he died on the Cross at Calvary as the supreme sacrifice for our sins. I believe that Christ rose from the dead after three days and that He will return soon.

As I grew older and went into adulthood my faith was pushed aside by a preoccupation with higher education, getting started on a career and making a success of myself. I knew I was not a good example of a Christian. It was politics that opened the way for a life-changing acceptance of Christ which helped me carry the burdens of office.

Korovou prison gave me a special experience. There, among those regarded by many as the outcasts of society, I found a depth of spiritual commitment and love of the Saviour which in turn gave me added strength. I believe I walked out of Korovou a better person, with a new depth of understanding of Christ's love and mercy.

Looking back, I can see that neglect of my faith began in earnest at RKS and QVS. My inclination was to concentrate on my studies; the Bible was not a priority. I knew some basic stories from the Holy Book but sadly had no real knowledge of both the Old Testament and New Testament.

When I started work in 1959 in the civil service my spiritual life actually deteriorated. It was the same story in my university years from 1963 to 1966. I returned home consumed with an ambition to move up in the civil service as quickly as I could.

I had the mistaken belief that good deeds and a basic belief in God were sufficient to guarantee eternal life. Over time I came to the realization that much more than this is required. Every Christian needs to develop and maintain an intimate relationship with God, love him with all your heart and mind and strength and obey his commandments.

The full awareness of the huge gap in my spiritual life came home in 2003 when I was serving my first term as elected prime minister of Fiji. The responsibilities of office weighed heavily on me. I realized I could not carry them alone. I needed God to help with the load.

I was assisted by the late Rev Maikeli, from the Centenary Church in Suva and Rev. Koyamaibole of Raiwai church. They began to visit me at the prime minister's residence in Richards Road, Suva, to share the Word of God and offer prayers before I left for the office to start work at 8am. It was through their counsel and guidance that I decided to offer my life totally to Jesus and accept him fully as my Lord and Saviour. This happened at a brief function during a Sunday service at the Centenary church. I felt a great weight had been lifted from my shoulders. I was able to tackle the job of PM with greater confidence and conviction.

At the Methodist Church conference on Cicia, Lau, in April 2006, I took another momentous step in my Christian journey. Exercising his discretionary authority, the president of the church, Rev. Laisiasa Ratabacaca, conferred on me the designation of lay preacher. I was honoured and humbled.

Another significant event occurred in February 2008 when Leba was critically ill in Suva Private Hospital. As I sat beside Leba's bed one day, Pastor Poate Mata and Pastor Esekaia of the Pentecostal Church, Nokonoko, came to visit us.

They shared God's Word and then offered up prayers for us and, in particular, for Leba's recovery. Their visit was the start of regular Bible study and devotion with the two Pastors, their wives and occasionally with other church colleagues.

These encounters have had a tremendous and positive impact on Leba and I. A year after they began, I was baptized by Pastor Poate.

Leba and I have been blessed by prayers from many individuals and prayer groups around Fiji. This happened before I was appointed interim prime minister in 2000, during my term as elected prime minister (2001-2006), and in the years following the 2006 coup, especially during my imprisonment.

Brother Tukana who leads a group of young prayer warriors, is a regular visitor to my home at 6 Moti Street in Suva. I admire the warriors' strong faith, their commitment and their good work in evangelizing.

I cannot find the words to fully express our gratitude to all those who have kept us in their hearts and prayers.

As Prisoner No. 302 I wondered what religious life would be like in prison. What level of spirituality would there be among the inmates? I was surprised to find among these men, many of them hardened criminals, a very high degree of devotion to God, worship and prayer. Some had a remarkable knowledge and understanding of the Bible, with the ability to recite entire passages with ease and confidence.

I was also astonished to discover that Korovou was something of a training ground for aspiring pastors. It took prison to make them into men of God. Quite a few past and present ministers of the Methodist Church took their examinations to enter the ministry while they were in prison.

What greater testimonial could there be to Christ's closeness to sinners?

At weekends between meal times some inmates gathered for Bible studies. There was plenty of spare time as meals only took about 15 minutes. There was little else to do but read. So I had ample opportunity to go deeply into the contents of the Bible.

In fact I read both the Old Testament and the New Testament at least four times before my release. Additionally, I studied particular sections of the Bible that were of specific interest to me.

The Seventh Day Adventist Church delivered several volumes of literature. An Australian couple sent me a Bible commentary by the US preacher Pastor John Hagee. Rev. Tuikilakila Waqairatu, the late president of the Methodist Church, gave me a copy of Rick Warren's bestseller The Purpose Driven Life. I read it several times. After much consideration, I concluded that God's purpose for me had always been to serve others.

Morning and evening prayers were integral to our prison routine. My cellmates and I conducted devotions every day before breakfast. We took turns to lead with a format comprising a short message based on Bible verses followed by prayer. We had evening devotions just before lights out following the same pattern.

As I sat in my cell in the evenings, I would hear inmates singing hymns in faultless harmony. The distinctive rhythmic vocalising of the Lauan "*polotu*" by my kaivata (relatives) from Vanuabalavu lifted my heart as always and took me back to my island home.

I looked forward very much to the Sunday church services. I had assumed, for some reason, that we would be permitted to wear civilian clothes for worship. This was not the case. We remained in our prison garb. Before 9am the prisoners gathered in the dining hall. Pastors from different Christian denominations arrived. One of them would lead a short devotion before the assembly broke into separate denominational groups. The Methodists, easily the largest, used the prison chapel for their services. The other groups went to their allo-cated places. For us Methodists, the services followed the normal pattern in any Methodist Church. The only difference was that the service lasted for just an hour from 10-11am.

As always, I was amazed at the quality of the singing. There was no equivalent of choir practice and yet what I heard was as powerful and uplifting as anything from any Fijian male choir in the world outside.

Many senior ministers conducted our services. They included former presidents of the Methodist Church, Rev. Tomasi Kanailagi and Rev. Ame Tugaue, and the late president Rev. Tuikilakila Waqairatu. My diary tells me that Rev. Kanailagi officiated on 19th September 2012 when his sermon was based on Matt 5:1-12. Rev. Ame Tugaue preached on 4th November 2012 with a sermon drawn from Joshua 24:14-24 and II Samuel 1:1-28. The Rev. Tuikilakila Waqairatu spoke to us on 28th October 2012 from Luke 15:11-24 and Isaiah 49:19. On a number of occasions Pastors from other denominations – Assemblies of God (AOG), Seventh Day Adventists (SDA), Christian Mission Fellowship (CMF) - visited me to offer prayers and Bible messages. A Ghanaian, Rev. Jacob, was another visitor. Regrettably these visits were stopped by the prison authori-ties. For security reasons, I suppose.

I tell relatives and friends that prison is an ordeal. You are consigned to a confined and strictly controlled environment. You lose your freedom. Your entire life is turned upside down and you are separated from those you love and depend on.

In my case, those 243 days produced a virtual spiritual rebirth and awakening. I gained greater knowledge and understanding of the Bible. My personal relationship with God and Jesus Christ intensified further. My faith, which was already strong, became unshakeable. I regret that this happened so late in my life. I suppose it is a great irony that it took prison for this to occur. We mortals can never understand the workings of God.

# 49

# RUPERT AND KING KONG

For a few nights the sound of rats scurrying in the ceiling kept me awake for hours. From the noise they made I imagined they were huge. They ran to and fro playing or fighting. It was probably their mating season? Whatever was happening they certainly kept me awake. During morning walks I came across many mongooses slipping out of the sides of buildings or running back through holes or gaps. They were huge; obviously were well-fed from the left- overs from the kitchen.

The mongoose reminded me of my time at Ratu Kadavulevu School during 1953/54. Lunch and/or dinner usually consisted of *cassava*, boiled *"bele"* enlivened with the smell of tinned fish. Some of us used to supplement this monotonous, tasteless diet on Saturdays with some "lovo" mongoose. We would set traps and normally caught what we wanted. A "lovo" with *cassava*, "lairo" (mud crab), mongoose and eel ("duna") was a feast. At first, I was hesitant about consuming mongoose but once I tasted it I quite liked it.

One morning I decided to have breakfast in my cell. With half a loaf of bread and a cup of tea I sat down for the meal. After a while, I saw a baby mouse coming into the cell rather cautiously. He must have seen me. Slowly, he moved towards a small cupboard at the side of the door, which sometimes contained some fruit and other food-stuff. I threw some small pieces of bread towards the tiny creature. But he ran away quickly. After a short time he would re- appear and head for the cupboard again. I threw some more bits of bread and the mouse would again disappear quickly.

I took note of the time I encountered my visitor. It was always before 8am. My cellmate had left for work. I did not start work in the office until 8am.

There was an opportunity for me alone to quietly befriend the mouse. I would offer more bread pieces, but he always ran away quickly. This performance was repeated each morning. Finally, the two of us did seem to come closer. The mouse was not as nervous.

During a visit from Leba and our two granddaughters I related my experience with the mouse. Fane was quite excited and wanted to know more. I had assumed that the mouse was a "he" and asked Fane to suggest a name. Immediately she said "Rupert". So Rupert it was.

Some weeks passed and I noticed that my friend Rupert was growing. He was healthy and active. Fane was obviously interested and keen to know all I could tell her about Rupert. I would relate his activities to her each time they visited. Fane was well disposed to Rupert even though she did not see him. Following some heavy rain and flooding Rupert failed to turn up at the usual time. I feared the worst. He may have been swept away by the flood and drowned. But I did not want to believe that. I thought perhaps now he was growing up, Rupert had became occupied with many mouse friends. I made the huge mistake of suggesting to Fane that Rupert might have died. Fane was quiet, and I could see tears welling in her eyes. I tried to comfort her and suggested that Rupert would be back soon after spending time with his friends. Thankfully, he did re- appear and seemed to possess a new confidence. Fane of course was very happy when I told her he was alive and well.

After the prison authorities gave me approval to walk around the courtyard in the morning I started a daily walking routine. The walks were generally uneventful. I would walk past three or four prison guards during each round of the yard. We would greet each other with "good morning" during the first round, and then I would continue on until just before 6am.

I would walk past the dining hall and then up to one end of an unused two-storey concrete building, constructed in 1910. It had been declared unsafe for human occupation. From one end I would turn and walk towards the other end of the building, about 30 metres. About half a metre from the ground a flat concrete strip a few centimeters wide ran right along the length of the building.

One morning, as I started to walk from one end of the building in the dim light, I noticed something moving along the raised flat concrete.

I stopped and took a closer look. It was a big rat, about eight inches long. I started to walk again and the rat did the same. Half way along the building the light was brighter and the rat hesitated. It stopped and I stopped too. It turned around, ran away and disappeared into the darkness. For several mornings the big rat and I became walking partners. I decided to name him "King Kong". I was sure the big rodent was a "he" because of his size. He was obviously well fed from kitchen leftovers.

I told Fane about King Kong. She was excited and pleased for me. First I found a mouse companion. Now I had a rat for a friend! King Kong and I were regular companions. At times, during our walks, we would stop. He would look at me curiously and I would do the same to him. It seemed there was an understanding that this small part of the world belonged to us. I never had a liking for mice and rats. But in the prison environment Rupert became my friend and King Kong doubled as friend and walking partner. They gave me some kind of comfort.

Then I remembered Genesis 1:24-25 in the Old Testament which says:

*And God said, 'Let the land produce living*

*creatures according to their kinds:*
*livestock, creatures that move along the*
*ground, and wild animals, each according*
*to its kind'.*

*And it was so. God made the wild animals*
*according to their kinds, the livestock*
*according to their kinds, and all the*
*creatures that move along the ground*
*according to their kinds. And God saw*
*that it was good.*

So I reminded myself that Rupert and King Kong were both created by God just as I was. God created them for a purpose. God also created me for a purpose. I thanked Him for the opportunity of making special friends who made my life a little easier, in a difficult time and in an alien environment. I reminded myself that Rupert and King Kong were free. I was not.

# 50

# NO WORDS CAN DESCRIBE HOW MUCH I LOVE YOU

O ur children and their families had followed my trial very closely. They were concerned about my health and welfare. Those living overseas visited me when they could. There was a memorable gathering on 4$^{th}$ February 2013, my 72$^{nd}$ birthday. The prison authorities were kind enough to allow family members to have a small celebratory dinner for me in the visitor area. Leba, Senikau, Fane, Josefa from Dubai, his sons Josateki, Jerry and Benjamin were all present. We had a good time and there was plenty of food which we shared with the guards.

I received many letters from home from those that I care for very much. They kept me in touch with myself and who I was, bolstered me when I felt down and renewed my faith in the future. The love that radiated from every word of those letters – no matter how mundane the topic - was a powerful emotional support. They uplifted my spirits and gave me comfort and joy.

The most regular correspondents were Fane and Senikau, my granddaughters, who lived with us at our house, 6 Moti Street, Suva. They always addressed me as Tua, the Lauan word for grandfather. When they came visiting on 18$^{th}$ August 2012, it was the first time they had seen me in my orange prisoner's uniform. They were shocked, but at the same time happy to be with me. Of course, I was happy to be with them. They were accompanied by Leba and Fiona and Seini, their first cousins. It was the start of the second term school holidays and also the beginning of the Hibiscus festival. Leba and I decided to give them some pocket money. There were smiles all around.

Fane, especially, had always been very close to me. She was the child who clung to me in despair as I left the courtroom for Korovou prison on 3$^{rd}$ August 2012. A photo of Fane hugging me and weeping, appeared prominently in the media the following day, 4$^{th}$ August 2012.

This is what Fane wrote just before Christmas 2012. She was 14 at the time.

---

Dear Tua,

It's me Fane. I just wanted to tell you how much I miss you. I also want to thank you for everything that you have done for me throughout my life. There are no words in the world that could describe how much I love and miss you. I know I can't give you much but right now; all I have is my love and how much I care for you. I know you are going through a lot right now but all I can say is Hang in There. God has a purpose for everything and I know he has a good reason for making us go through this. I remember at your 70$^{th}$ birthday I said "you are 1 in a million" I was wrong Tua, YOU ARE 1 IN A BILLION. I will always love you no matter what happens. Merry Christmas and Happy New Year.

Love you Fane.

---

I am not a demonstrative person, but Fane's letter of love to support her grandfather in his difficulties touched me very much. It still does.

Senikau is the shy one. She was in form six at Adi Cakobau School, Sawani. Her form teacher and classmates were kind enough to send me a large card covered with individual messages and good wishes. I noticed that nearly all of them drew on Bible verses. I sent a short response to the form teacher. Senikau told me later that what I wrote was photocopied for each student.

Her reply to my note said this:

---

Dear Tua,

This is Senikau. Hope you're healthy and strong. I gave your letter to my form captain and they all loved it. ☺ They all have a copy each now, they were so happy and excited to get it and that it was signed. Our form teacher went on maternity leave last week. Me and Fane already have our materials, "sa soli vei Nei Togi me cula". Hope you enjoy your dinner today. We are all excited to see you tomorrow.

Love, Senikau.

---

Although the students were thankful and happy for my reply to them, my happiness was even greater. The students did not know me personally. I did not know them either.

And yet there was a connection between us. The common element was the Almighty God we believe in and worship, and the Holy Scriptures.

'Love your neighbor as you love yourself', says the Bible. The messages on the card from the ACS pupils showed love, compassion, respect and care for me in my situation. I thank God for their concerns.

From Fane:

---

Dear Tua,

I hope you are well and doing ok. We miss you a lot since we don't get to see each other everyday. Today is Saturday and we are having another 'vuli meke' at home and we went to town today to buy our material for next week. The Mavana material is really nice. Daddy sent us some money so we just bought the material with our own money. We hope you are well and enjoying your dinner that we drop off everyday. School is going well and I have started studying for the annual examination which is in week 9. Everything is going well at home apart from us missing you. I have filed the things you put in the bag and mummy has sent out the e-mail you wanted her to send. Oh and yesterday was teachers day but Grammar is celebrating it next week Tuesday and I am organizing the one for my form. Well we just wanted to let you know about everything that's happening at home and please reply to this letter.

Love from: Nau, Senikau and Fane.

---

From Fane:

---

Dear Tua,

It's me Fane. I just want to let you know that we miss you and everything else is ok. After I just drop your food I'm going to town with Kaji to go buy some things for my task which I have to give in tomorrow cause I'm not going to school starting from Wednesday. Please reply to my letter. Hope all is well and how was your court case? Love you and miss you.

Fane. Please reply.

From Senikau during a cyclone warning:

---

Dear Tua,

Sorry we can't see you today because the weather might be worse in the afternoon so we're delivering your dinner early. We miss visiting you today. Everything is alright at home, all shutters are up and all containers filled with water. Candles and our solar lights are ready. We also have our food rations ready. The car is parked inside the garage. Tata Teki and aunty Berni had left, they called this morning before they boarded and they are sending their regards and best wishes to you. Stay safe Tua. We all Love you. May God Bless You.

Love from: Nau, Senikau and Fane and small Leba.

---

Leba, my wife's namesake, who is our granddaughter from our youngest son, Josateki Lagilagi Qarase of Sydney, also visited me and later corresponded.

From small Leba:

---

Dear Tua,

I miss you very much and hope to see you soon. This is from Leba. I will leave soon but still think of you. And thank you for all the good times. Love always from Leba.

---

From small Leba:

---

Thinking of you and I love you. From Leba

---

Visits from relatives made a lot of difference to me. I looked forward to them and it was good to keep in touch with family members on a regular basis. From 4$^{th}$ August 2012, to one week before I was released, visits from Leba and the two granddaughters were regular. In addition, my family members who now live overseas were allowed to visit me whenever they were in Fiji. During my first week in prison, our third son, Isoa, his wife Kiri and their two sons, Josua and Lai (my namesake) were in Fiji. They are citizens of Australia and live in Griffith, New South Wales. They came to visit me before they left for Australia.

In November 2012, Josefa, our eldest son was on leave from Dubai where he worked. He came to visit me before he returned to Dubai. Josefa had moved to another job. He is a marine engineer in a large oil company. I was happy for him and his family. In December 2012, Josateki, our youngest son, his wife Bernie, and their daughter small Leba were in Fiji. Josateki and his family are citizens of Australia and they live in Sydney. They visited me before they returned to Australia.

Our only daughter, Seini and our eldest granddaughter Talei lived in different cities in the USA. But they phoned me a few times to find out how I was getting on. They were also concerned with my health. I assured them that I was reasonably comfortable in prison and there was nothing to worry about. Seini was expecting a second son. I congratulated her and wished them well. Talei had given birth to Eliana who is our first great grandchild.

On Sunday, 9$^{th}$ September 2012 Leba, Senikau and Fane visited me again. It was Fathers Day. Fane brought a large handwritten card with the message: "Do not be afraid! Be strong and courageous!" It was similar to the words of encouragement I gave to Fane when she was clinging to me as I was led off to prison. From then onwards we would greet each other with this exhortation. My cellmates and I agreed to fix the card on a wall.

The 4$^{th}$ of December 2012 was Leba's birthday. It was celebrated at a Suva restaurant with some friends. I gave her my greetings. On

Christmas day, 25$^{th}$ December, I was allowed to have Christmas dinner in the visitors' room with Leba, Senikau and Fane. They brought plenty of food, including "lovo". We shared with the prison guards and all enjoyed the day.

I have mentioned elsewhere that visits were restricted to close family members, three each time except for a few occasions when my children and grandchildren from overseas were in Fiji. For my personal friends, only three visits were allowed.

The first was from my long-time friends Hari Punja, Bachu Patel and Ajay Amrit. Hari Punja is a business tycoon and head of a number of large companies, including FMF Foods Limited, Rice Company of Fiji Limited, Blue Gas and a large packaging company. Bachu Patel is a director of Vinod Patel & Co. Limited and general manager of the company's Laucala Beach complex. Vinod Patel & Co. Limited is one of the largest hardware distributors. Ajay Amrit is a real estate investor and was presenter of a Bollywood television series. We had a good get together. It was lively and informative for me. We talked about many issues from business to Bollywood to politics. Between the four of us we could have solved many of the problems of the world! My friends visited me again on Thursday, 25$^{th}$ October 2012. We talked for about one hour. It was a good update for me on what was happening around the country.

My friend for decades, Matt Wilson, visited me on Monday, 24$^{th}$ December 2012. I have known Matt for a long time since my appointment as managing director of the Fiji Development Bank in 1983. The bank used his services as public relations consultant, speechwriter, and on other assignments. During my term as prime minister of Fiji (2000-2006) Matt was engaged as one of my speechwriters. He also assisted in other assignments required by the Office of the prime minister. I thanked Matt for the visit and I was happy to meet him. We talked for about an hour. It was again a good opportunity for me to be updated on what was happening in the outside world.

The only other visit from outside the immediate family was from

Ratu Tevita Rasiga of Mualevu. I was thankful for his concern for my welfare. We talked for about 30 minutes.

Requests from many other friends and prominent people to visit me were futile. Early during my imprisonment, the OC asked me for a list of 20 people for a list of potential visitors. I submitted the list, but nothing came of it, even after repeated reminders.

Ratu Epeli Nailatikau, the President of Fiji, visited the prison on Christmas day, 25th December 2012. We knew each other very well and had a special link.

Ratu Epeli had been my loyal deputy and Minister for Fijian Affairs when I was leading the unelected interim government. As Ratu Epeli did his Christmas rounds of Korovou, we had a brief encounter and exchanged greetings. I wondered what was going through his mind as he shook hands with Prisoner No. 302. He was a competent enough minister, although sometimes he had to be chased up a bit on his ministerial assignments.

I entrusted him with a particularly sensitive task following the death in a shootout of one of George Speight's civilian supporters, Kolinio Tabua. Speight and his followers had insisted that Tabua should be buried in the parliamentary grounds. There had been a large funeral for him. But as a government, we knew it was not appropriate for Tabua's remains to stay in the parliamentary complex. Ratu Epeli's job was to manage the exhumation of the body for reburial in Korolevu village, Namara in Tailevu. I was pleased with the way he handled the assignment with care and in accordance with protocol.

We were told to be ready in our cells before he arrived. He came to Makosoi dormitory first and our cell was first in line. He probably did not expect to see me but he enquired how I was and wished me Merry Christmas! Ratu Epeli was Speaker of the House of Representatives when I was prime minister. He was also commander of the Fiji Military Forces in 1987 and has served as a diplomat.

I thank those who were able to visit me at Korovou. It is regrettable that others were apparently barred. I fail to understand why.

# 51

# TRAINING FIASCO

Towards the end of 2012 I ran out of vanguard sheets. They were necessary to enable me to keep the Information Board up-to-date. I asked for a new supply, but it never came. During a family visit I asked Fane to bring me some new sheets and a few ball point pens. She brought them during her next visit and I was then able to update the information board.

At times there was little to do. This allowed me time to read the books given to me by friends and well wishers. In December 2012 the officer-in-charge asked me if I could take a training session for prison officers on a relevant and useful topic. I asked for time to think it over. I considered the request and thought that the subject of savings and investments would be useful. The officer-in-charge agreed, and I then began to prepare some training material. The stationery items I needed, such as photocopy paper were not available. Neither was a typing service. I had no alternative but to ask Fane, my granddaughter, to act as my secretary. She was happy and excited to take this on. It would be a good test for her secretarial abilities.

It took me two to three weeks to prepare the material. I passed the drafts to Fane to type, using the computer at home. The typed drafts were given to me for checking during family visits.

Fane passed the typing test. I then asked her to prepare 50 copies of seven pages each. I also asked her to prepare 50 files, with each containing one set of training materials. I had to spend about $400.00 - from my own depleted pocket - on stationery items such as photocopy papers, computer ink, and files. You might describe this as service to country above and beyond the call of duty. My secretary did not receive any pay; just a big "thank you" kiss. But she was glad to do the job.

I gave one set of training materials to the officer-in-charge and one each to two assistants.

Then I waited for the training session to be arranged. This was not easy because the prison officers worked in shifts. The training session was to be held outside working hours. The aim was to get 20 officers for each training session. This meant that the officers had to be off-duty and "free" all at the same time. It took quite a while to get the first session organized. It took place during February 2013. I believe the training went well. Remarks by many of them were positive and encouraging. I then waited for the next session. It never happened. I learned later that higher authorities in the Prison Department were not happy about my involvement. I should have billed them for the $400 I had spent. I felt bad. I thought about the effort Fane and I put into the project, only to be treated in this way. But in reality, the incident was nothing but a passing irritation.

# 52

# THE UPS AND DOWNS OF A
# MENACING DISEASE

I have been a diabetic for more than 20 years. My time in prison presented special challenges in the treatment of this menacing disease. I went through two threatening crises which landed me in the Korovou infirmary. But surprisingly in the end I found that life in Korovou actually helped to improve and stabilise my condition!

Like many thousands of Fiji people who suffer from an ailment which has reached epidemic proportions, I am guilty of not paying enough attention to managing it. My symptoms got worse as the years passed and I was forced to start taking medication.

It is very easy to be lulled into a false sense of security because most of the time you don't have any noticeable symptoms. In that sense diabetes is "invisible." I am familiar with the formula for dealing with the type 2 variety with which I am afflicted; diet, exercise and, usually later, medication.

The exercise part for me is achieved through vigorous daily walks lasting about an hour. But I'm afraid I was not very responsible about following medical advice on diet. I often tended to eat the wrong kind of food, containing too much sugar.

The result was my blood sugar was often too high. I use a hand-held monitor to provide the data. Generally, the closer your sugar levels are to those that people without diabetes have, the healthier your readings. This range is between 4 to 7.8 mmol/L.

Keeping the levels healthy is at the core of managing the condition. If you have a sugar "high" you are in danger. You may feel drowsy and thirsty and generally unwell and tired. You pass a lot of urine and may have blurred vision. In rare instances you may have to be hospitalised. A sugar "low" is also very threatening. Symptoms included hunger; feeling shaky or sweaty, trembling or tingling hands, loss of concentration, anxiety or irritation.

My sugar had been running high for weeks before I entered prison. It was registering between 13 and 18mmol/L, and sometimes over 20mmol/L. I sensed that this was probably to do with the stress of the court case. Stress is known to elevate sugar levels.

Our family doctor, Dr Ami Chandra, had written a comprehensive account of my diabetes. This was tendered in court during mitigation and also given to the prison authorities. Dr Chandra made some suggestions for my diet and exercise requirements. On the day I was admitted to prison – 3$^{rd}$ August 2012 - my sugar was at 21 mmol/L; this was dangerous. I was determined to get it down to between 5 and 6 mmol/L as soon as possible. The prison diet with a lot of dhal, greens, (mainly *bele*), *roti* and rice with curried tinned fish, was reportedly good for diabetes. But the half loaf of bread and tea for breakfast and lunch was a bit high on calories. I quickly learned that some inmates were permitted to supplement prison fare with food from home on medical grounds; so I applied and got permission.

One of my first tasks after breakfast on the second day was to visit the prison infirmary to collect my prescribed pills. The next step was to gain approval to walk around the prison courtyard in the mornings as part of my diabetes regime. There was no problem about this. A pair of canvas walking shoes from home completed the arrangements. I was striding out by 5am daily. Several guards patrolled the courtyard perimeter for normal security reasons. But this did not detract from my enjoyment of the exercise

The quiet and coolness of dawn lifted my spirits. When the moon was full and setting in the west it would light up the entire complex. It was marvelous to witness this; I saw God's hand at work. I would do 30 rounds of the courtyard, taking about 50 minutes, and be back in my cell just before the wake-up alarm at 6am. When it rained I did circuits around the dining hall.

These walking exercises combined with strict diet control had a dramatic effect. Within two months my sugar level was down to between 5 and 6 mmol/L as planned. I felt good physically.

My weight was around 96kg, which was about right for a person my height. I made sure that my sugar levels, weight, and blood pressure were checked regularly.

Then something went wrong. During December 2012, I noticed that my sugar was below a healthy range although my blood pressure was not a problem. By 3$^{rd}$ of January I felt sick, dizzy, and weak and had body pains. I did not want to eat.

In the evening I went to the infirmary where I was given panadol and vitamin pills. I took some as directed but did not sleep well. The following morning, I had a running stomach. I was advised to consume some sugar to get my sugar level back to normal. I did this and later in the day I was feeling better, but not 100 percent. I was then admitted to the infirmary where I joined four other sick inmates. After about a week I had recovered fully, but was told to remain in the infirmary for a while longer.

On 18$^{th}$ February 2013 the duty officer at the infirmary told me to move back to my cell at Makosoi. No reason was given for my transfer, but I was glad to team up again with my former cellmates. But the way I was treated annoyed me. Two high profile prisoners who preceded me were allowed to stay in the Infirmary the whole time they were at Korovou, with many privileges not given to any other inmate. Later I learned that the instruction to move me back to Makosoi came from higher authorities. The OC apologised for moving me back to Makosoi, but I told him not to worry since I understood the situation well.

Two weeks before I was released on 3$^{rd}$ April 2013, I became ill again and went back into the infirmary. Next day my sugar level was down to 2.4 mmol/L; this was in the danger zone. My blood pressure was not good either at 150/110. I took some sugar with tea and was allowed some chocolate bars from home. A day later I was still in hazardous territory. My sugar had gone up to 9.2 mmol/L. This was too high. My blood pressure was registering at 150/100. Things started to improve, until my readings were acceptable again. By 2$^{nd}$ April, I was fine.

For some reason on the day of my release, my sugar level and blood pressure soared again. I attribute this to last minute uncertainties about precisely when I would be freed. On balance though, I give Korovou a pass grade for diabetes patients. It gave me a diet, which worked.

My advice to victims is to follow medical advice. Get on the right diet, do your daily exercises and you are in with a chance of living long. As many people in Fiji have found to their cost, to ignore diabetes is a sure course for disaster and possibly death.

---

On 6$^{th}$ February 2013 the daily routine was disrupted when a tsunami warning was issued at about 3pm by the meteorological office. Apparently, a strong earthquake had occurred near the Solomon Islands. We were told to evacuate to higher grounds. Within minutes some remand prisoners were moved to St. Giles hospital up on the hill beside Korovou. The rest of us were told to wait for some transport that would take us to Naboro prison located away from the coast. I tried to ring Leba but could not get through. However, at about 4pm the tsunami warning was cancelled for the whole of Fiji.

# DEVELOPMENT PASSION GOES OVER THE PRISON WALLS

My intense and lasting interest in initiating and implementing community development projects began soon after I started work in December 1959. The career I followed gave me the opportunity to give full rein to this calling. It reached a milestone in the most extraordinary manner when I was in Korovou Gaol in Suva in 2012.

I had been appointed chair of a big local and overseas fundraising event for the entire island of Vanuabalavu to be held in Suva during a Vanuabalavu Day Festival to be held, (not just on one day, but for three days), from the 11th to 13th of October, 2012. All the complex arrangements for this were well under way and excitement among the islanders was rising.

At this critical time, I was facing charges as a result of High Court Case HAC no.26 about my involvement in some Fijian Holdings share transactions. On the 3rd of August I was sentenced to 12 months in prison to be served at Korovou. We did not allow this to impede the organization of the Vanuabalavu festival. I decided I would not step down as chair of the organising committee. The prison walls would not contain my ambitions to help my home island.

A core group of committee members quickly took responsibility for pushing forward with our plans. I was kept briefed on progress and eventually received permission to hold committee meetings in the visitor's room at the gaol. I knew exactly how much money was coming in during the celebration and prepared the final accounts in my cell.

My intense commitment to community affairs and fundraising began in the 1960s when I used to attend meetings in Suva of Mavana people who had relocated to the city. I was one of the younger generation following in the footsteps of our elders. Occasionally I would suggest a particular village project and, once it was approved, I would be delegated to produce the necessary documentation, organising fundraising and then implementation.

When I returned from university education in 1966 I continued to attend our Suva Mavana meetings. I increasingly felt that many projects were not properly organised. They were a bit haphazard and dependent on random initiatives emerging from our Suva discussions.

During the early 1970s I proposed the idea of a more structured and planned approach and encouraged discussion on this. Afterwards the idea was taken directly to the villagers at Mavana. The response was overwhelmingly positive. A village development committee in Suva spearheaded the new approach. It was led by Col. Mosese Buadromo, a former permanent secretary in the Fiji public service, and at one-time commanding officer of the Fiji Military Forces territorial force. A few years later he was succeeded by retired school teacher Mr Neli Vuatalevu, until Mr Vuatalevu passed away in 1986.

I took over as chairman until 2013 when I handed to Mr. Tevita Vuatalevu, who was assisted by younger members. The process I had initiated and which won support was fairly simple. The first step was to sit down with the villagers to find out what improvements they wanted that would enhance their way of life.

I would make a list of their suggestions and lead discussion on advantages and disadvantages of each one. The list would then be prioritized and documented as five-year plans. Each would have a budget on project costs, possible sources of finance and a time scale for implementation. The plans would be presented to the village meetings for approval.

We had five of these from 1976 to 2010. Not all projects in each plan would be completed on time, usually due to insufficient funds. In these instances, these would be rolled over into the next plan. Currently Mavana has a 10-year plan to 2020.

Major schemes we managed to complete included a large church building and a big community hall; piped water; electricity generation supplying each household; foreshore reclamation of an area 250 x 30metres; a 250 metres long seawall; four separate facilities each containing a flush toilet and shower for one half of the village; two teachers' quarters for the village school; a village drainage system; and two shop buildings, one at the village and another at Lomaloma for the retail business owned and run by the village company, Qalitu Enterprises Ltd. Additionally there were minor works mainly featuring repairs and maintenance of all community fixed assets in the village. The bulk of what we have achieved was financed by community fundraising with the balance coming from the government and overseas aid. The villagers made further contributions through free labour.

The people of Mavana appreciate the results of development planning. It has also brought together and unified the people who reside in the village and those living elsewhere in Fiji and abroad. The statistics tell a story of migration. About 200 people live in the village; Mavana natives living abroad total more than 2000. Many more live in other parts of Fiji. This demographic pattern is attributed to limited village resources, more people acquiring higher education and the lure of a better material prospects elsewhere.

Our underlying philosophy is to encourage self-reliance, initiative and traditional community effort rather than simply waiting for the government to provide everything. Our village investment company, Mavana Investments Limited and our trading enterprise Qalitu Enterprises Limited were products of these beliefs.

My enthusiasm from my years in the Department of Co-operatives for advising on and promoting the principles of savings and investments had never left me. This, too, became important for Mavana. During the 70s, 80s and 90s these concepts were still fairly new among many indigenous Fijians. Not many had invested in commercial properties, in equities, in unit trusts and in other secure investments. I was asked by many groups to explain the principles of savings and investments especially the management aspects. In many cases this was followed by the establishment of appropriate investment organisations. Many of these groups have now invested in shares, unit trusts and in commercial properties. Some of them have gained substantial and growing investment portfolios. I am happy for them.

The message I shared was always the same: We have to save, invest and use investment as a permanent source of income. Spreading this message has been a large part of my life and will continue to be. For some years I have been one of the business development advisors to the Mualevu Tikina Council, covering the larger district of which Mavana is part. Some years before we had established Mualevu Tikina Holdings Ltd (MTHL) as the investment vehicle for the people of the *tikina*. Its shareholders are individuals, funds from village trusts and village and family companies. MTHL has paid consistently good dividends.

The Vanuabalavu Island Council approved my appointment as business development adviser in September 2011. I suggested the setting up of two entities – the Vanuabalavu Island Trust (VIT) and Vanuabalavu Holdings Ltd (VHL). They were incorporated in early 2012 – VIT under the Trust Act and VHL under the Companies Act.

VIT's mission was to accumulate capital from the community and invest this. Income earned would be for further education and projects of general benefit for the islanders. VHL was to be a commercial company investing in ventures suited for our community, which would generate profits and dividends. Its shareholders would include VIT, *tikina* and village funds and individuals from Vanuabalavu. Funds raised from the share capital would be placed in assets to produce income for the benefit of shareholders.

The Vanuabalavu Day Festival to be organized in Suva was to be our way of raising capital required to launch VIT and VHL. Vanuabalavu Island has two *tikina*, Mualevu and Lomaloma. I was appointed chairman of the festival committee with members drawn from the tikinas' 17 villages. Each of the nine bigger villages would be expected to contribute $25,000; the eight smaller ones were levied

$15,000 each. From the amounts of $25,000 raised, $20,000 would go into VIT; the balance would buy shares in VHL. A similar breakdown with smaller amounts was applied to the smaller villages.

The next step was to spread the fund-raising net wider by inviting Vanuabalavu natives living in other southern hemisphere countries, such as Australia and New Zealand, to open the festival. Those domiciled in the northern hemisphere, the USA and United Kingdom in particular, would be requested to close it.

A delegation of chiefs, led by the Turaga Sau kei Mualevu, Tui Mavana Ratu Viliame Kaba went to Fiji's western and northern divisions to solicit support from Vanuabalavu people living in those areas. My role was to spread the word about the festival and its purpose to our Vanuabalavu expatriates in Australia, New Zealand, the UK and the US. We wanted as many as possible to be in Suva for the occasion. Everywhere the chiefs' delegation travelled in Fiji they were received warmly. I was welcome enthusiastically overseas. The support was strong.

A large number of villagers were expected in Suva for the event. Each village was requested to contribute coconut oil, mats and other artifacts for sale. The scene was now set. Then I was consigned to prison for offences I deny committing.

As I have mentioned, a group from the festival committee carried things forward. Its members included Ratu Jone Korovou, Ratu

Apenisa Dakuna, Peni Mau, Jeke Pai, Sekope Matasau and Mesake Koroi. The women involved included Adi Pasepa Korovou, my wife Leba and Tailasa Mau. All of them carried out their tasks with dedication and efficiency. Leba and my granddaughters kept me fully informed when they visited me. Everything was proceeding according to plan. It was heartening to hear of many extra volunteers stepping forward to assist.

Then I was told by some inmates that two company executives in prison were allowed to hold board and management meetings in allocated areas under strict supervision. I quickly applied to be given the same privilege as chair of our Vanuabalavu Festival committee. The application was approved. Now Prisoner 302 could more fully carry out the duties entrusted to him by the people of Vanuabalavu.

On Friday, 5th October, at 11am, one week before the festival, Ratu Korovou, Ratu Apenisa and Mesake Koroi arrived to meet with me for our first committee meeting within the prison walls. They gave me a comprehensive account of the festival preparation. We discussed various issues.

I heard that the people from Vanuabalavu were expected to arrive in Suva on the 8th of October 2012. A Vanuabalavu traditional 'polotu' performance was to be held on Sunday 7th October 2012. Visitors and supporters from overseas were expected to arrive by the weekend. Our meeting lasted for about one hour. I was happy and thankful for the preparations and had no doubt that the fundraising would be a huge success.

On Wednesday, 10th October 2012, the day before the festival would begin committee members Ratu Apenisa, Ratu Korovou, Mesake Koroi, Peni Mau and Jeke Pai came to meet with me at 11am. I was given another full briefing on the festival. All was in order for the big occasion. It was all systems go!

People from Vanuabalavu and from overseas had arrived. At our place, 6 Moti Street, villagers from Mavana were staying for the duration of the festival. The weather was looking good. Preparations for receiving and banking cash collected were complete.

Day one of the festival dawned. I talked by mobile phone to Leba, a prominent Lau businessperson, Dr Mere Samisoni, and Mesake Koroi. It looked like everything was beyond expectations. The visitors from the Southern Hemisphere opened the soli (fundraising). There was a large crowd at the festival ground. At Korovou, a prison officer married to a Vanuabalavu woman was probably more excited about the festival events than the Vanuabalavu locals. He would return each day to the prison from the festival grounds with stories of the current happenings.

Each of the 17 villages had a shed (vakatunuloa) to accommodate their people. These were packed to capacity and people overflowed into the immediate surrounding areas.

There were many meke, and lots of singing, food, merry-making and general fooling around in the Vanuabalavu way. Total cash collected at the end of the day was $150,000.00.

Day two was a great success as well. As each village was called out to give their "soli", the villagers would gather at the end of the ground and then moved slowly towards the main dais singing and dancing. Their "soli" would be followed by their meke and then the next village was called. The total cash collected rose to a total of $270,000.00.

The winning streak continued on the final day. It was then that our Northern Hemisphere contingents made the final contributions. The Southern Hemisphere visitors and the Northern were presented with mats, oil, sasa and other gifts to thank them in the traditional way. On the next day, a farewell *polotu* was staged. It was witnessed by a full house.

During the three days, we had brought in a total of $375,000.00. I was disappointed not to have been present but that was more than offset by the result. It boosted my spirits; I was grateful to those who had given me the detailed feedback from the festival.

The following Wednesday, Ratu Apenisa, Ratu Korovou, Mesake Koroi and Peni Mau arrived at Korovou at 11am for a discussion on the financial outcome. I had a look at the preliminary accounts and volunteered to prepare the full statements when they gave me all the relevant information. We talked about the options available for possible investment of the funds raised. I asked Peni Mau to obtain specific information on certain companies and securities. Another meeting was set for 24th October. Jeke Pai, our treasurer, came by the prison on 19th October 2012 at 10.30am, with documentation and records that enabled me to prepare a full set of accounts. I signed some cheques for payments of bills.

I had another meeting on Wednesday, 24th October, with Ratu Apenisa, Ratu Korovou, Peni Mau, Jeke Pai and Mesake Koroi. They were accompanied by Ratu Viliame Kaba, Turaga Sau kei Mualevu, and Tui Mavana.

Peni Mau and I were authorized to proceed with investing funds as capital in Vanuabalavu Island Trust (VIT) and Vanuabalavu Holdings Limited (VHL). The committee would be leaving the next day for Vanuabalavu to present the financial statements, the preliminary investments and details of some proposed development projects. I wished them well on their mission. They had worked tirelessly to ensure success. Special gratitude goes to the prison authorities for allowing me to continue with my obligations from within Korovou gaol.

When we combined the 2012 Vanuabalavu festival results with the finance raised at the next festival in 2015, we had accumulated a total of $795,000. This has been used to build a portfolio of shares in listed companies including Amalgamated Telecommunication Holdings Limited; Fijian Holdings Limited; Fiji Television Limited; Rice Company of Fiji Limited; FMF Foods Limited; and RB Patel Group Limited. Some of the funds have been utilized to purchase units in the FHL Unit Trust.

All the money raised was used initially to capitalize Vanuabalavu Holdings Limited (VHL), the commercial investment vehicle for Vanuabalavu. All investments mentioned here are held by the company. The trust funds of all villages on the island are shareholders of VHL. Shareholders of VHL have received dividends on their shares for 2014, 2015 and 2016.

I have written in detail about Vanuabalavu fundraising and investment initiatives in view of the on-going national problem of the lack of indigenous success in business. The underlying message is that indigenous communities can mobilize capital and earn income from investments. They can do this through the power of their communal social networks and traditional leadership. Wrap into this a collective commitment to a cause and some elements of individual commercial and managerial expertise and you have a recipe that works, and you can have some fun doing it!

The communal savings by the people of Vanuabalavu and their investments via VHL are a clear application of the principles of savings and investments that I have long propagated and promoted among indigenous Fijians. The partnership between the festival committee and the people of Vanuabalavu is exemplary and an excellent indicator of what a small community can achieve by working together to achieve a desired goal.

There was no way my confinement to a prison cell would curb my passion for the development of my community.

To you whom I owe all my love

My mother- Vika Fane          My father- Josateki Mate

Paradise

Naivaka- Our Mavana home built in 1986

Leba & I on a Easter resurrection Sunday

Qarase the farmer

At our 2018 Naivaka family reunion

Visiting our children, grandchildren & great grandchildren in the US

Leba & I, with our youngest son Josateki, his wife Bernie & small Leba in Sydney

Leba & I with our loyal driver- Kaji

My brother, Kepa & his wife Milika at Leba & I's anniversary celeboratory dinner

Granddaughters Senikau, Fane & Small Leba at one of my Court hearings

Korovou jail

Heading back to Korovou

Back in Suva after nine months
of exile in Mavana

Leba & I's first Sunday back in church
after returning from exile

Some family time while on a break from Korovou gaol

Thessalonians 5 16-18 Rejoice always, pray without ceasing,
in everything give thanks for this is the will of God for you in Christ Jesus.

# PART III

# 54

# CONFRONTING THE LAW, AGAIN

In the *HAC. No. 26 of 2009 FICAC vs Laisenia Qarase* (FHL case), which had resulted in my prison sentence, I had to exercise my right of appeal within 30 days from the day the sentence was imposed. I had to consider the issue very carefully. I had to take into account Leba's views and I needed to consult with my lawyers on the pros and cons if I decided to proceed with the appeal. The cost was also a major consideration as I was running low on funds. For 6 years to 5th December 2012 government, for reasons known only to Prime Minister Bainimarama and Minister Khaiyum, refused to pay my pension and other legal entitlements. These are provided for in an Act of Parliament. I had fully earned what was owed to me as prime minister elected by the people in two general elections. I was in dire financial need.

On Saturday, 18th August 2012 my lawyers Ms. Tupou Draunidalo and Ms. Silika Waqabitu met with me at 9am. Ms. Draunidalo said they had identified a woman QC to defend my NLTB case which was still pending. They would provide full details about her later. Also, they would write to me about appealing the high court decision on the FHL case. There were strong grounds for appeal, but the final decision would be mine. There were risks, particularly with the present illegal regime now bent on keeping me out of the 2014 general elections. In any case, Leba and I would need to consider the matter thoroughly before we made a decision. On Friday, 24th August 2012 during a family visit I told Leba that we had to make a big decision that weekend - to appeal or not to appeal. On Monday, 27th August 2012, Ms. Waqabitu called at 3.15pm with an application to appeal the FHL case decision. She would call again the following day for my decision. I discussed the matter further with Leba. We decided that I should lodge an appeal.

I studied the grounds for doing so and I was happy with them. Ms. Waqabitu called again on 28th August 2012 to collect the appeal papers with my signatures for filing at the Fiji Court of Appeal (FCA) registry.

On 4th September 2012 Ms. Waqabitu gave me a filed copy of my application to appeal and we could expect a decision from the FCA within a week or so.

On Saturday, 15th September 2012, Ms. Draunidalo, Ms. Waqabitu and a senior lawyer colleague were with me again. The appeal hearing would begin at the FCA on Wednesday the following week. They also proposed to file an application for bail. The lawyers told me that discussions in Sydney for a QC to lead the appeal went well. They had identified a QC for the FHL case and another for the NLTB case. On Wednesday, 19th September 2012, Ms. Draunidalo and Ms. Waqabitu called at 8.30am to advise that the appeal application would be heard at 9.30am. They returned after court at 10am to say that both sides were required to file submissions within 14 days, and a court hearing will take place on 31st October 2012. My lawyers called again on 2nd October 2012 to deliver the final submission for my appeal to be filed by 5th October 2012. My application for bail was to be filed on the same date.

I went to the Fiji Court of Appeal on 12th November 2012 at 9am regarding the FHL case. Leba, Senikau, Fane, Atelaite Cama and Manase Nukuvou were there in support. Leave to appeal was granted and Ms. Draunidalo would file a motion later that day for the case to be heard in the current session. My bail application would be decided on 21$^{st}$ November 2012. The FCA sitting could be before the end of 2012 or during February 2013. I advised my lawyers that I would prefer February 2013. On 20$^{th}$ November 2012 Ms Draunidalo called to deliver a copy of the submission to FCA on my bail application.

On 21$^{st}$ November 2012 I went to the Fiji Court of Appeal at 9am. Leba, Rev. Josateki Koroi, Senikau, Fane, Josefa, Josateki, Jerry, Kaji, Peni Mau, Jeke Pai, John Samisoni, Semisi, Joeli, Atelaite Cama and others were there. Ms. Draunidalo made an excellent submission. The decision would be given on notice. On Tuesday, 27$^{th}$ November 2012, Ms. Draunidalo and Ms. Waqabitu called to inform me that the QC from Sydney would not be available for the February 2013 hearing.

However, another QC from Melbourne was willing to take on the case with little cost. I was delighted at the information, particularly on the cost.

On 4$^{th}$ December 2012 I received notice that the decision on the bail application would be given at 9.30am. I rang Leba to tell her and also Ms. Waqabitu to confirm. On 5$^{th}$ December 2012 I went to the FCA for the decision. Leba, Fane and others were there. The FCA refused bail. I would be going back to my cell. Fane cried. I returned to Korovou soon after.

On 14$^{th}$ December 2012 Ms. Draunidalo called to inform me that the FCA appeal hearing would be from 8$^{th}$ to 22$^{nd}$ February 2013. She would be travelling to Australia to discuss the case with our QC. Ms. Draunidalo came to visit on 21$^{st}$ December 2012 and advised that the appeal was set for the 1$^{st}$ and 2$^{nd}$ week of February 2013. The QC's papers for admission to the Fiji Courts had been received and arrangements were made to obtain the necessary approvals. The appeal hearing by the FCA was to begin on 25$^{th}$ February 2013. I arrived at the FCA at 9.00am. I was introduced to QC Remy by my lawyers.

# 55

# ENTER QC REMY VAN DE WIEL

Ms Tupou Draunidalo had held discussions with a number of QCs in Australia with a view of obtaining the services of one to take my appeal to the Fiji Court of Appeal on the FHL case. The problem was to get a QC who would be available during the period set aside for the appeal hearing.

Remy Van de Wiel QC of Melbourne, Australia, was willing and available to take on the case. His cost would be approximately

$40,000, which will be paid from my savings, which by then would be nearly exhausted. I'm not complaining about the cost. It was reasonable. The main point was that legal costs incurred through what I considered to be persecution were having a ruinous effect.

Mr de Wiel had been in continuous practice for over 30 years. His practice encompassed pleas, committals, trials and appellate matters in all Courts and Tribunals in every state in Australia. Areas of expertise include criminal law, intervention and compensation.

Mr de Wiel had been involved in numerous trials for murder, computer fraud, drug cases and tax appeal. Although predominantly criminal, his practices also include civil cases.

Over the years he had been chairman of the Victorian Criminal

Bar Association. He has also served on many committees. Mr de Wiel is admitted to and has practiced in all states of Australia.

Mr de Wiel began his submission at 9.30am. He took the whole morning and then another one hour after lunch and completed by 3.30pm. The FICAC QC then began his submission before the adjournment at 4pm. Leba, relatives and friends were there. The hearing resumed the next day, 26th February 2013, at 9.30am. The FICAC QC continued his submission and took the whole day. Leba, Peni Mau and Tailasa, Robert and Lupe Wolfgramm (daughter of Mesake Koroi), and Isireli Koyamaibale were in Court. FCA would sit again the next morning, 27th February 2013, to hear Mr de Wiel's right of reply. My lawyers and all of us thought that his presentation was excellent. Many local senior lawyers thought so too.

I was confident that all things being equal, we would win the appeal. The FCA decision was expected on or before 13th March 2013. I gave my thanks to Mr de Wiel before I returned to Korovou.

# 56

# END OF THE NLTB CASE

A s Minister for Fijian Affairs I became chairman of the Native Land Trust Board (NLTB) and also the Fijian Affairs Board (FAB). Meetings of the NLTB were always chaired by His Excellency the President in his capacity as president of the NLTB. In his absence the Minister for Fijian Affairs would chair the meetings. During 2003/2004 the NLTB discussed the formation of Vanua Development Corporation (VDC) as the investment vehicle of the board. The objectives of VDC included land development and management, investments in commercial and industrial activities and in other business ventures. VDC was to become an additional source of income to the NLTB. It was registered as a company fully–owned by the board. The company had its own board of directors appointed by the NLTB.

After the formation of VDC the NLTB also discussed the company's funding. At one of its meetings the board approved the investment in VDC of some trust funds held by the board. The investment of trust funds was approved after seeking legal advice on the use of such funds in this way. It was this investment that became the subject of the charges laid against me by FICAC. I was accused and charged with "abuse of office" based on the investment decision made by the board. At the same time FICAC also laid charges against the late Mr Kalivati Bakani, general manager of NLTB, and Mr Keni Dakuidreketi, a member of the NLTB and also a director of VDC. The charges related to their involvement in VDC.

The decision of the NLTB to invest in VDC was a collective responsibility of all members of the board including His Excellency the President. I have often wondered why I was singled out and charged with "abuse of office" while my colleagues on the board were exempted. It was a board decision and not one that I made alone as chairman of the board. Was it fair that I should be targeted? Was it just? I believe that it was most unfair and most unjust. But it demonstrated the extent to which the authorities would go to remove me from the political scene.

The case against me was first heard in the Suva magistrates court on 13th May 2008. I was interrogated by FICAC the whole day. I was charged with abuse of office and taken to court about 8pm that night. I had no idea why the case required a court to sit at night. Maybe FICAC wanted to avoid the publicity that would obviously follow.

I had asked Mr Qoriniasi Bale of Q. Bale & Associates to be my lawyer. He had also been my attorney general in government. He agreed and Ms. Salele of his office appeared on his behalf. A lot of disclosures were required. The magistrate court sat another seven times before the case was transferred to the high court. I was granted bail.

The first hearing at the high court was held on 5th March 2009. Judge Shameem presided. Mr Bale appeared for me. The court restricted my travel overseas and I had to surrender my passport. My local travel was also restricted, including visits to my home island, Vanuabalavu. Several judges presided over the case. Judge Gounder sat for a few hearings between June 2009 and December 2010. On 24th January 2011 the case was transferred to Judge Priyantha Fernando who dealt with the case until the judgment in June 2013.

The delays in finalising the case earlier were caused by both sides, by FICAC on one hand and my lawyer on the other. It took quite some time to gather all the disclosures required. Also Mr Bale was trying to confirm the services of a QC to take my case.

In the meantime, FICAC was trying to get the approval of the court to combine the hearing of my case together with the case against Mr Bakani and Mr Dakuidreketi. Arguments from both sides took a few more weeks before the Court approved FICAC's application for a joint hearing.

From 24th January 2011 to 16th June 2013 there were about 15 more hearings by Judge Fernando.

In prison on Wednesday, 8th August 2012, Ms. Draunidalo and Ms. Waqatabu briefed me on the NLTB case. They had taken it over from Mr Bale who had withdrawn as explained earlier. The next day, 9th August 2012, I left prison for a hearing of the High Court No. 4 at 8.45am. Leba, Rev. Josateki Koroi and Nola Koroi, Mesake, Manasa and Mosese were there. Co-accused Keni Dakuidreketi and Kalivati Bakani and their QC were there too, as well as Ms. Drau-nidalo. The Judge came in at 9.30am and after a short proceeding the court was adjourned to 14th November 2012 for the next hearing and discussion on the pre-trial conference. The trial was likely to take place during June/July 2013. I kissed Leba, said goodbye to other relatives and friends, then returned to Korovou.

On 16th June 2013 Ms Draunidalo represented me at the high court hearings. My co-accused, Mr Bakani and Mr Dakuidreketi were also there with their lawyers. Leba, Peni Mau and Tailasa, rela-tives and supporters were present. And so were the relatives and friends of Mr Bakani and Mr Dakuidreketi. The court was full.

It so happened that on this particular day my hearing was quite bad. I could not hear what the judge was saying. Nor could I hear what the lawyers were saying. Then I saw people looking at me. They were smiling and nodding with approval. I leaned forward and asked my lawyer what was happening. She smiled and said that my case has been withdrawn. Apparently, FICAC had filed a "nolle prosecui" and there was no case to answer. Leba and I were over-joyed, and so were all our relatives, friends and supporters.

As I looked back I wondered why this case was brought up in the first place. There were no grounds to support the allegation. The prosecution must have spent hundreds of thousands of dollars on the case. I spent a lot of money on costs. I was virtually broke. I wondered whether the whole purpose of the aborted prosecution was really to make a pauper out of me and my family. If this was so, how could people in national leadership harbour such pernicious ill- will?

My wife, Leba, and I and our children and grandchildren, suffered irretrievably from the adverse publicity of this case. Between 13<sup>th</sup> May 2008 and 16<sup>th</sup> June 2013 there were 40 court hearings altogether, eight at the magistrate's court and 32 at the high court.

The day after each hearing the details would be splashed across the news media, including television, radio and newspapers. For Leba and me, it was hard to endure the humiliation, frustration and depression during the entire episode.

It was our faith in God and the love and support of our family, relatives and friends, reinforced by my own strong conviction that I had not committed any of the allegations orchestrated against me, that kept our spirits up.

Mr Dakuidreketi was sentenced to six years in gaol. His appeal was dismissed. Mr Bakani was sentenced to a prison term as well. He died in hospital while still a prisoner. In my view, neither of them were guilty.

# 57

# ON AGAIN, OFF AGAIN

The jail term I was serving was for 12 months. However the law requires that one-third of the sentence should be deducted for every prisoner who behaved well during imprisonment. Accordingly, I was due to be released on 2nd April 2013 and not on 2nd August 2013, provided I did not misbehave. I had conducted myself well and was determined not to spend one more day in prison beyond 2nd April 2013.

Part of my work in the office was to update the names of prisoners who were due to be released during the following 30 days. As the 2nd April 2013 drew closer, my anticipation of release naturally increased. I would be free again! On the day itself I ensured that my name was on the notice board for release. Just to make doubly sure I checked the actual calculation in my personal file. My release date was certainly 2nd April 2013.

As I have mentioned, I had been admitted to the Infirmary as the end of my sentence approached. I was instructed to take a rest for a few days. There were issues with my blood sugar and blood pressure, although I felt good physically and mentally.

On 1st April the officer-in-charge came to tell me that I would be released on or before 12 noon the next day, 2$^{nd}$ April. The OC explained that two senior prison officers would accompany me home as a matter of prison procedures. I was to provide my own transport. I called Leba to explain the plan and she was obviously happy and excited. I asked her to contact Mesake Koroi to arrange for a welcoming party with *"sevusevu"* and lunch or tea whichever was appropriate. The OC left but called me after lunch to say that my release on 2$^{nd}$ April was off. The Attorney–General had intervened and wanted to study my case. I thought it was a joke since 1$^{st}$ April was April Fools' Day. I rang Leba and told her. She was very unhappy. I assured her that everything would be done to secure my release as scheduled on 2$^{nd}$ April.

On the morning of 1$^{st}$ April, the news of my release the following day spread quickly. The OC came into the Infirmary before breakfast and we talked for the best part of the morning. He was interested in planting yams. I told him that I would supply him with planting materials.

The Infirmary is almost directly opposite the dining hall. As inmates marched to the hall and back for meals all eyes were on the Infirmary wondering what was happening. On the morning of 2$^{nd}$ April, the same happened. By late afternoon it was clear that I would not be released that day. On the morning of 3$^{rd}$ April there was still no news. Many inmates were disappointed just as I was, but there was nothing we could do but wait and hope for the best.

According to the provisions of the Prisons Act and the Regulations made under the Act the authority to release prisoners on due dates rests with the officer-in-charge at Korovou. When a prisoner is to be released on the due date he returns his uniforms and bedding to the storeman and changes into civilian clothes. According to the regulations the prisoner is expected to be released on or before 12 noon that day. As far as I knew there was no requirement to refer a case to higher authorities. I witnessed this procedure when I worked in the prison office. But in my case, it appeared that there was an attempt to interfere with the provisions of the law from higher authorities.

I rang Leba to tell her. She told me that Mesake Koroi, Peni Mau, Tevita Vuatalevu and our village committee members were at home. She said that everything was ready, including the "*sevusevu*", "lovo" food etc. Meanwhile, the OC had spent the whole morning at head office in discussion with the Commissioner of Prisons and other senior officials. After lunch the OC advised me that I would be released by late afternoon. I was becoming sceptical.

However I was told to change into civilian clothes and returned my uniforms and bedding to the storeman.

In the meantime, media personnel were virtually camped outside the prison walls expecting my release sometime during the day.

Quite a number of people were also at home expecting my arrival. They were all to be disappointed.

By 7pm the OC called me to explain that my release that day was off. Apparently, senior officers had been trying to meet with Attorney General Sayed–Khaiyum who made himself unavailable for the day. A late message from his office confirmed that he would meet them at 10.30am the next day 3rd April. I relayed the bad news to Leba and all at home were disappointed.

I could not change back into prison uniform since under the law I was no longer a prisoner from mid-day 2nd April 2013. In the meantime I had lost my toilet bag. It was a small occurrence, but in the prison world small things sometimes loom large. I stayed at the infirmary in civilian clothes. I was restless and could not sleep.

According to legal advice, I was held in prison illegally by government from mid-day on 2nd April 2013. I was told that the penalty was $1,000.00 for each day held illegally. It was good information for possible legal action in the future.

Then at 11.15am on 3rd April the OC called me to his office. He told me that I would be going home within 20 minutes. I asked to ring Leba to tell her. She was happy but wondered whether it was true. About 10 or 15 minutes later I arrived home in a prison vehicle accompanied by the officer in charge and another senior officer. I kissed Leba, Senikau and Fane. Mesake Koroi, Peni Mau, Jeke Pai, family members and other friends were there, along with village committee members. The media was not aware of my release until later in the afternoon. The people who had gathered at home the previous day were also not there.

But there was joy and happiness all around from those present.

My escorts from the prison were accorded the traditional welcome of *qaloqalovi*, *sevusevu*, and a *tanoa of yaqona*, followed by a presentation of yams as *vakasoso ni waqa*. They stayed with us for about two hours. We continued the *yaqona* session until early evening when food was served.

I enjoyed being at centre stage relating some of the highs and lows of my time behind bars. I issued a media release, which went out quickly. I took a couple of interviews. Radio and TV evening news covered the story.

On 4th April I woke up at 5am and took my normal morning walk along Rewa Street, the first after nine months. It was good to be free.

After breakfast I went to the bank and then had a haircut. Later at 3pm the SDL executives called including the Roko Tui Dreketi, Ro Teimumu Vuikaba Kepa, Ratu Jone Kubuabola, Col. Sakiusa Raivoce, Pio Tabaiwalu, Tupeni Baba. Also, Professor Biman Prasad (later to become leader of the National Federation Party) and Dr Wadan Narsey (the renowned economist and commentator) were there. We had a good *talanoa* and *yaqona* session before they left. I thank God for their concern and kindness. Later in the day more relatives and friends called to greet me.

For me, life was certainly back to normal. I settled gladly and happily back into the domestic routine. I became busy with public and political life again; many people wanted me to continue serving in parliament, although government legal restrictions would make it difficult for me to stand for elections.

Village development and commercial ventures, as always, took a large part of my time. One of the most inspiring projects I was invited to lead was the creation of a commercial enterprise for the Methodist Church from its extensive property holdings. In 2014 the church asked me to head a committee to achieve this. The church is an important part of my life and I'm always ready to help it. I see that as a calling from God.

I was joined on the committee by Ratu Jone Y. Kubuabola; Mr Tui Mailekai, a former Commissioner of Inland Revenue; and Hon. Josefa Dulakiverata, a SODELPA member of parliament and a land development specialist.

The church did not have a co-ordinated and professional approach to managing its properties which, in total, could have a current market value of up to $100 million. Our committee drafted a comprehensive report for the setting of a management company Lako Yani Management Limited (LYML), with a brief to organize and direct the development of church real estate for maximum returns.

I became chairman of LYML. The other directors are Ratu Jone Kubuabola; Mr Mailekai; Ratu Meli Saukuru, a former vice president of the church; and Ms Sereana Qoro, previously chief executive officer of Fijian Holdings Limited. By January 2017 LYML was fully operational. Its asset base is held by the Methodist Church in Fiji Holding Trust (MCFHT).

The trust owns significant properties transferred to it by the church. Further property will be transferred over time. The trust is managed by a seven-person board appointed by the church.

In the first six months of LYML operations, three tourism sites were advertised internationally, with proposals from prospective developers to be evaluated. Some agricultural lots should be on the market by early 2018. Options for commercial areas are being assessed. A 10-year corporate plan to guide strategy and annual plans for immediate goals has been established.

To me it was very clear that God was telling the church to make the best use of what it owns. This message is driven especially by the lessons of the Parable of the Talents (Matthew 25:14-30). The extra income that will be earned by the church from leasing or selling of the property will be used in many ways. It will support church programmes of teaching and training, founded on spiritual principles and beliefs in line with guidelines from our annual conferences. There will be funding for the encouragement of good citizenship and the advancement of social, cultural and community activities of church members and other groups. Some income will also be invested in strengthening the church's ability to effectively manage the affairs of a ministry serving over 200,000 members.

When I look back at the numerous projects I have helped to start, the Methodist property initiative is one of the most exciting. I hope I live long enough to see it producing the returns we are projecting.

# 58

# PENSION MALICE AND PUNISHMENT

I n one of his most infamous acts Bainimarama had decided to withhold government pensions from former civil servants and parliamentarians who may in the past have spoken against his government. The decree which gives him the power to stop payments also applies to judges. This is another blow to judicial independence. Will a judge nearing retirement have the courage or the stomach to criticise the government or find against it in a court proceeding, if this might lead to loss of retirement income?

I also had to fight my own pension battle over Sayed-Khaiyum and Bainimarama's decision to withhold what was owed to me from my time as prime minister.

The oppressors saw that pensions could be converted into weapons. Withholding them was a means of intimidation and control; making the targets mend their ways and start to support their government. If they did, the dictators might restore their entitlements. If they failed to reform themselves, they would presumably be happy to see them reduced to penury for the remainder of their twilight years.

The first to suffer under the more generalised pensions attack was

former prime minister Sitiveni Rabuka. He was joined by a significant number of other pensioners who had served as ministers, senior
diplomats and civil servants. In many cases they were losing their
only regular source of finance.

The treatment of the late Berenado Vunibobo was especially
cruel. His pension was stopped after he had served the military
regime as representative at the United Nations, where he had many
contacts from an earlier stage of his career. It was a bitter blow to
someone who had taken on the UN job knowing it would damage his
reputation. Presumably he felt he could help Fiji get through this
latest coup ordeal.

It was said that he earned the regime's disfavour because he was
unable to persuade UN decision-makers to accept a nomination from
Fiji for Pita Driti, one of Bainimarama's henchmen, to take up a security post. Driti had a notorious reputation as a Fiji military hardman
and rights abuser. Following the principle that coups sometimes
devour their own, he ended up serving a prison sentence for incite-
ment to mutiny. I believe he has now completed his sentence.

Eventually the monthly cheques of the ministerial pensioners
and others resumed. One of the victims recalled that he had been
deprived of his main source of income for up to seven months. It had
been stopped without warning. There was no compensation for what
he had lost.

In February 2010, senior army officer Pio Tikoduadua, then
permanent secretary to the prime minister's office, gave an inexcus-
ably inadequate public explanation for the assault on pensions. He
said it was not to save costs but was "something that just had to be
done". That's all he was quoted as saying. He did not explain what he
meant. Lieutenant Colonel Tikoduadua in 2017 became president of
the National Federation Party.

Lieutenant-Colonel Neumi Leweni spoke bluntly in a newspaper report in January 2010.

He announced that pension payments to former civil servants
who did not back the government would be stopped that week. This

would be done, he said, to "change the mindset" of people who were against the Bainimarama led government. "We will stop pension payments to all those who speak against the government or all citizens seen to halt the government's work on moving the country forward."

"Moving the country forward" was a favourite expression of the regime at a time of terror, torture and repression. There was usually a double meaning to the statements of regime spokespersons.

The decree empowering Bainimarama and Sayed-Khaiyum to halt pensions must surely have no parallel. It was full of malice and vindictiveness. It was certainly unprecedented in the South Pacific. It left the Bainimarama administration well outside the ranks of civilized governments and further separated the regime from the conventions and principles of the Pacific Islands Forum, the Commonwealth and the EU.

It was inevitable that I would become enmeshed in the Bainimarama pension obsession. He and Sayed-Khaiyum and their colleagues made the decision to deprive me of my legal prime ministerial pension entitlements as set out in Act No. 16 of 1994.

They were mistaken if they thought this would make me cower down into subservience. They did however succeed in placing me in a vulnerable financial position.

Sensing their intent I staked out my position early. Bainimarama and Sayed-Khaiyum claimed they believed in the rule of law. I would therefore base my position on that.

In line with the 1994 Act, a prime minister who had served in the position – as in my case – for more than five years was entitled to pension and other benefits.

A few days after my evacuation to Mavana I wrote to the Secretary to cabinet, the late Jowasa Volavola, requesting payment of my pension and other entitlements due to someone who had served as prime minister for more than five years.

The cabinet secretary acknowledged receipt of my letter by 'phone and said he would act on it. That was the last I heard from him at that stage. My understanding was that he had been instructed that my entitlements were on hold and no payments should be made. In the end the pension due to me was withheld for eight years. It was finally paid to me on 16th December 2014. Monthly payments have been maintained since then.

Section 9 (1) of the Prime Minister's Pension Act sets out some additional benefits which include: provision of a telephone, rental, maintenance and cost of local calls' a ministerial-type vehicle and driver; free travel on scheduled trips on government ships; medical expenses; provision of an allocation of $30,000 annually to meet the cost of maintaining a small staff; security protection at the discretion of the prime minister. At the time of writing I had not received the vehicle I was entitled to with a driver and the allocation for staff. I have applied for these two important benefits many times, through the Cabinet office, without success. I do not want security protection.

I acknowledge the payments for telephone bills were finally reimbursed on request, as well as some costs for medical consultations and prescribed drugs.

On 29th July 2009 I had taken a new approach and appealed for justice to the President, Ratu Epeli Nailatikau. His reply came on 12th of August. He said I had been "dismissed" as prime minister and was therefore not entitled to anything under the Act. Consider this: I had been forced from office by fully armed soldiers and the regime described this treasonous act as a "dismissal". I wondered what Ratu Epeli thought as he put his signature to this nonsense. We had worked closely together when he joined my interim administration as a minister. Whoever advised the president to sign the letter to me on the issue either did not know the law or simply ignored the relevant provisions.

There was absolutely no case for my dismissal under the constitution. The provisions for dismissal of a prime minister are set out clearly in the 1997 constitution which remained the supreme law of the land as confirmed by the Fiji Court of Appeal on 9th April in the case L Qarase and Others vs J V Bainimarama and Others. Also the

Prime Ministerial Pension Act No. 16 of 1994 does not say that a dismissed prime minister is not entitled to pension benefits. Any change to the Act would, in my view, require parliamentary approval.

I kept doggedly following up with the office of the prime minister and the cabinet office. On 16th of December 2013, I received a letter of approval from the PM's office. Bainimarama must have concluded that he could not stick with his pension sanction against me for much longer. But even then he fought a rearguard action and nothing was paid until a year later. His final, partial, surrender was probably brought on by questions that had been asked in the newly- constituted parliament. The issue was not going away.

I have provided some detail here so the reader gets a relatively clear picture of how far the Bainimarama-Sayed-Khaiyum regime was prepared to go to hurt its opponents, or potential opponents. In my case they would have been motivated by a heavy element of personal animosity, pure spite, malice and vindictiveness. Revenge was necessary because I did not conform to the expectations of Bainimarama. I had won electoral mandates and set my own course accordingly. It was not necessary for me to follow military dictates. This is what made him angry.

I was not sure whether the other former prime ministers, Sitiveni Rabuka and Mahendra Chaudhry had received their full entitlements.

In May 2011 Bainimarama-Sayed Khaiyum and their ministers embarked on another project of pension aggression that left many people bitter, disillusioned and in despair. Their retirements turned into nightmares of uncertainty and dread as the Bainimarama and Sayed-Khaiyum oppression machine moved against them.

This time it was aimed at several thousand hapless victims, members of the Fiji National Provident Fund (FNPF), who fought hard to escape the clutches of the regime. They could not, however, prevail against a military dictatorship, which was used to imposing its will and had the means to do so. It was a mark of enduring shame for the FNPF, its board and senior management, that they became willing accomplices of the dictators.

A certain Laisenia Qarase was among those at the receiving end. I was not only being deprived of my PM's pension.

As an FNPF pensioner I was also caught in this new onslaught on senior citizens. It was a double hit.

I have documents about the disgraceful betrayal of FNPF dependants. I was pleased to join many others in signing a petition calling for an independent inquiry into the joint government-FNPF plan to cut pensions of some 3600 recipients. Those selected for discriminatory treatment were mainly the poor, retired working people and some from the middle class.

The petitioners said that for the first time in its history, the FNPF had broken binding pension contracts. The FNPF had additionally ignored advice from its own consultants to honour contracts to existing pensioners and to allocate funds to continue to meet these payments. They knew the FNPF could afford to pay and that it should pay.

The FNPF, with the support of the dictatorship, argued that pensions had to be reduced to ensure the FNPF was sustainable. But its case fell apart on the details. In fact, it seemed to be making things up as it went along.

The petition spoke of a widespread suspicion that the whole episode was aimed initially at a group of less than 50 pensioners who received large monthly payments. Bainimarama and company felt these should be cut because they were too high. But these recipients were legally entitled to their payments in accordance with the law and rules of the FNPF.

Bainimarama had also referred to the "handsome amounts" paid to about 10,800 pensioners and said these could not be maintained. He was wrong. The FNPF corrected what he had said. It disclosed that approximately 89 per cent of the 10,800 received amounts below the FNPF poverty line.

The FNPF then adopted a new and lower poverty measure. This

meant that 3,600 - about 11 per cent of the total – would face reductions, including some who had been promised they would be exempt from cuts.

Their bitter reality was of a future on substantially lower incomes than they had been receiving through "irrevocable" arrangements with the FNPF. They contended, with justification that the fund had never proven that the continuation of their pensions at the existing contractual levels would send the FNPF into bankruptcy.

The government and the FNPF further undermined their case when they stressed that the fund as it stood, was sustainable for up to 45 years; that was half a lifetime. The aggrieved pensioners said this did not provide any foundation for default on current payments. Their conviction was reinforced by the claim of the then FNPF CEO Mr Aisake Taito that the fund was acting from a position of strength. Bainimarama also told the nation the FNPF was "in a strong financial position". This projected the FNPF as well able to meet its commitments.

I quote directly from some powerful comments in the petition: "All of us will be long gone before 40 or 45 years has elapsed. Our plea is for the FNPF to leave us alone in our final years, without inflicting on us the disruption and stress caused by savage reductions in income for citizens who will find it difficult to re-enter the workforce to make up for their loss. Our retirements were planned on the basis of contracted pensions. The government and FNPF have, without justification, cut away the foundation of the last phase of our lives."

The FNPF came up with a new ploy. It offered refunds of the original amounts pensioners had in their accounts. A refund is not a pension. The offer was seen as a "sweetener" to soften the impact of what the fund had done.

In the circumstances a good number of pensioners decided to take refunds. The question I saw was, when the money is gone, which in many instances was likely to be sooner rather than later, what will happen to the recipients? Destitution will stare them in the face. The petition described this as a social and human disaster for the pensioners concerned. That's exactly what it was. In fact, the entire business was a disaster.

To make things even harder for the innocent pensioners, Sayed-Khaiyum tossed into the arena a dreadful piece of legislation called the Transition Decree. Not only did this endorse the rescinding of contracts; it also denied the fundamental right of seeking redress through the court system. The 1997 constitution properly addressed this. It provided that every party to a civil dispute had the right for the matter to be determined by a court of law or an independent and impartial tribunal. Sayed Khaiyum's transition decree completely ignored this basic legal principle. It put an end to a civil action already started by a courageous pensioner from Suva Point, the late Mr David Burness. How shameful that Mr Burness was prevented from seeking justice before he died.

Well-known citizens who joined me in signing the petition were former prime ministers Mahendra Chaudhry and Sitiveni Rabuka; Taufa Vakatale, who had served as Fiji's first woman acting prime minister; Mick Beddoes, former Leader of the Opposition; Dr Mere Samisoni, a parliamentary backbencher; Poseci Bune, previously one of Bainimarama's ministers; Amraiya Naidu, retired senior civil servant and ambassador; Rev. Akuila Yabaki, former chief executive of the Citizens Constitutional Forum; social justice advocate Father Kevin Barr; and chief executive of the Consumer Council of Fiji, Premila Kumar.

In October 2012 Ken Giblin, 82 and frail, of Namadi Heights, Suva, spoke before Professor Yash Ghai's Constitution Commission, mandated to propose a new constitution for Fiji. Mr Giblin, a signatory to the petition who was on a modest pension, spoke to the commissioners on behalf of the pensioners.

He said the FNPF remained indifferent to their plight. He thought it was an example of growing disrespect for the elderly. Mr Giblin complained that the FNPF made it plain "that if we live too long, that is an 'adverse circumstance'".

So far our pleas for a fair hearing and a full commission of inquiry into the circumstances of the action taken against us have been ignored. The doors of the prime minister's office remain closed to us. There is just a deathly silence.

Mr Giblin died in 2016 without receiving justice.

After all the submissions and the arguments, Bainimarama declined to use his power to help the pensioners. He didn't even bother to reply to their petition. He doesn't much like this form of expression and protest. Two years earlier, he had described a petition for an election in 2010 as "toilet paper". Later he made it more difficult for petitions to be debated in parliament.

# 59

# YASH GHAI PROJECT ENDS IN TEARS

O n 3rd August 2012, the day I entered prison, the process of constitution–making was under way. Professor Yash Ghai, an eminent constitutional expert living in Kenya, had been commissioned to come up with a new draft constitution. For Bainimarama and Sayed-Khaiyum the international pressure to return Fiji to constitutionality kept on building. They knew they could not survive indefinitely as an illegal regime. Professor Ghai was selected by Sayed-Khaiyum to take on the detailed work required for producing a draft constitution. Sayed Khaiyum knew Professor Yash Ghai from his student days at the University of Hong Kong. The Professor had played a supervisory role when Sayed- Khaiyum wrote a controversial thesis on aspects of Fijian culture.

The other members of Professor Ghai's Commission, all appointed by the government, were: Christina Murray, an expert on human rights and constitutional law, who had acted as an advisor to the South African Constitutional Assembly; the late Penelope (Peni) Moore, first co-ordinator of the Fiji Women's Rights Movement (FWRM), and a former commissioner in the Fiji Legal Aid Commission; Professor Satendra Nandan, former Fiji MP and minister, and well-known author; and Taufa Vakatale, also a former MP, cabinet minister, and prominent educationist.

It was of concern to me, and many others, that Bainimarama and Sayed-Khaiyum had decreed that some of the provisions for the constitution were "non-negotiable". In other words, these provisions had to be in, even if the people did not agree. This, of course, ignores the cardinal democratic principle that the public has the final say.

It was reflective of our reality in Fiji that an illegal dictatorship was issuing such an instruction. I reminded myself that they were doing this at the point of a gun. The non-negotiables included a common and equal citizenry and a secular state. The citizenry requirement, on the surface, seemed extremely democratic.

But the interpretation of it ignored the complexities of Fiji's situation, ruling out Fijian group rights and recognition of indigenous rights. Secularism would not sit well with many of the majority who were dedicated Christians. It was the high chiefs of Fiji who insisted that the promotion of Christianity should be part of the Deed of Cession of 1874 which brought our islands into the British Empire. Since the missionaries brought the divine teachings of Jesus Christ to Fiji, Christianity has been at the very centre of indigenous belief; it became part of us.

# Arrogant dumping of the Deed of Cession

The Deed of Cession is the founding document of modern Fiji. It is therefore an integral part of the country's history. The Deed was endorsed on 10<sup>th</sup> October 1874 by 13 high chiefs of Fiji led by Ratu Seru Cakobau, styled Tui Viti and Vunivalu. Ratu Seru Cakobau had emerged as the leading political figure at a time of change and uncertainty. When he died in February 1883, the *Fiji*

*Times* described him as "the greatest warrior and statesman that the Fijian race has had".

Ratu Sir George Cakobau, the first local Governor General of Fiji, was his direct descendant. He had associations through marriage with other chiefly families, including that of Ratu Sir Kamisese Mara, Fiji's first prime minister and later president.

A key factor in the decision to become a British colony was a dispute with the United States about the burning of the US Consul's house at Nukulau island. Cakobau could not pay for the damage caused and feared that the US might invade and takeover the country. Negotiations began with representatives of the UK, leading to the Deed of Cession.

The chiefs with Cakobau on that momentous day were Maafu, Tui Cakau, Ratu Epeli, Vakawalitabua Tui Bua, Savenaca, Esekele, B. V. Tui Dreketi, Ritova, Kato-nivere, Ratu Kini, Matanitobua, and Nacagilevu. Sir Hercules Robinson signed on behalf of the British Crown. Copies of the Deed were prepared and signed in English and Fijian.

IN AGREEING THAT FIJI WOULD BE RULED BY BRITAIN, THE CHIEFS TOOK THE FRAGMENTED AND DISORGANISED COUNTRY INTO THE GREATEST EMPIRE THE WORLD HAD EVER SEEN. IT WAS A PIVOTAL MILESTONE FOR THE ISLANDS. CAKOBAU AND HIS FELLOW LEADERS WANTED A CIVILIZATION UNDER CHRISTIANITY; THEY ENVISAGED A NEW FORM OF GOVERNMENT FOUNDED ON PRINCIPLES OF JUSTICE, SOUND PUBLIC POLICY, AND INCREASING TRADE AND INDUSTRY. FROM THIS WOULD COME LAW AND ORDER, A SYSTEM OF ADMINISTRATION, THE BEGINNINGS OF EDUCATION, ORGANIZED HEALTH CARE, AND OTHER INFRASTRUCTURE.

WHAT THE CHIEFS COMMITTED TO UNDER THE GOVERNANCE OF BRITAIN AND QUEEN VICTORIA, SET THE STAGE FOR FIJI'S GRADUAL TRANSITION TO INDEPENDENT NATION. THE FAR-REACHING SIGNIFICANCE OF WHAT HAPPENED ON 10TH OCTOBER

1874 WAS RECOGNIZED IN FIJI'S CONSTITUTIONS OF 1970, 1990 AND 1997.

THE CONSTITUTION OF 1997, WHICH BAINIMARAMA-KHAIYUM PROCLAIMED THEY WOULD CONTINUE TO RECOGNISE, NOTED IN ITS OPENING DECLARATION THE DEED OF CESSION'S ROLE. IT SAID:

ACKNOWLEDGING OUR UNIQUE CONSTITUTIONAL HISTORY: (A) FIRST, THE DEED OF CESSION OF 10 OCTOBER 1874 WHEN RATU SERU EPENISA CAKOBAU, TUI VITI AND VUNIVALU, TOGETHER WITH THE HIGH CHIEFS OF FIJI, SIGNIFYING THEIR LOYALTY AND DEVOTION TO HER MOST GRACIOUS MAJESTY, QUEEN VICTORIA, AND THEIR ACCEPTANCE OF THE DIVINE GUIDANCE OF GOD AND THE RULE OF LAW, CEDED FIJI TO GREAT BRITAIN, WHICH CESSION WAS FOLLOWED IN NOVEMBER 1879 BY THE CESSION TO GREAT BRITAIN OF ROTUMA BY THE CHIEFS OF ROTUMA.

IT IS A SIGN OF SAYED-KHAIYUM'S EGOTISTICAL SELF-IMPORTANCE THAT HE, WITH BAINIMARAMA'S BACKING, DECIDED THAT THE DEED OF CESSION WAS NO LONGER IMPORTANT ENOUGH TO WARRANT CONSTITUTIONAL RECOGNITION. SO IN HIS OWN 2013 CONSTITUTION HE SIMPLY DUMPED IT, JUST LIKE THAT. I WONDER WHY HE THOUGHT HE HAD THE RIGHT AND AUTHORITY TO DO THIS? I SUPPOSE IT GETS BACK TO THAT SENSE OF SUPERIORITY THAT MARKS MUCH OF WHAT HE DOES.

We felt the entire process to develop a new constitution was fundamentally flawed. For instance, members of the commission had been appointed without any consultation with the stakeholders. There were serious reservations about the independence of certain members who were perceived to be too close to the military regime. We also thought the constitutional process was not inclusive or participatory.

Professor Ghai and his colleagues travelled widely to gather the views of the public. They reported receiving more than 7,000 submissions from right across society. Their report on their work said that many of these were made by organisations including villages, political parties, faith groups, professional and business associations; trade union, women's and youth group, academics and the diaspora. This meant the number of people who engaged in the process ran into the thousands.

I know that as Professor Ghai met with different groups and individuals to familiarize himself with local conditions and sentiments, he was warned privately that he would eventually run intro trouble with Bainimarama and Sayed-Khaiyum. He would cross a certain line, and when that happened his project would probably be over. These predictions came to pass; the Ghai commission's work was cut short, Professor Ghai was reduced to tears and his draft constitution literally reduced to ashes.

As party leader I was among those who provided ideas for the submission to the Ghai commission by the SDL party (before it was forced to change its name). I was also part of a delegation that had a preliminary meeting with Professor Ghai and his members. But by the time our party made its full presentation I was in prison, although I still remained in contact with other party leaders.

We declared in our submission that we had reservations about taking part in a process proposed by a military government but noted that it was what the military favoured for facilitating its return to the barracks and to democratic rule for Fiji. This was why we were participating.

The SDL document was comprehensive and well researched. It raised many issues relevant for the nation. I do not intend to give details of them all here. However, I will touch on some of the points it made.

The party stressed that Fiji's ability to forge a durable sense of national unity depended on the nation's ability to recognize the

importance of affirming our diversity. Any attempt to force unity by denying Fiji's diversity would simply not work. Achieving peace and security in our multi racial country was a commitment for the long term to be vigorously pursued. The SDL acknowledged the need for compromise. Its leaders were prepared to talk through the difficult issues in dialogue with other communities.

It was our hope that Fiji could once again adopt a constitution that addressed the concerns and hopes of all. We said that it must be by the people and for the people and could not be imposed. Only then could Fiji move forward as a united nation with a united vision.

We asserted that the contribution to nation building by Fiji's different communities must be recognized and appreciated. We emphasised that peace and harmonious multi racial living in a small country like Fiji could only be fully achieved when the indigenous communities were confident their fundamental interests were protected and they did not feel left out of national development.

The SDL proposed that the extant 1997 constitution should be used as the basis for a revised document, with amendments to be agreed with the people of Fiji. We stressed that the 1997 pact was a compromise arrived at by the country's communities and their leaders. It enjoyed broad multi racial support through an elected parliament and had been hailed as one of the best in the world for governing multi ethnic societies and the difficulties involved in that. We pointed out that the Bainimarama-Sayed-Khaiyum regime had also positioned themselves as big believers in that constitution which formed part of their so-called People's Charter.

To further reinforce our view, we quoted the then secretary-general of the Commonwealth, Chief Anyaoku who noted that the 1997 constitution enjoyed national consensus and conformed with the Commonwealth's Harare Principles.

A guarantee of fundamental rights and freedoms for every citizen and their equal protection under the law was an essential part of the SDL vision for Fiji. We said feelings of personal and group community came about when people had the confidence that breaches of rights would be addressed with impartiality and speed. We advocated affirmative action, not only for indigenous peoples but for all those disadvantaged in some way. Particular importance was given to the right to practice freedom of conscience, religion and belief. The party favoured Fiji Islander as a common name drawing on the recommendations of the Reeve's commission, which helped prepare the 1997 constitution.

The SDL felt it was important to cut through the regime's propaganda and bring out the truth. It was evident to the party that the 2006 coup was not about the imperfections of the 1997 constitution. The coup was a personal agenda of the head of the regime. He was now trying to give some moral justification for his illegal action.

We highlighted the words in the court judgment by Justice Anthony Gates when he referred to the 1997 constitution: "It is not possible for any man to tear up the constitution. He has no authority to do so... The constitution remains in place until amended by parliament, a body of elected members who collectively represent all of the voters and inhabitants of Fiji. The fundamental law represented in a constitutional document may only be changed in accordance with that constitution."

We protested about the regime's insistence that the state should become secular, meaning it should not prefer, lean towards or advance any particular religion. In other words, the state should be neutral. Our position was that secularism has no place here. We stood for Fiji becoming a Christian state. We stressed that Christianity introduced by missionaries and accepted by Fijians in 1835 convinced the chiefs to put aside their war clubs and choose a way of life based on the teaching of Christ and the Holy Bible.

The high chiefs who ceded Fiji to Great Britain in 1874 wanted to secure "the promotion of civilization and Christianity" alongside trade and industry, order and good government. More than half the population was now Christian, making Christianity the largest religious faith in the country and central to the social order of the indigenous people.

We stressed, of course, our proposal did not take away religious liberty - the right of every citizen to practise their religion and beliefs.

We quoted from a speech by David Cameron, then British prime minister, commemorating the 400<sup>th</sup> anniversary of the King James version of the Bible. The Anglican Church is the state religion of England. "We are a Christian country. And we should not be afraid to say so," declared Mr Cameron.

---

> Let me be clear: I am not in any way saying that to have another faith – or no faith – is somehow wrong. I know and fully respect that many people in this country do not have a religion. And I am also incredibly proud that Britain is home to many different faith communities, who do so much to make our country stronger.
>
> But what I am saying is that the Bible had helped to give Britain a set of values and morals which make Britain what it is today. Values and morals we should actively stand up and defend. The alternative of moral neutrality should not be an option. You can't fight something with nothing ... Because if we do not stand for something we cannot stand against anything.

---

Mr Cameron went on to say that the Judeo-Christian roots of the Bible also provide the foundations for protest and for the evolution of freedom and democracy. He argued that societies do not necessarily become more secular with modernity but rather more plural.

The British PM shared this quote from another former British prime minister, Baroness Margaret Thatcher:

---

> We are a nation whose ideals are founded on the Bible. Responsibility, hard work, charity, compassion, humility, self sacrifice, love ... pride in working for the common good and honouring the social obligations we have to one another, to

our families and our communities ... these are the values we treasure.

---

Mr Cameron submitted that those who say being a Christian country is doing down other faiths,

---

simply don't understand that it is easier for people to believe and practise other faiths when Britain has confidence in its Christian identity.

Many people tell me it is much easier to be Jewish or Muslim here in Britain than it is in a secular country like France. Why? Because the tolerance that Christianity demands of our society provides greater space for other religious faiths too.

And because many of the values of a Christian country are shared by people of all faiths and indeed by people of no faith at all.

---

Mr Cameron went on to say that he had never understood the argument some people make about the church not getting involved in politics.

---

To me Christianity, faith and religion, the Church and the Bible, are all inherently involved in politics because so many political questions are moral questions.

---

The 1997 Constitution Bill of Rights stated specifically that every person had the right either individually or in community with others and both in public and in private to manifest his or her religion and belief in worship, observance, practice or teaching. This right extended to religious communities providing religious instruction in schools. Additionally, the constitution provided that someone attending a place of education was not required to receive religious instruction, or take part in a religious ceremony or observance, if these related to a religion that was not his or her own.

We intended to recommend that the president of Fiji be given powers to protect religious freedom. Our final statement on this question summarized our thinking like this:

---

To honour our heritage; to guarantee our inherited liberties, rights and principles of justice; and to secure our national future under a sovereign God, the constitution should establish Fiji as a Christian state.

---

That is a reasonable and logical proposition. There is nothing extremist about it.

We proposed that Fijian be the national language of Fiji. Again, I see nothing radical or extreme here. The SDL argued that there were only some 600,000 indigenous Fijians in the world, and their language is central to their survival as a distinct race. As the official language of the country, it would become a strong unifying factor not only for a multicultural Fiji but also for the continuing existence of the Fijian people. If every Fiji Islander was able to converse in the indigenous language, this would likely have a far-reaching and positive impact on community relations and national cohesion. It is well known that in those parts of Fiji where many ethnic Indians are fluent in the local Fijian dialect, there is a more tolerant and accommodating relationship among the communities. It would be very natural for Fijian to be the language of the national anthem.

In the Fiji of 2017 when I am writing this, what is the position on this crucial issue of the Fijian language? Under the regime, Fijian has been targeted for special treatment. Fijians are not allowed to use their language for the name of a political party. They are not allowed to speak Fijian in parliament. I remember an incident in the campaigning for the 2001 election, which illustrated very well the need for a more understanding attitude towards public communication in Fijian. I was part of a panel of election candidates taking part in a debate in Suva. I made my opening remarks in English and then explained that I wished to make some comments in Fijian. The reaction from other panelists told a story. There was a stir in the room and visible concern. One non-Fijian participant complained that he wouldn't be able to understand what I was saying – I thought it was a pity he had not learned enough Fijian so that he could understand, at least, something of what I expressed. Another panelist – an indigenous Fijian – appeared to be annoyed and said he could speak in Fijian too, if he wished. (I thought, why doesn't he?) I think someone else might have made similar comments. I recollect that the chairperson, lawyer Richard Naidu, said there were no debate rules about prohibitions on use of a language. Then he added that I obviously wanted to address my constituents. That was exactly the point. I was told that afterwards a minority community citizen, asked for his reaction, said his first thought was: "Here we go again". I took that as an expression of disapproval because I had somehow engaged in Fijian nationalism. He did not respond when he was told that I was talking for a while in my own language and why should that be a problem?

A plural country like Fiji with a culturally distinct indigenous population should appreciate the native tongue. Making it the national language would help the indigenes to sustain their identity, their heritage and traditions in a world where first peoples have been oppressed, marginalised and eclipsed.

This is not racism. It is about survival in the great flowing tide of humanity. In this tide the Fijians are among the smallest of the indigenous groups. Our submission quoted a Pacific linguist, Dr Melanaite Taumoefolau, as saying:

Our language is like a container; inside the container is a set of values and beliefs that make us what we are as a people. Our behaviour, customs, traditions, our ways of thinking, our fa'a Samoa, our anga faka Tonga, are all packaged into this container called language. We lose the container, we lose also the contents. We lose our language; we lose also our distinctive ways that define us to ourselves, and to the world.

---

With Fijian as the national language the nation would have a new focus for national unity and inclusivity. The first language would be like a "glue" holding together the rich, diverse cultures of those who call Fiji home. People could speak freely and easily with their neighbours; some of the misunderstandings and suspicions that occurred would be taken away. Everyone singing the national anthem in Fijian would stand as a stirring symbol of togetherness. Naturally English would still flourish as a common language and as Fiji's means of discourse internationally. Fiji Hindi would continue to be part of our linguistic heritage although more of us speaking Fijian would contribute to a Fiji ethos of multi-racialism.

We expressed our view that the revised 1997 constitution should reflect the Biblical teaching that marriage is a divine ordinance of God between a man and a woman. It symbolizes God's union with humanity and carries the divinely-ordained responsibility to multiply the human species through family and parenting. Our position was that gay persons have a rightful expectation for love and companionship like anyone else. But this did not extend to a right to avail themselves through same sex marriage of the blessing and benefits of Biblical, Christian matrimony. We noted that the provision in the 1997 constitution, which opened the way for gay marriage, was not in the report of the Reeve's Commission. It appears to have been slipped in by the legal drafters.

On the military we stressed that the role and functions of the RFMF must be established clearly and without ambiguity.

The coup cycle had to stop. Constitutional provisions were required to effectively deter the RFMF from contemplating the illegal removal of future governments. We insisted that the RFMF should be subservient to the government of the day. There should be no room whatsoever for the military to intervene in the political leadership and governance of Fiji. We pushed home the argument against coups, saying they have had a disastrous effect on the country. There was enough evidence to show that after each coup the economy slumped, unemployment and poverty levels increased, education and health services were badly affected, and repairs and maintenance of public infrastructure was often neglected. To this can be added the toll of human rights abuse and torture – sometimes lethal - leaving deep scars on individuals and the national psyche.

We said that the cost of the military was a heavy burden on the nation and this was unsustainable. A reduction in military personnel would make it possible to divert financial resources to productive sectors of the economy and to assist programmes for the poor and disadvantaged. We submitted that the commander of the army should be appointed by the president on the advice of the Cabinet, and that the minimum qualifications for the position should be reviewed.

The SDL stood strongly for the reinstatement of the GCC which had been banned by Bainimarama because it refused to endorse his military takeover and nominee for vice president, Ratu Epeli Nailatikau. Bainimarama came up with various excuses for his actions against the GCC, including the spurious claim that the council was irrelevant and "politicised." (It was the army itself that was truly politicized in that it had crossed illegally into the politics of the nation). When he was venting against the GCC, he came out with his infamous declaration that the chiefs "should go and drink homebrew under a mango tree". That was an insult that will be long remembered.

Our party stated that the GCC was at the pinnacle of the Fijian social structure, that it had provided good leadership, had played a unifying role and was a stabilizing influence during uncertain times. We felt that the GCC should have its own legislation.

We reiterated our belief that native land should be administered by the Native Land Trust Board (NLTB), and no other agency, and that the Native Land Trust Act (NALTA) should be the foundation for arrangements between Fijian landlords and their tenants.

We called for Fiji Islander to be the common name for the citizens of Fiji, pointing out that from as far back as the 19th century, "Fijian" had been used to identify indigenous Fijians, rather than the word *"iTaukei"* decreed by the regime. The relevant part of our submission said: *"Taukei* is a prefix meaning "owner of", for instance *"taukei ni lori"* (owner of a vehicle) or *taukei ni sitoa* (owner of a shop). Indigenous Fijians are now called "owners of". Of what? They have no idea! The indigenous Fijians feel that they have become a "prefix" rather than a substantive entity in their homeland."

*iTaukei*, according to our thinking, was no substitute for the word "Fijian". The SDL said:

---

You really have to be an indigenous Fijian, speaking their language, living their way of life, dressing the way they dress and relating to others in the way they do to really appreciate the sense of loss in the removal of a name that identifies them with all these.

---

We referred to a survey by the Citizens Constitutional Forum (CCF) in which the majority of respondents said they felt Fijian should be reserved for Fijians.

The SDL argued against immunity being granted unilaterally to coup perpetrators, pointing out that the illegal overthrow of an elected government is one of the most serious crimes. "The coup cycle in Fiji must stop. It cannot stop if immunity is granted each time an illegal overthrow of government takes place. Those involved in a coup must account for their actions before the law.

The principle of 'no man is above the law' must be applied equally to everybody. There should be no exception to this principle."

Amnesty was an act of forgiveness granted by the president. It was like a pardon and was often used in other countries for offences that were political in nature. We envisaged a Special Commission on Coups to determine amnesty. It would only do this if it was satisfied that all the facts regarding individual participation or involvement were fully documented. We have asserted that if amnesty was given, all military leaders be terminated from their positions and dishonorably discharged from the military including all military personnel taken into the civil service after a coup; stripped of all military awards, medals and honours/decorations; not be allowed to take part in political elections for life; and not be allowed to take up any public office for life. Finally, we proposed all plaques or public monuments in their name to be removed.

We added:

---

All these measures should be pursued vigorously by the incoming government considering that a coup is a treasonous act and is punishable by death or life sentence. The perpetrators should know that they committed a crime on the nation and do not deserve any accolades. They are soldiers under oath to protect the constitution and provide security for the ordinary citizens of this country and they violated this honorable duty with arrogance and impunity. If they want amnesty they must accept these conditions.

---

Referring to the 2006 coup, we said an alarming feature was the number of Fiji citizens who supported it. These were often people of high standing in public life, diplomacy, in politics, commerce and in the judiciary. We proposed that those who aided and abetted or actively supported the coup should be: immediately terminated from public positions in government or statutory organisations; be prohibited for life from taking part in political elections; and barred from taking up any public office.

We had seen, when we were in office, that the environment was a looming issue, requiring strong government intervention.

It was this that led to our enactment in 2005 of the Environmental Management Act (EMA).

A statutory body, the National Environment Council, would coordinate the formulation of environment related policies and plans, and provide policy direction. It would ensure compliance and that government environment commitments made internationally were met. Environmental impact assessments would be carried out on developments which had a significant effect on the environment. It also had a role in ensuring the functions of the Litter Promulgation 2008.

We had started to take strategic action on solid and liquid waste in 2006, and climate change in 2005. There were plenty of warning signs by then about the destructive effects these phenomena would have. (It took the Bainimarama regime a long time to appreciate the significance of it.)

One of my key concerns was that the Environment Management Act (EMA) seemed to be sidelined, even as the environment became more of a pressing issue. Little was heard from the National Environment Council. That applies at the time of writing this in August 2017. In fact, the EMA itself had largely vanished from the public eye. There were reports in 2017 that the Department of Environment was reluctant to disclose the outcome of environmental impact assessments (EIA). It was known to sometimes take the position that they were "confidential", despite the legal provision for public access to such documents.

A well-known legal firm reported that in theory the EMA protected the environment from unsustainable environment, but in practice "anything goes". The Department of Environment, it said, did not have enough resources and was not clear on its own law.

The EMA provides for the appointment of environmental officers to police the Act. This is obviously a crucial clause for any government truly concerned about environmental management and protection. But if appointments have been made, little has been heard of the work and achievements of such officials.

To me this is another case of the regime neglecting their responsibilities on the conservation of our environment.

Yet the hypocrisy is continuing. Bainimarama travels constantly making set piece speeches about the climate change crisis, global warming, and rising sea levels. Remarkably, as president of the COP 23 climate change organisation, he sees himself as the voice for 7.5 billion people on the planet when he has failed to act in a timely and decisive way to tackle Fiji's own serious environment/pollution issues. He is saying he is dedicated to fashioning a great international consensus to defeat the effects of all these environmental threats. However, at home, he has never expressed any real interest in seeking consensus on anything, especially among parliamentarians. Essentially, he isn't really interested in working with those who might have different views. He is only really comfortable with those who agree with him.

Our Yash Ghai Commission submission recommended constitutional environmental rights. We felt that people were entitled to an environment not harmful to their health and/or well-being. The environment should be protected for the benefit of the present and future generations through legislative and other measures that prevented pollution and ecological degradation; promoted conservation; and secured ecological sustainable development and use of natural resources while promoting economic and social developments.

The regime's 2013 constitution has environmental provisions, but in my view, it has constantly breached these. There is also a section for limitation of these rights, meaning they can be diminished.

We expressed to the Yash Ghai commission our objections to the dismantling and marginalization of indigenous institutions and proposed measures to reverse this. We said there was nothing racial or discriminatory about people upholding their birthright, their right to indigenous land ownership and the right to be identified with a particular race or tribal group. To deny this was in direct violation of the United Nations Declaration on the Rights of the Indigenous People 2007 and the ILO Convention on Indigenous and Tribal Peoples. The challenge was to balance indigenous rights with the rights of others, so that one does not topple the other.

The Fijians comprising the majority of the population were never consulted on their representation on the Native Land Trust Board, the decision on the name Fijian, reduction on the entitlements of chiefs and termination of the GCC. The recognition of indigenous rights was not lost when the indigenous population became a majority. The self-identification criterion of being indigenous or tribal is sufficient for protection in line with international agreements.

SODELPA was not surprised that our well thought out submission angered Bainimarama. He criticised it publicly.

As predicted by some, the Yash Ghai commission finally came into conflict with the regime. The report of the commission was brushed aside. In a shameful spectacle, a proof of the document was burnt while a visibly distressed Professor Ghai watched. It was the first time such an episode had ever been seen in Fiji. The military regime then went ahead and imposed its own constitution after so-called consultations. I believe these were quite inadequate and could not compare with the consultations engaged by the Yash Ghai commission and the earlier Reeves commission, which led to the 1997 constitution.

Professor Ghai was scathing in his criticism of Bainimarama following the termination of his commission by the regime. He complained there was "massive interference". Bainimarama was telling him in emails to "do this or not do that". It was, he said, a kind of harassment. Of course, it meant the process of constitution-making was not independent.

When the Bainimarama-Khaiyum constitution came into force, Professor Ghai said he doubted that Bainimarama had read it. "He just repeats what his attorney general tells him to say". Samoan prime minister Tuilaepa, a constant Bainimarama critic, described as "despicable" the burning of the proofs of the Yash Ghai document.

# 60

# A NEW FORM OF DICTATORSHIP

After the trashing of the Yash Ghai draft, Bainimarama – Sayed- Khaiyum got started on making their own constitution. This was imposed on the nation on 6<sup>th</sup> September 2013. It fell far short of the critical need for openness and wide consultation. The people did not have a full oppyortunity to make their views known on the supreme law that was to govern them. The government said that just over 1,000 or so written submissions – a low number - were received by the attorney general's office. But we do not know what views were expressed because they were kept secret. (In contrast the Yash Ghai commission received more than 7,000 submissions. All of them were posted on its website.)

Bainimarama-Sayed-Khaiyum were sloppy and less-than-precise in their approach. For instance, when the document was released on 22<sup>nd</sup> August 2013, it was understood to be the final version. But when the assent was given, on 6<sup>th</sup> September, by the President, Ratu Epeli Nailatikau, revisions had been included, but there were no proper explanations about this.

The constitution was written to serve the interests of the principal coup makers. It was tailor-made for the continuation of their dictatorship. The commentator Professor Wadan Narsey described it as the final stage of a "successful" coup.

One of its defining characteristics is the inclusion of constitutionally mandated direct military intervention. In fact, this gives the army ultimate,overarching control, although the regular exercise of power is largely concentrated in the hands of Bainimarama and Sayed-Khaiyum, with Sayed-Khaiyum dominating.

The oft-stated claim that for the first time Fiji has genuine democracy could not be further from the truth. Confirmation of what many citizens already knew came from someone uniquely qualified, someone who knows much about the working relationship between Bainimarama – Sayed-Khaiyum and how their government functions.

Lt. Col. Pio Tikoduadua had been Bainimarama's loyal servant in the military government. He became permanent secretary in the prime minister's office and had also served as a minister in Bainimarama's 2014 parliamentary government.

There was a public stir when in April 2017 he joined the National Federation Party and became its president succeeding Tupou Draunidalo who had resigned. Lt. Col. Tikoduadua made it plain that he had simply had enough of the Bainimarama – Sayed-Khaiyum dictatorship. This is what he said publicly:

---

Fiji's biggest problem at the moment is not that my opinion does not matter. It is that nobody's opinion matters except those of the prime minister and attorney general ... No one else can ever be right and they can never be wrong.

---

Bainimarama's response to this was typical. He essentially described Lt. Col. Tikoduadua's remarks as "rubbish". There was silence from Sayed-Khaiyum.

Lt. Col. Tikoduadua rammed home his message again at the

NFP's convention in June when he declared that the national will to grow was determined by the people and "not by two people only".

He said he had witnessed how the governance of Fiji was slowly sliding back into "that space where the darkness that led to 2000 and 2006 (was) prevailing and rearing its ugly head again". "We have all experienced or witnessed the suppression of rights of the people to be heard."

Then he added another penetrating comment: "The nation, in my view, has been held to ransom by a dictatorial rule exploiting the very democratic process of parliament." He should have added that the imposed constitution provides the framework for this new parliamentary dictatorship. Perhaps he needs to explain also why he gave Bainimarama his loyalty for so long, especially during the height of the abuse and torture. The same question should be answered by other army officers.

It is notable that the parliamentary backbenchers of Bainimarama- Sayed-Khaiyum's Fiji First party are kept on a leash. If they break ranks, they run the risk of losing their seats in accordance with Section 63 of their constitution. (The same applies to Opposition MPs.)

The Fiji First MPs rarely make public comments of substance. It's been said that they act as mere ornaments. The two leaders do not encourage their backbench subordinates to speak out because they like to control virtually everything that is said by Fiji First representatives. In a parliamentary democracy, of course, robust comment and criticism from the backbenches is all part of the process. Not with Bainimarama and Sayed-Khaiyum. They dislike dissent intensely.

There has been an obvious trend for Fiji First to use its parliamentary majority to curtail debate which is at the heart of democracy and to fast-track legislation. This speeding up of the parliamentary process also reduces debate. The scope for petitions from the people to be fully debated and decided on, has been narrowed. Petitions are a time-honoured device for public expression and advocating causes.

They communicate the voice and the feelings of the electorate to those in power.

The opposition complains about the difficulty of introducing questions. The government has turned question time into an extension of their propaganda machine by filling it with "tame" queries on the order paper that give ministers an opportunity to recite boring summaries of government "achievements".

The sitting time of parliament has been reduced; this is another limitation which cuts back on the fabric of democracy. Parliament is where democratic business is debated, amended, approved and made ready for implementation. Bainimarama has described it as the peoples' house. It should be honoured as such by ensuring that it meets frequently. It is not honoured when its meeting schedule is cut for no good reason.

The regime did not like Professor Biman Prasad of the National Federation Party occupying the crucial role of chairman of the public accounts committee (PAC), as the nominee of the leader of the opposition. The PAC was traditionally chaired by the opposition as part of the checks and balances that prevent the abuse of power, especially through the accumulation of excessive authority by the few. As chair of the PAC Professor Prasad was forthright and open. Bainimarama-Sayed-Khaiyum were agitated about this. The professor was removed as chair and replaced by a Fiji First backbencher regarded as a favourite of Sayed-Khaiyum. It was felt by many that the PAC, from that point, lost its cutting edge and that accountability was reduced.

There are efforts to elevate the speaker (Ms Jiko Luveni) to a new and higher status which somehow places her almost above criticism. MPs have to be careful about what they say about her in case they breach parliamentary protocols. This has a chilling effect on debate. (A speaker, like every other member of the House, is accountable and can and should be criticised when this is warranted.) Ms Luveni made a noteworthy comment in an interview on September 20th with the *Fiji Sun*, which specializes in publishing pro-government propaganda. Asked whether she thought that Fiji now has true democracy,

Ms Luveni did not confirm this. But she said: "We have reached a level which we have not reached before. The level of democracy is higher than before I reckon." I do not understand how the speaker can make that statement in light of what has transpired since the 2014 elections.

The circumstances of the suspensions from parliament of three opposition members were criticized by the Inter Parliamentary Union (IPU), of which Fiji is a member. The IPU felt the suspensions were arbitrary and contrary to the governing rules of the parliament. It expressed the view that the house could be turned into a 'rubber stamp' institution which failed to carefully scrutinise government policies or other actions. The criticisms of parliament by IPU were ignored by the government.

Many profoundly serious questions about the fair and even-handed treatment of MPs were raised when Sayed-Khaiyum on November 18th, 2015 disgraced himself in parliament by imitating an ape. His gestures, accompanied by deep, barking grunts, were directed towards Ratu Isoa Tikoca sitting across the chamber. He was one of the opposition members who suffered suspension for comments he made in parliament.

Ape or monkey imitations are well-known throughout the world as a particularly obnoxious form of racism. In this instance Sayed-Khaiyum's actions were aimed at an indigenous Fijian member. What he did was unprecedented in the history of Fiji's parliament. Nothing like it had ever been seen before. It marked a new low in standards of public behaviour by MPs.

But amazingly no action was taken against Sayed-Khaiyum. In fact, some government members were amused by what he did. They were seen on video laughing at his shameful antics. I say shame on them. In his defence Sayed-Khaiyum claimed to have been impersonating the Star Wars character Darth Vader. Sayed-Khaiyum gets points for creative thinking but his explanation does not stand up.

When Ratu Isoa later raised a point of order demanding that Sayed- Khaiyum apologise, the Speaker ruled against him, saying he should have acted at the time. Ratu Isoa said he had raised the matter at the earliest opportunity. Sayed-Khaiyum never apologised.

So, a shocking racial slur against an indigenous member of the house was acceptable, but certain comments by Opposition members – including the victim of Sayed-Khaiyum's racist performance - saw them removed from the House. That tells its own story.

# 61

# SQUEEZING DEMOCRACY

The slow squeezing of democracy is also manifested in the proposed Bill No. 28 of 2016 (Parliamentary Powers and Privileges Bill), which as I write is still to be approved by the House of Representatives. This is a dreadful law-in-waiting. It envisages new laws and rules which will have a dampening or chilling effect on the processes of parliament. Fines and prison sentences of up to ten years face those members of the public who fall foul of it. The bill also increases the special status and protection of MPs, so that they would become even more elitist and distant from the people.

MPs are already protected by parliamentary privilege for their utterances in the House. Bill 28 appears to be doubling down on that. For instance, a member cannot be prosecuted for words spoken before a parliamentary committee or written in a document presented to parliament. I assume this means total freedom of expression for MPs but different and inferior standards for the ordinary people addressing a committee or with their names in a document submitted to parliament. It is possible, of course, that a member of the public's name might appear in a document without that person's knowledge. But at any rate this is all about discrimination.

The bill adheres to the ancient, and now outdated, British convention of "strangers in the House". The term was used to describe non-members, meaning the public, who were in the parliamentary chamber either to watch debates or meet someone. The offending Bill 28 specifies that "a stranger" who breaches an order by the speaker to control the admittance of strangers to parliament commits an offence and on conviction can be fined $100, or sent to prison for three months, or both.

How then does this rule square with Bainimarama's public declaration that parliament is "the people's house"? And the comment by the Speaker, Jiko Luveni, in a TV programme, that people must feel that they "own" parliament.

They are both right. The people own parliament. They pay for it and foot the bill for the salaries of the MPs and ministers. Its job is to enact laws and measures to improve their lives. But Bill 28 classifies the people who might wish to go into the house as strangers who might face a jail sentence if they break a rule about admittance to the premises. Bainimarama and the speaker should explain how this can be. The people can never be strangers in their own parliament. My advice is for the house to update its rules so that they are in accordance with Sayed-Khaiyum's ambition to transform Fiji into a "modern nation state".

Under the 2013 constitution, the people also have the right to freedom of movement. Even ex-convicts like myself have that right. Is that to be curtailed to give parliamentarians extra privileges that serve to "separate" them from the citizens they work for? I remind Bainimarama and Sayed-Khaiyum that Section 72(2) of the constitution they drafted and imposed declares that parliament "may not exclude the public, from any sitting unless, in exceptional circumstances, the speaker has ordered public exclusion on grounds that are reasonable and justifiable". With this provision in the constitution, why are they going to such lengths to bring in additional rules governing "strangers".

Section 17 of the Bill sets financial and prison sentences for a person who publishes a document "or other evidence" presented to parliament, the publication of which has been prohibited by parliament or a committee. I sense here a desire to keep secret documents the government does not want to be published. Some documents, of course, may need to be confidential for security reasons. But there is no mention of this in Section 17. It seems any document can become prohibited if the government so decides. This raises the issue of how much information should be made secret in an open democracy.

It also raises questions about Section 17(1)(a) of the imposed constitution, giving citizens the freedom to seek, receive and impart information. That provision can easily be blocked by introducing parliamentary rules prohibiting publication of certain documents. So what is it to be – freedom or prohibition?

In light of this tendency towards secrecy, I wonder why Sayed-Khaiyum and Bainimarama included in their constitution Section 72 (1)(a). This says parliament must conduct its business in an open manner and hold its sittings and those of committees in public. There is a disconnect and contradiction between these sentiments and the intentions of their constitution as expressed in Bill 28.

Section 20 of Bill 28 is very troubling. It provides for a term of imprisonment for up to ten years or a fine not exceeding $50,000 for persons who commit fraud or threats against members of parliament. The offence is spelled out in the context of an attempt to influence a member's vote, opinion or action in relation to a question in parliament or a committee. It also extends to attempts to influence a member to take a particular position on a parliamentary matter. In normal circumstances members of the public should be perfectly free to lobby MPs on issues that interest them. This is part of democracy. They may be vigorously outspoken about their pleas and arguments, and even remind an MP that the response will influence their votes in the next elections. Under Bill 28 this may be construed as a "threat" leading to 10 years in prison.

In these circumstances, who would even wish to submit their political concerns to MPs and ministers who might choose to interpret them in a particular and threatening way. It would be natural for people to be extremely cautious about making an approach to advocate their views. Who would want to risk a fine or a prison sentence?

I discern that this is a move to increase the power of the government by perceived intimidation and creating legal danger for the people. By limiting the scope and likelihood of political pressure that might be contrary to the wishes of the government, it has better prospects of having its own way. At the same time democracy would be further squeezed.

Section 24 presents another big problem. It proposes large fines and prison terms – up to $100,000 and five years - for those whose "words or actions defame, demean or undermine the sanctity of parliament, the speaker or a committee....".

The business community and company directors do not escape. They, too, are picked out as a target.

The savage provisions are a warning to those citizens who employ their right to freedom of speech by commenting publicly on the business of parliament. The regular writers to the letters columns of the newspapers had better watch out; so should contributing writers, news reporters and corporate managers who want to have their say on parliamentary topics. Step out of line and a prison cell awaits.

I make the point that there are already defamation laws; why introduce another one? The answer again is that this is a means of adding another layer of threat directed at limiting dissent.

I ask what exactly is meant by the "sanctity" of parliament? The popular definitions of sanctity are holy or sacred. Who said our parliament had been sanctified and is now sacred? How was this decision made and under whose authority? Why were the people not involved in this? I can find nothing in the constitution that refers to parliament as sacred. Parliament is not a church. It is certainly the highest political institution in a country and should be respected in that sense. It is also a place for the cut and thrust, the rough and tumble of debate between competing political parties. It is a forum for straight and often blunt speech; telling it like it is; criticism; truth-telling and robust expression of ideas and comments the opposing side may not want to hear. Importantly parliament is also where consensus and cooperation can be negotiated and achieved for the national good, although that concept of togetherness is foreign to Bainimarama and Sayed-Khaiyum.

My final comment is that the speaker is granted the right to decide that certain words spoken by members should not be published. Where will this end? How many words will be banned and what effect will this have on forthright debate? Surely this is censorship in another form?

Those who wrote Bill 28 should explain why they decided to relegate parliament to where it has never been before and where it does not belong. The result will be a weak institution for an emasculated democracy, suited only for a new kind of dictatorship.

The best place for Bill 28 is the waste paper basket.

---

The Fiji military's position of ultimate power in the 2013 constitution reflects the grandiose notions of some senior officers of their mission and purpose. In a 2012 constitutional submission, it stated that it was the "last bastion for law and order in Fiji" (although it has consistently broken the law) and would continue to provide "guidance of the governance of this country ensuring that peace, prosperity and good governance is practised and adhered to". This is not the statement of an army that sees itself as subordinate to civilian authority. It is just the opposite.

Section 131 of the 2013 constitution gives the army its power. It specifies that the overall responsibility of the RFMF is to ensure at all times the security, defence and well being of Fiji and all Fijians. The wording is similar to the 1990 constitution. But the provision was dropped in the 1997 constitution on the grounds that the armed forces should be constitutionally subordinate to parliament. The Reeves Commission, which did the ground work for that constitution and consulted widely, said it believed there was full acceptance that the military forces existed solely to serve the purposes of the government. Any deployment for a particular purpose must be in response to decision taken by the appropriate minister. This was approved by an elected parliament.

The inclusion of the military power section in the 2013 document was part of a scheme for perpetuating in a different form a dictatorship that had been in charge of the country for nearly eight years.

As of now, the military's constitutional right to ensure the well-being of Fiji and all Fijians is a blanket mandate. It is not subject to the authority of the president, the government or the parliament.

(If it is not accountable to them, how then can it come under the jurisdiction of the courts?) I submit that under the 2013 constitution the military, not parliament, reigns supreme in deciding what is best for Fiji. That is not democracy. It is military rule/dictatorship.

"Well-being" is defined as being healthy, happy and prosperous. "Ensure" means to make certain something happens. So, based on these definitions, the army has the task of making sure Fiji and its people are socially, economically and politically advanced to the extent that they are in a state of happiness, enjoy good health and have the income for a high standard of living. One might say it's the army's job to take us to paradise on earth. Now those who support the government will take issue with what I am saying; that I am exaggerating. I advise them to study the words of Section 131 (2) of the constitution. They are very clear.

I wonder where the RFMF will get the expertise, wisdom and resources to accomplish its constitutional mission. It has a record of bad governance, overspending and is politically inept. Of course, our history shows that it is capable of getting its way through the barrel of a gun. But this is not an acceptable, civilized means of accomplishing our well-being and everything that goes with it. It can hardly argue that a coup is for the public well-being, can it? Remember though that more than one leading figure felt the Bainimarama coup, although treasonous, was justified. It was supposed to be a good coup.

The army leaders seem to be confused about their role. Occasionally they flex their muscles by issuing a statement usually to do with what they define as security.

Sometimes they claim they are not involved in politics and do not wish to be. Those arguments do not work in light of their defined role. Ensuring the well being of the people can only be achieved through politics. If the military leadership insist they are non- political then surely, they are in breach of their constitution. It is all a tangle, a confusion of law and misconceptions. Bainimarama has always said the military is "all powerful". But he has to be sure that power will work for him.

I agree with the proposition that the military in a proper democracy, should have no part in government. Bainimarama and Sayed-Khaiyum clearly do not agree. They must also know the risk to which they have exposed themselves through their military "insurance" clause. Their worst nightmare would be an army commander, with the same traits as Bainimarama, who is not ready to toe the line.

I can only assume that the army constantly monitors in detail the state of affairs in the nation, but it is not known what their measure is for "well-being". It obviously had no concern about Sayed- Khaiyum's "ape" imitation, although it would be reasonable to assume that to a lot of citizens this was very provocative, inflammatory and insulting, and not conducive to promoting the national welfare.

At what point might the soldiers declare that the deplorable state of the environment does not add to our national well-being. A similar question could be asked about the health service, the condition of some roads, frequent water cuts and electricity blackouts, the increase in death and injury on our roads, low wages, violent crimes and unemployment, the high cost of holidaying in Fiji... and so on.

I ask what sort of system is in place for the army to impose its authority. Is there an army-ministerial working group? Does the army commander simply call the head of government and give him an instruction about what he must do to make things better? What if the head of government declines to follow orders? What happens if the RFMF insists that to further the public well-being it must be represented in Cabinet? I ask these questions in the absence of any details about how all this works.

# 62

# DOING AWAY WITH CHECKS AND BALANCES

T he 2013 constitution largely does away with the checks and balances of the earlier documents. It gives the prime minister huge and disproportionate powers. These undermine democracy as a system of governance of the people and by the people.

A useful assessment of the constitution by lawyers for the Fiji public advocacy organisation, the Citizens Constitutional Forum (CCF) says the prime minister's authority relative to the legislature, the judiciary and supposedly "independent" offices, is perhaps "unprecedented in modern constitutions". It observes that in most countries executive powers are given to Cabinet as a whole and not just the prime minister (and never the attorney general).

The analysis describes the attorney general's powers as "remarkable and wide ranging" and far wider than in constitutions of other Commonwealth countries. It states he has extensive control over the judiciary and "independent" bodies. The prime minister and the attorney general, says the CCF, have "significant control" over the judicial branch, including all the independent legal offices and the vitally important judicial services commission. For instance, the two highest judicial offices, chief justice and president of the court of appeal, are appointed by the prime minister after consultation with the attorney general. The judicial services commission comprises the chief justice as chair, the president of the court of appeal and the permanent secretary for justice who are all appointed by the prime minister, again after consulting the attorney general. The chief justice then nominates another two members, a legal practitioner and a non-practitioner, after consulting the attorney general. Their remuneration is set after the chief justice consults with the attorney general.

The CCF points out that judges and magistrates are essentially appointed and disciplined by the judicial services commission after consultation with the attorney general.

Among other things the judicial services commission has responsibility for the efficient functioning of the judiciary; a very broad and flexible mandate. It provides regular updates and advice to the attorney general on "any matter relating to the judiciary or the administration of justice". Again, this is a very flexible provision. For the record, the constitution stipulates the commission shall be "independent".

I am familiar with the public service commission from my time as its secretary. In my view the 2013 constitution has effectively removed the independence of the PSC. It has been politicized bringing it under the political control of the government in power.

Under the 1997 constitution the PSC consisted of a chair and not less than three, nor more than five, other members appointed by the president. Appointments were made on the nomination of the minister (prime minister). The nominations then had to be approved by the appropriate sector standing committee of the house of representatives before the minister submitted the nomination to the president. This ensured that the prime minister did not have too much unfettered authority.

Now, consistent with the 2013 constitution, the PSC, with the same membership numbers, is appointed by the president on the advice of the constitutional offices commission (COC). The government has a substantial majority in the COC, so its appointments are effectively government appointments.

The 1997 constitution provided that permanent secretaries were appointed by the PSC with the agreement of the prime minister. The 2013 constitution also says that the appointment of permanent secretaries by the PSC must have the agreement of the prime minister. However, the appointment of members of the PSC under the 1997 constitution was made by an independent COC. Under the 2013 constitution the members of the COC are effectively appointed by the prime minister and the attorney general.

These provisions make the prime minister into the appointing and dismissing authority. He can determine who should occupy these important positions and who should be sacked. He even has the power to decide their pay. All this means his grip over the machinery of government is therefore tightened.

Section 127 of the 2013 constitution gives the permanent secretaries large powers. Section 127 (7) confers on the permanent secretary the authority to appoint, remove and institute action against all staff of the ministry. But the minister, a politician, must agree. Both the permanent secretary and his political minister therefore have full authority to determine all matters relating to the employment of all staff in their ministry. This includes: terms and conditions of employment; qualifications for appointments; salaries, benefits and allowances; the total number of staff required within the approved budget.

It is very obvious that the government in power has total control politically and administratively of the public service. The use of this power is visibly demonstrated in the numerous political appointments in all levels of the service. Such power encourages corruption, nepotism and cronyism. There are many examples of these. The public service will never regain its accountability as long as the 2013 constitution is in place.

The constitutional offices commission (COC) has the important job of making crucial state appointments such as the commissioner of police, secretary general to parliament, governor of the reserve bank, supervisor of elections, auditor-general and commander of the Republic of Fiji Military Forces.

The COC is supposed to be independent but, like the PSC, is highly politicised. It is another good example of how the regime constitution has been engineered to give the PM greater power. Independence for the COC in the 1997 constitution was achieved by providing for a chairperson and two other members to be appointed by the president.

But in their constitution Bainimarama-Sayed-Khaiyum have rid themselves of the independence of the COC. They have given themselves freedom to appoint whom they wish. The CCF assessment says the prime minister through the COC controls appointment to ten significant offices or commissions.

The prime minister is the chair. The attorney-general is a member. So are two persons appointed by the president on the advice of the prime minister. The leader of the opposition is also a member and has the power to advise the president to appoint one member. (Note that the general powers of the leader of the opposition – the alternative prime minister – have been drastically reduced.)

Despite the one-sided composition, section 132, sub-section (5) of the constitution states that the COC "shall be independent and shall not be subject to the direction or control of any person or authority". How can it be independent when it is led by the prime minister as chair, supported by the attorney-general and two other hand-picked supporters as members? The leader of the opposition is left with just one appointee. Interestingly, even with such a preponderance of power favourable to the PM, the COC has not been functioning properly. The leader of the opposition has criticized its way of operating, with too much reliance on last minute emails rather than full meetings. Richard Naidu, a prominent lawyer who accepted appointment from the leader of the opposition, was so dissatisfied with the COC that he resigned, saying he did not wish to become a "rubber stamp". The leader of the opposition, currently Ro Teimumu Vuikaba Kepa, then nominated Sitiveni Rabuka, former prime minister, 1987 coup leader and leader of SODELPA, to replace Mr Naidu. But at the time of writing this there had been no announcement of Rabuka's appointment. That probably means the COC is incomplete and unconstitutional. This is no way to manage a government.

The CCF study highlighted a specific concern about the operations of parliament, stemming from the PM's dominance of the COC. It points out that the COC, led by the PM and his majority, appoints the secretary-general of parliament.

According to the CCF this means parliament is not even in full control of the person responsible for organising its administration. I can relate to the CCF reasoning.

The electoral commission and the supervisor of elections are vital for the conduct of "free and fair" elections. This also goes to the very centre of democracy. Under the 1997 constitution, checks and balances governed appointments. A chairperson was appointed by the president acting in his or her own judgment. The four other members were appointed by the president on the advice of the prime minister following consultations by the PM with the leader of the opposition. The supervisor of elections was appointed by the constitutional offices commission (COC) following consultations by it with the relevant minister. Under the new constitution, the checks and balances have been thrown out. Authority for appointments of the chairperson and members of the electoral commission lies with the prime minister through the COC. He has the majority. It is notable that Fiji's opposition political parties had expressed no confidence in the electoral commission, perceiving it as less than impartial. They mean it is not independent. I agree. The same goes for the supervisor of elections. The parties in 2017 announced a vote of no confidence in this official. The CCF analysis of the Bainimarama-Sayed-Khaiyum constitution went as far as to assert that elections under their constitution will challenge the principles of a "free and fair" poll.

Previously the pay of MPs was set independently. That idea has been scrapped by the two men at the top. They wanted to determine their own salaries. There is no limit on the levels of increase that can be granted but MPs are prevented from taking a voluntary pay cut. For the record when I was PM my salary was about $106,000, well below what I was paid in my last private sector job as head of Merchant Finance. I understand that under the Parliamentary Remunerations Decree, Bainimarama is getting a salary of nearly $329,000. This works out at more than $900 a day and is well over 200 per cent more than the PM's salary I received. Bainimarama also, reportedly, gets a $3,000 a day allowance when he's overseas.

I suspect this will be in addition to government paying for his accommodation and meals. You can imagine the sort of money he is earning in total in light of all the travelling he does.

I have heard Bainimarama virtually bragging about how difficult it is to change their constitution. That is not necessarily a virtue, especially when there are sound reasons for amendments. I have in mind in particular the lack of strong protection for indigenous land ownership. It will be almost impossible to correct this because of the stringent requirements for amendment. There is an additional problem. If there was to be a referendum it would presumably have to be limited to the landowners?

The CCF submits that the 2013 constitution might be the hardest in the world to amend. If that is the case, Bainimarama and Sayed- Khaiyum have cemented in the provisions they have implemented to serve their interests.

Amendments can only come through a bill debated three times in parliament and voted on twice by at least three quarters of the members with these votes separated by at least 30 days. A referendum must then be held which three quarters of registered voters must approve. The CCF analysts argue that future governments may need to revisit the amending mechanism. Without this ability, they say, citizens may well be stuck with a constitution that does not work or cannot respond to change.

# 63

# SWEEPING IMMUNITY

A section of the constitution is devoted to sweeping provisions to grant those who committed treason immunity for their crime. (Note well that these coup immunity provisions can never be changed even by amendment. That underlines the obsessive and understandable preoccupation of the coupsters with protecting themselves and those who helped them to commit treason.) They knew that for their own self-preservation and future, it was imperative to give themselves as much protection as they possibly could. If they didn't they would likely end up in Naboro gaol with George Speight.

According to the CCF assessment the constitution's immunity arrangements seemingly exceed the permissible scope of amnesties under international law. They also flew in the face of what the Yash Ghai commission heard when it was listening to the people in its Fiji-wide discussions. There was unhappiness about the immunity already established by decree by the regime. The Yash Ghai commission reported that immunity was raised repeatedly, and the government was "heavily criticised" for the way it had granted immunity to itself as well as the scope of it. The renewal of previous immunities was seen as favours to friends of the government.

Said the commission:

---

Many expressed their dismay that the government had not attempted to secure immunity through a process of discussion and reconciliation.

---

People knew that immunity could be a virtual free pass to coup makers. It also gave confidence to those contemplating a coup or engaging in one. When immunity was embedded in a constitution, the signal was clear.

I will quote some more from the Yash Ghai commission on this issue of coups because these have been such a destructive part of our history. The commission said it was frequently asked whether or how the constitution could prevent coups.

Some suggested that a constitution should prohibit coups. Others called for the abolition of the armed forces (since Fiji has no enemies) or deploying the forces to protect Fiji's maritime resources. It was even suggested that weapons should be stored in Australia to be collected as Fijian soldiers went abroad as peacekeepers. There were calls for active recruitment of military personnel from all communities so that the army's membership was representative of the population. A few citizens recommended that sanctions by the UN should be activated as soon as a coup happened and that all Fijian peacekeepers should be sent home immediately. Calls came for severe penalties for coup makers, including disqualifications from public office and the death penalty. Some people cautioned that in all coups, the military was used by other interests: politicians, business people, chiefs – which made it harder to predict or prevent coups. The commission asked why coups happened. Its answer:

---

There must be a military willing and able to conduct a coup and there is usually some situation within the country or the government that gives the willing military the opening or excuse, or that persuades it to step in.

---

As submissions to the commission noted, in Fiji there's always been a third factor: behind-the-scenes actors who use, manipulate or persuade the military to take action. The commission went on:

---

In most democracies, the military does not take over in times of crisis. This requires a military that takes pride in its role as defender of the country against outside attack and accepts that role as ... subordinate to the civilian government.

The commission knows that a constitution on its own cannot prevent coups. But it believes that in a vigorous democracy in which citizens participate in decision making and value their democratic institutions, coups are less likely.

---

The Yash Ghai commission's answer was to state in its draft constitution that coups are illegal and that trying to establish a government except in the ways the constitution provides is unlawful and no immunity could be granted for any future coups.

It emphasised that the military does not have any role as a guardian of the constitution or conscience of the nation and it was under civilian control. The draft did not give the president any role in relation to the military because it was the democratically elected government that must direct the army.

Importantly it stated that members of the security services must not obey manifestly illegal orders. This was of particular relevance to the military in a country with a record of coups. Soldiers must not use "superior orders" as an excuse for behaviour that they knew was clearly wrong. (Such as abducting people, bashing them up or otherwise tormenting them.)

There is another reference from the CCF that is relevant. It cited the example of Turkey whose constitution was approved by 91.4 per cent of Turks in a 1992 referendum. In 2010 it was amended to abolish immunity provisions and allow for prosecution of members of the previous regime.

The Yash Ghai document included an Oath of Reconciliation and Allegiance for the security services requiring the oath-taker to accept the sovereignty of the people as the only legitimate source of authority. The person swearing the oath must renounce "any actions in my past that may have promoted, assisted or protected attempts to establish a government otherwise than in accordance with the law".

I cannot find any special oath for the military in the 2013 constitution. It is not designed specifically to prevent future coups. The immunity provisions are, in reality, an incentive to those who have treason in mind.

Like the Yash Ghai commission, I believe there is never any justification for a coup in a democratic society and offer further thinking on this in the final reflections chapter of this book.

# 64

# BILL OF RIGHTS PROBLEMS

Sayed-Khaiyum tends to boast often about his constitution's Bill of Rights and its emphasis on socio- economic rights. What he fails to say is that the 1997 constitution also had an elaborate Bill of Rights. It covered many areas such as the right to life and personal liberty, freedom from servitude and forced labour, cruel and degrading treatment; and from unreasonable searches and seizure. There were rights relating to arrest and detention and legal charges, including the right to be presumed innocent until proven guilty, and the right to a fair trial, equality before the law, and other related rights. Freedom of speech, expression, association, movement, assembly, access, and union membership were granted along with religion and belief. Citizens could not be discriminated against although the inclusion of sexual orientation in the non- discrimination provision raised the issue of possible same-sex marriage. (The same applies in the Bainimarama-Khaiyum constitution.) The right to basic education and equal access to educational institutions was specified and protection against compulsory acquisition of property. In those cases where limitations might apply, these had to be reasonable and justifiable "in a free and democratic society". This was an important protective condition, which is missing completely from the limitation provisions of the regime's constitution. It is another indication of the sidelining of democracy.

In the 2013 constitution, a limitation, or escape, clause is used frequently. Rights can also be delayed. I counted at least 19 that could be changed, reduced or postponed.

It works like this. Bainimarama-Sayed-Khaiyum gives us the right to take part fully in the economy (sect 32) of the Bill of Rights. But then when you read on it becomes evident that this right is not instant. Read further and you see that a law might be enacted to place a limit on the right to economic participation. So when is a right not a right? When enough progress is made towards making it real?

But will it happen if some law limits it to the point of extinction. It is very clear that these sorts of provisions devalue the 2013 constitution's rights.

There is another serious problem. In the introductory section of the Bill of Rights section 6 (5) (a) (b) (c) spell out how rights and freedoms may be limited and therefore changed. This appears to apply not just to specific rights mentioned in the document, but to the entire Bill of Rights, further weakening it. I believe section 6 (5) (c) is the most threatening part of the 2013 constitution on the Fijian land issue, and for freehold owners.

In previous constitutions, there were special provisions providing extremely strong safeguards for this, along with protection for Fiji's Banaban people and the natives of Rotuma. The 1997 constitution laid down very detailed and entrenched procedures for altering the following: *iTaukei* Lands Act (Cap 133), *iTaukei* Land Trust Act (Cap 134), Rotuma Lands Act (Cap 138), Banaban Lands Act (Cap 124) and Agricultural Landlord and Tenant Act (Cap 270).

All these safeguards were dumped. There's never been a proper explanation for this. It was astonishing and inexplicable that the first draft of the 2013 constitution had no reference at all to native land. It was left out completely. I can only speculate on why this inexcusable omission occurred. In light of the extreme sensitivity over Fijian ownership of land, surely it is beyond belief that it could have been mistakenly overlooked. Bainimarama and Sayed-Khaiyum must have viewed the first draft before it was released publicly.

The omission caused great fear and uncertainty among the owners. It is only when supporters of SODELPA began to speak out that Bainimarama-Sayed-Khaiyum decided they had better include a specific reference to native land. I am convinced that without the SODELPA protests they would likely have enacted their supreme law with no particular mention of it. Now, after inserting Fijian land as an apparent afterthought, the two of them constantly claim that it has greater protection than before. This is absolutely untrue.

They have achieved their illusion of greater protection by simply placing indigenous land ownership (section 28) among the long list of rights in their constitution. These are the rights that can be limited and changed according to Section 6. This could be done by a simple majority in parliament.

The CCF analysis provides an imaginary example of how change could happen: "Parliament makes a law allowing for the grant of 99 years mining licenses over *iTaukei* land without requiring consultation with customary owners. Such a law would limit the constitutional protection of *iTaukei* land set out in Section 28 in the Fiji government constitution. If the law is challenged before a court, the State could argue that the granting of mining licenses was necessary for the economic well being of Fiji. This would likely pass the necessity test set out in section 6 (5) (c), in which case the law would be valid."

That is an example produced by experts of what could happen to Fijian-owned land. The CCF lawyers conclude that the Bill of Rights offers no real protection to *iTaukei* landowners. So do I.

Bainimarama and Sayed-Khaiyum have seized on a specific and isolated transaction expedited by my government to create the false impression that we had a policy of regularly changing Fijian land to freehold and that this was a loss to landowners. There was no such policy. I have gone on record on this issue a number of times and do so again here.

The land transaction in question involved the exchange of 68.7hectares of native land owned by Tokatoka Nasau, with freehold land of equivalent area and value owned by Matapo Ltd developer of Momi Bay Resort project. This was done to help facilitate the development of the resort which, in the event, was delayed by Bainimarama's coup. Upon exchange the native land was to be converted to freehold and the Matapo freehold to native land and registered under Tokatoka Nasau. There was no "loss" of land in this arrangement because of the equivalent freehold land and other benefits in exchange. Everything was done with the voluntary agreement of the two parties Tokatoka Nasau and Matapo Ltd.

The Native Land Trust Board gave its approval and the land swap was sanctioned under the Land Transfer Act. The terms and conditions of the swap are recorded in an Agreement between the two stakeholders dated May 31st 2005. The bottom line is that the landowners agreed to exchange their asset with a similar one of equivalent value. It was a voluntary act on their part. Conversion of native land to freehold was never the policy of the SDL. The Momi transaction was an isolated case carried out legally and completed in good faith.

There are two precedents for similar transactions. One was for the Hyatt hotel and the other for the big Denarau resort; both occurred during the leadership of the SVT. I stress that without the entrenched protective legislation for native land – scrapped by Bainimarama-Sayed-Khaiyum – any amendment to the Native Lands Trust Act, for example, would just require a straight majority in parliament. Without entrenchment, it becomes easier to alienate native land.

Bainimarama has claimed more than once that his constitution, for the first time, stipulates that landowners, or customary fishing rights owners, shall be entitled to receive a fair share of royalties or other money from extraction of minerals from land or seabed. This is not true. The 1997 constitution contains a similar section.

Many indigenous people were not happy that the 2013 constitution failed to recognize group rights which are integral to *iTaukei* culture. Fijian land, for instance, does not belong to individuals. It is owned by groups such as *tokatoka, mataqali* and *yavusa*. This was clearly recognized in the 1997 constitution which dedicated a full chapter to group rights; these are also recognized as human rights. But cultural awareness and sensitivity towards the indigenes is not a strong point of Bainimarama and Sayed-Khaiyum. They just dropped group rights altogether from their constitution.

# 65

# WHERE STANDS THE SECULAR STATE?

A s they had intended, Bainimarama-Sayed-Khaiyum insisted on Fiji becoming a secular state, meaning that the state is neutral in matters of religion. I have already explained that in light of Fiji's history and the transformational, civilizing, influence of Christianity amongst the first people, there is a sense amongst the indigenous Fijians that our islands should become a Christian state. With this would come full religious liberty and recognition of other faiths. But the dictatorship would not move from their misconceived notion that the country should become secular.

The 1997 constitution, which had been unanimously endorsed by a multi racial parliament, did not declare a Christian state, but it did highlight the conversion of the indigenous inhabitants to Christianity

through "the power of the name of Jesus Christ". It recognized the enduring impact of Christianity in Fiji and its contribution, along with that of the other faiths, to the spiritual life of the country. There was prominent acknowledgement of the high chiefs of Fiji ceding Fiji to Great Britain and their acceptance of the "Divine guidance of God".

---

Bainimarama and Sayed-Khaiyum removed our God from their supreme law. They declared that the State must not prefer any particular religion, religious denomination, religious belief or religious practice over another or over any non-religious belief. In other words, the State would become neutral in matters of religion. To the indigenous Fijians, this means the constitution is God-less. In practice secularism is supposed to mean that State employees on duty, especially at meetings or formal occasions, should abandon Christian prayer. But it is quite evident that it is not taking hold. For instance, the army, a State institution, still had a Christian chaplain last time I checked. If that still stands, that means the institution rejects the Bainimarama-Sayed-Khaiyum secularism.

The government clearly can do nothing to end this breaking of the secular rule. Some gatherings organized by State officers still begin with a Christian prayer; again, that is a repudiation of secularism.

I wonder about the significance of a government minister who might be a practicing Hindu, attending in an official capacity a Hindu religious gathering and maybe giving a donation? Is this permitted under the Bainimarama-Sayed Khaiyum secularism?

At one point, Bainimarama was encouraging children in government schools to pray a neutral prayer, which to me was a prayer, to an unknown God. Ro Teimumu Vuikaba Kepa, the current Leader of the Opposition and former leader of SODELPA, issued a public statement dated 17th March 2014 about the confusion surrounding the issue of school prayer. This is what she said:

---

The government has created a web of confusion over its

policy of a secular state. Since I raised the issue of school prayer, Commodore Bainimarama and the Attorney General, Mr Aiyaz Sayed-Khaiyum, have both made statements. They are still not spelling out their policy precisely. The question I ask is one that is also of concern to many thousands of others.

Will Christian prayers and observances referring to Jesus Christ be allowed in government schools? Will the specific prayers of other religions be permitted? I ask another question: Are schools that are owned and operated by religious denominations safe from secularism? I know there is a fear that the government will try to extend its religious authority to all schools on the basis of the extra funding it has provided for free education.

My understanding as of now is that Commodore Bainimarama and Mr Sayed-Khaiyum are promoting "neutral" prayer. This would remove Christ from school prayer. Commodore Bainimarama recited his "neutral" prayer at Kalabu High School, which is non-government. It is not for Voreqe Bainimarama to tell us what prayers our children should say at school. Did Voreqe Bainimarama and Mr Sayed-Khaiyum think they could tamper with school prayer without any reaction from the public?

Commodore Bainimarama needs to explain to the nation how his policy of secularism affects the Fiji Military Forces and the Police Force. Are the members of these two state institutions also expected to say only "neutral" prayers? There was no sign of that at the church service at the military headquarters to farewell Commodore Bainimarama as commander.

When I addressed the SODELPA general assembly I spoke out strongly on secularism. I criticized the decision of Voreqe Bainimarama and Mr Sayed-Khaiyum to take God out of their constitution and then claim that we the people supported it.

Commodore Bainimarama is trying to twist what I said to infer that I believe God has been removed from our national life. He knows very well that I did not make that claim. I was speaking about their constitution, its secular provisions and the impact on school prayer.

It is a fact that Mesui C Volau, a senior official from the Ministry of Education's ethics and disciplinary unit, advised that Christian prayers at Suva Grammar School, a government school, are unconstitutional. By extension this would obviously apply to the other government schools. Mr Volau went further and also advised that all schools would be affected.

He was reprimanded by Mr Sayed-Khaiyum for giving unauthorised "legal advice". But his advice was not legal. It was the considered opinion of a senior civil servant interpreting the Bainimarama-Khaiyum constitution.

Mr Khaiyum sent a letter to the minister for Education, Mr Filipe Bole, telling him about the constitution's secular provisions and that this was to be circulated to all education officials and schools. It seems very strange that Mr Bole needed this advice from Mr Khaiyum. Did he not understand the government's secular policies?

It is also extraordinary that there should be so much confusion over these sensitive religious issues. It tells us something about the workings and incompetence of the Bainimarama-Sayed-Khaiyum government.

Our different religions are woven deep in the fabric of Fiji. When Christianity came to these islands it changed forever the nature of indigenous society. We were converted and saw the light of Jesus Christ. Other faiths came and contributed to the life of the country.

This fundamental role of religion was recognized in previous democratically approved constitutions. But not in the Bainimarama - Sayed-Khaiyum constitution.

The advice by Mr Volau was contained in a letter of January 28, 2014, about Suva Grammar School. He signed it as a representative of the Education Ministry's Ethics and Disciplinary Unit. He stated that employees of the school were public office holders.

They must not therefore advance any particular religion over others. Therefore, it would be unconstitutional if any public office holders continued to conduct school devotions and prayers at the school in the Christian faith "as this would be construed as Christianity subjugating other religions".

Would it? Christianity for the vast majority of its adherents is a tolerant religion. Mr Volau went on to argue in favour of stopping all public officers at Suva Grammar from conducting any form of religious teachings or education at the school. He then said all schools must adhere to the constitution regardless of whether they were "religious based" or otherwise.

# 66

# 2014 POLL FAIR AND FREE OR A FRAUD?

The non-government organisation, the Citizens Constitutional Forum (CCF) prepared a submission arguing that in the 2013 constitution the central concept of free and fair elections is undermined by constitutionally-protected decrees that severely restrict the media and political parties. The contradictions are effectively described by the CCF. It says that while electoral rights are granted, they can be limited by a simple decree. The CCF goes on to say that citizens have a right to vote and stand for election, but trade union leaders are restricted from being candidates. It notes that an Electoral Commission will administer elections. But, of course, the prime minister exercises authority over it with the power of appointment through the Constitutional Offices Commission.

While media can report on elections, the media decree and limitations of freedoms can be applied by law to control media behavior. Political parties must be transparent and peaceful; but limitations can be drawn to define definitions of transparency.

The CCF underscores other problems such as parties having to gather 5,000 signatures across the country to register. This, in my view, does not help to create a democratic environment. It is an obstacle to democracy.

The outcome of the controversial 2014 election, gave Baini-marama, Sayed-Khaiyum and the Fiji First Party a majority in parliament. This was questioned by the opposition parties including SODELPA, National Federation Party (NFP), Fiji Labour Party (FLP), Peoples' Democratic Party (PDP) and One Fiji Party. They prepared a detailed report explaining and illustrating their reservations. It was signed by Ro Teimumu Vuikaba Kepa, for SODELPA, Mahendra Chaudhry, leader of the FLP and Tupou Draunidalo, then president of the NFP. The report they endorsed was based on election incidents, irregularities and issues witnessed, described and highlighted by sundry party officials and polling agents. The leaders felt that the report contents pointed to a "systematic and co-ordinated effort to alter the ballots cast at various polling stations." They said:

---

The information we have at hand is compelling and suggests beyond reasonable doubt that the election process was compromised. It is therefore not unreasonable to conclude that the extent of this compromise may well have contributed to the final outcome.

---

Signed statutory declarations were included from individuals who testified to witnessing irregularities. Details were included of breaches of the law that the parties alleged had ocurred.

I am including some detailed extracts from the parties' report because I believe it should be read widely. To this point it has been flicked away by electoral commissioners "for lack of evidence". As someone said, the content was not pulled from thin air.

One of the central issues was that according to witnesses a number of polling stations closed without reason at the end of voting and stayed closed for up to two hours. Party polling agents were ushered out of the stations and in some cases police were also not present. This was highlighted as a breach of sec 89 (1) of the Electoral Act. The scenario the parties envisaged was for unsecured ballot papers to be placed in ballot boxes during the time a polling station was closed. When the party polling agents were readmitted, the count would begin.

They included specific instances of irregular closing:

- • St John Bosco Primary School Nadera. Presiding officer reportedly sent agents away for an hour. According to the parties, there were no police inside the polling station for this period. Statutory declaration prepared by party agent at the station.
- • Drasa Primary School, Raviravi Sangam School station no. 5156, Lovu Sangam School, Satya Sai School.
- • Statutory declaration of Luseyane Ligabalavu.
- • Signed letter from Ravendra Chand, Fiji Labour Party.

The party investigations led to their discovery of what they called a "ghost call-centre". They alleged that presiding officers were instructed to call their results into a certain person identified only by initials.

This had been independently verified by four separate agents at different locations as well as by a polling official and a counting supervisor at a count centre. There was reportedly established confirmation from a count supervisor that the results they were receiving did not come directly from the polling venues but from an unknown person or persons. An example was provided involving Kalokolevu to ATG (Army Training Group Nasinu) where the presiding officers were required to call in their results to someone called RT and not to the count centre. This was interpreted by the parties and their agents as a variation from normal procedures. But no reference about an amendment to the Electoral Decree was referred to by either the chairman of the Electoral Commission or the supervisor of elections.

The report verified that a Vodafone owned by a supporter was used by a presiding officer to call 9993975 to give polling results to an unknown person receiving the call. The presiding officer did not know who he was calling; he was just given the number to call in the results. It was not to the count centre. The report said it had been established that the number called by the presiding officer was one of 16 listed as belonging to the Elections Office.

The parties alleged that the Elections Office knowingly broke the requirements of Section 97 (1) (Electoral Decree 2014), and was operating Ghost Call Centres to which results were first relayed and not the count centres:

- • Statutory Declaration of Polling Agent Saini Nabou of NFP
- • Statutory Declaration of Jolame Uludole Polling Agent for SODELPA
- • Statutory Declaration of Peter Waqavonovono Count Agent for SODELPA
- • Statutory Declaration of Marika Naseqai supporter of SODELPA

The parties report there was a sworn statement of an agent of the One Fiji Party who was suspicious of a parked Kia Sorento motor vehicle no. FR852, registered to a well-known company, parked at the Andrews Primary School Nadi at 3pm on Wednesday, September 17th.

The One Fiji agent approached the vehicle and noted stacks of ballot papers in the boot of the vehicle. He signaled his associate to take pictures and when an individual handling the ballot papers saw the One Fiji agent, he closed the boot and drove off. The incident was reportedly witnessed by two other agents from the NFP.

The parties report quoted the response to this incident from Mr Chen Bunn Young, who was then chairman of he Electoral Commission. He identified the Kia Sorento number FR852 as owned by

Tappoos Limited trading as Bula Rentals. The contents of the vehicle's boot were contracts for polling day workers and the vehicle was used to deliver them to various polling stations. The party leaders rejected Mr Young's explanation.

They drew Mr Young's attention to section 42 (7) (*Electoral Decree* 2014) stating: a person appointed under this section must not begin to perform his other duties unless he or she had signed a declaration or a code of conduct in the approved form.

The parties said the incident at Andrew's Primary School took place at 3pm on September 17$^{th}$, 2014; the elections ended at 6pm. So 70% of the voting may have been concluded at that time (3pm), hence the question:

1) Why was an election official (not in uniform) delivering employment contracts to polling stations ... when 70% of the time of polling had already lapsed?

2) Section 42 (7) related to all appointments by the supervisor and therefore if Mr Young's explanation is to be considered, then hundreds of elections officials were performing their tasks in breach of Section 42 (7).

3) Mr Young dismissed the parties witnesses accounts as false. And according to the parties, the documents were day workers' contracts. The report said the parties were not mistaken and that the witness knew the difference in size between a A4 paper and the 2014 ballot paper.

4) The report went on to ask a number of other questions including the numbers of day workers; how many were performing their duties in breach of section 42 (7); why was the election official not in uniform; how many contracts did he deliver that day; how many other polling stations required contracts to be delivered after polling was almost over and how many other cars and election officials were engaged in a similar way on election day.

The Statutory Declaration of Pauliasi Rokosawa Bulawa of the Fiji One Party:

The parties reported a second sighting of an unsecured ballot paper on Thursday 18th September 2014 at the Nasinu Forestry Station. It was discovered after counting had been concluded. The ballot paper was reportedly a vote for candidate 255. The report said with sightings of unsecured ballot papers in the west and the east this gave rise to how many other areas were involved.

---

## Statutory Declaration of Peniasi Daveta of Sabeto:

---

Agents from SODELPA and NFP had noted discrepancies in some pre- polling containers as they were off-loaded on September 17th at 3pm in the Vodafone Arena in Suva. They gave the number of ballot boxes involved as follows: Ba-Tavua-Rakiraki 73; Lautoka 42; Keiyasi 38; Eastern 155; Northern 124; Navua 44; Nausori 14; Korovou 19; Vunidawa 40; Suva 0; Total 549.

The Suva container was opened after protest from the polling agent and there were no ballot boxes inside. All ballot boxes had additional documentation and files and other objects inside them, suggesting that they would have been opened in order to place the additional material inside the box.

---

## Statutory Declaration of Peter Waqavonovono of SODELPA:

---

A summary of counting irregularities was attached. The parties were also attempting to verify information that in some instances polling boxes were removed from polling stations.

There was an account of trucks full of ballot boxes arriving from the north after the announcement of the election result.

Mick Beddoes, former Leader of the Opposition, has provided a supplementary report in which he raises issues about the software programme used by the office of the supervisor of elections. Mr Beddoes said party representatives have been informed that the software responsible for the final vote count was shown to members of the Electoral Commission on the day of the count. It was understood that the persons involved in managing the software worked in the office of (name withheld) and that the owner of the software was an associate of (name withheld).

Mr Beddoes provided a summary of points from an interview with one of the data agents, who was reportedly one of several clerks entering voting results into the computer system located at the count centre. The SOE would bring in the results with a police escort and following various checks by supervisors and auditors; data clerks would be given result sheets to input into the system. According to the supplementary report, the clerk noticed that whenever they put in the results for 317 (Ro Teimumu Vuikaba Kepa) and other candidates, these votes would be "lost" whenever there was an attempt to retrieve them for verification. The clerk(s) stated that this occurred multiple times throughout the night and in the end they would be instructed to leave the lost votes inputted and process the next batch of results. It was also noticed that the SOE came in with lots of results without police escort and not all these results have been verified.

It was alleged that on the Saturday (presumably the final day of elections) the operators of the count software and supervisors asked those present to leave the room as they needed to "reset" the computer. On their return, and after the restart of processing the "loss of votes" for 317 and other candidates continued.

---

The report from the parties was dismissed out of hand by the Chen Bunn Young electoral commission which conducted the election. A newly appointed commission led by a lawyer, Mr Suresh Chandra, was also dismissive. In June 2017, he made comments that were antagonistic towards the parties, many of whom he and his colleagues will have to work with in the 2018 election. This smacked of partisanship and lack of judgment that will have soured the commission's relationship with important stakeholders.

Mr Chandra declared that since the parties have failed to provide any evidence in their report on the 2014 poll, all their allegations lacked merit and were falsely designed only to undermine the public's faith in the electoral process, which the commission was committed to strengthen and uphold. Mr Chandra was making a serious allegation that the parties were perpetrating a falsehood.

I have a question for Mr Chandra: How are the parties supposed to go about actually gathering evidence? They can report on what they have seen and observed (which they have), prepare statutory declarations (which they did), and provide relevant details (which they have). But collecting evidence in itself is a specialized business requiring trained investigators with the appropriate powers and funding. The point is, it is the job of those in authority to take note of allegations and accusations and then ensure that a full investigation happens. So were the allegations from the parties ever officially investigated?

A Multinational Observer Group (MOG) co-led by Australia, Indonesia and India was in Fiji to observe the elections. The MOG, in its report of its work, concluded that the election "broadly represented" the will of the voters and that conditions were in place for them to exercise their right to vote freely. However the group's analysis and conclusions were written with caution. Reading between the lines and studying some of their actual words, indicated to me they felt there had been significant problems that might very well have influenced the results. But they were only prepared to go so far in their criticism.

Here are some examples taken from the MOG document which I will comment on.

- • Changes to legislation and new rules introduced in the lead up to elections had a negative impact on political parties and prospective candidates' confidence in their ability to campaign freely and effectively under Fiji's legal framework. That, to me, sounds like a very serious issue. It meant those affected were not fully confident about the fairness and freedom of the election.
- • The MOG observed that late changes to the legal framework for the election left little time for explanations, created confusion and the perception that changes were aimed at disadvantaging certain parties or individuals and decreased confidence in the electoral process. This is another indictment of the way the election was organized and raised issues about how free it was.
- • It was "unusual" that there was no political party identification on either the ballot paper or the national candidate list. These were the only sources of information available to voters inside polling stations. The ballot paper did not include candidates' names, photos, party name or symbol. The candidate list did not include political party names or symbols.
- • The MOG mentioned penalties for certain offences such as taking any type of paper into a polling station or mobile phones. These offences were punishable by a maximum penalty of a fine of up to $50,000 or a jail

term of up to 10 years, or both. Such savage sentences are a mark of the Bainimarama-Sayed-Khaiyum years. They add to public fear of their regime. The MOG addressed this legal extremism, but in polite, diplomatic terms. It said the range of penalties for electoral offences should be "proportionate and appropriate and comparable to international standards and practices". Translation: Your punishments are too severe and out of line with normal international standards. They should be eased.

- • For the MOG to describe as "unusual" the absence of political party identification on the ballot papers or the national candidate list means this was abnormal. Bizarre can be substituted for abnormal or unusual. Why should an aspiring modern democracy choose to be abnormal in its ballot paper? Or its candidate list? Again, I saw in this a further sign that all was not well with the election. The MOG felt so strongly about the problems with the ballot paper that it recommended it be redesigned; alternatively, party identification should be on the candidate list and voters should have the right to bring how-to-vote material inside the polling stations. This looked to me like another slap in the face of the government.

- • In a reinforcement of its dislike of the ban on paper in the polling station, the MOG pointed out that it was common practice for observers, party polling agents and police officers to carry surveys, checklists and notebooks into polling stations. However, the restrictions imposed by the government covering "any type of paper" limited the rights of international observers, polling agents and the Fiji Police Force to undertake and record observations.... (This might appear to be a small issue, but I have included it in some detail because it underlines the extent of the control Bainimarama-Sayed-Khaiyum had imposed on the elections.)

- • Neutral domestic observers were not allowed to be part of the poll. Strong concern was expressed about this by civil society and faith-based organisations. MOG noted that a coalition of 15 civil society organisations did not receive approval to undertake domestic observation of the elections with up to 300 local observers.

- • The MOG stressed that non-partisan domestic observers greatly increase the degree of scrutiny of elections and served to improve public confidence. Their participation, it said, was necessary to ensure the credibility of the electoral process. This, of course, raises doubts about whether the election was credible.

- • The MOG emphasized again that the presence of local observers would have strengthened public trust and helped alleviate "the high degree of uncertainty about electoral processes and suspicion of election officials by some stakeholders in the lead up to and during the election". Strong words. Hardly an endorsement.

- • There was a recommendation for the Electoral Decree to be revised to encourage civil society engagement in elections and for the removal of restrictions on organisations receiving foreign funding. The Elections Office should provide clarification on the reasons for rejecting civil society applications.

- • Under the decree, the minister for elections (in this case Sayed- Khaiyum) has to approve observation of an election. I submit that Sayed-Khaiyum had a conflict of interest. The conflict arose because Sayed-Khaiyum was performing in the role of minister when he was also secretary-general of Fiji First. He justified this by claiming that Fiji has always had a minister for elections. That title was never held previously in Fiji by any minister in any government. Sayed-Khaiyum's inaccurate explanation does not remove the conflict of interest.

- • The MOG reported that representatives of some political parties and civil society expressed lack of confidence in the independence and impartiality of the Electoral Commission and the Supervisor of Elections, Mr Mohammed Saneem. I contend their concerns were relevant in view of the circumstances. The MOG explained that questions were asked about the appointment of the Supervisor, given that he had not applied for the position and had no experience of administering elections. (He was introduced into the recruitment process at the last minute. It appears to me he was handpicked by Sayed-Khaiyum. There is continuing talk that the Supervisor is related to the attorney general but this has not been substantiated. Neither Sayed-Khaiyum nor the Supervisor have publicly denied this.)

- • The MOG made it plain they were concerned about impartiality. They said, however, they had not received any credible evidence of anything that compromised the impartiality of electoral administrators or the conduct of the election. (That does not mean there was no evidence.) Then the MOG came back to the theme. It said the government and electoral authorities "should make an effort to strengthen the impartiality of these bodies as well as increase citizens' trust in the election institutions". Translation: There was a problem of impartiality and public trust.

- • There was comment about the Fiji Independent Commission Against Corruption (FICAC) which is headed by a former army officer who served under Bainimarama at the time of his coup. There are suspicions that FICAC has sometimes been used to persecute regime opponents like me.

- • The anti-corruption agency did not show up well in the MOG report which detailed complaints. Some of the issues involved "destroying handouts and posters, displaying posters in non- designated public places, misbehavior in polling stations etc". Six people were charged over alleged breaches of the Electoral Decree.
- • MOG noted that if convicted, the accused could face fines of up to $10,000 or prison for five years or above. Again, MOG noted that these penalties were higher than common international practice and hoped that such penalties would be applied "justly and lawfully. So, once more, Fiji was picked out for severe laws.
- • MOG referred to allegations of intimidation by FICAC. It recorded that a FICAC investigation into the Citizens Constitutional Forum (CCF) included a search of the CCF premises. FICAC also searched offices of members of the Electoral Commission. MOG politely said this action raised questions about the appropriateness of FICAC investigating electoral offences, rather than the police.
- • FICAC had also executed a search warrant at the offices of the vice chancellor and a senior academic at the University of the South Pacific. This was thought to be in response to a CCF- hosted forum at the USP on the topic of free and fair elections. After this, CCF cancelled other planned public seminars. The Electoral Commission advised that the CCF event breached the Electoral Decree, because it was held without an application being made.
- • Raids on the offices of the head of the region's top university and a well-known non-government organization such as the CCF, plus searches of office

premises of Electoral Commissioners, are not the
hallmarks of a free and fair election. Some might say that
these were police state tactics.

- • Fiji's notorious political party registration procedures
came in for scrutiny. MOG mentioned the requirement
for existing parties to re-register under the Political
Parties Decree within 28 days of the decree's
promulgation or face dissolution and forfeiture of assets
to the state. In contrast, new parties were given a period
until the issue of the writ of election to comply with
registration requirements. My own party, *Soqosoqo
Duavata ni Lewenivanua* (SDL), decided to dissolve
itself and re-register under the name SODELPA. We
decided to do this because we were banned from using
the Fijian language for a political party name.

This, to me, represents severe and racist discrimination against
the indigenous community and their language. It surprises me
that the MOG did not criticise this. Is an election free and fair if a
nation's numerically largest community the indigenes, are banned
from adopting a party name in this manner?

MOG highlighted the registration requirement of 5000 members
from all four administrative divisions, a $5000 fee, and setting up
branch offices. But it was very muted in its comments on these outrageous conditions.

It did however express criticism of the "large number" of signatures required within such a short period. This placed Fiji, again,
outside standard international practice. We were once more odd man
out, an example of procedural anti-democratic extremism.

Bainimarama-Sayed-Khaiyum's constitution declares that each
citizen has the freedom to make political choices, and the right to

form or join a political party. But with Bainimarama-Sayed Khaiyum political freedom and rights come at a price.

In this instance, it is a fee of $5,000 plus the considerable cost of establishing branch offices, combined with the huge effort and funding required to send volunteers to all parts of a scattered island nation to collect 5,000 signatures. Add to this the completely unreasonable deadline of 28 days or face dissolution.

Consider the position in Australia and New Zealand, prosperous countries with mature democratic systems. Both have a political party registration fee (in their currencies) of $500. The stark contrast between Fiji, and Australia and New Zealand is also heavily underscored by the number of voters required for registration in these neighbouring nations. It is 500.

The Bainimarama-Sayed-Khaiyum rules were not established to promote a vibrant and free democratic culture. They were imposed to make it extremely difficult and costly for people in a small and poor country to exercise their political rights. (These rights were granted by the same people who then made it difficult for them to be accomplished.)

A thought: what about those who would like to exercise their so-called political freedom to set up single issue parties such as the right to life, cleaning up Fiji's pollution, the rights of pensioners, curbing drug abuse, or opposing domestic violence? Such parties do not usually win enough votes to get into government, but they provide an opportunity for those dedicated to certain causes to champion them to the electorate. That is what political freedom is about. Under the Bainimarama-Sayed-Khaiyum system, that freedom is denied. It is absolutely obvious that they don't want too many groups seeking votes, and coming out with different ideas; their autocratic inclinations lead them to favour the least number of parties.

I salute the parties who did manage to beat the odds, overcome the barriers thrown against them, and succeed in registering. It goes without saying that all the cost, the sacrifice, and effort would have been better employed campaigning amongst the people.

The MOG concluded that the broad definition in the Political Parties Decree of public officer holder meant that "large numbers" were effectively excluded from the political process. It said specifically that the prohibition on trade union officials being members of political parties was a limitation on political freedom.

In other words, Bainimarama and Sayed-Khaiyum's decree denied these unionists the rights supposedly granted in the 2013 constitution. It's like giving with one hand and taking away with the other.

The MOG did manage to make a recommendation that public office holders, including trade unionists, should be allowed to be party members. However it could only bring itself to recommend that "consideration" should be given to reduce requirements for party registration.

I can only conclude that in this instance the MOG members were wearing blinkers.

Professor Yash Ghai, whose draft constitution was trashed by Bainimarama-Sayed-Khaiyum, is one of the numerous critics of the Political Parties Decree. He said it was particularly objectionable that it should be drafted by a regime that had shown little respect for, or even understanding of, democracy or political parties. Professor Ghai described the Decree as "so biased in favour of the government". He said rules for political parties should not be introduced and determined by an unelected regime which might well have plans for continued political and administrative control of the country. Professor Ghai obviously could see the larger intended scheme of things.

The MOG criticized the short period between the national candidate draw and the election. This curtailed the length of time political parties had to conduct widespread campaigning. It said the Public Order (Amendment) Decree 2012 restricted the ability of political parties to organize public gatherings in the lead up to elections.

Rumours of civil unrest and possible military action increased on social media in the days before the elections. According to MOG, comments by the prime minister and the then head of the military, Brigadier-General Mosese Tikoitoga, that the military would be on "standby" might have been seen to "play into the political debate and possibly added to a climate of apprehension". (Another word for apprehension is fear).

I recollect that Bainimarama made statements to the effect that Suva would not be allowed to burn again as it did in 2000. This was certainly interpreted as an attempt to frighten people. There was definitely apprehension after he made his comments. Of course, the army, under Bainimarama's leadership, failed to prevent the 2000 fires and disorder in Suva.

The MOG highlighted what it called the "restrictive and vague media framework" for the elections, including potentially harsh penalties. According to MOG, this limited the media's ability to rigorously examine the claims of candidates and parties. It spoke of threats of penalties under the Media Industry Development Decree (MIDA). (This includes prison sentences for journalists, which obviously is an impediment to media freedom.) The MOG recommended the establishment of an independent institution to adjudicate complaints about MIDA, and an independent procedure for dealing with complaints about biased media coverage.

The regime talked a lot about Fiji having its first one day election. This did not happen. Before the main voting began some 51,000 voters cast their ballots in a process described for some inexplicable reason as pre-polling. This was a misnomer. It should have been called early voting. The inaccurate description confused some voters. In some areas they only learned about the schedule for "pre- polling" when officials arrived in their village to start the process. Pre-polling mostly took place in remote locations, military sites, detention centres and prisons. Some pre-polling stations had insufficient voting material and incorrect voter lists. Pre-polled voters had less time to get information about parties and candidates.

When I ask myself whether the election was credible, and taking into account everything I have related about the poll, this is the picture that emerges:

Allegations of FICAC intimidation; raids on university, CCF and electoral commissioner offices by FICAC; cancellation of public seminars; an army, known for its oppression and violence, placed on standby; references to Suva burning shared in the media by the commander who led the 2006 coup; lack of confidence; fear; bias, uncertainty; suspicion; concerns about fairness and freedom, impartiality and trust; gross conflict of interest by a key minister; electoral laws with savage penalties inconsistent with international standards; late changes to laws and new rules creating confusion; restrictions on ability to organise public meetings; denial and limitation of political rights and freedoms; insufficient time for campaigning; banning of 300 local election observers; no party or candidate identification in polling booths; media faced with threat of imprisonment and fines; extreme and unfair requirements for registering political parties introduced by an unelected regime; a discriminatory ban on using the Fijian language - spoken by the majority of the population - for party names.

I should add also the numerous issues raised by the political parties in their report on what they considered to be election irregularities, as witnessed and noted by their agents.

Finally, I cannot ignore that the election was supervised by an Electoral Commission whose appointment was dominated by the prime minister. In my view this raises obvious queries about its independence. It should come as no surprise that in view of the above I find it impossible to declare that the election was free, fair and credible. It puzzles me that the Multi National Observer Group thought the election was credible despite all the serious flaws it highlighted.

The 2006 election, which my SDL party fought and won, had a large number of observers. Problems were reported about such things as complaints procedure, voter registration, some missing names, invalid votes and wrong constituencies. However, an observer group from the Commonwealth declared that it was "struck not so much by what went wrong during the voting, but by how much went right."

Postscript: International observers of the Kenya presidential election in August 2017 praised the poll as "free, fair and credible". Less than a month later, the country's Supreme Court ordered a new vote to take place, declaring the result was "invalid, null and void." The court said irregularities had affected the integrity of the poll.

# 67

# A THESIS TOO FAR

Sayed-Khaiyum became the number one supporter and adviser of Bainimarama, eventually wielding power that many people felt was in excess of that held by the commander. The academic thesis he authored - Cultural Autonomy, its implications for the nation state. The Fijian Experience - is thought by many to form part of a Bainimarama plan to erode the culture and traditions of the indigenous people. Sayed-Khaiyum tends to avoid talking about this.

This "super minister" who became Bainimarama's attorney general and simultaneously held many other major portfolios, has stamped an indelible mark on Fiji. As a young and relatively inexperienced corporate lawyer he emerged as the brain of the Bainimarama governments. Many people feel that without him Bainimarama would be lost. It is also said that they need each other; that they can only survive by remaining joined together politically.

Sayed-Khaiyum has a voracious appetite for work. I believe this is fuelled by the knowledge that he must stay in power so that he can ensure he continues to benefit from the immunity against prosecution he enjoys along with Bainimarama and others. This immunity is extensive. It is contained in the 2013 constitution of which Sayed-

Khaiyum was the principal author. If it is taken away, Sayed-Khaiyum, Bainimarama and their main aiders and abettors, with be face-to-face with treason. That is what they committed when they removed an elected government at the point of a gun in December 2006. George Speight was found guilty of this offence, received the death sentence, and is now in prison for life.

Sayed-Khaiyum's arrogance, know-it all attitude and closeness to the dictator have earned him numerous enemies, even in the ranks of the Fiji First government. His parliamentary party colleagues are too frightened to openly criticise him. He has seen off all rivals, and all challenges including from members of the military. As I write this he wields probably more legal and ministerial power than anyone else in Fiji. It is sometimes a bit difficult working out exactly what portfolios he holds.

But I think the following list is probably accurate: Attorney General and Minister for Justice, Anti-Corruption, Climate Change, Public Enterprises, Civil Service, Communications, and Civil Aviation. In the last part of 2017, he also acted as Minister for Education and Minister for Health. The icing on his cake comes when he acts as prime minister during Bainimarama's frequent absences overseas. I sense he dreams of the day when he will be substantive prime minister.

In my view no one else in our contemporary history, has accumulated governmental authority like Sayed-Khaiyum. I would go as far as to suggest that even the "father" of our nation, Ratu Sir Kamisese Mara, was probably not as politically dominant as Sayed-Khaiyum has become, although it is difficult to gauge the depth of his true support from key stakeholders like the army, the business sector and grassroots voters. Observing Mr Khaiyum it is very easy to discern that he relishes his role, and his confidence knows no limits. He thinks he always knows best. But I can imagine he sweats at night over succession arrangements. Will he be able to prevail without Bainimarama? Will his opponents then feel free to move against him?

In 2002 Sayed-Khaiyum published an academic work that

became Fiji's most famous thesis. It was a product of his studies at the University of Hong Kong. Interestingly and coincidently, he received academic supervision from Professor Yash Ghai, an eminent constitutional scholar from Kenya. The professor was recruited undoubtedly on Sayed-Khaiyum's advice, to write a new constitution for Fiji when it became obvious that the days of the Bainimarama-Sayed-Khaiyum military governments were numbered and they would have to return Fiji to parliamentary rule. The relationship between Sayed-Khaiyum and Professor Yash Ghai had a predictably unhappy ending, which is described elsewhere in these pages.

I am among those who see Sayed-Khaiyum's thesis as a form of undeclared manifesto for the Bainimarama – Sayed-Khaiyum governments. Ideas it contains have been put into practice and are central to their agenda.

When I reflect on this, it is extraordinary to me that Sayed-Khaiyum as a relatively young man produced an undistinguished flawed thesis, which he managed to transform into a foundation stone for a "new Fiji".

I have read every line in the thesis. The burning issues for Sayed-Khaiyum are the arrangements for governing the indigenous people that were put in place during the colonial period and continued into independence. He asserted they were separate and independent centres of power and thus a threat to the integrity and unity of the nation.

I am not enough of a historian to go into all the complexities of Fiji's colonial past. I will touch on it briefly to give some context to what Mr Sayed-Khaiyum submitted and advocated in his thesis. Britain's colonial policy was to bring immigrants from India to help with the establishment of a sugar industry. This profoundly changed Fiji. Two distinct and very different communities populated the same land but lived apart. Additionally, Fiji had small numbers of Europeans, Chinese, people of mixed heritage and other Pacific islanders. The differences between the two main groups, the indigenous Fijians and the settlers from India, were many. They spoke their own languages and had their own distinctive cultures, traditions, customs and food. The Fijians were Christians; the Indians were mostly Hindus and there were also communities of Muslims and some Sikhs. There was little intermarriage between the immigrants and the Fijians. That is still the case today. Official colonial policy in many ways was to keep them apart. It was natural that the Fijians should become nervous about the new community. These days Sayed-Khaiyum, Bainimarama and some of their cheerleaders would falsely brand such a reaction as "racist," just as "indigenous rights" are portrayed in the same light.

The indigenes obviously began to wonder whether they would end up in a subordinate position. This feeling intensified when, for a time, they were outnumbered, although that demographic changed through birth rates and emigration. When a new national system of politics began to emerge as Fiji moved towards independence the Fijians feared that democracy's one man-one vote elections would overwhelm them. It was said that Fijians feared one man-one vote "like the devil."

The democratic way had nothing in common with their long-established system of rule through hereditary chiefs. This had features in common with hierarchical forms of chieftainship which evolved in the history of Polynesia and most of Micronesia and which survive to this day. Among our immediate regional neighbours, Samoa, Tonga, Vanuatu, the Cook Islands and Wallis and Futuna have customary chiefs. Rotuma, the Polynesian Island, which is governed as part of Fiji, has the same. All these structures of authority are an integral part of culture and history. Many are adapting to western style politics. That is certainly the case in Fiji where chiefly political leadership was a critical factor in the peaceful transition to independence and providing on-going guidance for progress.

Sayed-Khaiyum, and others as well, questioned the need for the indigenous people to come under a separate Fijian administration. He wrote critically and at length about this in his thesis. There was a Great Council of Chiefs, Native Land Trust Board, Fijian Affairs Board; Fijian provinces; district administration, Fijian Development Fund Board and Native Lands Commission. Sayed-Khaiyum also mentioned the Native Affairs Ordinance of 1876 and the establishment of the Native Regulation Board. These were the early organisations charged with managing the welfare of the indigenous people.

Sayed-Khaiyum thought there was merit at the time of colonialisation for such institutions to protect indigenous rights. But the thrust of his thesis was that the so-called cultural autonomy – indicating independence or self-government - which applied to them, was an obstacle to the development of a national polity with a unified sense of nationhood. In his mind cultural autonomy raised many questions about national allegiance, identity, loyalties and patriotism. He submitted that it must have an ending, a "sunset clause". This expression became the most quoted phrase from the thesis. It was seen as pointing to the setting of the sun on the indigenous population.

Sayed-Khaiyum appears to be cautious about his thesis and the role it is playing in Fiji. I cannot recollect him ever speaking publicly about it and his call for a "sunset clause".

The prolonged continuation of cultural autonomy he wrote,

---

will place a stranglehold on the very members it seeks to protect, and it will concomitantly disallow the critical cultural space in which a just vibrant and coherent nation state can flourish while embracing diversity.

---

It was evident, said Sayed-Khaiyum, that cultural autonomy had its limitations. Cultural autonomy for the long term .... was in doubt since it "entrenches particularism and a divided nation state".

Cultural autonomy (and its institutions) must "devolve or at least evolve to not only reflect changes in society but also to ensure the development of a common citizenship". It promoted culture/ethnicity as the modus operandi leading to the politics and constitutions of ethnicity. This was at the expense of addressing "pertinent citizenry" concerns.

Cultural autonomy, Sayed-Khaiyum wrote, potentially could lead to communal politics since it is vulnerable to the dictates of elites who are prone to manipulating symbols around which ethnic groups coalesce. These symbols made inter-ethnic violence appear "just, honourable and legitimate".

Sayed-Khaiyum stressed that by placing too much emphasis on culturally autonomous institutions "individual and groups could have the tendency to not only become insular but also to have negligible levels of allegiance to the nation state."

The institutions of autonomy could become completely independent at the expense of superseding the institutions of the state – coming into direct conflict with the state and creating and perpetuating the ethos of the particular and difference. This, argued Sayed-Khaiyum, created a weak state and also stunted the growth of nationhood. He thought culture-based institutions could get caught in a time-warp and subsequently not be responsive to the changes and needs of the group with autonomy.

He argues that common and equal citizenship does not necessarily mean the erosion of culture and identity. He has difficulties with the idea of people having only one culture, arguing that they are influenced by and subject to "a whole gambit of ideas, values and cultures". He wrote that concerns of discrimination and possible subjugation could be addressed by a comprehensive Bill of Rights.

Sayed-Khaiyum acknowledges that the 1997 constitution, which the military government of which he was a crucial part claims to have overturned, does have a comprehensive Bill of Rights. But he added, "its viability is questionable given the heavy emphasis on group rights and what he said was a lack of a healthy jurisprudence pertaining to individual rights". (The 1997 constitution has no such emphasis. My copy of it has only two pages on group rights out of 153 pages. Its biggest section by far is on rights for all.)

His thesis also makes it evident that he is not sympathetic to chiefly leadership based on inherited rank. This, he said, creates a system of rule by an elite, privileged few. (That's what we now have in Fiji with the Sayed-Khaiyum and Bainimarama style of government. Bainimarama and Sayed-Khaiyum are the leading elitists.) Maintenance of culture, he thought, was for the self-preservation of the chiefs and a "convenient tool for the management of the masses" within the nation state. He felt leaders like the great Ratu Sir Lala Sukuna had a vested interest in keeping things as they were. Sayed-Khaiyum did acknowledge that Ratu Sukuna "was an educated and articulate member of the indigenous elite". But he was reluctant to give any real credit to the high chief for his careful and measured leadership, his substantial contribution to Fiji's development and to his sweeping land reforms.

It is significant that the Bainimarama, Sayed-Khaiyum military regime dropped Ratu Sukuna Day from the national calendar. This was an annual celebration of the chief's life and achievements. I sensed that the removal of the holiday in his honour was part of a plan to downplay his historical significance and it was certainly in tune with the thinking of Sayed-Khaiyum.

Sayed-Khaiyum went into a controversial area when he advocated in his thesis that all Fiji citizens should be known as Fijians. The issue of a common name in Fiji is complex given that the indigenous people had been referred to as Fijians from the time Fiji was ceded to Britain in 1874. They felt the word "belonged" to them. To me it is an affront that "Fijian" should be imposed by a military dictatorship as a common name; such a sensitive issue should be referred to the citizenry for a decision.

I highlight as well that the 1997 constitution, which the Bainimarama-Sayed-Khaiyum regime committed to protect, opened the way for the common name Fiji Islander, similar to Cook Islander or Solomon Islander. A constitution review commission comprising the late Sir Paul Reeves, the late Tomasi Vakatora and Professor Brij Lal, acknowledged that 'Fijian' was used to describe the indigenous people. They did not recommend that this should change. As the commission was recommending that the name of the state should be the Republic of the Fiji Islands, they thought the citizens should have the right to use the common name 'Fiji Islander'. The commission felt it was not necessary to make provision for this in the constitution. In other words, it should not be prescribed by law. But, of course, Bainimarama-Sayed-Khaiyum did not uphold the 1997 constitution, as they had pledged to do, and purported to remove it.

Their new name for the indigenous people was to be *iTaukei* (owner) in accordance with the Fijian Affairs (Amendment) Decree No. 13 of 2010. They were not asked whether they agreed with this. It is clear to me that my government, the Chaudhry government and those of Sitiveni Rabuka were remiss in not actively promoting Fiji Islander as the national name. We did not concentrate on doing this. We should have.

It is also notable that Sayed-Khaiyum not only repudiates the Fijian administration and has little regard for chiefly leadership. He also expressed in his thesis stinging criticism of the performance of the Fiji Military forces in dealing with the crisis caused when George Speight and his accomplices took prime minister Mahendra

Chaudhry hostage in parliament along with members of his government.

Sayed-Khaiyum wrote:

One would have thought, given the few numbers of kidnappers, a rescue of the prime minister and cabinet, in particular by the Fiji Military Forces, which prides itself in its military prowess, was obvious and a relatively easy task.

However, this was not to be. The ineptitude, inertia and reluctance displayed by the military and other law enforcement agencies in the first few weeks of the crisis allowed the kidnappers a freehand in mustering support at the parliamentary grounds for their cause, holding the prime minister and his cabinet in captivity for 56 days.

---

This was an attack by Sayed-Khaiyum not only on the army but on its leader, Bainimarama, who is famously intolerant of criticism. But in this instance he appeared to tolerate what Sayed-Khaiyum said in his thesis and continued to stand by him.

The central point of Sayed-Khaiyum's thesis relates to this issue of the "autonomy" of Fijian institutions, meaning of course that they were and are independent or self-governing. He is wrong about that. His reasoning is far-fetched and flawed.

In the colonial days the institutions he complains of were accountable to the British, to the law and the legislature. Since independence in 1970 they were answerable to the constitution, to cabinet, and to parliament. Their financial affairs were subject to scrutiny of the Public Accounts Committee. So how does Sayed- Khaiyum's autonomy claim fit in? It doesn't.

The GCC was not in itself a standalone independent institution. It came under the Fijian Affairs Act and its membership, functions, operations and procedures were prescribed in that Act. So where was its autonomy?

The 1997 constitution gave the GCC power to appoint the president and vice president. However, it could only do this after consultations with the prime minister. So, again, it did not possess the kind of autonomy referred to by Sayed-Khaiyum.

If circumstances arose requiring the removal from office of a president or vice president, the GCC was bound to follow a procedure involving the prime minister, the chief justice, a tribunal or medical board. The PM had considerable discretion in the matter. Sayed-Khaiyum's autonomy did not apply.

The GCC had power to make 14 appointments to the Senate. However, the Senate, as a house of review, did not possess the same authority as the House of Representatives. The power of appointment in this case only related to the senate which had limited authority. The GCC appointees, however, had an important role to play in protecting Fijian rights. The Senate was scrapped by Bainimarama-Sayed-Khaiyum.

It is true that at times of great crisis when governments were not able to function, the GCC has come forward to attempt to use its authority to seek a path out of chaos back to order and stability. On those occasions it was filling a vacuum and responding to events. I do not see that as the GCC exercising the kind of autonomy envisaged by Sayed-Khaiyum.

The military regime in which Sayed-Khaiyum was a central figure began to take steps quite quickly that were consistent with the thinking in his student thesis. His "sunset clause" had become reality but without the permission of the community directly concerned. There was no discussion, no consultation, just enactment of illegal actions by an illegal regime to weaken the illusionary autonomy which had driven Sayed-Khaiyum to write his thesis[vii].

Bainimarama was enraged because the GCC refused to support his coup. It was, therefore, suspended by the Fijian Affairs (Great Council of Chiefs) Regulation 2007. Later its existence was terminated. That fitted in very well with Sayed-Khaiyum's thinking. The rage of the dictator was converted into the sinking of the sun on the GCC. He thought its members should "drink home brew under a mango tree".

The Bainimarama-Sayed-Khaiyum constitution removed any reference to group rights, which form an important part of indigenous culture and land ownership. This was properly addressed in the 1997 constitution as was provision for the application of customary laws. When a majority of a population practise group rights and that is not reflected in a nation's constitution, what does that say about that constitution?

Along with many others, I assert that the oppressive measures I mention here are, in their totality, in breach of Fiji's international obligations under the International Labour Organisation (ILO) Convention 169 ratified by Fiji in 1998 and the UN Declaration on the Rights of Indigenous Peoples (UNDRIP). The Bainimarama-Sayed-Khaiyum government has refused to ratify UNDRIP. The ILO Convention means the government is bound to protect and maintain customary institutions, indigenous language and customary rights, and to obtain prior consent when it wants to change any policy or law affecting native Fijians under those rights.

The UNDRIP received overwhelming backing in the UN General Assembly in September 2007. It was seen as a landmark declaration that ended nearly 25 years of negotiations over the rights of native people to protect their land and resources and to maintain their unique cultures and traditions. It set out the individual and collective rights of native peoples everywhere, called for the strengthening of their cultural identities and emphasise their right to pursue development in keeping with their own needs and aspirations. It also prohibits discrimination against indigenous peoples and promotes their full and effective participation in all matters that concern them.

"The importance of this document for indigenous peoples and, more broadly, for the human rights agenda, cannot be underestimated," said General Assembly president, Sheikha Haya Rashed Al Khalifa.

The SODELPA MP Niko Nawaikula spoke to the UN Committee on the Elimination of Racial Discrimination (CERD) in Geneva in 2012. Mr Nawaikula reported that the Fiji government representative was asked why decrees had been passed to terminate the GCC, to take away the name of the indigenous people and other issues. The Fiji representative, according to Mr Nawaikula, answered that Fiji did not recognise indigenous rights because native Fijians were in a majority.

The Fiji representative's attention was then drawn to Bolivia and Guatemala. My information is that some 62 per cent of the population of Bolivia was of indigenous ancestry, yet the government of that country approved UNDRIP. Indigenous inhabitants of Guatemala make up approximately 60 per cent of that country's population. It, too, voted in favour of UNDRIP. Bainimarama and Sayed-Khaiyum's notion that UNDRIP should not apply when an indigenous population is in the majority is illogical. The principles involved of protecting indigenous heritage, culture and rights is not dependent on population statistics.

Bainimarama and Sayed-Khaiyum and their government tend to brand anyone who stands up for indigenous rights as a racist. There is nothing racist about such rights. By extension they are accusing the UN of racism by its endorsement of conventions on indigenous rights. They do not wish to recognize that these international instruments give full recognition to the rights and interests of indigenous communities everywhere, without denying equal rights for all citizens. We can enjoy equal citizenry in Fiji while being a party to these internationally approved UN agreements.

When Sayed-Khaiyum warns about cultural autonomy potentially leading to communal politics, he seems to be out of touch with reality. Communalism – and the separation that arrived with it - came into being from 1879 when the first migrants to Fiji from India arrived. It was a reflection of British colonial policy. The complexities inherent in this and their resolution would be for the local political leaders to deal with after independence.

Modern Fiji is an infant country. It achieved independence only 47 years ago. This means we are still involved in the complicated task of making Fiji into a unified nation. Countries do not become complete at the stroke of a pen. When, like Fiji, they are freed from colonialism they must then start out on a new journey to find themselves and to decide what sort of society they want to become. We have suffered grievously from the legacy of division handed to us.

Those divisions cannot be closed at the point of a gun. It will take time, patience, dialogue and goodwill. Together we can do it so that we can once again become what Pope John Paul II called a "symbol of hope for the world".

The indigenous institutions which are the target of Sayed-Khaiyum and Bainimarama are likely to change and evolve through a consensus of the chiefs and people exercising their constitutional and God-given freedoms and in line with recognised international principles. It does not require a coup, its attendant oppression and Sayed-Khaiyum's thesis to make this happen. It was a thesis too far.

The government I was leading in 2006 was on the right course, with elected leaders with substantial backing from the main groups coming together in a multi-racial, multi-party Cabinet. It was an important step. But it was sabotaged by the Bainimarama takeover which substituted force for dialogue and consensus. Bainimarama-Sayed-Khaiyum embarked on a military-backed plan to make Fiji into a "modern nation state" giving expression to Sayed-Khaiyum's half-baked student theories about cultural autonomy and the way to unity. In the process of attempting this it has opened new wounds and created fresh challenges and problems.

Many thoughts come to mind when I consider Sayed-Khaiyum's fears that allegiance to institutions which in his view are culturally autonomous will detract from and diminish national loyalty and patriotism. I agree with him that patriotism and national consciousness are critical for any nation and that in Fiji we have to achieve a greater focus on this, reflecting a more complete sense of oneness. But this does not mean we are a country without patriots. When Fijian rugby stars show their emotions as they sing the national anthem before a big game their hearts are moved by their love of Fiji not their feelings for the "culturally autonomous" Great Council of Chiefs, or the Fijian Affairs Board. They are showing their patriotism for the nation.

Consider again a couple of lines from the lyrics of Ratu Mara's song 'Ciri Koto' expressing sentiments about home by a young Fijian soldier,

> *Don't cry for me my beloved Fiji ... My*
> *beloved land, land of life.*

Those are expressions of pure patriotism by one of our greatest patriots.

Independence celebrations brought thousands of our people together to celebrate the birth of a new sovereign nation. That was a time of patriotism and allegiance to Fiji. Some of the other great gatherings and parades at Albert Park have been filled with patriotism.

When the national flag is raised at schools, little children feel the stirrings of what it means to be part of this country. That is the beginning of their patriotism and national loyalty.

I call for the understanding of Fiji's other communities of the desire of the indigenous people to survive and flourish. We do not want to go the way of other indigenous races who are now marginalised minorities. Ratu Mara got it right when he said: "The Fijian people have learned from history and wish to make history in their own country and not become history..."

# Super Decree

THE BAINIMARAMA- SAYED-KHAIYUM REGIME'S APPROACH TO FIJIAN LAND IS ILLUSTRATED IN THE LAND USE DECREE OF 2010 AND ITS LAND BANK. THESE ARE EXTRAORDINARY EXAMPLES OF LEGISLATION AND MEASURES WHICH DISADVANTAGE LANDOWNERS, DENY THEM CRUCIAL RIGHTS AND DISCRIMINATE AGAINST THEM. ONCE LANDOWNERS DECIDE TO

PLACE THEIR LAND IN THE LAND BANK, THEY HAVE LOST THEIR
OWNERS' RIGHTS.

SECTION 15 OF THE DECREE PREVENTS THE LANDOWNERS FROM
LEGALLY QUESTIONING THE VALIDITY OR LEGALITY OF A LEASE
OR ANY LEASE CONDITIONS; THEY CANNOT TAKE ANY GRIEVANCES
TO COURT. THIS IS A GROSS DENIAL OF THEIR RIGHTS. IT IS ALSO
IN BREACH OF SECTION 26 OF THE 2013 CONSTITUTION WHICH
STATES THAT EVERY PERSON IS EQUAL BEFORE THE LAW AND HAS
THE RIGHT TO EQUAL PROTECTION, TREATMENT AND BENEFIT OF
THE LAW. THE DECREE IMPOSES A STATE OF INEQUALITY ON
INDIGENOUS LANDOWNERS. IT DISCRIMINATES AGAINST THEM.

SECTION 6 GIVES THE PRIME MINISTER COMPLETE POWER TO
UTILISE NATIVE LAND ACQUIRED UNDER THE DECREE. THE PRIME
MINISTER IS NOT REQUIRED TO CONSULT WITH LANDOWNERS ON
THE UTILISATION OF THEIR LAND. HIS POWER IS TOTAL AND
DICTATORIAL. HE CAN ALSO MAKE REGULATIONS UNDER THE
DECREE - WITH NO APPARENT PROVISION FOR LANDOWNERS TO
HAVE A SAY IN THIS.

SECTION 9 (1) OF THE LEGISLATION STATES THAT IT IS SUPERIOR
TO ALL LAWS RELATING TO FIJIAN LAND. IT'S LIKE SOME SORT OF
SUPER LAW. SECTION 10 STATES THAT LEASES ISSUED UNDER THE
LEGISLATION SHALL BE FOR A PERIOD OF NOT MORE THAN
NINETY- NINE YEARS. LANDOWNERS CAN THEREFORE BE
DEPRIVED OF USE OF THEIR LAND LEASED UNDER IT FOR NEARLY
A CENTURY.

ANOTHER MAJOR ISSUE IS THAT THE 2013 CONSTITUTION PUTS
FIJIAN LAND INTO A LONG LIST OF RIGHTS IN ITS BILL OF
RIGHTS. BECAUSE FIJIAN LAND IS OWNED COMMUNALLY, IT DOES
NOT BELONG IN THIS PART OF THE CONSTITUTION WHICH DEALS
WITH INDIVIDUAL RIGHTS.

BY CONTRAST, THE 1997 CONSTITUTION'S CHAPTER ON GROUP
RIGHTS CONCENTRATED ON FIJIAN LAND AND THE ENTRENCHED
PROTECTION FOR IT IN THAT CONSTITUTION. THESE
COMPREHENSIVE SAFEGUARDS HAVE BEEN REMOVED. UNDER THE

Bainimarama-Sayed-Khaiyum constitution any changes to these formerly entrenched laws can be approved by a simple majority in parliament. In the opinion of many observers, whatever protection has been given to Fijian land in the Bainimarama-Sayed-Khaiyum supreme law can be limited or removed.

Ratu Sukuna must be turning in his grave at what Bainimarama, Sayed- Khaiyum have imposed on the landowners.

# 68

# A DEVOTED SERVANT AND LEADER

Ratu Sir Lala Sukuna was a great leader with an astonishingly varied career. In the minds of the Fijians, he had an almost heroic quality. Some thought he was God-like. He had foresight that projected well into the future and was instrumental in the development of Fiji. I felt it was important for me to include in this book some comments and facts that illustrate the role he played, especially in light of attempts to minimise his achievements. I came across the draft of a speech I made at Ratu Sukuna Memorial School which captures my thinking on what he meant to Fiji. The following are extracts from that draft:

*In Ratu Sir Lala Sukuna, we have a towering figure who contributed immeasurably to the welfare of our country in the time of colonialism. Much of what he did and achieved helped lay a foundation for the future. The positive effects are still felt today.*

*And yet we have tended not to give full enough recognition of what he meant to Fiji and his illustrious place in our history. We mark Ratu Sukuna Day each year but without the commitment and scale worthy of this great and heroic leader... We want to change this and transform our annual Sukuna Day ceremonies into a truly national occasion, something worthy of a man so eminent in the annals of Fiji.*

*Ratu Sukuna was a Fijian leader, but he was also a leader of Fiji. His legacy is lasting and of value for every citizen, no matter their ethnic community. We can all take pride in what he stood for, the example he gave, his courage, loyalty, commitment to duty and service to Fiji.*

*Ratu Sukuna's horizons and vision went far beyond the Fijian community, far beyond the vanua and his role in it. He felt that his chiefly responsibilities extended to Fiji as a whole and that he had an obligation to promote the welfare of all citizens.*

*Ratu Sukuna embodied the virtues of chiefliness, captured in the concept of vakaturaga.*

*He had natural authority and powerful mana. Indeed, to many Fijians he was almost a god. There was wisdom in him and an innate dignity. This was combined with kindness and caring concern for others .... When we think about Ratu Sukuna, it is natural to consider the role of chiefly leadership and its significance for Fiji. Critics of the system argue that in this modern age there is no place for chiefs; that they are an anachronism.*

*I believe that the chiefs of Fiji have relevance for all our citizens, not just the Fijians. They still represent stability, order and continuity. To a Fijian, a chief is a symbol of identity and a cultural inheritance which stretches far back into the mists of time. The Fijians without their chiefs would be incomplete, for it is rightly said that the chiefs and people are one. If the chiefs were diminished, the entire nation would be weakened and vulnerable. Let us not forget that since we became a sovereign state, chiefs have acted as a stabilizing factor.*

*When I was growing up in the village, children felt chiefs were to be feared and honoured. Even now I still feel reverence and respect for those of customary rank. This is part of me and part of my custom.*

*"I gave strong traditional allegiance to the late Ratu Sir Kamisese Mara, na Turaga na Tui Nayau, Ratu Sukuna's nephew. Ratu Sir*

Kamisese was much influenced by Ratu Sukuna. They both personi-
fied the best qualities of hereditary Fijian leadership.

Today, not everyone endorses Ratu Sukuna's approach to governance for the Fijians. They think he was too conservative and protective. My view is that he was a man of his times, who saw that Fijian
progress should be managed carefully.

We live in a period of great and sweeping change. So did Ratu
Sukuna. He could see the dangers this represented to the social cohesion, the culture and the identity of the Fijians. It was therefore necessary to proceed with prudence. Dr Deryck Scarr, author of two major
books about Ratu Sukuna, said the chief felt you could not safely ask a
people to leap a thousand years in a few decades.

Ratu Sukuna broke through the barriers of colonial thinking and
attitudes which assigned an inferior status to the Fijians and the Indians. He was recognised early for his intelligence and ability and
became the first Fijian to go to university, gaining degrees in arts and
law. During his time at school in New Zealand and at university and
studying law in Britain, Ratu Sukuna became more closely acquainted
with the precepts of western civilisation and the ways of the Europeans. It was this knowledge that enabled him to be an effective bridge
and mediator between the colonialists and the colonised.

He was just as much at ease talking with classically educated
members of the British gentry and the mandarins of the colonial secretary's office, as he was with villagers around a tanoa. But the strain
sometimes showed. A revealing entry from his diary of 1933 said he
had gone to bed on 7$^{th}$ August tired out by conforming to the demands
of two entirely different social systems.

Study Ratu Sukuna's career and you will be amazed at the extent
of his service to Fiji and the numerous roles he was able to fulfill. Ratu
Sukuna was a lawyer, administrator, teacher, politician, parliamentarian, first speaker of the Legislative Council, a school boxing champion
and rugby player, a policeman and a soldier.

His exploits in the great war of 1914-18 are legendary and are not
often mentioned. When he wanted to enlist, he was rebuffed by the

British army. So, he fought with the French Foreign Legion and received the Military Cross for bravery. In one instance he charged a strongly entrenched German position with fixed bayonet and ran forward with "tremendous zeal" ... in spite of stubborn resistance by the enemy, and in the face of machine gun fire. Later he launched an assault on enemy trenches with what was described as superb courage, taking many prisoners and seizing several machine guns. There are other accounts of the incredible bravery of Ratu Sukuna. Eventually he was wounded in the arms and head and hospitalised.

Reading his letters home, it is clear that Ratu Sukuna was sickened by the killing. He felt he was doing his duty, but to him war was hell. The sight of blood caused pain in the stomach and it was hard to stop vomiting. He admitted being reduced to tears by the effect of the conflict on the population. He wrote a long letter to a fellow chief which poignantly conveyed his feeling that he might not survive. He said, quote: "I do not know whether we will meet again."

When he returned to Suva, his head still in bandages, he received a hero's welcome."

I cannot here relate all that Ratu Sukuna did in his lifetime. But whenever there are tributes to him, we should always single out his most outstanding achievement. For someone who tended to be conservative, it was indeed a radical move.

Ratu Sukuna could see that land policies were needed which reflected the needs of a multi-cultural community. It was this that led to the formation of the Native Land Trust Board, regarded at the time as a milestone for customary land ownership and tenure in the entire British empire. The NLTB would ensure that the Fijians had enough land for their maintenance and support, with the surplus available for leasing by members of the Indian community and others.

Through the influence and persuasive power of traditional authority, as expressed in the person of Ratu Sukuna, the Fijians agreed to give up direct control of their lands. This was vested from then on in the NLTB.

Ratu Sukuna said these were unmatched acts of goodwill and co-

*operation. The then governor described the setting up of the NLTB as one of the greatest acts of trust in colonial history.*

*What Ratu Sukuna accomplished has served Fiji well. The NLTB is sometimes criticised. But it cannot be denied that it serves as a cornerstone for economic development, consistent with Ratu Sukuna's thinking.*

The high chief did not hesitate to speak bluntly to the Fijian landowners about their responsibilities. He told the Legislative Council in a debate on the Native Land Trust Bill in 1940 that landowners had duties as well as rights.

---

Travel the country and you see small patches of native cultivation here, long stretches of unused land there, further on, more scratchings. Is the native, is anyone, justified in holding up large tracts of land in an agricultural country with a quickly growing population? On this point I heartily endorse the remarks of the honourable mover of the motion. I recall the story of the ten talents and not far away I seem to see a writing which looks like tax on undeveloped lands and consequential effects.

---

Again and again, he was an advocate for making land available to others. He understood that other races needed access to this Fijian resource for their livelihood and for the sake of the economy. This was particularly so for members of Fiji's Indian community who were, by tradition, farmers. Many of them earned a living from growing sugar cane which was Fiji's most important crop. However, they lacked secure arrangements for leasing their farms. Ratu Sukuna saw there had to be a fair balance between the interests of the landowners, and the Indian farmers. He said the Indian desire for more permanent tenancy was a natural and legitimate consequence of an agricultural community settling in any country. It was this thinking that led to the establishment of the Native Land Trust Board.

In 1936 he told the Council of Chiefs that there was a growing demand for land, both from indigenous people and the Indian community. He urged that land not required by Fijians for their maintenance be determined and demarcated.

He said that as leaders of the Fijian people, it was the duty of the chiefs to use their influence and power to open up waste *mataqali* land for agricultural purposes, whether they be taken up by Europeans, Indians or Fijians.

He stressed the importance of education saying the chiefs were unanimous in their desire for the Fijians to be educated so they could thrive and grow.

---

We wish then to earn and save money. To use their land and to live peacefully with all. Hence it is our duty to show those we lead the straight and narrow path.

We cannot in these days adopt an attitude that will conflict with the welfare of those, who like ourselves, wish only to live peacefully and increase the wealth of the colony. We are doing our part and so are they. We wish to live; they do the same.

---

He said that if the Fijians obstructed other people without reason from using their land "there would be no prosperity".

---

Strife will overtake us and before we realize the position, we shall be faced with a situation beyond our control, and certainly not to our liking. I have stressed it once and I will do so again, we the leaders must take guard on two points, restrain the hasty and inspire the weak.

---

Ratu Sukuna was not an office-bound administrator. He was always ready to go out to the people. He travelled to every part of Fiji, often on foot, to talk with the landowners about co-operating with a new land scheme to be centred on what became the NLTB.

Finally, after countless meetings, Ratu Sukuna won the acceptance of the Fijians for what he was proposing. They agreed to place control of their land with the new organization. This achievement was chiefly leadership at its best.

Ratu Sukuna told the Legislative Council in 1940 that he believed the Native Land Trust Bill was unique. He spoke of a native policy which had produced the sort of "faith that removes mountains".

When passed the legislation would be a monument of trust in British rule, of confidence in its honesty and of hopes for the future—hopes that the seeds for disruption would disappear and that Europeans, Indians and Fijians would settle down to labour, sacrificing if need be community interest for the benefits of the whole.

In Legislative Council, six years later, Ratu Sukuna defended the Fijian landowners, who he said were frequently blamed for retarding settlement.

---

If truth be known he has done a great deal, probably more than any other section of the community, at any rate measured in ethical terms. He has given up his right of bargaining, dear to the heart of every one of us; he has abandoned premiums; he slowly swallowed the sentiment to which the first Indian nominated member so feelingly referred in his speech, that is, the attachment to land; he has also handed over the control of his inheritance to a Board.

These, Sir, are acts of goodwill and cooperation which, I believe, are unmatched in our time.

_____

And so Fiji acquired a unique system of land ownership and tenure that became a cornerstone for development. It was Ratu Sir Lala Sukuna who laid the foundations for it.

# 69

# SIDESHOWS

The years of incompetent and abusive military rule had their particular moments of strangeness, drama and humour. I have called them Sideshows. One of them - Esala Teleni's determination to infuse the police force operations with evangelical fervor as a priority rather than modern crime prevention – is reported elsewhere in this book. I write here about some others.

## Master deceiver, deceives the military

Peter Foster is a renowned international swindler, conman and jailbird. Dubbed a "man of mystery" he has been involved in scams in many places and at one point even managed to get himself involved controversially in the personal affairs of former British Prime minister Tony Blair and his wife Cherie. He persuaded the Duchess of York and the model Samantha Fox to endorse one of his phony slimming products.

He eventually ended up in the South Pacific. In Fiji he thought he saw an opportunity in tourism development and winning favours by getting involved in politics. Both these endeavours ended in controversy. Foster was arrested over fraud and immigration offences.

Then he mysteriously emerged in January 2007 as a "source" for the military of allegations of corrupt behaviour by my SDL government. Foster purportedly tape-recorded conversations with SDL officials which were supposed to confirm vote rigging and other illegal activities. Bainimarama's army was so desperate to prove we were corrupt that they formed an alliance with a known liar and cheat, a master deceiver, and eagerly awaited his "evidence". This would justify the Bainimarama coup. Comments from a military spokesman confirmed the regime believed that what Foster had come up with was proof of corruption and explained why the coup was staged.

Of course, despite the army's belief that Foster would demonstrate wrong-doing on our part, the episode was a farce from start to finish, leaving the military looking naïve and foolish. I told the ABC from Mavana there was absolutely no way I would support actions that were illegal or even encourage them. I said in other media interviews that the videotaped conversations produced by Foster could have been set up by the military to bolster its support. The timing of the videotape release after the coup also raised questions about its validity. In my view it could all have been a staged show, with the aid of a supreme trickster, supported by the military, to try to discredit the SDL. There was very obviously an arrangement between Foster and the Bainimarama government. The mystery is why Bainimarama and his officers thought they could trust a serial fraudster?

# Dramatic escape to the Kingdom of Tonga

. . .

Lieutenant Colonel (Lt. Col.) Ratu Tevita Uluilakeba Mara (Roko Ului) was one of Bainimarama's top commanders as head of the important 3rd Fiji Infantry Regiment (FIR). He had a reputation, deserved or otherwise, as one of the military's hardmen. But gradually he became alienated from the regime to the point where he was allegedly part of a plot to replace Bainimarama's government with the hope of speeding up the return to democracy. He was joined by Brigadier General Pita Driti, who now languishes in jail following his conviction for sedition. Driti too was close to Bainimarama. Coups devour their own.

There was no way Roko Ului would surrender himself to the Fiji legal system. He knew what the outcome would be.

On 9th May 2011, he vanished from Fiji and ended up in Tonga under the protection of the royal family to which he is related. The late King George Tupou V reportedly made it known privately that there was no way he would stand by and allow his relative to fall into the hands of Bainimarama.

Roko Ului was on a purported fishing trip when he was picked up by a Tongan naval vessel off Cape Washington, Kadavu. He had been snatched away just 100 km from Suva. In Nuku'alofa he was immediately accommodated by the King, and today is private secretary to King George's successor, King George Tupou VI.

Bainimarama was furious about Roko Ului's abduction but the Tongans, under the guidance of King George V, played a subtle diplomatic game. The Tongan authorities claimed to have picked up Roko Ului after responding to a distress signal. Bainimarama railed against the "illegal extraction" of the fugitive officer, adding that his government took "strong exception to such breaches of Fiji's sovereignty". He would seek Mara's extradition to Fiji to face charges.

On May 21 the Tongan government issued a statement saying it had received no request for Roko Ului's extradition. It only had a note from the Fijian authorities containing what it called "unsubstantiated assertions" and a "personal statement" by Bainimarama. Subsequently acknowledging receipt of an extradition request, the Kingdom's government indicated "it will have to go through the proper channels for legal advice before proceeding any further". There would be no interference with the judicial process. In early June, Roko Ului was granted Tongan citizenship and a passport. In late June the Fiji government was formally informed that Tongan law made it impossible to extradite Roko Ului.

Roko Ului, from his base in Nuku'alofa, is presumably waiting the right moment to return to his home. He has said on a number of occasions he is ready to face the consequences of his actions in the coup (but I doubt he would give himself up while Bainimarama and Sayed Khaiyum are still in power). For a brief period Roko Ului launched a *Thumbs Up For Democracy* campaign with the intention of achieving regime change. He travelled overseas mostly to Australia and New Zealand addressing groups of regime opponents and giving many media interviews about what he called a hateful dictatorship. However, his efforts came to nothing.

# Irregular

For a few years during the height of military rule, an irregular system was used for the payment of ministerial salaries. Somebody decided that they should be disbursed through the accountancy office of Ms Nur Bano Ali, who just happened to be Sayed-Khaiyum's aunt. This arrangement was surrounded by secrecy, amid talk of large salary increases. It broke all the financial rules of the civil service. There has never been a proper explanation of why this was done. The secrecy remains in place. It was just another example of misrule by a dictatorship. Interestingly, Ms Ali was my enthusiastic supporter when I was head of government. But these days she is not in touch.

# 70

# ROCKY ROAD TO RECONCILIATION

F iji desperately needs to be reconciled. It carries wounds and scars from brutality and oppression. It has been hurt by ethnic division, extremism, intolerance, tension and distrust. People have been killed and murdered. During the George Speight uprising, when Fiji came close to anarchy, terror was abroad, and innocents suffered. The eight years of military rule, and its reign of terror, added to the national trauma.

When we were in power and before the Bainimarama coup and its effects, our government could see clearly how damaged and divided the country was. We therefore gave urgent priority to reconciliation, with the intention of setting the country on a new pathway to national unity. As I have earlier emphasised, I gave so much importance to this that I made reconciliation part of my ministerial portfolio.

We decided to introduce legislation representing a bold and new approach to peacemaking. It was centred on a draft Reconciliation, Tolerance and Unity (RTU) Bill based on the concept of what is termed restorative justice. This has been employed elsewhere in divided, strife torn countries, notably in South Africa. That nation had to struggle to come to terms with the legacy of cruelty, bitterness and injustice of the apartheid system of separate racial development. Restorative justice helped in that difficult and emotional process.

We were to quickly find out that in Fiji attempts to bring about national reconciliation can provoke outrage and protest. Those against what we were proposing thought it was some sort of trick to hand out amnesty to those who belonged in goal. Bainimarama jumped on the bandwagon. His opposition was so vocal that it stirred rumours of another coup. He thought the bill was a product of "warped and corrupt minds" intent on destabilizing Fiji. I believe he used the bill as a partial justification for the coup he was already planning.

During its first and second readings in parliament he ordered military personnel in uniform to occupy public seating in parliament. They sat there as a rather threatening, intimidatory presence. Baini-marama declared that the RFMF "must stop the bill from passing or get rid of the government if it is passed". This was treasonous talk, but Bainimarama didn't care. Our opponents joined him in demonizing the bill and other legislation – the Indigenous Claims Tribunal and the Customary Fisheries Bill, also known as the proposed Qoliqoli law that I have already described. I think they gave him comfort and encouragement for what he intended to do.

There was a kind of pack mentality at work, with some pronouncements verging on the hysterical. The dissenters, with the army in the vanguard, seemed to believe that if the RTU Bill came into effect Fiji would be plunged into instant anarchy. The many people in favour of the Bill were even accused of following a doctrine of evil!

Some NGO's (non-government organisations) sought overseas assistance to bolster their opposition to the bill. The aim, in some instances, was to encourage international punishment to be imposed on Fiji. Even some normally sober and restrained professional organi-sations were caught up in the fever of the moment. One or two governments also expressed concern about the bill.

Here's a reality that I saw: our government had opened up a legitimate democratic procedure for our citizens to have their say on legislation that was still in draft form. We had consistently said we were listening and indicated changes would be made if necessary. It was frequently asserted that our government wanted to ram the legislation down the throats of the people. This was not so. After I had introduced the bill in parliament, it was referred to the Parliamentary Sector Committee on Justice, Law and Order, which organised public consultations. The committee received 124 formal submissions and another 148 oral presentations. These covered views for and against the draft legislation. In its report the committee made many valuable observations and suggestions.

It also made the crucial point that in the deliberations of South Africa's Truth and Reconciliation Commission, 70,000 amnesty applications were received. Only 7,000, or 10 per cent, were successful.

I told the country that we had not adopted a rigid position on everything and that there was room to discuss details and the significance of certain clauses. I gave an undertaking that we would ensure that the bill was not in conflict with the constitution.

In August 2005, I said in parliament that our Fiji communities had to honestly face up to the issues associated with living in a multiracial country. The country would need to look deeply within itself and confront some painful truths. I spoke of the tendency to gloss over these or brush them aside completely. It was necessary, I said, for people to examine their own fixed communal attitudes and acknowledge there are other views.

"We must become open-minded enough to talk candidly about our fears and grievances, but without being racially insulting or provocative. I don't mean just speaking through newspaper columns and ethnic radio, but face to face through personal dialogue."

I expressed the view that the bill had already started this. An editor's forum, which I attended, brought together citizens with all kinds of attitudes and emotions. We heard extremist indigenous

Fijian points of views. A young lady – a non-indigenous Fijian - who contributed to the discussion also came across as being an extremist. I did not agree with her conclusion, but I learned something by listening to her. To me that young woman provided further evidence of how much we have to do to overcome our differences and close the gaps between us.

All in all, I found the questions and observations at the editor's forum helpful because they were honest and candid. I felt that when we appreciate the way people think about racial and related issues, we were on the way to greater understanding. When there is greater understanding, fear and distrust starts to diminish.

Then true reconciliation is possible. We needed more mixed meetings where people feel confident about saying what they feel in the knowledge that it will be accepted in the right spirit. I pledged to continue to do all I could to encourage a political climate where this could happen.

I said in parliament:

This does not mean that those who have opposing positions – such as the government and the opposition – should hold back from expressing them. Party politics is competitive. It is a hard business. All the protagonists must vigorously defend and advance the principles and policies they believe in. When they are attacked politically, they must counter what is being said and done against them. Sometimes hard words are necessary. Similarly, there must be a readiness to make adjustments and to compromise for the greater good.

The free expression of different views is fundamental to democracy. Our country will find added strength and harmony when we use this freedom well. I repeat, however, that we cannot engage in the difficult dialogue on reconciliation if we go into denial about what sepa-

*rates us. Those who try to argue that race is not important are adopting a position at odds with the very nature of our society.*

*Fiji has two main races, with different languages, outlooks, cultures, religions and customs; and it has many other distinct ethnic groups. These differences of ethnicity and multi-culturalism have to be managed and accommodated. That is one of the principal roles of leadership in our multi-racial land. It is about the difficult task of balancing the interests of all communities. We must ensure, for instance, that development takes place so no particular group is disadvantaged. If we do not do this and help those who have fallen behind, we produce fertile ground for future upheavals. Nobody wants that to happen.*

*Our late President and Prime minister, Ratu Sir Kamisese Mara, also believed that we could not ignore race. That principle underlined his approach to politics. He was a realist. So am I.*

The restorative justice featured in the RTU Bill involved the victim, the offender and the community. It was concerned with repairing broken relationships and establishing lasting peace, instead of lasting hurt or conflict. It sought to reconcile the victim and the offender. Emotional healing is regarded as crucial not just for victims but also for offenders who must be rehabilitated and integrated into society. An underlying theme is that crimes or wrong doings are violations of people and relationships, rather than offences against the state. Acceptance of responsibility by the accused is required before the process of restoration can begin. The victims are free to obtain answers, express their anger and seek compensation.

Fiji's existing system of justice was based on retribution – "an eye for an eye" and "a tooth for a tooth". Offenders got what was coming to them; they received their just desserts.

Ever since we came to office, we had insisted that the system of law in place must take its normal independent course in connection with the offences related to the terrible disorder, terrorism and persecution of 2000. We did not interfere with the authority and independence of the judiciary, the police and all the agencies of the law. It was important that justice be done. During our six years of rule, about 3000 police investigations into the 2000 insurrection and associated matters were completed. Some 800 offenders were prosecuted.

However, we believed that the length of time investigations were taking was hindering our progress towards greater national unity. Wounds were reopened when cases went to court and resulted in convictions. Further tensions and resentments were created which inevitably had an impact on race relations. As investigations and court hearings dragged on with so many still to be concluded, there would be further strain, uncertainty and apprehension. The healing and advancement of Fiji would be delayed, if we could not bring the people together sooner and concentrate all our energies on developing the country. So with the agony of 2000 continuously haunting us we advocated a new approach, a process of justice that went beyond simply meting out punishment.

In the view of our government the RTU bill would help us to face and deal with the challenges of living together in our common homeland. It provided a means of laying to rest the memories and nightmares from when our nation came very close to complete collapse. The bill would help to find the truth and the facts behind unanswered questions. It would give the victims a new avenue for justice, including a convenient process for seeking speedy compensation for the harm they had suffered. This responded to the calls of those who felt there could be no justice without compensation. It would especially serve the interests of those who did not have the money to seek redress.

The compensation victims received, meeting with those who hurt them, and exchanging forgiveness, would become part of the restoration of Fiji. These important elements were missing from conventional methods of justice. I told the nation that restorative justice was finding favour in other countries and was endorsed by the United Nations.

There were two key parts to the bill. One of these aimed to establish an independent Reconciliation and Unity Commission. The other part was about a promotion of Reconciliation, Tolerance and Unity Council.

I stressed that the Unity Commission would not be permanent. It was likely to function for just 18 months with the mandate of dealing with specific aspects of the aftermath of 2000. The Unity Council would be a permanent statutory body with membership representing a cross section of the community. Its many obligations included adopting and implementing a national policy on reconciliation designed to bring unity among the people.

Sadly and understandably, many of those who suffered in 2000 were not yet able to reconcile. Their hurt and sense of violation went very deep. There was a recurring sense that the entire project was an attempt to grant amnesty to the offenders who had caused virtual anarchy. Most of the criticism was directed at the proposed Reconciliation and Unity Commission.

This would possess the powers to make recommendations to the president on the granting of amnesty in cases of violation of human rights judged to be politically motivated. Although amnesty would obviously be an important part of reconciliation, there was no plan at all for making it available to all those under investigation, or who were charged and had been convicted. The Bill was not intended to provide relief for the people who used the coup for their own gain or criminal intent. People who joined in the 2000 upheaval with clear criminal purpose, as established by the police, would still be subject to the full force of the law.

In my many public pronouncements I hammered home constantly the crucial point that there was no general amnesty. If the Unity Commission felt an amnesty should be granted, it would advise the president who had the statutory power to act. People who chose to apply for amnesty would have some decisions to make. They had to give full disclosure of all the relevant facts and express a genuine willingness to accept that they did wrong and that they wished to reconcile and seek forgiveness. If they didn't do this, they would not get amnesty.

The Parliamentary Standing Committee on Justice, Law and Order, which was bipartisan, also saw that the Bill was not meant to simply hand out amnesty or to free persons already convicted for coup offences. Neither did it aim to free those already charged or were likely to be charged. The committee stressed that people could apply for amnesty but pointed out there was a procedure to be followed. The Reconciliation and Unity Commission, presided over by a judge, would have to be satisfied that conditions were met before an amnesty was granted. They would have to prove, for instance, that what they did was for a political purpose. It would be for the judge to decide whether someone had genuinely acted out of political belief. If a claim of political intent was rejected, there would be no amnesty.

Applicants had to give a full and truthful disclosure, under oath, of all relevant facts. It had often occurred to me that some people would be very uncomfortable about telling everything they knew. They might decide to keep their secrets and remain in custody.

Applications not approved, would be referred to the criminal justice system in the normal way. The committee, however, did have some reservations about the amnesty guidelines which it thought were not clearly defined. It gave particular attention to what categories of crime would be considered as political and suggested further clarification of this. Its views were to be given full consideration by Cabinet.

I had to explain that what we were proposing was neither unique nor unusual. Amnesty had been provided in many countries, especially for offences that were political in nature. One of the most notable and controversial examples of amnesty formed part of the peace process in Northern Ireland. Amnesty was included in the settlement of the hostilities in our neighbour, the Solomon Islands. I recalled that in India, amnesty had been introduced to help resolve a long-standing dispute between the region known as Nagaland and the Indian government.

The Philippines government proposed amnesty for a peace plan for areas under conflict. Other amnesties in recent history include those in El Salvador, Mozambique, Sierra Leone and South Africa. I assured our critics that we were very much aware of the rule that amnesty must be used sparingly and be limited by legislation and law to avoid abuse. This was reflected in the RTU bill.

I could appreciate that the idea of political offences was difficult for some people to understand. However, it was a fact that history recognizes it. It was applied in particular to countries which had experienced deep-seated and destructive internal division and dissent, based on such things as class, ethnicity and ideology. Governments of all types have held political prisoners. Even the US faced allegations that some offenders there were in that category.

I gave an assurance that our government would look carefully at how the final draft of the Bill defined politically motivated wrongdoing. Generally, someone who was jailed for a wrong committed in pursuit of certain political ideals, beliefs, purposes or objectives could be classified as a political prisoner. Much would depend on the specific circumstances of the case.

I imagined, for instance, that someone who took part in certain activities out of a traditional sense of duty and obligation, but without criminal intent, might be categorized as a political prisoner.

I explained repeatedly that the principle of amnesty was linked to the concept of restorative justice which formed the foundation for the Bill. The critics who kept insisting that the real purpose of amnesty provisions was to provide a ticket out of prison for coup offenders, had either not read the Bill or did not understand it.

Amnesty, I reiterated, was accepted internationally and had been applied many times to offences considered to be political in nature, even when these involved acts of extreme and persistent terrorism. I pointed out that in the United States, one of the world's most advanced democracies, the president had wide powers of pardon but what we were seeing in our own country was a significant body of opinion that appeared to be totally against forms of amnesty that had been widely used elsewhere. This section of the public favoured strict application of punishment as retribution or revenge.

Another important point ignored by the critics is that the legislation relied on voluntary participation by victims and wrong-doers alike. The ordinary criminal and civil processes were left to the courts. Citizens who did not wish to take advantage of the provisions of the bill were at liberty to pursue their grievances through the normal judicial system. There was no question of them being forced to take their case to the Unity Commission.

I felt it was crucial to emphasise that the ideals of restorative justice were not new to the Fijians. These are built into their culture. The whole community takes part in finding solutions to problems and imposing sanctions. This is reflected in customary practices such as the veisorosorovi and matanigasau. It is about recognizing that a wrong has been committed and then asking for forgiveness. All the parties, the offender, the victim and the whole community are involved. At the end of it, relationships, dignity and mutual understanding are restored. A new start is made.

This community system of conflict resolution was reinforced with the coming of Christianity and the instructions of Jesus Christ for forgiveness without condition. I stressed to the country that the teachings of forgiveness were common to all the great religions followed in Fiji. No one said forgiveness was easy. In the context of what happened in 2000, it touched on very deep emotions arising from painful and harrowing experiences. But we could hope and pray that one day the reasons not to forgive would be overcome and the bitterness would fade.

The Lord Jesus Christ tells us in Luke's Gospel: "grant pardon and you will be pardoned".

In Mark's Gospel, Jesus says: "And whenever you stand praying, forgive, if you have anything against anyone: so that your Father also who is in heaven may forgive you your transgressions. But if you do not forgive, neither will your Father who is in heaven, forgive your transgressions"

The Lord's Prayer is clear. "forgive us our sins as we forgive those who sin against us"[viii]

---

F ather Michael Lapsley, is an Anglican priest, born in New Zealand. He spent time in South Africa campaigning against the apartheid system of segregation and white supremacy. He earned the enmity of the government.

Father Lapsley has one eye, shattered eardrums and metal claws instead of hands. He suffered his terrible injuries in Harare, Zimbabwe, when a letter bomb delivered to him from South Africa exploded. This was an act of revenge from some hate filled individual (or individuals) who did not like Father Lapsley's active opposition to apartheid. The courageous priest returned to South Africa when it became free and became involved in the difficult mission of helping to bring an end to the bitterness and hurt left by the horrors of the past. In Cane Town, he helped to launch the Institute for the Healing of Memories.

We brought Father Lapsley to Fiji to assist in our own reconciliation efforts through the legislation we were proposing. The initiative began with New Zealand's then prime minister, Helen Clark. I accepted immediately when she offered to help arrange for Father Lapsley to visit. He would bring a very powerful perspective to forgiveness and building peace. Surely there was something we could learn from this remarkable man who was ready to extend friendship to those who had tried to kill him and had left him so severely crippled.

Father Lapsley made several trips to Fiji. The people listened to him with the respect and admiration he deserved. His message came through in seminars and other meetings. Participants shared their experiences in groups of five or six, giving them an opportunity to have their pain heard and acknowledged. Father Lapsley, in a *Fiji Times* article, said this was necessary in the journey to healing.

"People have this poison in them," he said. "If there is to be healing, there has to be storytelling and a letting go of that which is poisonous and painful. We make very modest claims for what we can do and in a sense, we can't do anything. We create the space where healing can take place." Seminars and workshops were "a small but powerful step towards healing the wounds of the past."

Father Lapsley recalled Jesus Christ declaring that he came for the sick not the healthy.

He went on: "So its in the acceptance of the truth that 'yes. I do have a dimension of brokenness, incompleteness' that there's a possibility of healing."

The priest recalled that he received the best medical care in his recovery from his injuries and added the crucial point: "Of equal importance was that I was prayed for, I was loved and supported by people all over the world."

He emphasized that one of the important aspects of the Truth and Reconciliation Commission in South Africa was that it acknowledged and recognized all communities, the pain of all sides of the conflict. It did not help if one sector's pain was heard but another's was not.

It was crucial for a Truth and Reconciliation Commission to be fair and balanced and for those who led it to be people of integrity.

I valued my own discussions with Father Lapsley and listening to what he had to say. He wrote to me summarizing some of his impressions of Fiji. He commented that many people spoke as though only political leaders were responsible for building the nation. All citizens, he said, had a role to play. This mirrored my own view that reconstruction of Fiji must involve everyone.

He also commented that our Fiji debate was almost exclusively focused on amnesty and felt some consensus should be reached on this. He felt there might be some merit in separating amnesty from truth and reconciliation, thus allowing these different elements to be evaluated separately. This was something we would be prepared to look at.

Then Father Lapsley shared something that reinforced my view that, despite the opposition, we were on the right course with our proposed legislation. He told me that he had asked Professor Piet Meiring, who had served on South Africa's Truth and Reconciliation Commission, to comment on our draft legislation.

The professor felt there was no reason why our Bill should not work. He highlighted the role of faith, or religious communities in guiding the South African Commission, and wondered whether our religions could contribute to what we wanted to achieve. I was sure Cabinet would be happy to consider this.

It was extremely interesting to me that about 36 representatives of Fiji's military, police and prisons service attended one of Father Lapsley's seminars in Suva in November 2006, just before the Bainimarama coup. According to the *Fiji Times* it was organized in response to specific requests from the military and police to help participants deal with the trauma they experienced during the 2000 coup. A major complaint seemed to be that they hadn't had this kind of workshop earlier - that this would have helped in the healing process.

According to Father Lapsley many in the disciplined forces had deeply traumatic experiences and never had the opportunity to work through them.

The significance of this is that Father Lapsley's engagement with the community was within the context of the draft legislation that was so reviled by Bainimarama and some others in the military. Clearly that revulsion was not necessarily shared by the members of the security services who attended Father Lapsley's seminar.

We planned to invite Father Lapsley to return in 2007 to continue his work of reconciliation. But that never happened. Bainimarama staged his coup a few weeks after the seminar for the military, police and prison representatives. This deepened the need for the healing of the country. There was more trauma and more bitterness.

# 71

# 'SOMETHING OF A MIRACLE'

**B**ainimarama and his colleagues, especially the Attorney General, Aiyaz Sayed-Khaiyum, have tried very hard to discredit and demonise the SDL and its performance in government. We were accused of corruption, racism, nepotism and bad governance. At one point it was alleged we had committed crimes against humanity! Such was the extent of the propaganda against us by the coup-makers and their accomplices.

I can say, without hesitation, that the SDL achieved a great deal in both rehabilitating Fiji after the 2000 insurrection and in setting our nation on a sound course. I want to comment in some detail about what we accomplished because it is important to establish the truth, correct misrepresentations, and to set the historical record straight.

It is a matter of public record that our government earned excellent reviews for its accomplishments generally and specifically for economic management. The Asian Development Bank described growth under the SDL as solid and noted the strong performance by the private sector. It listed our external debt outstanding as the lowest among 12 Pacific Island states. The International Monetary Fund commented favourably on Fiji's economic progress from 2000. Mr

Bob Lyon, who was then a senior executive with the ANZ Bank, described Fiji as a bright star. He was quoted as saying that growth and recovery in our time in office had been tremendous.

One of the most glowing testimonials came from Mr Adrian Simcock, the New Zealand High Commissioner to Fiji from 2001 to 2004. In a *Fiji Times* report of 3rd November 2003, Mr Simcock said he thought we had worked "something of a miracle". His statement was important because he was a senior diplomat representing a near neighbour with close links to us. New Zealand followed events and developments in Fiji very closely. Talking to Lautoka Chamber of Commerce, Mr Simcock was quoted as saying no other country had executed such a rapid recovery toward democracy since the unlawful overthrowing of a democratically elected government. This achievement, he said, had paved the way for future investment.

While there was still a lot of work to be done economically and politically, the restoration of the rule of law was something to be admired by the world. He said that with some very important issues before the courts being closely monitored locally, as well as internationally, our government's commitment to respect the law had brought about widespread stability and progress. The country had achieved economic buoyancy that was readily apparent. He went on to say that with economic indicators predicting more growth by the end of the year, this certainly established Fiji as the "economic tiger" of the Pacific.

I was surprised when in 2005 the *Fiji Times* itself also saw Fiji's recovery as "nothing short of miraculous." This was praise from an unexpected quarter because I had been critical of much of the Times' coverage and comment. I believed it was biased. But on this occasion, I was naturally happy to acknowledge the newspaper's accolade. I said that I thought we had worked a miracle in light of the grave crisis that almost destroyed the country just five years earlier. But it was a miracle created out of the support and purpose of the people co-operating with government that had a clear set of objectives and a guiding vision.

A sharp decline in economic performance always follows an illegal takeover of a government. This happened in 1987, 2000 and 2006. Our commitment was to get the economy into a recovery phase as quickly as possible. We pushed strongly for growth in tourism, one of the strong pillars of the economy; measures were taken to remove obstacles to setting up businesses; foreign investments were assisted and encouraged; the sugar industry was reviewed and plans adopted for significant expansion, with the assistance of the European Union. There was support for forestry and fisheries. Major capital expenditures in infrastructure, such as roads and water supplies, were included in national budgets. The outcome of these priorities was positive.

The SDL manifestos give the details of our principles and goals. As I carried out my duties as prime minister every day, these statements of our thinking, policy and intent were always close to hand.

I referred to them regularly to ensure we were on track to meeting our promises. They show that we had a very broad vision for Fiji and all its people. We had a particular focus on helping the poor. I felt that for Fiji to develop with justice, we must as a community concentrate with a fixed sense of purpose on defeating poverty. I felt that when people were beaten down and in despair because they did not have enough money for their basic needs this should be an issue of pressing concern for everyone. Full employment in our view was possible, when the poor were poor no more and living standards throughout Fiji were on the rise. This was, and is, about equity, a society's moral values and its humanity.

In our nearly six years in power, we never deviated from what we promised and our vision for the country. We wanted ethnic rivalry and suspicion to be replaced by co-operation, trust and understanding and a relaxed acceptance of differences. We saw a Fiji where people were proud of their own distinct cultures and traditions, but united by a powerful surpassing loyalty to our islands. Stability was essential for what we wished to achieve; without it we would fail. Everyone in Fiji had experienced the economic and social cost of instability.

All those who felt alienated should be encouraged to look upon Fiji as their homeland; they had to be confident about their rights, their security and protection under the law and equality as citizens. It was important to acknowledge that all Fiji's ethnic groups had played a role in advancing the nation. Following the 2000 upheaval and renewed ethnic tensions and hurt, we believed it was essential to enhance inter-communal relations, especially through building understanding of diverse cultures, traditions and value systems. Young people coming out of schools should have opportunities for livelihoods and careers and the disadvantaged had to be assisted without others feeling that something was being taken from them.

We envisaged Fiji's children growing up in happiness and good health, looked after lovingly by their parents in a proper family environment and receiving an education to equip them for productive lives in a multi-cultural nation.

Given time, patience and political will all these things could be accomplished.

After what had happened in 2000, it was self-evident that we would have to devote a lot of effort to reconciliation. The country had been traumatized; people had been threatened and terrorized because of their ethnicity. I felt that as head of government I should take the lead in helping heal Fiji's wounds and, therefore, took responsibility for the portfolio of national reconciliation and unity. I could not have imagined how difficult reconciliation would become in the years ahead.

I told the United Nations national assembly in September 2004 that when I returned to Fiji, the country would be getting ready for eight days of prayer and forgiveness. The aim was to bring people together to create a sense of national purpose and patriotism. All the great faiths represented in Fiji would be part of this. I added:

Each contains in their teachings those jewels of truth which gleam for all humanity. Each has an important capacity for peace-making; each can make a valuable contribution to increasing understanding and resolving differences.

I concluded:

Mr President, just as this great organization seeks a world of harmony, bound together by common ideals, we, in Fiji, want our own UN – a united nation where our citizens live together happily, and nationhood is fulfilled.

A united nation not a broken one.

The SDL manifesto for the 2001 election specifically offered a creed of peace, tolerance and truth, caring for others, social justice, commitment to law and order, and honesty and integrity in public life. We spelled out the magnitude of the ordeal of 2000, the damage caused to race relations, the decline in the economy and political uncertainty, division and instability. These were the realities with which we were confronted and that had to be tackled.

The solemn assurance I gave was that we would work to remove the barriers that separated communities and replace animosity and fear with trust and co-operation. The pledge we made was to work for the betterment of everyone.

"When we say everyone, we mean everyone." Those were the words I used, and I meant what I said. I stressed that there was no racial boundary to our desire to serve Fiji.

As we went to the country for the 2006 elections, our pledge to the people was similar; peace, stability and harmony built on tolerance, understanding and respect, and strong families.

I reminded the nation that when we first came into office, Fiji was on its knees but quickly rose again. We had restored constitutional democratic governance, re-imposed law and order, started to repair the economy and encouraged reconciliation. Our party declared that it had given Fiji a government that put people first.

When I mentioned that we had encountered some difficulties and threats, I was referring to the aggressive and illegal interventions against our government by Commodore Bainimarama who was clearly intent on conducting another coup. He had become the biggest obstacle blocking the way forward.

# 72

# REFLECTIONS

At the time of writing, I am in my 77<sup>th</sup> year. According to the Bible, the normal life span is three score years and 10. So I am now a proud member of the Overstayers' Club and leave my future, as always, to my Maker. My life has been full. I have taken the opportunity to serve others whenever that has been possible and have tried to use whatever talents I have to the fullest extent. I think I know where I have fallen short.

I endured persecution and imprisonment by the Bainimarama-Sayed-Khaiyum military regime in the belief that it was part of the divine plan for my life. God never said our lives would be easy. I was tested by my legal challenges and imprisonment and those close to me were hurt. Frank Bainimarama and his senior officers wanted to shame me, break me, and drive me out of politics. They achieved none of these things.

Here I am, unbowed, with my faculties and energy intact and my health in reasonable order. I hope I have improved in knowledge and wisdom. I am busy again doing things I want to do.

The Letter of the Disciple James reassures me: "My brothers and sisters, consider yourselves fortunate when all kinds of trials come your way, for you know that when your faith succeeds in facing such trials, the result is the ability to endure. Make sure that your endurance carries you all the way without failing, so that you may be perfect and complete, lacking nothing." (Chapter 1, v 2-4)

I should add that I have too many flaws to ever be perfect but that does not prevent me from gaining inspiration from the Scriptures.

I felt it was important to include in these reflections some personal comments by my granddaughter, Fane. Her letters to me in prison – along with those of other family members – comforted me and lifted my spirits very much.

Fane found her way into the nation's conscience when she was photographed clinging to me as I made my way to a police vehicle to be taken to prison. Her face was contorted with distress. It was a very difficult moment.

Fane was 14 then. She is 20 now, married, and living in Santa Rosa, California. Towards the end of 2017 and into early 2018, she spent nearly two months with us with her six months old daughter Alona, our great grandchild. Most of the time we were in the Moti Street house; we also spent a few weeks at our home *Naivaka* at Mavana. Fane loves the village because of its relaxed atmosphere.

I thought comments by Fane about the trauma behind the photograph of us outside the court would add to my story. She agreed to talk to a family friend about that experience. What follows is her account, in her words. Some five years after my sentence, Fane still reacts emotionally to what happened. She related on her recent holiday with us that she had started to read the drafts of this book containing her letters and the stories about Rupert and King Kong. But she had to stop when her tears started again. She dabbed her eyes constantly with her handkerchief when she went into the detail of her recollections. This is what she said:

---

I found out about the guilty verdict indirectly from Tua's

driver Kaji. As he was driving me home, he did not reply when I asked him what had happened in court that day. So, I knew the outcome was not good. When we entered the driveway of Moti Street there were many people downstairs. The house was full. I looked for my mother, Atelaite. My father, Bale, was in the US at the time. I asked Mum what had happened, and she told me Tua had been found guilty and I have to be strong about it. Sentencing would be the next day.

How did I feel? I was angry. It was like, why is this happening? Then tears came with my anger. Tua was upstairs with Nau (Leba) having a conversation with Ro Teimumu (Kepa). I looked at him and he looked at me and I started crying.

I walked into my bedroom and closed the door because Ro Teimumu was sitting there with Tua. I pretended I was studying for my school examinations the next day. I had my books open, but I was really just

thinking...thinking about our life at home, how Tua would react to everything; would he be ok? Why had all this happened?

Next day, when the sentence was to be announced, my sister Senikau and I got ready for school. We dropped her at the bus stop to catch the bus for ACS (Adi Cakobau School in Sawani). Kaji took me to my school, Suva Grammar.

As soon as I got to school people were just staring at us. They knew what was happening. Mum was with me. When I got out of the car a bunch of my friends were waiting. Some hugged me and asked if I was ok and I said, yes. I went into class and sat down but I couldn't stay. I joined Mum in the car and told her I could not remain in the classroom. She told me, "Tua would want you to take the exam." As we were walking back to class the school principal came along; he was looking for me. He asked if I was ok and then said I could go to court and do the exams later. I passed them all, thank goodness.

We went back home and then got ready to go to court. Tua and Nau went ahead in their vehicle. Family members followed in a taxi including Mum, me and two cousins.

When we arrived, the courthouse was full; we could not go inside. So we sat on a bench.

I knew he would be going to prison. I just knew. Then we heard of the sentence and Tua came out of the courtroom, followed by photographers who also took pictures of us. We tried to hide our faces because it was kind of annoying; a policeman sent them away.

When Tua came I thought it was our time to say goodbye to him.

I remember standing and running towards him screaming "Tua, Tua!" I hugged him; I was just so distressed and weeping. I felt like I was never going to see him again. Who would look after him? Was he able to look after himself?

I remember that he touched my head. Then he said, 'Be strong and courageous. God is good'. That's all he said. I could not speak; I was just too emotional.

The police led him away down the stairs with me following right behind him. Nau walked with him to the police vehicle; he got into it and it drove away. After Tua had gone, Nau and some of her friends went to a coffee shop. I told Mum I would see them at Moti Street. I sat by myself on a bench and then went to the house by taxi.

I am pretty sure that night I went to town and was just walking around with a friend, Natalia, whose father was also in prison. I got to know her because Tua used to visit him there. When I got home, I cried myself to sleep.

Someone asked what I think of Bainimarama after the passing of time. I think he has a sad life. I am not mad at him.

I do not hate him. I feel bad for him. I feel like he will never be satisfied. He will never be happy.

Would I ever go into politics in Fiji? I've thought about it, but then I lost interest in politics and anything to do with Fiji. My main concern has been Tua, Nau and their wellbeing. But Fiji is where I was born and that can never change. However, I still don't know about going into politics. I would think there's about a 20 per cent chance that I will.

I think I might come back in two or three years. I have an idea of going into the real estate business in Fiji with my sister. But I'll have to see.

People have asked me why I have such an intense love for Tua. It comes from deep inside my soul. He, to me, is the definition of a real man and how a man is supposed to love and care for his family. When I was really young my parents separated, and we lived with my grandparents from that time. Tua showed me how a man is supposed to love a woman. The love he gives me and everything he sacrifices and does for me and Nau and our family is just amazing. Not only does he sacrifice for his family but for our village and our country.

Growing up and witnessing how much he would sacrifice for anyone my love for Tua grew and there's nothing in this world that can ever take my love for him away. Tua is a great man; in my eyes he is one in a billion.

---

All I can say is that I cherish the feelings towards me of Fane and all my grandchildren. I am thankful for their love.

Investigations against me by the Fiji Independent Commission Against Corruption (FICAC) started more than a year after the coup of 5th December 2006. It took over four years before I was finally convicted and sent to prison over the Fijian Holdings Ltd case. For much of this time I was also embroiled in the case brought against me relating to the Native Land Trust Board. This was finally withdrawn.

It was a long four years with many preliminary court hearings involving both cases. I was granted bail with restrictions. For instance, I had to inform the court registry of my travels from Suva to Mavana, Vanuabalavu and return to Suva. On one of my visits to Mavana I was whisked away at the airport on Vanuabalavu by local police who required me to sign a register at the police post. That was not a pleasant experience. My visits to other parts of Fiji were not so regulated. I did not have to inform the registry of my itinerary. I did not understand why there was a difference between the conditions for my visits home and other local travel. My passport was confiscated by the court and high court approval had to be sought if I wanted to travel overseas.

Because of all the uncertainty surrounding the future, and the legal threats and pressures, it was a difficult period for the family. The mental anguish weighed heavily on Leba and me. The adverse publicity about the two cases was merciless and ongoing. I remember a radio news bulletin one morning that said I was accused of fraudulent conversion amounting to hundreds of thousands of dollars. I couldn't believe my ears. But this was typical of the changing allegations against me by FICAC broadcast to the local community and the outside world. While all this was going on the regime withheld my pension entitlements as an additional means of punishment. Financial problems became part of my daily concerns.

---

I t was a joy to pick up the threads of my life following the prison punishment that gave me the number 302 as my identity. On 3$^{rd}$ April 2013, after some delays I suspect were deliberate, I became free again after 243 days of incarceration. No more bars, no more control and regimentation, no more depressing, dirty, run-down surroundings. No more separation from those I loved. I looked forward so much to rejoining Leba and the family and doing normal domestic things. The reunion at our home in Moti Street in Samabula, Suva, was everything I wanted it to be. There were celebrations by family, friends and well-wishers. The senior prison staff who had brought me home were given traditional thanks for delivering me to the house. Next morning, I was up and off early for my daily walk in the familiar surroundings of the Samabula neighbourhood. Then breakfast again with Leba. After that there were many personal and village matters to follow up. It was good to be greeted in the streets with smiles and handshakes and to welcome a delegation of my SODELPA colleagues.

It wasn't long before national affairs began to demand my attention through SODELPA, the political party that succeeded the Soqosoqo Duavata ni Lewenivanua (SDL). Under the Bainimarama-Sayed- Khaiyum regime Fijian language names for political parties were prohibited so SDL had to become Social Democratic Liberal Party (SODELPA).

SODELPA wanted me to be involved in its affairs and I was happy to oblige. In fact, if it had been possible, I would definitely have applied for a SODELPA ticket for the 2014 election. But as I have already explained, Bainimarama and Sayed-Khaiyum had enacted certain constitutional and legal measures that disqualified me from seeking a seat in parliament.

I stress again that I have been punished twice and at the same time some of my important political rights have been taken away. This is clear evidence that Bainimarama and Sayed-Khaiyum have not yet ended their Qarase personal vendetta. I wonder whether any other so-called democratic country has enacted the kind of legal devices that have been used against me. They are inconsistent with the very concept of political freedom.

When Bainimarama staged his coup in 2006, I was 65 years old. In normal circumstances I could have pursued my political career fully for another 10 years at least. The dictatorial duo has succeeded in blocking me from parliament. But I remain an active member of SODELPA and take on political assignments when I am asked. I intend to campaign in the 2018 election.

I have often reflected on the extent of the hate Bainimarama and Sayed-Khaiyum have for me. As I have said at the start of this book, I can find no other word that fits.

To be fair to Sayed-Khaiyum he has been restrained in expressing his feelings towards me publicly, but I have no doubt about the extent of his enmity. I represent much of what he opposes. In a democracy such differences are normal. But, like Bainimarama, Sayed-Khaiyum is not a democrat. He makes all the right noises while masterminding controls and anti-democratic legislation that have no place in a modern democracy. In his own way he is as despotic as Bainimarama. His behind-the-scenes influence is deep. The popular belief is that he runs the country. In fact, a visiting Muslim cleric referred to him as King Khaiyum. It might have been said as a joke, but the reality is that Sayed-Khaiyum is indeed a monarch of sorts.

With Bainimarama the very mention of my name was enough to set him off. His favourite description of me was that I was a liar. When Bainimarama and I met jointly with the late vice president, Ratu Jone Madraiwiwi, in a vain attempt to reach an accommodation, the word spewed out frequently. I apparently lied about everything.

A couple of episodes underscored the depth of his hatred.

He told the journalist, and later his speech writer, Graham Davis, in May 2009, that I was "finished". He added that I would only return over his (Bainimarama's) dead body. So, there it was, his hatred in its purest form. He would rather give up his life than see me come back to office.

His antipathy to me was such that he could not bear to see my photograph. It was hanging in the cabinet room along with pictures of other prime ministers and presidents. Not long after the coup it was removed and ended up in a rubbish bin. Bainimarama could then preside at Cabinet meetings without me gazing down on him accusingly. The headquarters of the Fiji Disabled People's Association (FDPA) at Brown Street in Toorak was named Qarase House. It had been refurbished by my second government and I had been invited to inaugurate the new-look premises. The nameplate later caught someone's attention. (I wonder whose?) It was taken down. My response is: what's in a name anyway? To me dumping my photos and removing my name from a building are like the spiteful actions of a wayward child.

Before 2000 I did not know Bainimarama, although Leba went to the same primary school as he did in Lautoka. I heard on the coconut wireless that when he was growing up, he tended to get his own way. The need for his will to prevail is a defining feature of his personality. I notice he tried to hide this at the COP23 climate change conference in Bonn in November 2017. He was busy promoting the false notion that he was a keen advocate of respectful, island-style, *"talanoa"* discussions, designed to reach consensus among those with differing viewpoints. On his return to Fiji, it didn't take him long to revert to his hard-line rhetoric demonizing those opposing him. No sign at all of the coalition- building consensus and inclusivity he spoke about so frequently at COP23.

After an undistinguished career in the navy, Bainimarama became commander of the RFMF on the recommendation of then Commander Ratu Epeli Ganilau. Many doubts were expressed privately about the appointment, especially in the military. It is a mystery to me why Ratu Epeli thought Bainimarama had the leadership and professional abilities qualifying him to head the army.

After his coup I knew Bainimarama was anxious to see me in prison. My information indicated he wondered impatiently why it was taking so long. I believe he was burning up with rage against me for a number of reasons. As far as he was concerned when I accepted nomination to be head of an interim government to get the country back on track after the huge disruption of 2000, that somehow made me the military's man. I would simply do what Bainimarana and his officers wanted.

I never saw things that way. The cabinet was not military; it was civilian in membership and had the endorsement of the Great Council of Chiefs. We set our own agenda for rescuing Fiji and followed it closely. The decision to contest elections in 2001 amazon.com

y 4, 2023

Prisoner 302

Carson Cname?   Paperback

B0B43Y5S7G

8:9798986147703

Return or replace your item
Visit Amazon.com/returns

0/G4vp5yVLb/-1 of 1 //TCY9 CART A/second/0/0107-05:00/0107 02.11

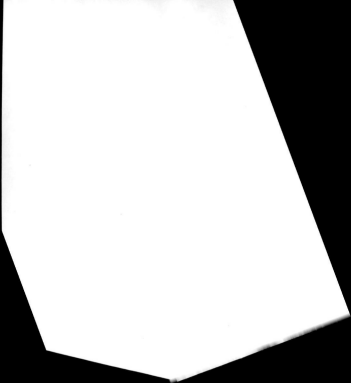

belonged to me and my ministers. The manifesto we put together was ours, not the military's. We drew on our joint experience, political judgement and the views of the people. The same applied to the manifesto for 2006.

Our independence of action began to agitate Bainimarama. He was angry and affronted by it. In his mind he should have been controlling me. His authoritarian instincts gradually expanded. As related in these pages, from at least 2003 he started to think about seizing power through a coup despite resistance and warnings from certain professional senior officers who stood by the established principle that in democracies armies are subject to civilian control. He finally became obsessed with removing me and my government from office. He wanted complete power, and he got it, with the support of some 3,000 armed soldiers. He also got the keys to the national treasury.

I believe greed for political power and wealth became a driving force for him, many of his military colleagues and other supporters outside the military. I rememember clearly that Bainimarama promised no military officer would benefit from the coup. But he went on to place military men in many senior government positions. They have done well financially. I question whether they would have earned their positions through merit and hard work.

This militarization of the public service provides Bainimarama with another layer of protection and influence that will have to be dismantled. By now he must be a wealthy man, with his salary of $329,000 (over $900 a day) plus $3,000 a day allowance on his very frequent overseas visits. Presumably the daily $3000 is in addition to other expenses met by the taxpayer. For the record, my PM's salary was approximately $105,000. I was careful to charge personal expenses to my private credit cards. Costs I incurred on days off were met by me.

Through his rebellious behaviour, Bainimarama also managed to put himself into a corner. His actions and words led to a police investigation. When he executed his coup, his arrest was imminent. It was necessary for him to take power through force to escape the law. In doing so he created an even bigger problem: treason, one of the most serious of crimes. George Speight had initially received the death penalty for it but this was commuted to life in prison.

Bainimarama's legal problems go further. He has questions to answer about the brutal murders of soldiers killed after the 2000 mutiny at the Queen Elizabeth Barracks. Those murders were horrific; I was told that a nurse who saw one of the bloodied and battered bodies had to receive trauma counseling.

For the rest of his life these issues will be his burden and his nightmare. Always there; always threatening. The immunity he has granted himself – a cowardly action - may not be as strong as he thinks. The same applies to Sayed-Khaiyum. I reflect also that the wide immunities they have put in their constitution will not help with the restoration of democracy. You cannot have equality and justice when some citizens are protected from their crimes.

At this point, Bainimarama and Sayed-Khaiyum enjoy dictatorial power. But that power will slip away from them. The night sweats come when, alone, they consider their future without the support of psychophants, favour-seekers and expensive p.r. people helping them to ride along on propaganda. No one stays in office forever. Bainimarama and Sayed-Khaiyum must think often of the moment when their authority has gone, and they can no longer command the structures and the power of the state. That will be their moment of truth.

In the meantime, if either one of them is unable to continue in office, what happens then? What will Bainimarama do without Sayed-Khaiyum? What will Sayed-Khaiyum do without Bainimarama, his patron and protector?

At some point both of them will find out that most of those who profess to be with them will begin to keep their distance. The members of the business community and other elites who have poured huge amounts of funding into their Fiji First Party coffers won't be in touch anymore and may not always return a call. For these opportunists it will be time to forge new relationships of convenience. For Bainimarama and Sayed-Khaiyum the arm of the law will beckon.

When I reflect on the military leadership that has unleashed so much unhappiness, fear and abuse, I see the spreading presence of evil. Soldiers brought up according to the principles of mercy, compassion and love for their neighbour, acted as agents and practitioners of thuggery, fear, force and torture. Evil had invaded their souls.

I saw men who, because of some misconceived sense of military loyalty, were ready to blindly maintain illegal authority at the point of a gun. We had some eight years of that.

However, I must add that there is still hope. Many of the RFMF rank and file know what is right and what is wrong and believed they were simply following orders. I don't think they were affected for the long-term by the brainwashing of their leaders to accept that the military is all-powerful and they may use that power against defenseless citizens.

I must add though that they should have known they did not have to follow illegal orders. They should have known they were not free to subjugate the populace by virtue of their weaponry.

The image and reputation of the army is now tarnished. To this day, citizens still fear being taken to the barracks with all that implies. Many who once looked to the army as a bastion of security, discipline, and exemplary behaviour now have doubts and second thoughts. Their admiration and regard for the institution have been replaced by indifference, some suspicion and even dislike.

It is still possible through sound, principled and professional leadership for the RFMF to regain its reputation and high standing of yesteryear. It will not be easy, but the task can be done. A strong government must be ready to purge the RFMF of leaders and other elements who do not affirm their commitment to the rule of law, democratic principles and civilian control of the army. A central purpose of this purge must be to remove the supreme political powers granted to the RFMF. This elevates it above the elected civilian leadership.

A question every concerned citizen must ask is whether the cycle of coups has stopped. Military people have declared there will be no more armed take-overs.

But in my view Bainimarama is less than emphatic about this, perhaps because he has convinced himself he did no wrong. There is nothing in the Sayed-Khaiyum-Bainimarama constitution to deter future coup-makers. The wide immunities in the document are actually an incentive to conduct a coup. Someone plotting intervention against civilian rule will be comforted with the thought that "if I do this I will get immunity like all the other perpetrators. I can also become rich and powerful." Put another way: the message is that it is ok to commit treason and related crimes as long as you can protect yourself as others have done.

Fiji needs a full review of every aspect of the RFMF. As a small and relatively poor nation, we must consider very closely the cost of maintaining a large army. The personnel numbers are a bit hard to pin down but, including territorials, it could be up to 10,000. It is impossible to justify the multi-millions of taxpayers' dollars spent annually to support all the needs of the RFMF. I calculate that in the five years ending in 2018, some $680 million of our money has been allocated in national budgets for this. Clearly that money could have been more productively employed catering to the needs of the poor; rehabilitating the victims of Cyclone Winston forced to live in tents; improving the broken health system; rescuing the crippled sugar industry; constructing and repairing more roads; upgrading schools; cleaning up the severely damaged environment; reviving the stagnant agricultural sector, and much more.

For specific context think of this: For the same five-year period of the military spend, only the equivalent of 45 per cent of the multi milions for the military went to assist women, children and poverty alleviation. Only 11 per cent was allocated to support young people. This tells a story of priorities.

I favour retaining a small, well-trained force to continue Fiji's tradition of peacekeeping, but with the international community promptly meeting the costs. This specialised role of the RFMF should only continue when we have set up a system of supervision that virtually eliminates the possibility of future coups. Never again must we send Fiji soldiers on international peacekeeping duties when the RFMF is suppressing and ill-treating its own populace. Rigorous security must be applied to the control of national arms and ammunition. That was shown to be completely lacking during the George Speight coup when large amounts of weaponry ended up in the parliamentary grounds. I recommend national armoury legislation for the purchase and issue of military hardware, according to strict guidelines. This would involve oversight by a bi- partisan Parliamentary Committee reporting to the prime minister of the day, who would have ultimate responsibility. The overriding principle should be that in view of Fiji's history of coups, it is far too dangerous and unnecessary to give authority to a single military person, such as the head of the RFMF, for the purchase and supervision of arms. The national armoury would be closely managed by a special security authority.

I support building up Fiji's navy into an effective tool for managing and protecting Fiji's large exclusive economic zone, with assistance from climate change funding. This makes sense in terms of the broad national interest, especially border security, conserving our marine and fishery resources and the great ocean itself which is threatened by pollution. At the moment, the rusting wreck of the Kiro on a reef not too far from Suva symbolizes the failures of our current naval force.

The inability of my governments to remove Bainimarama for insubordination and seditious activities lies on my shoulders. We were confronted by a rogue military leader, ruthless in his final determination to seize power by force, and we could not stop him. He demonstrated that the military was, in his words, "all powerful." The power was that of force.

But I was prime minister; the buck stops with me. I am account-able for our failure to contain him.

I am sorry in my heart for the enormous difficulties suffered by so many and for the human tragedies and deaths that occurred as a result of the actions of those who committed treason.

The country has had no closure for the 2006 coup; the families of the victims have had no closure. They grieve still. I think of the rela-tives of young Sakiusa Rabaka whose life, when he was just 19, came to an end after injuries inflicted on him at the Black Rock military base near Nadi. It is surely a cruel irony that Black Rock is being developed as a training camp for peacekeepers.

I think of the relatives of Nimilote Verebasaga and the others who lost loved ones and friends in cruel circumstances. They have received no real justice, no proper compensation. What about members of the population at large who endured threats, terror, intimidation, curtailment to their freedoms, police state tactics, finan-cial loss and general social distress. Some are in exile overseas.

Are the people not to receive even an apology?

I am convinced that what Fiji needs now is healing and reconcili-ation based on restorative justice, modeled on what SODELPA proposed to the nation as outlined in this book. The victims need the right to face those who acted so violently and with such malice; they are entitled to the answers they have never received. The question of compensation must be addressed. The perpetrators must be given the opportunity to explain themselves, to seek forgiveness and to apolo-gise. The human spirit responds to true contrition, and mercy often follows.

The people of Fiji are constantly fed propaganda that all is well in the country. That claim was punctured in 2015 when some 140 armed soldiers were deployed in Ra province. For legal reasons I will not discuss why this happened. What I can say is that such a deploy-ment is not a sign of normalcy in a democracy.

I reaffirm that under Bainimarama and Sayed-Khaiyum Fiji has veered away from democratic principles and now has a new style of dictatorship which has a grip on many aspects of life. Democracy is under continuous assault, starting with the constriction of parliament. The Bainimarama-Sayed Khaiyum imposed constitution was written to provide a foundation for the continuation of authoritarian rule. Essentially there is a formidable concentration of power in their hands. Standard democratic checks and balances have been removed along with the independence of key institutions. Oppressive legislation is a hurdle for those wishing to register political parties and in the practice of media freedom. Extreme penalties are a feature of other laws.

The practice in Fiji of local democracy has been tossed out. Since before independence, the affairs of municipalities were managed by locally elected councillors. Bainimarama-Sayed-Khaiyum ended this and closed the councils. There was a promise there would be new elections, but nothing has happened. It is obvious that they would see elected municipal representatives as a possible source of dissent and aggravation.

Localised democracy had a valued role previously when parliamentary candidates stood for certain constituencies often where they lived or were well-known. The result was that the voters had access to their own MPs from their area, who had detailed knowledge of local conditions and needs and who could be relied upon to raise these in parliamentary debate and follow-up with the relevant cabinet minister.

Sayed-Khaiyum scrapped this vital part of the democratic system. In its place he decided that Fiji would be just one constituency. He has tried to rationalize this without much success. Every MP, he says, has responsibility for the entire single constituency. The political parties – except Fiji First – largely ignore this and try to ensure that candidates are appointed for certain areas of the country broadly in line with the old constituencies, thus preserving something of the important system of local democracy.

The government functions under a great blanket of propaganda which seeks to paint a positive picture. Everyone is supposed to "get on board" and help the government through a "partnership". It's a one-sided arrangement of course with little or no room for competing views.

An increasing number of citizens recognise the truth of the state of the nation. They remain cautious however about expressing themselves. This means Fiji has much still to do as a country, including emancipating itself from authoritarianism, fear and frustration and achieving complete freedom.

One newspaper letter writer had the courage recently to say this: "Our democracy seems to be a leprous disease of power and force." There is nothing in his mind of the "genuine" and "vibrant" democracy Bainimarama talks about.

I have written at length about the marginalisation of the indigenous people and the sunset clause in Sayed-Khaiyum's thesis. It is a fact that their culture and traditions are now under threat. Indigenous institutions have been closed down, emasculated or taken over. I comment on this at length in the relevant chapters and how it is in conflict with the United Nations Declaration on the Rights of Indigenous Peoples which Bainimarama-Sayed Khaiyum, have refused to endorse. Even the idea of adoption of Fijian as a common name – without consulting the people - is taken from his thesis.

I have shared my thinking on affirmative action and why it is necessary, as a temporary measure, to build a well-balanced society. My thinking on this has not changed.

In appointments to statutory boards, committees and government companies a close circle of regime supporters, dominate. Members of a religious group which has a large world membership, but is a small minority in Fiji, hold a disproportionate number of top positions. People talk about this a lot. It has created some tension and suspicion.

I wonder whether the lack of diversity on boards is equivalent to discrimination against other communities. The appointees must always be straining to do exactly what the regime wants. Step out of line and consequences follow.

There is also an unprecedented degree of nepotism, most visible in the number of Bainimarama and Sayed-Khaiyum family members holding government or semi government positions.

As I reflect on my time in prison, I acknowledge the failure of my governments to devote adequate resources to bring standards and facilities to an acceptable level. The same applies to other administrations, including the current regime. When I was in prison a number of religious institutions and denominations were permitted to conduct certain teaching programmes and other activities. I commend them for this and believe their efforts went a long way towards encouraging inmates to become better citizens on their release. Based on my observations and conversations, the prison officers were the "poor relations" of the security services. I felt there was a need for relativity in their pay and conditions, with those of the police and military.

As I come to the end of my story, I must share my thinking about forgiveness. Have I forgiven those who persecuted me? As a Christian I place my trust in the only perfect and righteous judge, the Almighty God and Father. And I abide by the teachings of His Son and our Lord and Saviour, Jesus Christ, that we are to forgive one another. So yes, I have forgiven.

Yet as a human being with the failings of humanity, I would be lying if I said I have forgotten what happened to me; the persecution and imprisonment and the continuing vindictiveness and spite. I would be lying also if I said I did not want justice for myself, and for all who suffered at the hands of the usurpers. For me justice would be tempered with mercy.

I reiterate that I firmly reject the accusation that I am a racist. These days this label is thrown around freely. I am a product of my own culture. I am also a product of a multi-ethnic Fiji. My Fijian identity co-exists with the unique and complex diversity of our nation.

I make no apology for my concern about advancing the position of the indigenes in those areas where they have fallen behind. This can be achieved without in any way disadvantaging other groups. To some my commitment to uplifting the indigenous Fijians means I am some sort of prejudiced nationalist. I am not. I characterize myself as a moderate. I believe in tolerance, dialogue and peace-building for a unified and happy Fiji.

The extremists are those like Sayed-Khaiyum and Bainimarama who imposed a repressive military regime on Fiji and continue to be intolerant of dissent and dictatorial in their decision-making. All right-thinking people who want a return to democratic values and governance should come together in peaceful opposition to what they represent.

It is crucial now for the people and leaders to come together to find a formula of governance which allows democratic principles to co- exist with the traditional systems of authority. The 1997 constitution did this. It should be reinstated, with amendments where necessary. The 2013 constitution, never formally validated, must be rejected.

Above all Fiji's political leadership must fear God and manage the country's affairs in accordance with his Word. There must be acceptance that Fiji is a land of distinct and differing communities under Jehovah. I confess that my attitude towards the role of the Almighty in the state has become more fixed and pronounced in response to the secularism preached and imposed by Bainimarama and Sayed-Khaiyum.

I thank God for the privilege of leading the Government of Fiji from 2000 to 2006. I thank my colleagues in SDL for their support and confidence in my leadership. I thank my supporters throughout Fiji, and trust the governments I led contributed well to the development and welfare of the people of Fiji.

I want to record my big "thank you" to those who made my life reasonably comfortable in prison. I appreciate the support of all who followed my trial and extended their good wishes and prayers, particularly the large crowd that gathered around the high court during sentencing. They gave me moral comfort when I needed it. I thank the prison officers and inmates at Korovou for their kindness and respect. I thank friends who visited me in prison, as well as those who wished to but were not allowed. I thank the pastors and ministers who offered prayers in Korovou for me and the other inmates. I thank the many individuals and prayer groups who were concerned for my welfare. All these people and what they did helped me enormously in dealing with an ordeal.

Lastly, but not least, I thank my beautiful and loving wife, Leba, my children and their families who stood by me throughout. The love of my grandchildren was especially important.

I state once more that I remain unequivocally clear in my mind that I did not commit the offences that put me behind bars. I was sacrificed for revenge.

Now, in my remaining years, I look to the future with the love of Jesus Christ and the counsel of the Holy Spirit as my constant guide. For as that great Apostle Paul reminds us: "For what is life? ... It is Christ!" (Philippians 1:21)

# APPENDICES

# APPENDIX 1: SDL ACHIEVEMENTS IN THE ECONOMY

To keep us on course, we had adopted a five-year Strategic Development Plan setting out goals for jobs and incomes, and investment of at least 25 percent of GDP. The plan had detailed analyses of virtually every component of the economy and laid out many recommendations and projections for the advancement of the country. The first steps were taken by my interim government and carried forward on a participatory basis with the support of many willing citizens. They joined in eleven bipartisan consultative task forces comprising government officials and private sector and civil society representatives. People of different political persuasions and allegiances came together to pool their ideas for the national good. I commend this kind of co- operative inclusive approach to the Bainimarama government which continues to have great difficulty in working with those who have differing viewpoints and beliefs.

I have stressed often that an important part of governance is to take account of differing views, especially by listening directly to those who hold them. My governments truly believed in the partnership principle. The manifestations of this were widely evident especially in our strategic development plan, in education and in other social and economic sectors.

We planned to take this a stage further with the introduction of Public Private Partnerships for providing infrastructure. We were drafting a policy on this and intended to consult with private industry. It could have included power plants, roads, ports, airports, water supplies, education and health facilities and many other public amenities and services.

In our revival of Fiji, we had to deal with a virtual halt to investment. It was crucial for us to stabilize government finance. Our minister for finance, Ratu Jone Yavala Kubuabola, was in the right portfolio. He had worked as an economist for the World Bank, had been permanent secretary for finance, and governor of the Reserve Bank of Fiji. I worked closely with Ratu Jone in the early days to avoid a devaluation of our currency, which would have hurt the poor by causing price rises. (The Bainimarama military regime chose to devalue by 20 per cent, which predictably caused increased economic stress amongst the most vulnerable.)

Investment began to revive significantly. Private businesses that had previously been reluctant to invest were taking the lead role in the resurgence. Fiji has many able and successful business people. Their efforts have helped in no small way to establish Fiji as the nation with the most diversified economy in the entire Pacific Islands region. Through my own professional involvements, I developed relationships of trust with some of the best local entrepreneurs. As a banker, I loaned

them funds for expansion. The formula most of them followed for establishing and growing a business is a textbook study: save whatever money you can, a dollar at a time if need be; use your savings to get started; keep costs low; work hard to serve customers; forget about following a normal work day routine, if you have to start early and finish late, that's part of the price you pay; keep on saving; use savings as a base for borrowing for working capital; apply this to improving and expanding; never forget that profit is the measure of a successful commercial enterprise; keep an eye open for new opportunities; manage risk with care; and accept that it will probably take a long time to get to where you want to be - twenty or thirty years maybe.

I can think of businesses that are household names in Fiji such as Hari Punja's companies, Tappoo Group, Motibhais, Vinod Patel, which used this formula for building their empires. All had started with a small family enterprise and went from there.

Naturally I was keen to tap into all this local commercial knowledge and acumen to help us accomplish our mission of rebuilding the economy. I therefore decided to appoint Fiji's first prime minister's Think Tank dominated by the best and brightest from the private sector. I approached most of the potential members personally and explained why I needed their help and what I expected them to do. I invited them to contribute their ideas, thoughts and proposals for keeping the country firmly on the path to higher growth. I wanted them to tell us what more, in their view, had to be done to make better conditions for business and investment . How could Fiji earn a world reputation as a competitive and appealing centre of investment commerce and industry, where opportunities abound and returns were attractive?

Recommendations from the Think Tank would be followed up for consideration by Cabinet and parliament, when necessary. The link between the Think Tank and the National Strategic Development Plan would be through Ratu Jone who was chair of the National Economic Development Council (NEDC). This would provide a two-way flow of information between the NEDC and the Think Tank. I was very happy with the contribution of the Think Tank members. They came up with many recommendations for enhancing the business climate, especially by getting rid of unnecessary regulations and achieving our growth targets. They gave especially important contributions in undertaking comprehensive reviews of the structure and sectors of the economy. I was gratified when they collectively decided that Fiji had a "wonderful and bright future".

By July 2005 I was able to report to the Lautoka Chamber of

Commerce that Fiji was experiencing an unprecedented investment boom. Our target was for investment to be at least 25 per cent of GDP, or higher and we were confident of achieving this. At that stage the threatening, aggressive public statements by Bainimarama had not caused travel cancellations. That was to come later. Tourism was powering along and it was difficult to get rooms at some hotels. Another record total was expected for tourist arrivals. Construction companies were working at full capacity, adding several thousands new jobs to the national workforce. It was also important to push ahead with substantial investments in infrastructure improvements

Our overall economic growth target was five percent of GDP with an ultimate target of eight percent. We predicted that workers and rural people could expect more increases in wages and income opportunities as the economy got stronger. Reforms in the public service would make it investor-friendly. Changes had already been introduced to the investment approvals process to assist in reducing the cost of doing business. The processes needed to be further streamlined to remove bottlenecks.

I come here to another failure by the Bainimarama-Sayed-Khaiyum governments. During the SDL's first term, the World Bank ranked Fiji 34 out of 155 countries for ease of doing business. We were well ahead of some nations with developed economies. In a 2016 ranking Fiji had dropped from 34th to 84th place. The decline continued with Fiji plunging to 97th position. This is an indictment of the Bainimarama- Sayed-Khaiyum business and investment poli-cies. They brag often about how successful they are in bringing in investment but are incapable of making it easier for investors and businesses to operate. One of the reasons for this failure is their obses-sion with control and regulation.

In a four-year period in our term, economic growth averaged 3.5 per cent, up from 2.5 per cent over the last 25 years. The highest recorded growth we accomplished in a single year was over five per cent of GDP. At the time of our 2006 manifesto, the improvement in growth placed Fiji above other developing countries.

We decided to employ deficit budgets to help stimulate growth. These were funded from borrowings sourced mainly from the domestic market. The finance from borrowings was channeled towards capital expenditure to create economic expansion. At the same time, we maintained Fiji's economic fundamentals. The country had moderate debt, low inflation and a satisfactory level of foreign reserves. Deficits, ranging between three and six percent of GDP, were manageable.

We aimed to cut the deficit by about three percent of GDP or lower. Debt was to reduce to about 40 percent of GDP. Maintaining local borrowing at about 80 per cent of our needs would minimise the risk of exposure to foreign exchange fluctuations that had created problems for other developing countries. Foreign reserves were kept at an amount equivalent to between three to five months of the value of imports. There would be further concentration on improving tax revenue collection that had reached record heights. Company tax would be cut further to encourage investment. The combined impact of all our manifesto initiatives represented a total effort to defeat poverty in all its forms, among all our communities, and in every part of Fiji.

Funding for education, health, infrastructure and rural development reached record levels. We conceived and put into effect extensive and ambitious schemes for lifting the standards of rural communities. Combined, these formed a grand plan for remaking the economic and social landscape of the most deprived areas. Manifesto policy details provided the framework for widespread reforms in virtually every sector. All of these were high priority; rural development had special significance because it was obvious that standards of living in villages and settlements where more than half the population lived, should be improved. Their needs were not fully catered for.

I was able to report to the SDL annual meeting in May 2005 significant spending on roads, education grants, scholarships and school improvements. Finance and training for farming, fisheries, forestry, tourism and other small businesses was helping people support their families and themselves through their own initiatives. A small grant scheme had been largely dedicated to education, village and settlement development, welfare assistance, and support for young people, women, sports and provincial councils.

In response to a challenge from our government to extend banking services, a major commercial bank launched an ambitious rural banking scheme. The government itself also promoted schemes for rural savings.

I shared with the public statistics to underline the scale of rural work we were doing. Since 2001, 406 projects received funds for village improvement schemes comprising 151 multipurpose halls and evacuation centres; 16 beautification projects and 239 sanitation schemes. In three yeas 400 connections were made through our rural electrification scheme. An additional $6 million was allocated to this for 2005. Water supplies in the same period were provided to over 130 villages and settlements. In 2005 another 40 to 50 villages would get piped water. Funding was allocated for more water supplies in outer islands. Vanua Levu was very much part of our rural thrust.

# APPENDIX 2: SDL ACHIEVEMENTS IN EDUCATION

My own experiences at school and the struggles of my parents to educate my brother and I were on my mind as we introduced the most sweeping agenda for education reform in Fiji's history. We sought a better education at a reduced cost for all children regardless of race, religion, culture or economic status.

We were driven by a belief that public investment in education is one of the best ways of building a successful and prosperous nation. We regarded education as a ticket out of poverty for all those people struggling to support themselves and their families.

Specifically, we felt the most valuable assistance a state could give to every family in Fiji was to ensure every child had access to quality education to the highest possible level. A central intention was to assist each family to have at least one child attain university or other higher education qualifications. We committed to maintaining education funding to a minimum of 20 percent of the national budget. By May 2005, I could tell the nation, that over $1 billion had been invested by our government to provide more quality teachers, extra books and computers and improved school facilities in rural and urban areas.

In 2005 the education budget had increased by nearly $9million to $260million, the highest in Fiji's history. Parents had been freed from paying tuition fees for most classes and we had made a commitment to bring fee-free education to form seven. As a result, a record number of children were going to school.

We calculated that these policies had directly benefitted more than 60,000 students. Under the former system, parents would have had to pay $10 million annually for tuition fees. They no longer had to meet that cost. The way had been opened for many more disadvantaged students to receive higher education through increased funding for university and other advanced learning. From 2000 tuition fees assistance grants had been introduced to 55 poor and disadvantaged secondary schools, thereby providing assistance to approximately 3,000 students. This programme was extended to form six in 2002.

All children were exempted from paying external examination fees starting from the Intermediate Examination at class six to the Fiji Seventh Form Examination. It was estimated that removing these costs further lightened the financial burdens on families by a total of $1 million a year. We moved a long way towards our goal of giving every child the benefit of 12 years basic education from class one to form six. Fiji had reached near universal primary education and more children were receiving secondary education. At that stage, our compulsory education programme covered children at primary school and up to form four at secondary school. For forms five and six, the removal of fees and payment by government of school and building grants had made it possible and easier for many thousands of children to study to this level. Previously they would not have been able to go this far in school. We expected to reach the overall target of 12 years of education to form six within the next five years.

Since 2001 $9.6 million was granted for higher education scholarships through the Public Service Commission. This assisted 2,638 students from all ethnic communities and a total of $3.6 million had been allocated for 490 scholarships in 2006. Additionally, we had provided $6.5 million for a student loan scheme for those who could not afford to pay for their children's higher education. This had helped an ethnically mixed group of nearly 1,000 students who would otherwise have been denied this. More than $14 million was allocated to multi-ethnic scholarships particularly for poor and disadvantaged families from the Indo-Fijian and minority communities. We were on track to exceed our target of granting 5,000 scholarships in our first period in office. For 2006, another $4 million had been allocated for more than 1,000 additional scholarships.

We had invested in developing the Navuso Agricultural School which was to be linked to the Ratu Kadavulevu School and the Ministry of Agriculture. Construction was to start on a new form seven college at Nasinu, catering for academic and industry linked courses for students aspiring to further and higher education, those entering employment as technicians, as well as tutoring in basic skills for the workforce.

We ended discrimination against some 4,000 students from poor villages by introducing boarding school grants to non-government primary schools, largely in rural districts. Previously they have been denied this help. Additionally, we were making building grants to urban boarding schools serving poor children from the islands and other isolated locations. We fulfilled a pledge to pay lease renewal premiums for schools on native land.

In a three-year period, we upgraded many secondary and primary schools. A lot of primary schools, in particular, were in shocking conditions. But as a result of our assistance they received such basic items as desks and blackboards and better overall facilities. From 2002 to 2004, 185 primary schools and 84 secondary schools were supplied with new textbooks. Those rural schools that had previously been neglected were now also benefitting from a major project the government agreed on with the European Union.

We maintained a strong and unapologetic commitment to tackling the crisis in Fijian education which had seen Fijian children falling behind those from other ethnic groups in their school performance. Special assistance was largely concentrated on improving the poor conditions of Fijian schools and their lack of facilities. We were starting to see the results of our efforts with Fijian pass rates and examination results getting better.

There was opposition to our policies for lifting Fijian education. We believe they were absolutely justified in the interest of peace, stability and social justice. Let it be noted that there was no discrimination against other children. As a matter of fact non Fijian schools still received by far the largest portion of funding.

The never-ending barrage of propaganda from the current government gives the impression that no other administration had ever thought about reducing education costs. The truth is they are ten years behind, thanks to their 2006 coup. We were striding forward vigorously towards our education goals, when they seized our government by force and delayed our plans.

I would just add a further thought here. Bainimarama boasts constantly about how his government has delivered "free education". He is stretching it. Education can never be completely free. Governments can do much to minimise costs to parents – as we did - but there are always expenses that must be carried by the family, such as uniforms, lunch packs, footwear, sports gear, school bags, and so on.

# APPENDIX 3: SDL ACHIEVEMENTS IN HEALTH

The SDL launched important health service expansion and improvement programs providing better and cheaper amenities. Costs for the people were further reduced when we scrapped charges for outpatient services and costs in hospital general wards for treatment, beds and meals.

Four hospitals were built and a pharmaceutical centre in Suva; health centres and nursing centres were completed. We had proposals for more new hospitals and extension and upgrading of existing facilities. So, again, when the military struck, that slowed down the development of our health system. The people suffered.

The disgraceful and deteriorating state of the health services under Bainimarama–Sayed-Khaiyum governments is another very visible testament to their failure in office. The extent of the crisis unfolded steadily. One minister was transferred to another portfolio when it became clear the job was beyond him. The new minister, Mrs Rosy Akbar, disclosed that the "gaps" in the service were such that 879 new positions had to be approved. Think about that: after 10 years of rule by Bainimarama and Aiyaz Sayed-Khaiyum, the public was informed that the Health Ministry was short of 879 personnel! It took them a long time to realize this. In March of 2017 the crisis worsened when the health system itself became infected with bacteria. It was detected following the deaths of newborn babies at Suva and Lautoka hospitals. The CWM Hospital had to close its intensive care unit for infants. In June there was another flare up of the bacteria; more infants died although the Ministry of Health argued that this may not have been due to the bacteria.

The public were shocked when it was disclosed that mothers of babies had to sleep on the floor at Lautoka Hospital because of bed shortages. A new hospital opened at Navua but the kitchen could not cope and food had to be transported from the old hospital; this sort of monumental mess-up had never happened before. At Korovou a member of the public described the hospital in the town as being "like a garage".

The Ministry appeared to be incapable of solving chronic shortages of pharmaceutical supplies. A senior doctor confirmed at a health forum that there was a lack of drugs and other pharmaceuticals. The doctor said staff were reduced to using alternatives, but it was not clear to me what this meant.

And so it goes. The flood of controversies, accounts of deterioration in services, including severe, even lethal patient neglect caught on video, seem to be never-ending.

It became noticeable that the minister was ducking for cover as controversies mounted, leaving her permanent secretary to field questions. But even this official seemed to be confused in June about the direction in which the health service should be moving.

In mid June 2017, Mrs Akbar claimed that the problems besieging her ministry and department were not caused by a shortage of finance. This was not the issue, she said. It sounded as though this was an admission of complete ministerial incompetence.

A common public complaint is of the grubby, gloomy, dirty, and rundown state of the hospitals. On 23rd June 2017, Mrs Akbar finally admitted her government had neglected the improvement and upgrading of hospitals and pledged to do something about it. Her statement that finance was not the issue raised the question of why the neglect had been allowed to continue, especially in light of ceaseless complaints about the disgraceful state of affairs. It is an indictment of a government that was simply out of touch and completely separated from public concerns. This is what elitism does. Even the simple act of ensuring that all the health amenities had a new coat of paint got lost in the general flood of neglect.

# APPENDIX 4: SDL ACHIEVEMENTS IN INFRASTRUCTURE

The Bainimarama government is making massive investments in infrastructure. In the 2016 budget, it allocated a substantial sum of the public purse for this. This is presented as something of a breakthrough. At last a government has grasped the idea that infrastructure is vital for national development. Or so we are led to believe.

However, the reality is that the Bainimarama Sayed-Khaiyum government neglected infrastructure, especially roads and bridges, to the point that much of it was in a state of near collapse. The population knew about this, but the government appeared to be oblivious. Finally it dawned on them that they had a crisis and they would have to scramble to begin the long process of curing it.

In 2001 - that's 15 years ago at the time of writing – the SDL announced a comprehensive scheme to improve our roads, water supplies, sewerage systems and expansion of electricity. We pointed out all these amenities are essential for making life better and triggering economic growth.

One experience stays in my mind. When I was in Vanua Levu, I sat wth a group of villagers who wanted to thank my government because after waiting for 30 years they finally had a water supply. At the time I thought: "They are so grateful to us. But this is what we in government are supposed to be doing. It is our job. These villagers are entitled to their water and to very much more. We have to work even harder to help them and many others who need support."

These days community members frequently make public declarations of their deep gratitude to the prime minister for developments in their areas. I have a feeling that they believe it is wise to lay on the praise so that more development will follow. This is a sad reflection of our times. For a politician the opportunity to serve should be thanks enough.

So the long-suffering people of Fiji were again the victims when the coup makers couldn't come to terms with the need for timely investments in infrastructure. When it eventually started to come the record of achievement was spotty.

The SDL government invested some $427 million in upgrades and expansion of water and sewerage systems and put well over $350 million in five years into improving rural and urban roads. We planned to continue with roading and bridge projects through the Fiji Road Upgrading Programmes.

Our government vigorously pursued provision of affordable housing for middle and low-income earners and brought down the Housing Authority

interest rate to 3.99 percent, the cheapest in the market. For the immediate future, we envisaged a target of 3,000 low-cost homes annually. Towards the end of our time in office, current programmes included developing approx. 8,000 lots in Suva, Nausori and the Western Division. We promised a new drive to resettle squatters and announced substantially increased funding for a rural housing scheme.

# APPENDIX 5:SDL ACHIEVEMENTS IN TOURISM AND ENVIRONMENT

Tourism under our watch grew at a rate well above the world average. We were confident of meeting our target of 1.1 million visitor arrivals by 2014. I note that the Bainimarama-Sayed-Khaiyum government is still struggling to reach that goal. There is also a growing perception that Fiji might be pricing itself out of the market largely due to tax policies.

Encouraged by a much-improved investment climate during our term in office, foreign and local companies were proceeding with projects with a combined value of more than a billion dollars. By 2005, ten hotels had either been built, were under construction or ready to start at Denarau, that dynamic hub of Nadi investment. Fiji had never experienced an investment boom of this magnitude before.

Work on the Momi Bay and Natadola tourism schemes started during our time in office.

To build the industry's capacity, we gave a kick-start to a $20 million National School of Hospitality, Tourism and Aviation.

In manifestos for the 2001 and 2006 elections, we recognized the growing importance of environmental conservation and included policies to promote this. At that time climate change had not emerged as one of the dominant world issues but it was clear that pollution and many attendant dangers were on the rise. We had enacted an important Environment Management Act 2005 designed to protect natural resources, control and manage development and provide for waste management and pollution control. New litter legislation was in the pipeline. Other measures included a Marine Pollution Prevention Act and legislation to conserve mangrove areas. Construction of a modern landfill at Naboro to handle waste from Suva, Nausori, Nasinu, Lami and Navua was a major advance in environmental management. We planned to develop other landfills.

I have followed with a lot of interest and skepticism Bainimarama's record on the environment. Frankly it is very bad. I see a picture of severe negligence representing a serious indictment of someone who's managed to gain recognition as a leader in the international fight to reduce the impact of climate change and to generally save the world's environment. He has done this with the help of his high-priced international PR consultants. They have manufactured his image as an advocate for environmental conservation.

But here is the truth: Under his watch, many mangrove sites – a crucial part of the coastal eco-system - were destroyed. Just a few days ago, at the time of writing this, a social media commentator complained about the obliteration of mangroves at Denarau. Big areas of the Fiji landscape are strewn with plastic bags which look terrible, clog drains cause flooding, add to marine pollution and hurt sea creatures. Domestic rubbish and other forms of garbage are freely dumped at roadsides, creating eyesores and health hazards. Buses and lorries continue to spew poisonous black fumes. Marine oil spills occur with little public comment from the government. Industrial pollution is also a significant problem, threatening people and the environment.

In December 2014, broken Water Authority of Fiji pipes at Nabua let loose a huge torrent of sewerage for 16 days. It contaminated the Samabula River, moved into the Laucala basin and Suva Point seafront. The waste directly affected some 6000 people, plus those using picnic spots in Suva. A media report said the sea around Suva Harbour had become dark brown. It was an environmental catastrophe.

Even Sayed-Khaiyum has now recognized the crisis over which his government presides. He publicly described Fiji as "dirty". A vocal government supporter had earlier commented that tourists would now be visiting a dirty country. It was not clear to me that Bainimarama had even started to realize the potential embarrassment he faced as a so- called world crusader for a cleaner environment who was incapable of dealing with his own country's fundamental problems of pollution. (As the public began to make its views known, there was a belated move to get a handle on the plastic bag problem by charging 10 cents per bag. But it's too little too late.)

All this is a pathetic story for a country that prides itself on its beauty and image as a South Seas paradise. Unless Bainimarama gets a grip on the situation, how long will it be before tourism begins to suffer and we, as a people, face a real risk of losing our precious heritage?

Bainimarama meanwhile quietly let it be known in April 2017 that Sayed- Khaiyum had also become the minister for climate change. This was a further expansion of Sayed-Khaiyum's already formidable list of portfolios. Clearly in Bainimarama's mind Sayed-Khaiyum is still superior to everyone else in the government. Other government members simply can't compete with him. He is the minister without parallel.

# APPENDIX 6: SDL ACHIEVEMENTS IN LAW ENFORCEMENT

Law and order, which had suffered during the Speight coup, was one of our priority areas. Finance for the Police Force increased by 30 percent. This made it possible, among other things, to recruit more than 800 additional officers. We also provided funding for improved transport. Australian Andrew Hughes, the new police commissioner, added impetus to the fight against crime. Mr Hughes became a popular and effective leader of the force. We gave him our full support and he received strong backing from the public. His bold approach to preserving law and order and taking on criminals made a big impact.

Within weeks of his arrival and with the endorsement of our government, Mr Hughes launched a highly successful Operation Strike Back. It targeted robbery with violence, breaking and entering and vehicle theft – specific crimes on the increase in urban areas. The scheme was initially set up in Suva and then extended to the West. Up to 100 police officers were deployed to patrol well-known trouble spots, particularly at night. Operation Strike Back also focused on vital intelligence and investigative operations. It produced a substantial decrease in offences.

Mr Hughes was soon able to state that by global standards, Fiji had one of the lowest crime rates while detection was high. He stressed that Fiji had no gang or gun culture and no culture of hard drugs. He argued that with everything in perspective Fiji was a safe place to live, work, visit and invest in.

Mr Hughes led a drive to remove serious offenders from circulation. In a dramatic television appearance, he identified 10 people suspected of involvement in major robberies with violence, appealing for them to surrender and assuring them of decent treatment and a fair trial. Three gave themselves up, five were captured and there were negotiations for the surrender of one of the two who remained at large.

Special emphasis was then placed on reducing sex crimes and domestic violence. The drug trade and road deaths were the next priority.

His term in Fiji ended before his contract was finished when he found himself at odds with Bainimarama. Mr Hughes had instituted investigations into Bainimarama's treasonous behaviour.

My governments frequently declared a commitment to rooting out corruption, which we described as a stain on the integrity of a nation. The Public Service Commission established a special unit to investigate reports of corruption. We had started to draft anti-corruption legislation, which was to be enacted as quickly as possible. A Code of Conduct Bill was in the pipeline, as was a Freedom of Information Bill. During the entire period of the Bainimarama governments corruption has been a problem and there's been an alarming growth in speculation about corrupt activities at a high level. This has partly been caused by secrecy and a lack of accountability.

A report by the Commonwealth Business Council during our tenure classified Fiji as one of the best five performers in 2005 for introducing measures to reduce and eliminate corruption. The assessment was based on a survey of 32 Commonwealth countries. Fiji was ranked four for the reliability and effectiveness of its justice system. It was almost level with New Zealand for having balanced and effective business regulation. Fiji also did well in ratings for government–business relations, free media, effective government, efficient administration and future outlook.

It is noteworthy that in October 2005, Transparency International ranked Fiji at 55 in a corruption perceptions index covering 158 countries. Fiji was perceived to have less corruption than nations such as Brazil, Jamaica, Mexico, Poland, China, Sri Lanka, Romania, Argentina, Nepal, Philippines, Venezuela, Pakistan, Thailand, Trinidad and Tobago, India, Iran, Turkey and Russia. Papua New Guinea, the other Pacific island country listed, was at 130 on the perceptions list. For our government, Fiji's ranking gave us a benchmark for improvement.

The positive perception of Fiji was reinforced in a reference by the Australian National University (ANU) published in November 2004. This noted there was no sign in Fiji of the widespread corruption that affected some other Pacific Island countries.

# APPENDIX 7: SDL ACHIEVEMENTS IN SUGAR

The 2006 coup had a particularly devastating impact on Fiji's crucial sugar industry. Bainimarama eventually appointed himself minister. At the time of writing he has demonstrated an inability to reverse the fortunes of the millers, the farmers, and the many thousands of other people who depend on the industry. I can say with confidence that he is the most incompetent minister ever to hold the sugar portfolio. But judging by his statements locally and overseas he has convinced himself he is doing a sterling job. This shows how divorced he is from the reality of the disaster his leadership has inflicted on this important and historic agricultural enterprise.

In November 2013 when he was president of the International Sugar Organisation (ISO) – presumably by rotation – he outdid himself at an ISO consultation in London. At a time when the Fiji industry was near rock bottom, he made extraordinary and untrue claims of progress. He boasted that he and his government had achieved a "dramatic turnaround" for the industry. "We are producing better cane resulting in more sugar, putting more money into the pockets of our growers and diversifying our industry into ethanol production," he said. "They said it couldn't be done, but we have done it." This was fantasy.

In parliament in 2015 he further advanced his delusion about sugar's success. He said the FSC was able to stand on its own two feet and government did not have to provide it with any more funding. It was, he said, one of the most remarkable stories of the last two years. More fantasy.

The true story was that the industry had not recovered from a post-coup slump; the Fiji Sugar Corporation had been technically insolvent for years; farmers, who had been stripped of their industry voting rights, lacked confidence and were leaving the cane fields. There was no publicly visible plan for reviving sugar growing and milling. The minister and his officials seem to stumble along without any concentrated strategic direction. The diminished state of the industry was on show again in October 2016 when FSC engineers could not deal with mill breakdowns. Engineers from India had to be flown in to fix the problems.

Professor Biman Prasad, leader of the National Federation Party, effectively nailed many gross misrepresentations and falsehoods in an article in the *Fiji Times* on 26th November 2016. Professor Prasad quite rightly questioned the prime minister's comments in view of the loss of $31.7 million recorded by the FSC in the 2015 financial year. The publicity about the loss revealed that the government was continuing to support the FSC to keep it going. The corporation did not have enough cash flow to meet all its commitments and obligations. FSC auditors had significant doubts about the corporation's ability to continue as a going concern. In other words, it was not able to stand on its own two feet.

Professor Prasad ridiculed a statement by Sayed-Khaiyum about the "tremendous performance" of the FSC under its then management, especially its executive chairman, Abdul Khan. Sayed-Khaiyum said the government had given the FSC the guidance and support it needed to properly manage the industry! Another propaganda gem.

In November 2016 Mr Khan resigned. Shortly afterwards an investigation was opened into allegations against him relating to director's fees and possible abuse of office.

Professor Prasad, in his *Fiji Times* article, said it had become clear that the government was clueless about reviving the sugar industry. That was quite obvious to me a long time ago.

A new FSC CEO, Mr Graham Clark, from Zimbabwe, likened the industry to a jigsaw puzzle. The challenge was to make all the pieces fit. Bainimarama and his governments have been trying to do this for nearly 10 years. But the pieces of the puzzle are still all over the place. Listening to Mr Clark as he took over, it was very clear that the industry had to be rebuilt from top to bottom.

Our SDL governments recognized the need for decisive action for sugar to adapt to changing market conditions. Farming methods had to become more efficient and the mills modernized to focus production on the quality of cane rather than quantity. The annual crop at that stage was hovering around three million tonnes of cane from which we produced 300,000 tonnes of sugar. To be sustainable, however, we needed to achieve a crop of 4.2 million tonnes a year. The total aim of industry reorganization was to bring cane yield and production to world standards.

As prime minister, I also took responsibility for sugar, drawing on my knowledge of the industry, and driven by determination to help to reshape it for the future. We had extensive plans in place to guide the industry through transition. I was able to announce in September 2006 that we had been successful in securing assistance worth $350 million from the European Union to improve the entire cane farming sector.

However, this money was lost to Fiji and the industry when Bainimarama seized government by force of arms.

Also, in September 2006 it was announced that we had negotiated a loan from India to assist mainly with the introduction of modern technology and machinery into the four FSC sugar mills. This mill upgrading scheme was a failure. The Bainimarama government did not exercise proper oversight over the project. This was another big blow to a faltering business. Bainimarama, typically tried to pass the blame for this failure onto our government!

I explained to the Fiji Cane Growers Association AGM at the end of September 2006 that we would be aiming to increase land under cane by 10 percent and reduce production costs from $35 per tonne to $20.

A research institute would have available the latest scientific knowledge on such topics as development of cane varieties, with the highest sugar content. There would be investment in drainage, transport and roads and community amenities. Farmers leaving the industry would be given assistance with housing and access to land and credit to start new farming ventures.

We envisaged utillising sugar cane as part of a biofuel project for alternative energy. It had become clear that even with a complete restructure of the sugar industry, cane growing and milling on their own would not be commercially viable. Fuel from cane and sugar would give FSC a new source of profit for the mills and the farmers. In this transformation, the FSC would re-emerge as a maker of both sugar and energy. Electricity would be generated from bagasse (crushed cane) from the mill, while ethanol fuel for export and local use would be manufactured from sugar juice.

All these exciting plans were scuttled by Bainimarama.

Complementing the push to renew sugar was the Alternative Livelihood Project (ALP), backed by government and the Asian Development Bank, Fiji Development Bank and other institutions. It would cost about $100 million and take about six years to complete.

As well as giving support for cane farmers to move into other commercial crops if they wished to, the ALP would assist poor people to develop new livelihoods and improve their quality of life.

Naturally this very large plan to breathe new life into rural areas was another casualty of the Bainimarama coup. It was stopped in its tracks. Thousands and thousands of people were denied an opportunity to lift their living standards.

# APPENDIX 8: SDL ACHIEVEMENTS IN LAND TENURE

I was optimistic about the prospects for resolving the longstanding impasse over land leases. That optimism grew with the establishment of a multi party Cabinet of SDL and Labour MPs. We had already started discussions with the ministers from SDL and Labour based on the guiding principles of fairness to landowners and tenants. The SDL had made a proposal to parliament with the main provision as secure 50- year renewable leases for the tenant farmers with renewal to be determined within the 35th to 40th years. There would be higher rental income for the Fijian landowners.

When a landowning unit was not able to agree to a 50-year lease, shorter leases may be offered. I thought it might be feasible to get agreement for a 30-year minimum.

These proposals were a huge improvement over the existing tenancy arrangements.

I regularly expressed concern about the political standoff, which had hindered a solution to the lease issue. Our government was ready to talk and negotiate. But we could not break through the suspicion and the reluctance to engage on the part of those leading the farmers. The divisions were historical and political. Meanwhile farmers whose leases expired became victims, and their families suffered. Many joined an exodus from the cane areas to become urban squatters. To me this was a humanitarian, social and economic tragedy. But I was confident that the spirit of give and take in the new multi party cabinet would provide the answers we needed. Bainimarama's coup destroyed those possibilities.

Our Rural and Outer Islands (ROI) project was one of Fiji's most ambitious rural development schemes. It was to cost some $172 million over five years and be crucial in bridging the rural urban divide and reducing income inequality.

All its diverse parts combined formed a grand plan for remaking the social and economic landscape of the most deprived areas. It was essentially designed to create a new rural economy, with opportunity for people to earn a decent income and raise their families without being deprived of the amenities enjoyed by other communities.

We were working closely with the Asian Development Bank to get the scheme ready for implementation. But when Bainimarama executed his coup that was the end of it.

# APPENDIX 9: SDL ACHIEVEMENTS IN INDIGENOUS AFFIRMATIVE ACTION

Our government moved quickly to introduce affirmative action in support of the disadvantaged and the needy. This reflected our belief in the necessity for this form of government intervention and it was consistent with the social justice requirements of the 1997 constitution approved by all members of parliament.

Because of the opposition to these policies, we went to great lengths to explain the context for them and to reject the contention that they were racist. The core problem was that many people had the impression that affirmative action was for the sole benefit of Fijians and Rotumans and that it worked against our other communities.

I told the nation that the majority of our programmes were for the disadvantaged of all communities. They fell within the international definition of affirmative action as a "coherent set of temporary measures aimed specifically at obtaining effective equality". Article 44 of the 1997 constitution required parliament to enact social justice and affirmative action in education and training, land and housing, and participation in commerce, and in all levels and branches of State services. The compact chapter (Chapter 2) of the constitution, Article 6 (k) provided as follows:

"affirmative action and social justice programs to secure effective equality of access to opportunities, amenities or services for the Fijian and Rotuman people, as well as for other communities, for women as well as men, and for all disadvantaged citizens or groups, are based on an allocation of resources broadly acceptable to all communities".

These provisions of the 1997 constitution formed the legal basis for my government's approach and as required under the constitution, the details were set out in a special act of parliament.

The constitution came into force after very wide and credible public consultations conducted through a legal parliamentary system. It was hailed in Fiji and abroad. The then secretary general of the Commonwealth, Chief Emeka Anyaoku, said the constitution enjoyed a national consensus and conformed with the Commonwealth's Harare principles. These committed member states to the liberty of the individual under the law; equal rights of all citizens regardless of gender, race, colour, creed or political belief; the inalienable right of individuals to participate through free and democratic political processes in the society in which they live; recognition that racial prejudice and intolerance is a dangerous sickness, a threat to healthy development, and that racial discrimination is an unmitigated evil; opposition to all forms of racial oppression and a commitment to human dignity and equality; recognition of the importance and urgency of economic and social development to satisfy the basic needs and aspirations of the vast majority of people and the progressive removal of wide disparities in living standards among Commonwealth members.

It was important to note that Article 1 (4) and Article 2 (2) of the United Nations Convention of the Elimination of All Forms of Discrimination (CERD) were designed to exempt affirmative actions programmes from the definition of racial discrimination.

The SDL stressed that the objective of its affirmative action was not to gain a benefit for some at the cost of others. It was to overcome the burden of poverty for all those in need; discrimination would be removed and economic rights secured.

The overriding aim was to create an expanding economy with room for all and allowing for an equitable sharing of economic and commercial power. To me it had always been self-evident that accomplishing this was in the national interest. It was necessary for continuing peace and stability and attaining national unity.

Our approach was not designed to encourage a handout mentality. We were offering people an opportunity to lift their living standards and stand on their own feet.

Affirmative action programmes covering all communities included multi- ethnic scholarships and student loans; training; the disabled, pensioners, family assistance for the poor and destitute; small business schemes; rental subsidies for accommodation for the needy; poverty alleviation and self-help projects; agriculture; and housing and squatter settlements.

Many people in many countries support affirmative action. Many are against it. America had affirmative action, so did Canada, India, New Zealand, Australia, South Africa, Brazil, Malaysia and many more nations.

I was in New Zealand in 2003 when the results were announced of an affirmative action programme to improve the health of the indigenous Maori people. In response to public criticisms that it was a racist programme, the medical professor who led it argued it was fully justified by the very positive outcome produced for the Maori.

Ratu Sir Kamisese Mara, the father of our nation, believed firmly in affirmative action. He brought in special measures to address the lack of Fijian participation in the economy and to promote Fijian education. The 50/50% sharing of government scholarships between Fijians and Fiji's other communities, and the policy of 50/50% recruitment in the Public Service came in during his time in office. He paid a high political price for them.

Our government agreed with Ratu Sir Kamisese's view that there was no quick and easy answer to closing the gaps; it was about making sure and steady advancement over the longer term.

A researcher in education named Dr Whitehead warned in a report on education in Fiji that if nothing was done to narrow the divide that left Fijians lagging, there would be social strife and political instability. His views did not get the attention they warranted. These days in Fiji such statements which reflect uncomfortable truths are likely to be branded as hate speech and carry heavy penalties. But I believe a nation should be capable of discussing and debating sensitive issues without descending into racism and vilification. The tone and context for that should be set by the national leadership. It is plain foolish to pretend that in a multi- ethnic society differences either do not exist or should not be publicly debated. Those who think that way are living in a pretend world.

It is instructive that the critics who denounced our programmes as racist did not obtain a declaration from the courts. That's because there was no case for legal redress.

Any study of how we applied affirmative action demonstrated our resolve to be fair and equitable. Out of scholarship funds, for instance, between 50 and 55 percent were allocated for Fijian and Rotuman students. This was roughly in proportion to their numbers in the total population.

Additionally, annual budgetary allocations for government scholarships was substantially increased. As a result, the total number of Fijian and Rotuman graduates from universities and other tertiary institutions went up significantly during our term in office. At the same time more and more students from our other communities also earned university degrees and tertiary institution qualifications. A report on the scholarship scheme showed that my government had given far more scholarships to our non-Fijian students than any previous government.

In commerce, our main programme was the special loan scheme

by Fijians and Rotumans set up by Ratu Sir Kamisese Mara's Alliance government and administered by the Fiji Development Bank. We added more concessions under the scheme to help further boost the number of Fijian and Rotuman businesses. During our term in office we saw a significant and gradual expansion of indigenous commercial companies. Total loans granted to successful applicants represented only about 10 percent of the FDB's total portfolio. The vast majority were held by other communities and those few Fijians and Rotumans who no longer needed concessionary assistance. Contrast this ratio with the Fijian and Rotuman proportion of the population and it is very evident that affirmative action, in this instance, was extremely modest numerically.

Two other measures taken by the SDL were considered to have racial overtones. We believed that the landowners and the tenants would be best served by removing native land from the Agricultural Landlord and Tenant Act (ALTA). The reason for this was that native land was adequately covered under the Native Land Trust Act (NLTA). The other important consideration was that under ALTA the rental on native agricultural land was kept at six percent of the unimproved capital value (UCV). This was well below market rental rates. This made ALTA a most unjust piece of legislation from the landlord's point of view.

Our proposal was aimed at giving the landowner a right to have a say in determining rental for leasing. There was absolutely nothing racist about this. Similarly, we did not consider the controversial Qoliqoli Bill to be racist. It was about the rights of Fijians to their resources, in this case traditional fishing areas. The rights of indigenous people everywhere are covered by the International ILO Convention 169 which the Fiji government has ratified. Indigenous rights are also covered under the UN Declaration on the Rights of Indigenous Peoples (UNDRIP). Bainimarama's Fiji First government has refused to endorse this and has reportedly stated to the UN that it does not recognise indigenous rights.

I reiterate that the rights of indigenous peoples have nothing to do with racism. They are part of basic human rights.

For my part, I have never been a racist. My wish is to see all the communities which make up our multiracial Fiji moving forward together in harmony and increasing prosperity. I write more about racism in my reflections at the end of this book.

# APPENDIX 10: SDL ACHIEVEMENTS ON THE INTERNATIONAL STAGE

Our first task in Fiji's foreign relations was to repair the damage to Fiji's reputation caused by the George Speight coup, hostage taking and the associated anarchy. Then we focussed on boosting trade and attracting investors. It was important for our presence to be felt and our voice to be heard in the international community. We quickly consolidated our relations with our close neighbours Australia and New Zealand, and again became a full contributor to regional affairs through the Pacific Islands Forum.

As prime minister I felt it was crucial to build up international contacts to assist our government in gaining the maximum benefit from our diplomatic networks.

China loomed large on our horizons as an emerging and increasingly powerful international player. On four official visits to that fascinating country, I observed the astonishing transformation of its economy. It was on the way to becoming the manufacturing centre for the world.

I went to India, Australia and New Zealand cementing our relationships and exploring new opportunities for co-operation, trade, importing expertise, expanding aid, and establishing more people-to-people contacts.

I spoke at the United Nations general assembly on occasions and attended two Commonwealth Heads of government meetings. At one of these the delegates endorsed the reinstatement of Fiji into the Commonwealth after its suspension over the 2000 coup. The end result of our efforts was that between 2001 and 2006 our relations with other countries were excellent. Much of the work was carried out via our Ministry of Foreign Affairs and the minister Kaliopate Tavola.

One of our foreign affairs highlights was the hosting at Denarau, Nadi on July 18$^{th}$, 2002 of a hugely important gathering of the nations comprising the Africa Caribbean Pacific (ACP) bloc. Ratu Sir Kamisese Mara, our first prime minister, was an ACP pioneer and well respected by the ACP leaders. He attended the first ACP Summit in Libreville, Gabon, West Africa.

The ACP countries mostly comprise former colonies of metropolitan countries now part of the European Union. Main objectives of the ACP are sustainable development of its member states and their gradual integration into the global economy. There is a major focus on reducing poverty, partnership agreements with the EU countries, and establishing a new and fairer world order. Another overriding aim is establishment and consolidation of peace and stability in free and democratic societies, and promotion of unity and solidarity among ACP States.

The delegates at Denarau were from 78 nations and included heads of states and government representatives of the EU, and some non-ACP members. I read a message from Ratu Mara to the conference in which he underscored the critical role of the Lome Convention. The high chief was the central figure in the negotiations leading to the establishment of the convention which covered co-operation in economic matters, trade and commodities including sugar. Fiji was a major beneficiary of the Lome sugar protocols.

In his message for delegates Ratu Sir Kamisese said he rejoiced that the meeting would prepare for a new stage in the ACP partner-ship with the EU. He added that the ACP's Lome pact had brought enormous benefits to all member countries.

"Those of us from an earlier generation have played our part," he said. "We did our best. I pay homage to my colleagues who have passed on. Those of us who remain watch with special interest as the torch of leadership goes into new hands."

In my inaugural remarks as head of the host government, I took the opportunity of sharing our government's worldview and vision for the future of the planet. I touched on the unique and legendary oceanic legacy of Fiji and its neighbours. My remarks also reflected the concerns of the ACP nations.

This is what I said in my opening: "We are concerned for planet Earth. We see and experience its troubles and its turmoil. It is a time of crisis, of great tension and threats, of suffering and of fear. Our people carry a large part of the earth's burdens. We have come together in Fiji for their sake and for the sake of the world. We stand shoulder-to-shoulder to fashion a new order of economic and social justice. We seek an end to war, to poverty and disease. We want to make it possible for the distressed millions to have decent jobs, better shelter, enough food and education for themselves and their children. We would like the riches of the world to be spread with fairness, so that the dangerous gulf between the North and South is removed and the family of humankind becomes closer. We wish to protect this Earth and its natural resources from wanton depredation and destruction, threatening the very environment, which supports us."

I said that we of the Pacific were grateful to be the conference host. In terms of population, we were the smallest group in the ACP. Some of the Pacific states were the smallest in the world.

"Like so many of the ACP countries," I said, "we do not have monetary wealth. We struggle to develop our economies and to come to grips with wrenching, inexorable change. We must reconcile our traditions and culture with the onrush of modern systems of trade, government and mass materialism."

Then I went on to speak about our great heritage.

"There is something else very important to us. Although our countries are small and economically weak, we bring to you something unique – the great Ocean of which we are part. The Pacific covers a fifth of the planet's surface. It drew our forebears onward thousands of years ago, on mighty voyages of exploration and migration, which have had no parallel. They sailed in their canoes to where the sea met the sky and then kept going, for the horizons were endless. Did they come from Africa or Asia? "We do not know, for no one has yet sifted legend from fact. But whoever their ancestors were, these seafarers brought with them fortitude, imagination, courage and many skills.

"They made landfall on lonely slivers and dots of rock and earth and vegetation, which broke the surface of the sea. There they settled and made societies. But how could they possibly survive in this boundless stretch of water, isolated and cut off from the rest of humanity?

"We did make it, ladies and gentlemen. We evolved ways of life in our aquatic world, which endured. The Pacific separated us, but kept us together. It became the common link, formed by the tides, the currents, marine life, the stars and the wind. There was travel and trade between the islands. We became part of the Ocean. It was part of us.

"This Pacific defined us, shaped our cultures, created our myths and traditions, gave us bodily sustenance, made us what we are. It is the same today.

"Though the distances between us are long, we of the Pacific are close neighbours and friends. We have many shared traits and common features. There is a spirit among us, which makes us distinct. It is the spirit of the islands. You will have experienced it already."

I returned again to the new hazards from the environment which had increasingly become a critical concern:

"This relationship with the ocean will make it easy for you to understand why we are so adamantly opposed to any actions which expose it to threats of pollution, hazardous waste and the destructive effects of nuclear and missile testing."

"Rising sea levels from global warming are also a grave danger to the Pacific Islands, especially the low-lying atolls. It is quite conceivable that environmental refugees from Oceania will in future be seeking sanctuary elsewhere."

(It is a great pity that it took Bainimarama, his ministers and advisers so long to fully recognize the regional and international perils of climate change. And even then, they were negligent in protecting our local environment.)

I told the Denarau gathering that we were at a turning point in history.

"Fresh alignments are taking place in international affairs. The political maps are being redrawn and the course is set for change. This is particularly so in trade, investment and aid.

"It is our task to ensure that change improves life for both rural and urban dwellers alike in the African Continent. We must ensure it brings more prosperity for the ordinary people of the Caribbean and for the islanders of the Pacific. That is why we are here."

I went on to issue a reminder that international affairs were not necessarily warm and cosy.

"The richer and more powerful nations will act decisively to protect their own interests, if they have to. We cannot always rely on an accommodating attitude which takes account of our problems. "

I said we were told that free trade means an evening out of the market.

"All nations will trade from the same basis of equality and fairness. We know that is not true. We accept free trade as the ideal, but there is no level playing field for the ACP. The open market is more like a steep and slippery slope for the poorer states. This is why we must move carefully into an integrated system of world trade. It is a matter of savings some of our industries from decimation and protecting employment."

I turn towards China again expressing appreciation for its growing assistance in development aid. I asked whether it would consider an alliance with ACP to build international solidarity. It was crucial for the summit to fashion strategies for a world gathering on sustainable development later in the year.

This is how I finished my address:

"Brothers and sisters of the ACP, in some of our Pacific cultures the frigate bird has traditional and almost mystical significance. There is a song of great beauty from Kiribati which ends with these words:

Very low on earth are the frigate birds hatched, Yet they soar as high as the sun.

We cannot soar to the sun, but we can move forward with our people towards the far horizon and beyond. This is a journey we must make together, traveling onward, ever onward. Our aim is a new world where poverty is defeated, peace reigns and new hope blooms.

In a September gathering at Nadi marking the start of negotiations for renewed Economic Partnership Agreements I took the opportunity of putting the case for the Pacific Islands:" We urge special consideration for the smallest of our regional members. Their development difficulties are defined by their limited land areas, combined with the effects of remoteness in the vastness of our Ocean. Nowhere else in the world do these conditions apply."

I spelled out what isolation meant for Fiji's sugar industry: " Even when we sell to the EU on terms that are ostensibly equal to that of other ACP sugar producers, we are penalized by distance. The transport costs for delivering our sugar are much higher, and the return we receive is therefore less."

This would be a matter for our negotiators.

# APPENDIX 11: SDL ACHIEVEMENTS IN THE REGION

The South Pacific Islands Forum is the leading regional organization. Ratu Mara took the initiative for its formation in 1971 with the support of other island heads of government. Its purpose was to fill a gap in the regional system of consultation and joint action between the island countries and territories. The South Pacific Commission based in Noumea had since 1947 provided a forum for co-operation and action on issues crucial for Oceania. It was, however, a creature of the colonial powers of the day including Britain, France, the Netherlands, United States, Australia and New Zealand. They made the rules; politics were off the agenda. This was unacceptable to Ratu Mara and other island leaders. To give force to his view, Ratu Mara staged a walkout from a Commission meeting in Noumea. As far as he was concerned there was a clear and urgent need for a grouping of Pacific Islands where politics and everything else was on the table.

The South Pacific Forum – later to become the Pacific Islands Forum – met for the first time in Wellington. Participants included the heads of government from Fiji, Samoa, Tonga, the Cook Islands, and Nauru. Also, there were the Prime minister of New Zealand Sir Keith Holyoake, who acted as chair; and Australia's minister for

External Territories. Their presence fulfilled a decision from the leaders from the islands for Australia and New Zealand to be partners in the new forum. They decided there would be significant benefits from the full involvement of these two wealthy, developed states. They had resources and expertise not available to the small island nations. They were also very much part of South Pacific, with very close social, economic, trade, investment and financial ties with the islands.

The communiqué of that first meeting expressed on-going concern about French nuclear tests in the South Pacific. The leaders sent an urgent appeal to the government of France for the current test series to be the last in the Pacific area. There were decisions on trade issues and the possibility of establishing an economic union and a regional shipping line. The member states would co-operate closely in civil aviation, tourism and investment. The meeting welcomed an offer from Australia and New Zealand as members of the United Nations Seabed Committee to keep island governments informed of the committee's deliberations and to draw attention to the special needs of the South Pacific Islands. The Premier of the Cook Islands was to report back on a fisheries project; the new University of the South Pacific in Suva would be approached about taking account of traditional values in its curricula. The importance of technical training was stressed. Telecommunications, national parks, regional disaster funds and joint diplomatic representation also found their way into the communiqué. It became the practice for subsequent leaders meetings to be hosted by member countries on a rotational basis. The discussions and decisions helped greatly in the development of the region; relationships between the heads of government created a regional bond and a sense of common purpose.

In my role as prime minister I had attended the forum's heads of government meetings. This was at a time when it was engaged on issues such as maritime safety; drug trafficking; non-proliferation of nuclear weapons; co-operation among law enforcement agencies; strengthening development coordination, exploring bulk procurement of petroleum; getting the best returns from regional fisheries and their conservation and management; trade cooperation; sharing financial intelligence; renewable energy; and rationalization of the services of various regional institutions. Climate change was also emerging as a great challenge.

I was at the forum meeting in Tarawa, Kiribati, from October 30th to November 1st, 2000 when the Biketawa Declaration was put in its final form and approved. I remember clearly being a little embarrassed because at that time I was head of the interim government appointed after the George Speight rebellion. So, I had the distinction of being the only unconstitutional prime minister present. I sensed some people may have been a little uncomfortable about my presence and I thought Helen Clark of New Zealand might have been trying to avoid me. Maybe this was all in my imagination. I was pleased that the meeting communiqué welcomed the effort and commitment of the interim government I led to return Fiji to constitutional democracy.

The Leaders had Fiji very much in mind when they endorsed the Biketawa Declaration. It committed forum leaders to participatory, fair and open governance; and democratic political rights; upholding democratic processes and institutions, rule of law and the independence of the judiciary. It addressed the issue of threats to security and the importance of co-operation among members in dealing with such threats. It stressed the importance of resolving conflicts peacefully, including by customary practice. There was also reference to the importance of respecting and protecting indigenous rights and cultural values, traditions and customs. (This was to become a pressing issue in Fiji under Bainimarama's leadership. He and Khaiyum appeared to have scant regard for the rights and cultures of indigenous peoples.)

The declaration laid out options for the forum to follow in assisting in crisis resolution. The preeminent illustration of this was the Regional Assistance Mission to Solomon Islands (RAMSI). In a commentary on the imminent end of the mission in June 2017, Dame

Meg Taylor, secretary-general of the Forum Secretariat, described it as a true regional exercise in solidarity and a shining example of Pacific diplomacy and co-operation. RAMSI was set up after more than five years of internal unrest and armed conflict in the Solomon Islands.

Dame Meg acknowledged the people of the Solomon Islands for their widespread support for RAMSI, essential for the success of its mission. She said it was important to remember that RAMSI had required considerable resourcing. Australia and New Zealand stepped forward with both financial and personnel contributions complemented by Pacific nations personnel. (Fiji provided police and soldiers).

In August 2002, in Suva, I chaired the 33$^{rd}$ Pacific Islands Forum shortly after a major ACP summit at Nadi. The meeting ended with leaders calling for united stand on trade, good governance, environment, population, fisheries and HIV/AIDS. Briefing journalists, I identified one issue as being particularly vital. This was the agreement on strategy and structure for the negotiation of Economic Partnership Agreements with the EU. In my view the outcome would directly affect the lives of all the people of the region.

On another occasion I chaired a leaders' meeting, which I recollect, was in Apia. It was the first summit attended by prime minister Manasseh Sogavare of the Solomon Islands. He severely disturbed the usually calm atmosphere that prevailed at these meetings. On one issue - I recollect it was to do with RAMSI - he was very direct and blunt. There was a dramatic change in the atmosphere. It became quite tense and there were a few curt exchanges. As chair my job was to guide the meeting into calm waters, which I started to do. With great Pacific leaders at the meeting, the Pacific Way prevailed. The tension dissolved and we moved on to the next item.

One of the advantages of PIF meetings is that they provide opportunities for bi-lateral discussion between leaders. At this Samoa meeting, the then Prime minister of Australia, Mr John Howard, and I met briefly during a tea break. We discussed a long-standing request from the Fiji Garment Manufacturers Association for additional concessions for the entry of our Fiji-made garments into Australia. Our discussion was clear and to the point and Mr Howard assured me he would look at the request on his return to Australia.

I followed up with him when we met again in Townsville, Queensland, this time to farewell the Australian, Fiji and Tongan troops assigned under RAMSI to go to the Solomons. We spoke again about the garment manufacturer's request and a letter was handed to Mr Howard's secretary. Not long afterwards we got the concession we sought. It effectively reduced by 25% the Australian import duty on Fiji-made garments. It gave a significant boost to our garment exporters to Australia.

During the period 2000 to 2006, the PIF made great strides in terms of regional development and co-operation. Some noteworthy achievements were the approval of the first Pacific Plan for a joint co-ordinated approach to regionalism; the coming into force of the Pacific Islands Trade Agreement (PITA); the start of the prolonged negotiations for the Pacific Area Trade Agreement (PACER); and the finalisation of a seasonal workers scheme aimed at providing temporary employment for Pacific islanders in Australia and New Zealand.

I was privileged and honoured to represent Fiji at the PIF leaders' meetings, where I gained much new knowledge and always did my very best to contribute to the region. My associations with my counterparts were cordial. In particular I highly valued the contributions by New Zealand Prime minister Helen Clark, and John Howard, Prime minister of Australia. I sensed that their hearts were in the Pacific and that they were prepared to do whatever they could to help the forum and our island states, even at the risk of losing some of their own support at home.

When Bainimarama executed his coup, he placed Fiji in conflict with the forum, what it stood for and specifically the Biketawa Declaration.

# SOME RELEVANT DATES AND DEVELOPMENTS IN FIJI'S POLITICAL HISTORY

## 1835

First Christian missionaries arrive in Fiji waters. They established a base in Lakeba, Lau, before setting up
missions in Rewa, Taveuni and elsewhere in the Fiji group.

## 1874

Through the Deed of Cession, Fiji colonized under British rule by mutual agreement between a representative group
of tribal chiefs and consuls for Queen Victoria.

## 1879-1916

Indentured labourers from India brought in to work in the newly established sugar industry. This created a multi-racial, multi-cultural country of two main communities – the immigrants from India and the indigenous people - with very different customs, traditions, languages and beliefs.
Over time the Fiji Indians outnumbered the indigenes, although that trend was reversed and the Fijians again
became the majority.

## 1939-1945

Fijian soldiers served in World War 2 in Coral Sea theatre of war – mainly Guadalcanal with Corporal Sefanaia
Sukanaivalu posthumously awarded the Victoria Cross.

## 1920-1958

Ratu Sir Lala Sukuna establishes himself as a pre-eminent figure in Fiji's pre-independence development; his work led directly to the establishment of Native Land Trust Board (NLTB), a historic initiative in land and lease reform. He was a key adviser to the British colonialists on the governance of
Fiji.

## 1970

October 10<u>th</u>
The instruments of Independence are handed over by Prince Charles, representing the British Crown, to Ratu Sir Kamisese Mara, in an impressive ceremony at Albert Park,
Suva.

## 1972

In first post-colonial election, Ratu Sir Kamisese's Alliance Party wins a majority. He is to remain in elected office for 17
years and becomes the dominant figure in modern Fiji.

## 1977

The Alliance Party loses majority when Fijians voting along nationalistic lines take about one quarter of the Alliance votes. Opposition National Federation Party (NFP), led by Siddiq Koya, delays in moving to form a new government and Ratu Mara is controversially re-appointed. In a second
election that year the Alliance regains a majority.

## 1985

Fiji Labour Party formed to contest the next election. It is led by Dr
Timoci Bavadra, but is perceived to be dominated
non-Fijians.

## 1987

Dr Bavadra's Labour Party, in coalition with the NFP, wins the election of 1987. On May 14$^{th}$, Colonel Sitiveni Rabuka overthrows the
Bavadra government in Fiji's first military coup. The Great Great
Council of Chiefs [Bose Levu Vakaturaga] supports Rabuka.
International sanctions are put in place against Fiji. Tensions are
high; human rights
offences take place.
September 25$^{th}$
Following negotiations to form a new government, Rabuka executes a
second coup and takes power again until December. He then handed
authority to the high chiefs Ratu Sir Kamisese Mara and Ratu Sir
Penaia Ganilau. It may have been the only time a coup leader has
voluntarily given up
power.
October 3$^{rd}$
Fiji declared a 'republic' formally ending ties with the British
Crown. Fiji is expelled from the Commonwealth.

## 1990

July 25$^{th}$
New controversial constitution promulgated, reflecting
indigenous political aspirations.

## 1992

May 30$^{th}$
Great Council of Chiefs backs Soqosoqo ni Vakavulewa ni Taukei
(SVT) Party led by Rabuka. SVT wins a majority in
general election and forms government.

## 1994

January 15th

Snap election when SVT MP Josevata Kamikamica challenges
Rabuka government with formation of Fijian
Association Party. SVT wins poll and returns to government.

## 1995-7

Reeves Constitution Review Commission produces the 1997
constitution – Fiji's third in three decades.

## 1999

May 19th

Election of this year produces government led, for the first
time, by a Fiji Indian PM, Mahendra Chaudhry.

## 2000

May 19th

After one year in office, Chaudhry's Labour government falls victim
to Fiji's third coup. It is led by civilian George Speight, and nationalist extremists, who appeared to be supported
initially by an ambivalent military.

July 28th

In July, Frank Bainimarama, Commander of the RFMF, out manoeu-
vres Speight, who is arrested and placed in detention. Laisenia
Qarase agrees to a request by the military to lead an interim government. Qarase receives
support of the GCC.

November 2nd

An army mutiny on this date fails to overthrow
Bainimarama, who escaped an assassination attempt.

## 2001

May 9th

Qarase launches new SDL party uniting SVT and FAP remnants.

iTaukei ethno-nationalists form Conservative Alliance Matanitu Vanua (CAMV). Qarase's SDL gets the most votes and forms coalition with CAMV in September
elections.

## 2002
February 18th
2000 Coup leader George Speight is convicted of treason and receives death sentence which is immediately commuted to life imprisonment.

## 2004
April 18th
Fiji's founding father Ratu Mara dies on this date.

## 2005
May 15th
Reconciliation, Tolerance and Unity (RTU) Bill released on this date.

## 2006
May 15th
Qarase-led SDL party wins its second election and forms constitutionally mandated multiparty government with Fiji Labour Party. Labour MPs become part of Qarase's Cabinet. This is a new form of multi-ethnic power sharing. War-of- words with military hots up in emerging confrontation
between elected government and aggressive military.
December 5th
Bainimarama stages Fiji's fourth coup: a state of emergency is imposed and the military rules by decrees. Army begins reign of terror, cracking down on dissenters. This continues
for approximately eight years.
December 28th

Jagannath Sami, CEO of Sugar Cane Growers Council and eight board members, sacked by new regime alleging manipulation of council's operations.

## 2007
In January 2007 a series of legal maneouvres sees Bainimarama first assuming the presidency, then relinquishing it and subsequently being appointed interim PM. A so-called 'clean-up' takes effect with removal, suspensions and/or resignations of numerous officials. Harassment, disruptions, and vendetta politics continue.
April 13th
The GCC is suspended by president in line with wishes of the military government.
June 14th
New Zealand High Commissioner, Michael Green, is expelled from Fiji on grounds of political interference.
September-October
Six high court judges resign citing political interference in their commissions.
November
Eleven arrested in alleged failed plot to remove Bainimarama and other Cabinet members.

## 2008
February 26th
Australian publisher of The Fiji Sun, Russell Hunter, deported on this date.
May 2nd
Australian publisher of The Fiji Times newspaper, Evan Hannah, deported on this date.
December 27th
Second New Zealand High Commissioner, Caroline McDonald expelled.

## 2009

January 24th
Second Australian publisher, Rex Gardner, of The Fiji Times
deported.

April 13th
Fiji judiciary is sacked ("Coup 4.5") after the Court of Appeal
rejected the October 2008 Gates high court decision which found
the coup justified. Fiji Methodist Church hierocracy is not permitted
to convene its annual conference.

Three foreign journalists - Sia Aston and photographer Matt Smith
from New Zealand's TV3, and Australian Broadcasting
Corporation's Sean Dorney - expelled from Fiji (on 13th).

May 2nd
Fiji is suspended from Pacific Island Forum.

July
Twenty-Seven Methodist Church senior ministers detained
and charged for meeting illegally.

September
Fiji is yet again suspended from the Commonwealth.

November 4th
Australian High Commissioner, James Batley; and New
Zealand High Commission envoy, Todd Cleaver, expelled.

## 2010

January
The Methodist Church again forbidden to convene annual
conference - this time until 2014.

June
Indigenous Fijians lose their historic nomenclature and identity as
'Fijian' when the military government approves a decree for all Fiji
citizens to be called 'Fijian'. Those formerly identified as indigenous
'Fijians' to be called itaukei – the
owners - effective 16 July 2010.

July 9th

Second Australian High Commissioner, Sarah Roberts,
expelled.

## 2011
August
The Methodist Church hierocracy is forbidden for the third consecu-
tive year by the military government to convene the
church conference.

## 2012
August– December
Work commences on fourth Fiji constitution by Professor Yash
Ghai's Commission – public submissions, process and drafting. Ulti-
mately a draft of the constitution produced by
the commission is burnt to ashes.

## 2013
January
Political Party (Registration, Conduct, Funding and Disclosure)
Decree proclaimed – existing parties given 27 days to re-register
under new names using new logos or lose their assets. All parties will
have to disclose full assets, income, liabilities, donations and financial
information on relevant standing politicians.
Government invites the international community to observe
2014 election preparations.
March
Video of brutal treatment of two men released and goes
viral.
April
Author released after serving eight months of his one-year jail term
for alleged abuse of office conviction. AG (and minister Responsible
for Elections) Aiyaz Sayed-Khaiyum to establish a Transparency
Commission to enforce public
service code of conduct.

September

Fourth constitution takes effect 7 September by presidential assent, but without public mandate.

## 2014

Election year but under what kind of rules? Parties await announcement of these.

September

Bainimarama's Fiji First Party wins election. Many questions unresolved about conduct of elections. Suspicions persist of rigging.

# GLOSSARY OF FIJIAN TERMS

**Bati** - *warrior*

**bele** – *nutritious green vegetable*

**bête** – *traditional priest*

**bula** – *welcome greeting*

**bure (pron. booray)** – *thatched house*

**dalo** – *root crop*

**Gujerati** – *Indian ethnic group*

**iTaukei** – *indigenous owner*

**cassava** – *root crop*

**kaivata** - *relatives*

*kirikiti* - cricket

*koro* - village

*kumala* – sweet potato

*lavo* - money

*leqa* - problem

*lotu* - church

*lovo* - earth oven

*makosoi* – scented flower - Cananga odorata, known as the caning

*masi* – bark cloth

*matanitu* - government

*matanivanua* -spokesperson

*mataqali* – traditional clan grouping

*nau* - grandmother

*polotu* – form of singing of Lau islands

*qai* - cordyline terminalis, used for making ceremonial skirts

*qaloqalovi* – equivalent to freedom of village

*Ratu* – chief

**Roti** – *a kind of flat Indian bread almost like a pancake*

**Sega** - *no*

**sevusevu** – *presentation of kava root as part of a welcome*

**taukei ni sitoa** – *shop owner*

**suki** - *tobacco*

**sulu** - *a kilt-like garment*

**tabakau** – *coconut leaf mat*

**tabu** – *forbidden*

**tabua** - *a whale's tooth, the most sacred of the objects in traditional ceremonies*

**talanoa** – *customary manner of discussion to achieve consensus*

**tikina** - *district*

**tokatoka** – *sub clan*

**tua** – *grandfather in the Lauan dialect*

**turaga-ni-koro** – *village head*

**ulidrano** - *Masomo lake special fishing expeditions*

**uvi** - *yam*

**vakasoso-ni-waqa** – *giving of gift*

***vanua*** – *the land, the people, the chiefs*

***yavusa*** - *clan*

***yawa*** – *mullet fish*

# MAPS

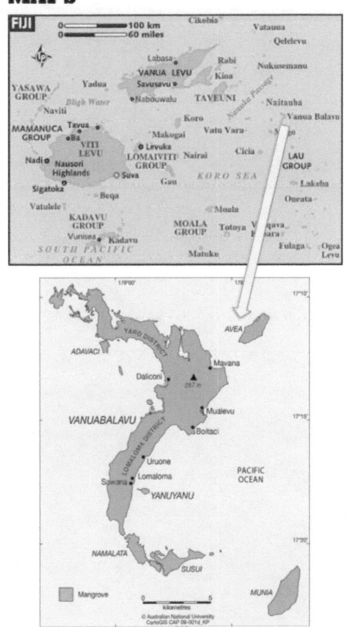

# END NOTES

i The extent of my commercial involvements over the years led to my appointment on many boards. Here are some of them: Fiji International Telecommunications Limited (FINTEL) (1978-1979; Financial Advisor, Fijian Affairs Board (1979-1999); Fiji Development Bank (1983-1997); Foods Pacific Limited (1985-1986) ; inaugural chair, South Pacific Fertilizers Limited (1985-1996); Fiji Forest Industries Limited (1988- 1997); Carlton Brewery (Fiji) Limited (1989-1999); inaugural chairman of Fiji Post and Telecommunications Limited (1990-1991); Unit Trust of Fiji (1990-1999); Voko Industries Limited (1993-1997); inaugural chair of Fiji Television Limited (1994-1998); Air Pacific Limited (1996-1998); Colonial Advisory Council (1996-1999); Samisoni Enterprises Limited (current) and Corporate Management Services Limited t/a The Hot Bread Kitchen (current). I still hold directorships in our local Lau companies – Mualevu Tikina Holdings Limited, Vanuabalavu Holdings Limited, Qalitu Enterprises Limited (Chair). I am also advisor to Mavana Investments Limited.

ii Here is the list: Laisenia Qarase, Prime minister and minister for

National Reconciliation and Unity; Mr Tomasi Vuetilovoni, a prominent corporate executive, minister for Commerce, Business Development and Investment; Mr Keni Dakuidreketi, qualified in property management and valuation, minister for Youth, Employment Opportunities; Mr Pita K. Nacuva, prominent town planner, minister for Health; Ratu Tu'uakitau Cokanauto, member of a prominent chiefly family, minister for Local Government, Housing and Environment; Mr Alipate Qetaki, well-known lawyer, Attorney General and minister for Justice; Mr Ilaitia Tuisese, high profile community leader, minister for Regional Development and Multi Ethnic Affairs; Ro Teimumu Vuikaba Kepa, teacher and holder of one of Fiji's highest chiefly titles, minister for Women, Culture, Heritage and Social Welfare; Ratu Talemo Ratakele, president of the Senate, minister for Home Affairs and Immigration; the late Mr Hector Hatch, well- known human resource specialist, minister for Public Enterprise and Public Sector Reform (Mr Hatch stepped down shortly after being appointed); Ratu Tevita Momoedonu, minister for Labour and Industrial Relations; Mr Apisai. V. Tora, long time union leader and politician, minister for Agriculture, Fisheries, Forests and ALTA; Mr Kaliopate Tavola, agricultural economist, minister for Foreign Affairs, External Trade and Sugar; Mr Joketani. W. Cokanasiga, prominent tourism industry leader, minister for Works and Energy; Ratu Jone Y. Kubuabola, economist and former governor of the Reserve Bank of Fiji, minister for Finance and National Planning; Mr Mitieli Bulanauca, land management specialist, minister for Lands and Mineral Resources; Ratu Epeli Nailatikau, brother of Ratu Tu'uakitau Cokanauto and former military commander and diplomat, minister for Fijian Affairs; and the late Mr Savenaca Draunidalo, also a former senior military officer, minister for Transport and Communication.

iii The leaders included the late Rev. Tuikilakila Waqairatu, the late Ratu Epeli Kanaimawi, the late Ratu Osea Gavidi, Rev. Pastor Poate Mata, Rev. Pita Cili, and Rev. Suliasi Kurulo.

iv The Cabinet team included me as Prime Minister, Ratu Naiqama Lalabalavu, who also holds the title of Tui Cakau, minister for Lands and Mineral Resources; Mr Kenneth Zinck, a well-known unionist and bank officer, minister for Labour, Industrial Relations and Productivity; Mr Pita K. Nacuva, a town planner, minister for Health; Ratu Jone Y. Kubuabola, minister for Finance and National Planning; Mr Kaliopate Tavola, an economist, minister for Foreign Affairs, External Trade and Sugar; the late Mr Jonetani K. Galuinadi, minister for Agriculture, Sugar and Land Resettlement; the late Mr Mataiasi V. Ragigia, minister for Local Government, Housing, Squatter Settlement and Environment; Mr Tomasi Vuetilovoni, well known business executive, minister for Commerce, Business Development and Investment; the late Mr Qoriniasi Bale, Attorney General; Mr Konisi T. Yabaki, who had served as conservator of forests, minister for Tourism, Culture, Heritage and Civil Aviation; Mr Isireli Leweniqila, a former businessman, minister for Youth, Employment Opportunities and Sports; and Ro Teimumu Vuikaba Kepa, holder of the Roko Tui Dreketi title, minister for Education.

v This was the line-up: SDL - Laisenia Qarase, Qoriniasi Bale, Ratu Jone Kubuabola, Ro Teimumu Vuikaba Kepa, Ratu Naiqama Lalabalavu, Ilaitia Tuisese, Isireli Leweniqila, Savenaca Draunidalo, George Shiu Raj, Tomasi Vuetilovoni, Ratu Meli Saukuru, Josefa Vosanibola, Adi Asenaca Caucau, Rajesh Singh, Ted Young, Samisoni Tikoinasau, Losena Salabula, Ro Suliano Matanitobua, Ratu Josefa Dimuri, Ratu Jone Navakamocea, Pio Tabaiwalu, Inoke Luveni, Paulo Ralulu; Senators – Kaliopate Tavola, Adi Samanunu Cakobau-Talakuli; FLP - Poseci Bune, Krishna Datt, Dr Gunasagran Gounder, Gyani Nand, Lekh Ram Vayeshnoi, Udit Narayan, Chaitanya Lakshman, Ragho Nand, Adi Sivia Qoro. Independent – Robin Irwin, Jioji Konrote.

vi The following signed: Simione Kaitani, Mitieli Bulanauca, Niko Nawaikula, Konisi Yabaki, Ratu Isikeli Tasere, Irami Matairavula,

Nanise Nagusuca, Joji Banuve, Mataiasi Ragigia, Ratu Jone Waqairatu, Asaeli Masilaca, Misaele Weleilakeba, Mere Samisoni, Ratu Osea Vakalalabure and Rajesh Singh.

vii Here is a list of decrees which show how thoroughly Bainimarama-Sayed-Khaiyum have put into effect the "sunset clause": The Fijian Affairs (Great Council of Chiefs) Regulations 2008 to bring the GCC under the complete power and authority of government (even though it was suspended); the Fijian Affairs (Provincial Council) (Amendment) Regulation 2008, that terminated the attendance at provincial councils of educated urban Fijian *iTaukei*; the Fijians Trust Fund (Amendment) Decree No. 38 of 2009, that brought the fund completely under the authority of government; the Native Land Trust (Amendment) Decree No. 31 of 2009, terminating the GCC's appointing authority to Ratu Sukuna's creation, the Native Land Trust Board and replacing with government authority; the Native Land Trust Regulation (Amendment) 2010, terminating the chiefs share of royalty income (thus making it harder for them to fulfill their traditional duties); Mahogany Industry Development Decree 2010 terminating Native Land Trust Board's power and authority over mahogany leases on native land and replacing the NLTB with a new council headed by Bainimarama and Sayed-Khaiyum; the Surfing Areas Decree of 2010, removing control of surfing areas by *iTaukei* and their trustee the Native Land Trust Board (renamed (iTLTB) *iTaukei* Land Trust Board); the Native Land Trust (Amendment) Decree of 2010 removing the president as chiefly representative and chairman of iTLTB Board and replacement by the prime minister; the Native Land Trust Act (Amendment) Decree of 2010 terminating the GCC authority over extinct *mataqali* land; the Native Land Trust (Amendment) Decree of 2012 terminating the power of the GCC to determine customary ownership of extinct *mataqali* land; the *iTaukei* Affairs (Amendment) Decree of 2012, terminated the existence of the GCC; the *iTaukei* Trust Fund (Amendment) Decree of 2012, ending the GCC administrative power over the Fijian Trust Fund; and the Bainimarama-Sayed-Khaiyum 2013 constitution removing formerly entrenched provisions protecting native land.

viii In parliament, I referred to David Kirkwood in The Christian Disciple's Manual that the wrongs people have committed against us may seem great. But compared to how much God has forgiven us, they are really no comparison. Then I referred to the heart-wrenching testimony of the late Corrie ten Boom, who had been a prisoner in the Ravensbruck extermination camp in Nazi Germany. She and her family suffered terrible cruelty and deprivation at the hands of the camp guards. Only Corrie survived.

After the war she spoke often of the love of God, and God's forgiveness. But she was still bitter at the Nazis for what they had done to her and her family. At a meeting in Munich, where she was speaking on Christian forgiveness and her experience at Ravensbruck, she saw a man walking towards her. Her heart froze. He had been a guard at the camp, one of the worst. Now he was in front of her, with his hands extended. Corrie's reaction is contained in a book by Dr James Dobson. The guard told her he had become a Christian, and that he knew God had forgiven him for all the cruel things he had done in Ravensbruck. Although Corrie had remembered him, he obviously did not know who she was. The former guard wanted to know if she would forgive him. Corrie stood there. She could not forgive. She could not take the man's hand. She said she was wrestling with the most difficult thing she had ever had to do. She knew the commandment of forgiveness, but she could not, at that point, act. "And still I stood there," she said, "with the coldness clutching my heart." But Corrie knew that forgiveness is not an emotion. It is an act of the will, and the will could function, regardless of the temperatures of the heart. She prayed for Jesus to help her. She describes what happened next. "And so, woodenly, mechanically, I thrust my hand into the one stretched out to me. And as I did, an incredible thing took place. The current started in my shoulder, raced down my arm, sprang into our joined hands and then his healing warmth seemed to flood my whole being, bringing tears to my eyes." "I forgive you, brother," I cried, "with all my heart." "For a long moment we grasped each other's hands, the former guard and the former prisoner. I had never known God's love so intensely as I did then. But even so, I realized it was not my love. I had tried and did not have the power. "It was the power of the Holy Spirit, as recorded in Romans 5:5, "because the love of God is shed abroad in our hearts by the Holy Ghost which is given unto us." I can add nothing to that story; it says everything that needed to be said.

# SOURCES

Source material for this book encompasses documents and speeches, news reports, and other data. Some of it is available online.

What follows are some of the specific sources I wish to mention:

1. The Holy Bible for inspiration and guidance and selected verses of Scripture.
2. My mind, memory and experiences.
3. Forum Eminent Persons' Group Report on Fiji – 29 January to 1 February 2007.
4. 2014 Fijian Elections, Final Report of the Multinational Observer Group.
5. Report of the 1996 Fiji Constitution Review Commission
6. Parliamentary Paper No. 17 of 1997 - Report of the Joint Parliamentary Select Committee on the Report of the Fiji Constitution Review Commission.
7. Documentation from Yash Ghai Constitution Commission 2012, including the draft Constitution it produced.
8. The 1997 Constitution.

9. The 2013 draft Constitution.

10. The People's Charter – 15th December 2008.

11. The State of the Nation and Economy Report Executive Summary, National Council for Building a Better Fiji 2008.

12. Cultural Autonomy. Its implications for the nation state. The Fijian Experience. – Aiyaz Sayed Khaiyum's thesis.

13. Message from Mr Justice Marshall 2012.

14. The rule of law and the independence of the judiciary in Fiji (A paper presented to the International Commission of Jurists, Queensland, July 20th 2004.

15. Report of Board of Inquiry into the involvement of the First Fiji Meridian Squadron in the illegal takeover of Parliament of 19 May 2000 and the subsequent holding of hostages until 13 July 2000.

16. Submission to the Pacific Islands Forum Leaders' meeting, 27-31 August 2012, Rarotonga, Cook Islands, by the SDL Party, Fiji Labour Party, United Peoples Party and National Federation Party on Fiji's constitutional process.

17. Various communiqués of the Pacific Islands' Forum.

18. The Deed of Cession making Fiji a British colony.

19. United National General Assembly Human Rights Council 7th session. Report of the Special Rapporteur on torture and other cruel, inhumane or degrading punishment; Human Rights Council 8th Session – Report of the Special Rapporteur on extrajudicial, summary or arbitrary executions.

20. Dire Straits: A report on the rule of law in Fiji – March 2009. An international Bar Association Human Rights Institute Report.

21. Soqosoqo Duavata ni Lewenivanua (SDL) Party submission to the constitution commission – 13 October 2012.

22. Persona Non Grata. Breaking the bond Fiji and New Zealand 2004-2007
- Michael Green.

23. Pensioners' petition for justice to the Prime Minister – March 2012.

24. FNPF Pensioners' submission to Yash Ghai Constitution Commission – 10th October 2012.

25. Ratu Sukuna. Soldier, statesman, man of two worlds – Deryck Scarr.

26. Fiji: The three-legged stool. Selected writings of Ratu Sir Lala Sukuna, edited by Deryck Scarr.

27. Mission Complete. The Fiji Interim Government's Achievements. – December 1987-April 1992.

28. The Power and The Promise. Electrification in Fiji. Published by the Fiji Electricity Authority in 1987.

29. Deed of Commitment by Government Members of Parliament – 5th December 2006.

30. International Senior Lawyers Project (ISLP) - Analysis of the Draft Constitution of Fiji released by the Interim Government of Fiji on 21 March 2013

31. Citizens Constitutional Forum - An Analysis: 2013 Fiji Government Constitution – September 2013

32. Back to the future: Qarase v Bainimarama – 27 November 2009 by R. A. Pepper.

33. Beating Justice. How Fiji's security forces get away with torture. © Amnesty International 2016.

34. 2001 and 2006 SODELPA manifestos.

Made in the USA
Las Vegas, NV
04 January 2023

64987547R00381